Handbook of Computer Networks and Communications

Volume I

Handbook of Computer Networks and Communications
Volume I

Edited by **Akira Hanako**

LANRYE
INTERNATIONAL

New Jersey

Published by Clanrye International,
55 Van Reypen Street,
Jersey City, NJ 07306, USA
www.clanryeinternational.com

Handbook of Computer Networks and Communications
Volume I
Edited by Akira Hanako

© 2015 Clanrye International

International Standard Book Number: 978-1-63240-262-2 (Hardback)

Contents

Preface

A communication is a method to exchange data of different types which is encoded and then transferred through wired connection, or wireless connection, a communication can be one to one, many to one, and many to many. A computer network on the other hand is a data network or data connection which allows two computer systems to exchange data.

Network computers when originate data, establish routes, and then exchange data followed by terminating the link; are known as network nodes. One of the most common examples of computer network is internet, and internet's applications such as World Wide Web (WWW), printers, messaging applications, cash cards use, etc. Computer networks can be applied in different physical media with different approaches.

This book studies the different computer networks used in different applications and for different purposes for the communications. This book contains some topics which study the problems in computer networks and communication processes, and these topics will prove to be good read for all those who are working in the field of communication setups and computer networks.

I would like to thank all the contributing authors who have put in their hard work and time in these researches. I also wish to acknowledge the extraordinary efforts of the publishing team in helping me at every step.

Editor

A DHT-Based Discovery Service for the Internet of Things

Federica Paganelli and David Parlanti

CNIT, Research Unit at the University of Firenze, Via S. Marta 3, 50139 Firenze, Italy

Correspondence should be addressed to Federica Paganelli, federica.paganelli@unifi.it

Academic Editor: Jae-Ho Choi

Current trends towards the Future Internet are envisaging the conception of novel services endowed with context-aware and autonomic capabilities to improve end users' quality of life. The Internet of Things paradigm is expected to contribute towards this ambitious vision by proposing models and mechanisms enabling the creation of networks of "smart things" on a large scale. It is widely recognized that efficient mechanisms for discovering available resources and capabilities are required to realize such vision. The contribution of this work consists in a novel discovery service for the Internet of Things. The proposed solution adopts a peer-to-peer approach for guaranteeing scalability, robustness, and easy maintenance of the overall system. While most existing peer-to-peer discovery services proposed for the IoT support solely exact match queries on a single attribute (i.e., the object identifier), our solution can handle multiattribute and range queries. We defined a layered approach by distinguishing three main aspects: multiattribute indexing, range query support, peer-to-peer routing. We chose to adopt an over-DHT indexing scheme to guarantee ease of design and implementation principles. We report on the implementation of a Proof of Concept in a dangerous goods monitoring scenario, and, finally, we discuss test results for structural properties and query performance evaluation.

1. Introduction

The research roadmap towards the Future Internet is envisaging novel services endowed with context-aware and autonomic capabilities to support end users in daily living activities (e.g., work, leisure time, travel). In such a perspective, the technological landscape is expected to be populated by a wide range of functional capabilities offered by heterogeneous types of devices (PCs, mobile phones, household appliances, smart textiles, etc.). Several research fields are expected to contribute towards this ambitious vision, including the Internet of Things, the Internet of Services, and Cloud Computing.

The "Internet of Things" paradigm aims at providing models and mechanisms enabling the creation of networks of "smart things" on a large scale by means of RFID, wireless sensor and actuator networks, and embedded devices distributed in the physical environment [1]. This paradigm will open up the possibility to create novel value-added services by dynamically assembling different types of capabilities (sensing, communication, information processing, and actuation on physical resources, just to mention a few examples).

Nonetheless, it is also well-known that the sustainable and efficient realization of IoT solutions requires the conception and development of dynamic adaptation and autonomic capabilities. Hence, the availability of mechanisms for discovering available resources and capabilities is of primary importance in the realization of the above-mentioned vision.

In the Internet of Things, "*data of real world objects and events will be available globally and in vast amounts. These data will be stored in widely distributed, heterogeneous information systems, and will also be in high demand by business and end user applications.*" [2]. Discovery mechanisms are thus required to enable a client application to obtain the location and addressing information needed to access these information repositories.

The contribution of this work consists in a distributed Discovery Service for Internet of Things scenarios. The proposed solution adopts a peer-to-peer approach for guaranteeing scalability, robustness, and maintainability of the overall system. While most peer-to-peer discovery services recently proposed for the IoT support exact match queries on a single attribute (i.e., the object identifier) [2], our solution can handle also multiattribute and range queries.

Indeed, while a one-attribute exact match query works well when a client application already knows the identifiers of the target objects (e.g., by means of readers that detect objects tagged with an RFID), the capability of handling multiattribute range query allows client applications to discover information and functional capabilities of objects that have not been detected yet and are not necessarily in physical proximity. The proposed solution is based on a layered architectural design that distinguishes three main aspects: multiattribute indexing, range query support, peer-to-peer routing.

The paper is organized as follows: in Section 2 we discuss functional requirements for discovery services in the IoT. Section 3 surveys related work. In Section 4 we describe the proposed distributed discovery service based on a P2P overlay. In Section 5 we present a Proof of Concept implementation in a reference application scenario and show testing results obtained by means of computational simulations. In Section 6 we draw the conclusions by discussing achieved results and future research directions.

2. Discovery Services in IoT Scenarios

The Internet of Things (IoTs) paradigm implies the perspective of objects and devices endowed with computational, sensing, and communication capabilities and capable of producing and disseminating a large amount of events. IoT applications should adapt their behaviour to changes in an extremely dynamic environment: users enter and exit from "smart environments" (e.g., smart homes [3–5], smart hospitals [6–8], smart offices [9, 10], and tourism locations [11, 12]), objects change their position according to specific application purposes (e.g., mobility of persons [13, 14], multimodal transport of goods [15], and maritime surveillance [16]). Discovery mechanisms are thus required in order to obtain up-to-date information about functional capabilities offered by devices distributed in the environment or information repositories storing information about a given object.

As argued by Atzori et al. [17], "key components of the IoT will be RFID systems." Radio frequency identification technologies (RFID) are typically composed by two types of hardware components: RFID tags and readers [18]. Tags store a unique identifier and, optionally, additional information. They can be applied to objects, animals, or persons (e.g., goods loaded on pallets or containers, smart bracelets worn by patients in hospitals [19]) to gather information about their status or surrounding environment (e.g., measurements gathered from sensors monitoring the status of goods or biomedical parameters of a target patient) and infer knowledge about the context (e.g., alarm and critical events) [20]. RFID and sensing technologies can thus be exploited in the development of context-aware applications in a wide range of application domains: logistic, e-health, security, smart cities [17].

As envisaged in a study promoted by the European Commission [21], it is foreseeable that any "thing" will have at least one unique way of identification (via a "Unique Identifier" or indirectly by some "Virtual Identifier" techniques).

Endowed with addressing and communication capabilities, these things will be capable of connecting each other and exchange information. Information and services about objects will be fragmented and handled across many entities (ranging from the creator/owner of the object to the entities that have interacted with it at some stage in its lifecycle). Available information could be provided either at the level of the single object instance (e.g., a goods item) or a group or class of objects (e.g., items of dangerous goods that are transported by land, air, sea, or a combination of these).

Although several low-level requirements could emerge in the manifold application areas of IoT, we elicited the following high-level functional requirements for a discovery service in IoT scenarios [2].

2.1. Flexible Identification Scheme. The discovery mechanism should be transparent with respect to the adopted identification scheme. For instance, in RFID applications for logistics, the Electronic Product Code (EPC) [22] is a widely adopted identification scheme. Other available identification schemes include URIs, IPv6 addresses, Universal Product Code, just to mention a few examples.

2.2. Multiattribute Query. The discovery mechanism should be capable of handling a query for an exact match of a given identifier as well as queries possibly containing other qualifying attributes (e.g., location and category).

2.3. Range Query. In addition to exact match queries, the system should support queries specifying lower and upper boundaries on a single or multiple attributes.

2.4. Multiple Publishers. Depending on the application purposes, several entities may be called to produce and publish information about a given object, besides the object's owner.

2.5. Management APIs. Authorized entities should be able to add, update and delete information associated with a given object.

3. Related Work

RFID systems are considered key components of the IoT [17]. A significant standardization effort has been performed by the EPCglobal consortium to establish principles and guidelines for supporting the use of RFID in trading and enterprise contexts. More specifically, the EPCglobal Network is a set of emerging standard specifications for a global RFID data sharing infrastructure built around the Electronic Product Code (EPC), an unambiguous numbering scheme for the designation of physical goods [22]. It aims at facilitating the handling, storage, and retrieval of information related to EPC-identified items.

The EPC is a universal identifier used for physical objects. It can take the form of a Uniform Resource Identifier (URI), thus enabling information systems to refer to physical objects. The EPC code is typically stored on an RFID attached to the referred object. Main components of the EPC Global

Architecture include the RFID Tags, the Readers, the EPC Middleware, the EPC Information Services (EPCISs), the Object Naming Service (ONS), and Discovery Services. The specifications define how Readers interrogate an RFID tag. The Middleware filters and processes data that are gathered by Reader components. Data are then stored in EPCIS repositories and made available to external clients via the EPCIS Query Interface. The ONS offers a name resolution service that translates an EPC code into the URLs pointing to the EPCIS repositories storing data about that EPC. More specifically, static and dynamic data about physical objects are stored in databases that can be handled by different actors (e.g., manufacturers, logistic providers, retailers, or third parties) and can be accessed via the EPCIS standard interface [23].

The EPC Object Name Service (ONS) is the service that provides clients with the EPCIS URL for a given EPC. The ONS is based on the Internet Domain Name System, which is characterized by a hierarchical architecture [24]. The ONS points to the manufacturer's EPCIS resources. Moreover, discovery services enable discovery of third parties' EPCIS repositories. The EPCIS Discovery Service is the lookup service providing clients with the URIs of EPCIS repositories storing information about a given EPC. The EPCIS Discovery specifications have not been published yet at the time of writing [25]. Several research contributions have thus attempted to fill this gap by proposing original solutions for discovery services.

The BRIDGE Project, funded by the European Commission, had the objective of investigating several issues related to the implementation and adoption of RFIDs in Europe. In the framework of the BRIDGE project, a prototype discovery service was implemented based on LDAP directories specifications [26]. The authors of [27] proposed an implementation of an EPC discovery service based on the IETF specifications of the Extensible Supply-chain Discovery Service ESDS [28].

More recently, some works investigated the use of peer-to-peer (P2P) systems to implement scalable and robust distributed discovery services. Schoenemann et al. [29] proposed a P2P-based architecture for enabling the information exchange among participants of a supply chain. Analogously, Shrestha et al. [30] proposed a peer-to-peer network, where each participant of the supply chain runs a node of the network. These nodes form a structured P2P overlay network with each node having a partial view of the other nodes. Manzanares-Lopez et al. [31] proposed a distributed discovery service for the EPCglobal network based on a P2P architecture, which offers item-level track and trace capabilities along the whole supply chain, also when items are not directly visible, since they are loaded within different storage systems (i.e., packages, boxes, containers, etc.). These peer-to-peer approaches typically adopt Distributed Hash Table (DHT) techniques. Distributed Hash Tables are distributed data structures where the information objects are placed deterministically, at the peer whose identifier corresponds to the information object's unique key according to a given distance metric [32].

In a DHT, each node is identified by means of a key (node-key), usually the MAC or IP address of the node. Analogously, content items handled by the network are identified by a key (content key). Both types of keys are mapped to an identifier of a given bit length by applying a hash function (e.g., SHA-1 or MD5). DHT overlay networks implementations differ in how nodes and contents are associated and how routing to the node responsible for a given identifier is defined. Well-known routing algorithms are Chord [33], Pastry [34], Tapestry [35], and Kademlia [36].

The study carried out by Evdokimov et al. [2] discusses some of the above-mentioned works [23, 24, 26, 29] by comparing strengths and weaknesses of these works and highlighting how P2P approaches better fulfil fault tolerance and communication scalability requirements. As discussed in that study, DHT peer-to-peer networks exhibit properties of scalability, efficiency, robustness, and load-balancing thanks to the adoption of consistent hashing. Typically, in a DHT of N nodes a lookup operation requires $O(\log N)$ hops. These networks show properties of self-organization and self-healing, since they are capable of handling joining and leaving events of participating members. For this reason, they also guarantee resilience to node failures and network malfunctioning. Load balancing is achieved through uniform hashing.

As highlighted in the state of the art analysis made by Evdokimov et al. [2], the above-mentioned works support queries providing an object identifier (typically the EPC code) as input, but they do not support more flexible query schemes based on object attributes, though these types of information queries could become very important in the future IoT.

4. A Discovery Service for the IoT Based on a Peer-to-Peer Network

This section describes our discovery service architecture based on a peer-to-peer overlay network. In particular, our approach aims to cope with the following functional requirements: flexible identification scheme, multiattribute query, range query, multiple publishers, management APIs. As discussed in the Related Work Section, most existing works do not support multiattribute and range queries. These contributions are able to solve an exact match query and thus they assume that the client knows the identifier of the target object. This assumption can be easily satisfied if the client application can acquire the identifier from an RFID reader that is close to the RFID-tagged object. However, such a physical proximity constraint would inevitably limit the scope of IoT applications. For instance, a good monitoring application might include the following desired features: (a) displaying on the map the current and past positions of a goods item with identifier I during a multimodal transport route, (b) displaying on the map the current and past positions of the items travelling from location X to location Y. In this example, feature (b) might be easily realized by relying on a discovery service capable of handling complex queries, in addition to exact match queries.

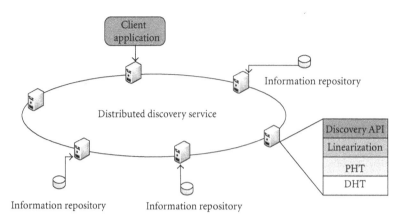

FIGURE 1: Functional view of the proposed Distributed Discovery Service.

Our work aims to address these limitations of related work by proposing a distributed discovery service capable of handling multiattribute and range queries. Hereafter, we describe the design of our DHT-based discovery service and our choice to adopt a layered functional architecture to promote modularity, ease of design and implementation, and maintainability of the system.

4.1. Existing DHT Implementations for Handling Complex Queries. Most widely adopted DHT implementations, such as Chord [33] and Kademlia [36], support one-attribute exact match queries. Several solutions have been proposed in order to handle range queries. The approach proposed in [21] is based on the adoption of the Prefix Hash Tree (PHT), a distributed data structure that can be built on top of a DHT implementation. The PHT overlay is based on a trie-based structure. A trie is a special tree in which each node represents a prefix of the target data domain. Interestingly, PHT relies merely on the DHT lookup() operation, and it is hence agnostic to the underlying DHT algorithm and implementation. The PHT solution presented in [37] supports only single-attribute range queries.

Mercury [38] supports multiattribute range queries by handling multiple simple overlays, one for each attribute, mapped onto a set of physical nodes. MAAN [39] extends Chord with locality preserving hashing and a recursive multidimensional query resolution mechanism. MAAN relies on a locality-preserving hashing function for each attribute, which has to be constructed using the attribute's values distribution (to be known in advance).

Squid [40] is a peer-to-peer information discovery system implementing a DHT-based structured keyword search. Each data element is associated with a sequence of keywords, the keywords form a multidimensional keyword space where data elements are points in the space and the keywords are the coordinates. In Squid, Space Filling Curves are used to map this multidimensional keyword space to a one-dimensional index space. Space Filling Curves can be defined as a continuous mapping from a d-dimensional space to a one-dimensional space, that is, $f : N^d \rightarrow N$. Examples of SFCs are the Morton curve (z-curve), the Gray code curve, and the Hilbert curve. Depending on the adopted mapping

rule, SFCs show different locality-preserving properties. SFCs are locality preserving in that points that are close in the one-dimensional space are mapped from close points in the d-dimensional space. In [41] a SFC-based technique is applied on an indexing scheme built on top of a generic DHT implementation to resolve multiattribute range queries.

4.2. Layered Architecture. We chose to use the Prefix Hash Tree (PHT) distributed data structure. Since a PHT data structure can be built on top of a generic DHT implementation, major advantages of this approach are the promotion of a layered design, and thus, modularity, ease of design, implementation, and maintenance.

Our design approach distinguishes the following layers: (a) an SFC linearization technique for mapping a multidimensional domain into a one-dimensional one, (b) a PHT search structure leveraging on the generic DHT get/put interface, (c) a DHT implementation based on the Kademlia algorithm [20]. By exploiting the distributed data management capabilities offered by this peer-to-peer overlay network, application-specific APIs for search and management of discovery-related information can be built.

Figure 1 shows the high-level architecture of the proposed system: each peer exposes a set of discovery APIs that can be invoked by client applications to search for some objects. The Discovery services returns the URIs of the repositories that handle information and services about those objects.

Below we describe our choices for the design of the three layers (a), (b), and (c), while Discovery APIs for a reference application scenario are described in Section 5.

4.2.1. Linearization of the Multiattribute Domain. We suppose that objects can be characterized by d attributes, including the object identifier (e.g., EPC, URI identification schemes). Consequently, our target data domain is a d-dimensional space. We applied a linearization technique based on Space Filling Curves to map a d-dimensional data domain onto a 1-dimensional data domain. The derived 1-dimensional data domain can thus be easily indexed in the PHT structure, as described below.

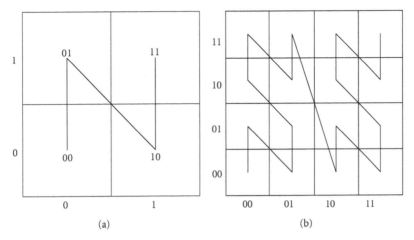

FIGURE 2: z-order curve approximations: (a) first-order z-curve; (b) second-order z-curve.

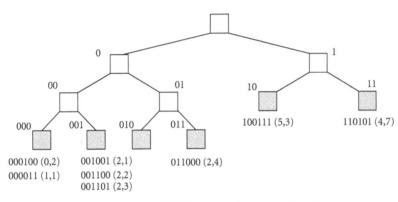

FIGURE 3: Example of a PHT for a two-dimensional data domain.

Among the existing types of SFC, we chose to adopt the Morton curve, known also as z-curve, since it is computationally simpler to generate than other known SFCs. A z-order-derived key is assembled by cyclically taking a bit from each coordinate of a point in d-dimensional space and appending it to those taken previously ("bit interleaving") [42]. For instance, the 2-dimensional point $P(x_1 x_2 x_3 x_4 \cdots x_d, y_1 y_2 y_3 y_4 \cdots y_d)$ is mapped onto the derived key $x_1 y_1 x_2 y_2 x_3 y_3 x_4 y_4 \cdots x_d y_d$.

A Space Filling Curve is constructed recursively and can be characterized by two parameters: the order of multidimensionality d and the order of approximation k. The first approximation (first-order curve) is obtained by partitioning a d-dimensional cube into n^d subcubes and connecting the subcubes to form a continuous curve. The kth approximation is obtained by connecting n^{kd} subcubes. Figure 2 shows an example of a SFC built in a 2-dimensional space over the binary domain $\{0, 1\}$: Figure 2(a) shows the first-order approximation and Figure 2(b) shows the second-order approximation.

4.2.2. PHT Data Structure. We assume that the data set to be indexed is some number N of D-bit binary keys. A PHT data structure is a binary trie, in which each node of the trie is labelled with a prefix. The prefix is defined recursively: a node with label l has either zero or two children, and the right and left child nodes are labelled with $l0$ and $l1$, respectively. A key K is stored at the leaf node whose label is a prefix of K. Each leaf node can store at most B keys. Consequently, the shape of the PHT depends on the distribution of keys: the trie depth is greater in regions of the domain that are densely populated and lower in sparsely populated domain regions. Figure 3 shows an example of a 2-dimensional data set indexed in a trie-based structure: first, 2-dimensional data objects are mapped into one-dimensional binary keys by means of the z-order curve linearization technique; then, the data objects are stored in the PHT leaf nodes whose label is a prefix of their one-dimensional binary key.

The PHT structure is an indexing data structure built on top of the DHT overlay network. As described in [21], the logical PHT structure is distributed across the nodes in a DHT. PHT prefixes are hashed and assigned to the proper DHT node, that is, a PHT vertex with label l is assigned to the node whose identifier is closest to HASH(l). The PHT can be built by relying on two basic DHT operations: put(key, value) and get(key) primitives. It does not require knowledge of the DHT routing algorithm and implementation details. Consequently, it can be built on top of any DHT implementation.

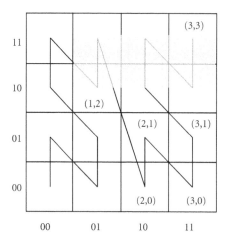

Range query: $1 \le x \le 3, 2 \le y \le 3$

FIGURE 4: Results for a range query over a one-dimensional z-curve.

PHT Lookup Operation. Given a key K of D bits, a PHT lookup operation shall return the unique leaf node whose label is a prefix of K. According to the algorithm proposed in [37], we adopted a binary search approach. The first step is to determine the prefix from which to start the search, so we consider the first $D/2$ bits of key K. Then, the get() operation is invoked on the DHT overlay with the $D/2$ key prefix provided as input parameter. The result returned by the DHT can be of three types: null, internal node, or leaf node. If the retrieved node is a leaf node, the search algorithm returns all the keys, along with the desired key, stored in the node; if the node does not exist (null), the prefix length is reduced. If the prefix is associated to an internal node, the search algorithm tries longer prefixes, repeating this step recursively until a leaf node is found. This kind of search has been preferred to a linear approach since it allows to considerably reduce the workload on the root and it requires $\log D$ DHT gets, thus making the lookup operation efficient [37].

PHT Insert/Delete Operation. The insertion or deletion of a key K in the PHT relies on the lookup operation to find the proper leaf node. In case of insertion, if the constraint on the number of maximum allowed children is violated, the node has to be split into two nodes, and the keys stored in the original node are distributed across the two novel leaf nodes.

PHT Range Query. In a one-dimensional data domain, a range query can be expressed as follows: given two keys L and H, where $L < H$, a range query shall return all the keys K that satisfy the condition $L \le K \le H$.

The PHT search algorithm first defines the smallest prefix that covers the whole specified range. If this prefix is the label of an internal node, then the query is forwarded recursively to the child nodes whose prefix falls within the specified range, until leaf nodes are reached [37].

An analogous approach is adopted for a range query in a d-dimensional domain. Minimal and maximal values for each coordinates are linearized to obtain minimum

and maximum derived keys. Then, the maximum common prefix of these derived keys can be obtained. The maximum common prefix thus allows locating the node the search is started from. The search is forwarded recursively to child nodes, selecting those nodes whose prefix falls within the monodimensional range delimited by the minimum and maximum derived keys, until leaf nodes are found.

The above-mentioned search algorithm can return leaf nodes that contain keys whose delinearized d-dimensional value does not fall within the original range query. This fact depends on the locality-preserving property of the adopted SFC curve. Points that are close on a linearized monodimensional space can be distant in the originating d-dimensional one. As shown in Figure 4, a range query in a 2-dimensional domain ($1 \le x \le 3$, $1 \le y \le 3$) can be mapped into a range query on a 1-dimensional binary domain ($0111 \le z \le 1111$) by applying the z-order curve linearization technique, but some results of the 1-dimensional query fall outside the original 2-dimensional query.

As searches of the left and right subtrees can be performed in parallel, the complexity of the algorithm is linearly proportional to the depth of the trie region that has been analysed.

If the query range is increased, the length of the maximal common prefix where the search starts from decreases. Consequently, the cost of the search increases since the trie region to be analysed increases. A typical example is when a range query is specified for a subset of attributes (e.g., x attributes), while for the remaining $d - x$ attributes any value is allowed, or a wild card query is performed. In order to reduce the cost of search, we introduced a mechanism that allows starting the search in parallel branches at deeper levels in the trie, by exploiting a simple pattern matching technique. First, we defined a "relaxed common prefix". Given the minimum and maximum derived keys, L ($l_1 l_2 l_3 \cdots l_k$) and H ($h_1 h_2 h_3 \cdots h_k$), respectively, the relaxed maximal common prefix P ($p_1 p_2 p_3 \cdots p_k$) is built according to Pseudocode 1.

```
Input:
minimum derived key L ($l_1 l_2 l_3 \cdots l_k$)
maximum derived key H ($h_1 h_2 h_3 \cdots h_k$),
Output:
relaxed maximal common prefix P ($p_1 p_2 p_3 \ldots p_m$) with m <= k
counter i ← 0;
counter j ← 0;
WHILE ($h_i \geq l_i$ AND i < n) DO
{
IF $h_i = l_i$ THEN $p_j = h_i$;
IF $h_i = 1$ AND $l_i = 0$ THEN $p_j = .$ (where . is the wildcard bit);
i + 1;
j + 1;
}
```

PSEUDOCODE 1

For instance, in a bidimensional data domain, the range query $2 \leq x \leq 4$, $2 \leq y \leq 4$ originates the minimum and maximum derived keys 001100 and 110000, respectively. While the maximum common prefix would be null, the "relaxed common prefix" is ".", where the symbol "." represents a wildcard bit (i.e., it matches any value {0, 1}). The search can thus be performed in parallel by starting from the prefixes matching the relaxed common prefix.

4.2.3. DHT. As mentioned above, the PHT indexing scheme is independent from the underlying DHT implementation, since a PHT relies on the basic put() and get() primitives offered by any DHT. The DHT that has been used for this work has been design and developed from scratch based upon the Kademlia specifications [20]. In addition, our DHT implementation supports data replication and versioning. Replicas of each data item are maintained in N nodes of the DHT network, where N can be configured. Replication is needed to improve availability and fault tolerance, while it introduces threats to the consistency of stored data. Our system implements an eventual consistency approach by handling multiple versions of a given data item. Conflicts arising from the presence of multiple versions of a data item in the system at the same time are handled and resolved by using vector clocks [43]. A vector clock is a list of tuples (node address, counter), and each version of an object has a vector clock assigned. Vector clocks can be analysed to infer causality between two events (i.e., different versions of the same object) and thus to decide if two versions of the same object are on parallel versioning branches (i.e., they are conflicting resources). When a versioning conflict is detected, the two resources are reconciled. In the current implementation, a basic reconciliation mechanism is implemented by merging the conflicting versions.

5. Experimentation

We performed a set of experimentation activities in a reference scenario for goods tracing and tracking in a multimodal transport chain.

In this reference scenario, several types of actors are involved, as shown in Figure 5: multimodal transport operators, road transport operators, shipping companies, intermodal terminal operators, and customers (the sender and addressee). These actors typically interact with tracking and tracing services to query for or to insert new information about the status and location of monitored good items. Moreover, also institutional actors (e.g., Port Authorities, Customs systems, etc.) and third-party actors (e.g., banks, insurance companies) can query for information about goods on transit [44].

In this scenario, we defined a set of attributes, in addition to the goods item identifier (i.e., the EPC number), that can usefully characterize the information acquired and stored during the steps of the transport route and that can be used to ease information retrieval tasks for different application purposes.

  (i) departure latitude;

  (ii) departure longitude;

  (iii) arrival latitude;

  (iv) arrival longitude;

  (v) type of goods (e.g., dangerous goods classification codes).

Our solution does not mandate any specific Object Identifier schema. For this experimentation activity we chose the EPC-64 numbering scheme (an EPC code encoded as a sequence of 64 bits). Latitude and longitude coordinates can be encoded into a sequence of 40 bits each [45]. For the type of goods attribute, we adopted the UN classification schema for dangerous goods, consisting in a 4-digit number, encoded in 16 bits. As the linearization technique has to be applied to sequences of bits of equal length, the shorter sequences are padded with zero bits on the left, so that they have the same length as the longer sequence (i.e., the 64-bit EPC code). The resulting PHT key is thus 384-bit long.

The information record stored for each key is a list of tuples (URL, timestamp), where the URL refers to an information repository storing the information about the target

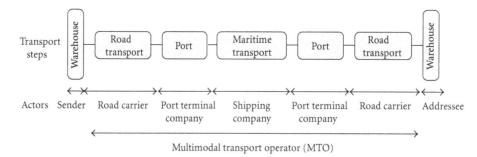

FIGURE 5: Actors involved in a multimodal transport chain.

object, and the timestamp marks the time when the record has been inserted in the system. As a matter of fact, during an object lifecycle, several information repositories handled by different actors could be associated to the object's identifier.

The API exposed to client applications can thus support the following operations.

(i) Inserting a new object: the client has to provide the values of the selected six attributes. These values are processed by the system to generate the corresponding PHT key. The system inserts the PHT key in the trie-based structure and the associated information (URL and timestamp) in the underlying DHT nodes.

(ii) Adding/deleting an information record associated to an object: the system uses the PHT key associated with the object to locate the information records stored in the DHT and update them by adding/deleting the given record.

(iii) Retrieving the information records for a given object: the system uses the PHT key associated with the provided query input parameters to locate the DHT nodes and retrieve stored information records.

(iv) Retrieving the information records for a set of objects that satisfy a range query over (a set of) attributes: the system exploits the trie-based structure to retrieve the PHT keys that are within the query range and to gather the information objects associated with the retrieved objects.

We performed a set of testing activities in order to analyse the structural properties and performance of the PHT. The object of our testing activities was the PHT overlay and not the underlying DHT implementation, therefore we adopted the testing methodology proposed in [41]. We used a DHT network of 20 nodes running on two physical hosts connected on a LAN environment. Since performance is measured in terms of DHT operations, we can abstract from the network characteristics.

To analyse the structural properties of the PHT indexing scheme, we conducted a set of experiments through computational simulations. We adopted two metrics: the average leaf depth of the trie and the average block utilization, which is calculated as the ratio of the number of elements stored in the leaf node to the value of block B, that is, the maximum number of keys that can be stored in a node [41]. We measured these properties on a data set of progressively increasing size (up to 20,000 keys) populated with randomly generated keys.

Figure 6 shows how the average depth of the leaf nodes varies with the block size. The average depth of the nodes decreases logarithmically with the increase of the block size. This is due to the fact that increasing values of B (block size) results in leaves containing more keys and thus a less deep trie structure. The average depth of leaf nodes increases with the data set size. Figure 6 shows the average depth measured for data sets of size 90 kB, 400 kB, 600 kB, and 1 MB. This behaviour is analogous to the one observed for other over-DHT indexing approaches [41, 46].

As shown in Figure 7, the block utilization exhibits a fluctuating behaviour as the block size increases. The bucket utilization shows how full the leaf nodes are with respect to the maximum allowed block size. Especially for smaller data sets (90 kB and 600 kB), the block utilization value fluctuates as the block size increases. As the data set size increases, the block utilization tends to increase with the block size. These results can be hardly compared with other approaches in the literature, since the behaviour of this structural property may vary with the type of the data set distribution [46].

We measured the performance of insert and lookup operations in the PHT by analysing the number of accesses to the underlying DHT for invoking get() and put() operations. We populated the PHT with 200,000 derived keys, and we measured the number of DHT operations that were performed at each level of the PHT trie for inserting a set of 1,000 uniformly distributed keys. As depicted in Figure 8, results show that higher levels in the trie are seldom accessed, thanks to the adopted binary search approach. Then, we performed a set of range query operations over a population of 200,000 keys stored in the PHT. For each iteration, we varied the range span of the queries (from wider ranges with a common prefix of zero length to an exact match query). Again, the results show that the workload in terms of accesses to the DHT seldom affects the root of the trie (Figure 9).

According to these testing results, our system behaves analogously to other over-DHT indexing approaches [41, 46]. Overlay-dependent indexing schemes can implement more efficient mechanisms for handling complex queries, since they can also modify the underlying routing mechanism, such as Mercury [38]. However, they are usually more

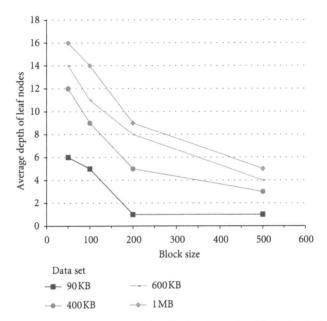

FIGURE 6: PHT structural properties: average depth of leaf nodes against block size for increasing data sets.

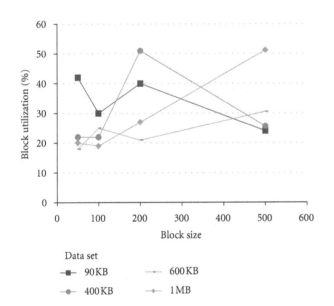

FIGURE 7: PHT structural properties: block utilization.

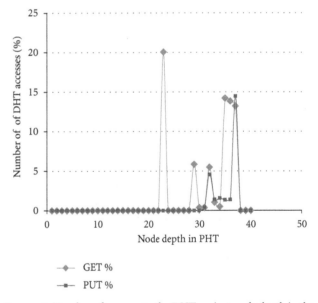

FIGURE 8: Number of accesses to the DHT against node depth in the PHT for the insert operation.

demanding in terms of complexity of design, development, and maintenance [46].

6. Conclusions

In this paper, we proposed a distributed Discovery Service based on a peer-to-peer overlay network for IoT scenarios. With respect to existing approaches implementing a DHT-based discovery service for the IoT and, in particular, for RFID-based scenarios, our original contribution consists in supporting more complex queries, that is, multiattribute and range queries.

Our design approach was based on the adoption of an over-DHT indexing scheme, thus easing the design of a layered functional architecture. More specifically, our discovery system design is made of the following layers: (a) an SFC linearization technique for mapping a multidimensional domain into a one-dimensional one, (b) a PHT search structure leveraging on a generic DHT get/put interface, (c) a DHT implementation based on the Kademlia algorithm. Although overlay-dependent indexing schemes can be more efficient in handling complex queries, they are usually more demanding in terms of complexity of design, development,

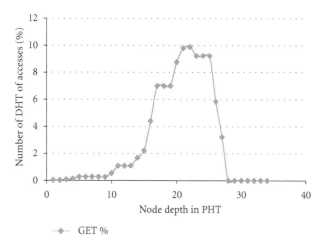

FIGURE 9: Number of accesses to the DHT against node depth in the PHT for the range query operation.

and maintenance [46]. Instead, our layered solution privileges ease of design and implementation.

We implemented a Proof of Concept in a reference application scenario for dangerous goods monitoring. We thus reported results achieved through experimentation activities regarding structural properties and query performance in an in-laboratory testing configuration. More extensive testing activities are planned in the near future. To this purpose, we are evaluating the possibility of exploiting the capabilities offered by PlanetLab, which is a large-scale distributed testbed [47].

Future research activities will also be devoted to carry out a case study on dangerous goods monitoring within a research project (SITMAR research project), funded by the Italian Ministry for Economic Development. To this purpose, we will also delve into security issues, ranging from secure communication to trust between interacting parties.

Acknowledgment

The authors thank Mr. Luca Capannesi from the University of Florence for his technical support.

References

[1] D. Guinard, V. Trifa, and E. Wilde, "A resource oriented architecture for the web of things," in *Proceedings of the 2nd International Internet of Things Conference (IoT '10)*, pp. 9–129, December 2010.

[2] S. Evdokimov, B. Fabian, S. Kunz, and N. Schoenemann, "Comparison of Discovery Service architectures for the Internet of Things," in *Proceedings of the IEEE International Conference on Sensor Networks, Ubiquitous, and Trustworthy Computing (SUTC '10)*, pp. 237–244, June 2010.

[3] G. D. Abowd, I. Bobick, I. Essa, E. Mynatt, and W. Rogers, "The aware home: developing technologies for successful aging," in *Proceedings of the American Association of Artificial Intelligence Conference*, 2002.

[4] F. Paganelli and D. Giuli, "An ontology-based system for context-aware and configurable services to support home-based continuous care," *IEEE Transactions on Information Technology in Biomedicine*, vol. 15, no. 2, pp. 324–333, 2011.

[5] F. Paganelli and D. Giuli, "A context-aware service platform to support continuous care networks," in *Proceedings of the 4th International Conference on Universal Access in Human-Computer Interaction (UAHCI '07)*, vol. 4555, part 2 of *Lecture Notes in Computer*, pp. 168–177, 2007.

[6] J. E. Bardram, "Applications of context-aware computing in hospital work—examples and design principles," in *Proceedings of the ACM Symposium on Applied Computing*, pp. 1574–1579, March 2004.

[7] F. Paganelli, E. Spinicci, A. Mamelli, R. Bernazzani, and P. Barone, "ERMHAN: a multi-channel context-aware platform to support mobile caregivers in continuous care networks," in *Proceedings of the IEEE International Conference on Pervasive Services (ICPS '07)*, pp. 355–360, July 2007.

[8] F. Paganelli and D. Giuli, "An ontology-based context model for home health monitoring and alerting in chronic patient care networks," in *Proceedings of the 21st International Conference on Advanced Information Networking and ApplicationsWorkshops/Symposia (AINAW '07)*, pp. 838–845, May 2007.

[9] F. Paganelli, M. C. Pettenati, and D. Giuli, "A metadata-based approach for unstructured document management in organizations," *Information Resources Management Journal*, vol. 19, no. 1, pp. 1–22, 2006.

[10] A. Kocurova, S. Oussena, P. Komisarczuk, and T. Clark, "Context-aware content-centric collaborative workflow management for mobile devices," in *Proceedings of the 2nd International Conference on Advanced Collaborative Networks, Systems and Applications (COLLA '12)*, pp. 54–57, IARIA.

[11] A. García-Crespo, J. Chamizo, I. Rivera, M. Mencke, R. Colomo-Palacios, and J. M. Gómez-Berbís, "SPETA: social pervasive e-Tourism advisor," *Telematics and Informatics*, vol. 26, no. 3, pp. 306–315, 2009.

[12] F. Paganelli, G. Bianchi, and D. Giuli, "A context model for context-aware system design towards the ambient intelligence vision: experiences in the eTourism domain," in *Proceedings of the 9th ERCIM Workshop "User Interfaces For All", Special Theme: 'Universal Access in Ambient Intelligence Environments'*, Lecture Notes in Computer Science, Springer, Königswinter, Germany, September 2006.

[13] D. Giuli, F. Paganelli, S. Cuomo, and P. Cianchi, "A systemic and cooperative approach towards an integrated infomobility system at regional scale," in *Proceedings of the IEEE International Conference on ITS Telecommunications (ITST '11)*, pp. 547–553.

[14] J. Santa and A. F. Gómez-Skarmeta, "Sharing context-aware road and safety information," *IEEE Pervasive Computing*, vol. 8, no. 3, pp. 58–65, 2009.

[15] S. Turchi, L. Ciofi, F. Paganelli, F. Pirri, and D. Giuli, "Designing EPCIS through linked data and REST principles," in *Proceedings of the International Conference on Software, Telecommuniccations and Computer Networks (SoftCOM '12)*, Split, Croatia, September 2012.

[16] D. Parlanti, F. Paganelli, and D. Giuli, "A service-oriented approach for network-centric data integration and its application to maritime surveillance," *IEEE Systems Journal*, vol. 5, no. 2, pp. 164–175, 2011.

[17] L. Atzori, A. Iera, and G. Morabito, "The internet of things: a survey," *Computer Networks*, vol. 54, no. 15, pp. 2787–2805, 2010.

[18] K. Finkenzeller, *RFID Handbook*, Wiley, 2003.

[19] W. Yao, C. H. Chu, and Z. Li, "Leveraging complex event processing for smart hospitals using RFID," *Journal of Network and Computer Applications*, vol. 34, no. 3, pp. 799–810, 2011.

[20] I. Zappia, F. Paganelli, and D. Parlanti, "A lightweight and extensible Complex Event Processing system for sense and respond applications," *Expert Systems with Applications*, vol. 39, no. 12, pp. 10408–10419, 2012.

[21] H. Sundmaeker, P. Guillemin, P. Friess, and S. Woelfflé, *Vision and Challenges for Realising the Internet of Things*, Cerp-IoT Cluster of European Research Projects on the Internet of Things, European Commission, 2010.

[22] F. Thiesse, C. Floerkemeier, M. Harrison, F. Michahelles, and C. Roduner, "Technology, standards, and real-world deployments of the EPC network," *IEEE Internet Computing*, vol. 13, no. 2, pp. 36–43, 2009.

[23] B. Fabian and O. Günther, "Security challenges of the EPCglobal network," *Communications of the ACM*, vol. 52, no. 7, pp. 121–125, 2009.

[24] EPCglobal, Object Name Service (ONS) 1.0.1, Ratified Standard Specification with Approved, Fixed Errata, 2008.

[25] EPCGlobal, http://www.gs1.org/gsmp/kc/epcglobal.

[26] BRIDGE Project, "Working prototype of serial-level lookup service," 2008, http://www.bridge-project.eu/data/File/BRIDGE_WP02_Prototype_Serial_level_lookup_service.pdf.

[27] U. Barchetti, A. Bucciero, M. De Blasi, L. Mainetti, and L. Patrono, "Implementation and testing of an EPCglobal-aware discovery service for item-level traceability," in *Proceedings of the International Conference on Ultra Modern Telecommunications and Workshops (ICUMT '09)*, pp. 1–8, October 2009.

[28] M. Young, "Extensible supply-chain discovery service concepts (Draft 04)," Internet Draft, IETF, 2008.

[29] N. Schoenemann, K. Fischbach, and D. Schoder, "P2P architecture for ubiquitous supply chain systems," in *Proceedings of the 17th European Conference on Information Systems*, pp. 2255–2266, 2009.

[30] S. Shrestha, D. S. Kim, S. Lee, and J. S. Park, "A peer-to-peer RFID resolution framework for supply chain network," in *Proceedings of the 2nd International Conference on Future Networks (ICFN '10)*, pp. 318–322, January 2010.

[31] P. Manzanares-Lopez, J. P. Muoz-Gea, J. Malgosa-Sanahuja, and J. C. Sanchez-Aarnoutse, "An efficient distributed discovery service for EPCglobal network in nested package scenarios," *Journal of Network and Computer Applications*, vol. 34, no. 3, pp. 925–937, 2011.

[32] Eng Keong Lua, J. Crowcroft, M. Pias, R. Sharma, and S. Lim, "A survey and comparison of peer-to-peer overlay network schemes," *IEEE Communications Surveys & Tutorials*, vol. 7, no. 2, pp. 72–93, 2005.

[33] I. Stoica, R. Morris, D. Liben-Nowell et al., "Chord: a scalable peer-to-peer lookup protocol for Internet applications," *IEEE/ACM Transactions on Networking*, vol. 11, no. 1, pp. 17–32, 2003.

[34] A. Rowstron and P. Druschel, "Pastry: scalable, distributed object location and routing for large-scale peer-to-peer systems," in *Proceedings of the IFIP/ACM International Conference on Distributed Systems Platforms (Middleware '01)*, pp. 329–335, Springer, London, UK, 2001.

[35] B. Y. Zhao, L. Huang, J. Stribling, S. C. Rhea, A. D. Joseph, and J. D. Kubiatowicz, "Tapestry: a resilient global-scale overlay for service deployment," *IEEE Journal on Selected Areas in Communications*, vol. 22, no. 1, pp. 41–53, 2004.

[36] P. Maymounkov and D. Mazieres, "Kademlia: a peer-to-peer information system based on the XOR metric," in *Proceedings of the 1st International Workshop on Peer-to-Peer Systems (IPTPS '01)*, pp. 53–65, Springer, London, UK, 2002.

[37] S. Ramabhadran, S. Ratnasamy, J. M. Hellerstein, and S. Shenker, "Brief announcement: prefix hash tree," in *Proceedings of the 23rd annual ACM symposium on Principles of Distributed Computing (PODC '04)*, pp. 368–368, ACM, New York, NY, USA.

[38] A. R. Bharambe, M. Agrawal, and S. Seshan, "Mercury: supporting scalable multi-attribute range queries," in *Proceedings of the Conference on Computer Communications (ACM SIGCOMM '04)*, pp. 353–366, September 2004.

[39] M. Cai, M. Frank, J. Chen, and P. Szekely, "MAAN: a multi-attribute addressable network for grid information services," *Journal of Grid Computing*, vol. 1, pp. 3–14, 2004.

[40] C. Schmidt and M. Parashar, "Squid: enabling search in DHT-based systems," *Journal of Parallel and Distributed Computing*, vol. 68, no. 7, pp. 962–975, 2008.

[41] Y. Chawathe, S. Ramabhadran, S. Ratnasamy, A. LaMarca, S. Shenker, and J. Hellerstein, "A case study in building layered DHT applications," in *Proceedings of the Conference on Applications, Technologies, Architectures, and Protocols for Computer Communications (SIGCOMM '05)*, pp. 97–108, ACM, New York, NY, USA.

[42] J. K. Lawder and P. J. H. King, "Using space-filling curves for multi-dimensional Indexing," in *Proceedings of the 17th British National Conferenc on Databases: Advances in Databases (BNCOD '00)*, Springer, London, UK, 2000.

[43] L. Lamport, "Time, clocks, and the ordering of events in a distributed system," *Communications of the ACM*, vol. 21, no. 7, pp. 558–565, 1978.

[44] Bollen et al., Sea and Air Container Track and Trace Technologies: Analysis and Case Studies, Project NO. TPTT01/2002T, APEC, July 2004, http://www.apec-tptwg.org.cn/new/archives/tpt-wg24/safe/its/itf-track-trace.pdf.

[45] IETF Dynamic Host Configuration Protocol Option for Coordinate-based Location Configuration Information, Request for Comments: 3825, http://www.ietf.org/rfc/rfc382.txt.

[46] Y. Tang, S. Zhou, and J. Xu, "LIGHT: a query-efficient yet low-maintenance indexing scheme over DHTs," *IEEE Transactions on Knowledge and Data Engineering*, vol. 22, no. 1, pp. 59–75, 2010.

[47] E. Jaffe and J. Albrecht, "PlanetLab—P2P testing in the wild," in *Proceedings of the 9th International Conference on Peer-to-Peer Computing (IEEE P2P '09)*, pp. 83–84, September 2009.

Admission Control for Multiservices Traffic in Hierarchical Mobile IPv6 Networks by Using Fuzzy Inference System

Jung-Shyr Wu,[1] Shun-Fang Yang,[1,2] and Chen-Chieh Huang[1]

[1] *Department of Communication Engineering, National Central University, Chung-Li 32001, Taiwan*
[2] *Telecommunication Laboratories, ChungHwa Telecom Co., Ltd., Yang-Mei 32601, Taiwan*

Correspondence should be addressed to Shun-Fang Yang, ysf@cht.com.tw

Academic Editor: Youyun Xu

CAC (Call Admission Control) plays a significant role in providing QoS (Quality of Service) in mobile wireless networks. In addition to much research that focuses on modified Mobile IP to get better efficient handover performance, CAC should be introduced to Mobile IP-based network to guarantee the QoS for users. In this paper, we propose a CAC scheme which incorporates multiple traffic types and adjusts the admission threshold dynamically using fuzzy control logic to achieve better usage of resources. The method can provide QoS in Mobile IPv6 networks with few modifications on MAP (Mobility Anchor Point) functionality and slight change in BU (Binding Update) message formats. According to the simulation results, the proposed scheme presents good performance of voice and video traffic at the expenses of poor performance on data traffic. It is evident that these CAC schemes can reduce the probability of the handoff dropping and the cell overload and limit the probability of the new call blocking.

1. Introduction

Since the next generation networks will be unified networks based on IP architecture, the design of IP-based mobility management schemes becomes necessary. The IETF MIPv6 (Mobile IPv6) [1] and its extension were proposed for efficient mobility management. HMIPv6 (Hierarchical MIPv6) [2] manages the mobility of an MN (Mobile Node) using both a router located in the MN's home domain and a router located in a domain visited by the MN. Local movements of the MN are hidden from the outside of the visited domain. The HMIPv6 can reduce the amount of signaling and improve the performance of handover latency. Although much research [3, 4] focuses on modified Mobile IP to get better efficient performance, there are few research papers to discuss admission control scheme when considering handover and mobility management [5].

CAC (Call Admission Control) has to be revised to deal with the anticipated new composite radio wireless environment [6]. The ratio of the reserved bandwidth is adjusted to make CAC in the Mobile IP networks in [7]. Because the blocking probability, dropping probability and

cell utilization are sensitive to the reserved bandwidth, it is challenge in deciding how to adjust this ratio. The utilization of the wire line link between HA (Home Agent) and FA (Foreign Agent) is used to make CAC in [8, 9]. Because the wireless links are much easier to be the bottle neck than the wire line link, it is not proper to use the utilization of the wire line link alone. Good CAC schemes have to balance the new call blocking and the handoff call blocking in order to provide the desired QoS (Quality of Service) requirements. Since the channel reservation can be adjusted dynamically, mobility-based call admission control schemes can be designed to provide QoS in the wireless networks [10].

The GCP (Guard Channel Policy), proposed in [11], keeps a certain amount of channels to handoff calls only while the rest of the channels can be shared by both new calls and handoff calls. It has been shown in [12] that the GCP can minimize a linear objective function of Pb (new call blocking probability) and Pd (handoff dropping probability). An enhanced version of guard channel policy, called FGCP (Fractional GCP), has proven to be optimal in minimizing Pb with a hard constraint on Pd and minimizing

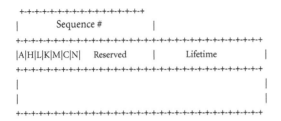

FIGURE 1: Local Binding Update message.

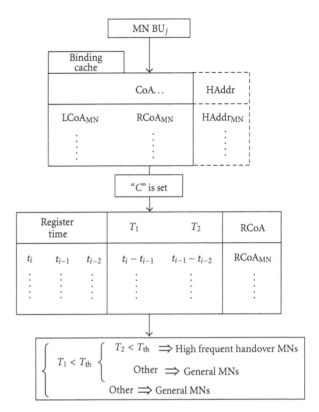

FIGURE 2: The operation procedure of the MAP.

the number of required channels with a hard constraint on both Pb and Pd. LFGCP (Limited FGCP), a combination of GCP and FGCP, is shown to be more effective than the basic guard channel policy in minimizing Pb and the number of required channels while holding the constraint on Pd.

In addition to much research that focuses on modified Mobile IP to get better efficient handover performance, CAC should be introduced to Mobile IP-based network to guarantee the QoS for users. The CAC schemes should handle packet-based applications that have highly burst and nonstationary traffic in modern communication networks. In this paper, we propose a CAC scheme which incorporates multiple traffic types and adjusts the admission threshold dynamically using FIS (Fuzzy Inference System) to achieve better usage of resources. The rest of the paper is organized as follows. Section 2 presents our previous work in the area of the HMIPv6-based CAC schemes. The proposed admission control algorithm is described in Section 3. The simulation architecture and result discussion are described in Sections 4 and 5, respectively. Finally, Section 6 concludes this paper.

2. HMIPv6-Based CAC Schemes

Some of the mobility-based CAC schemes that require extensive knowledge of the system parameters are not easy to implement; moreover, they sacrifice the scarce radio resources to satisfy the deterministic QoS bounds. The HMIPv6 extension headers can be combined with well-known CAC schemes, and the impacts of terminal mobility to the network performance are discussed. Our proposed method only requires few modifications on MAP (Mobility Anchor Point) functionality and slight change in BU (Binding Update) message formats.

The guard channel schemes are expanded to combine with the mobility information. A new call or a handoff call is identified from the new registered or updated HMIPv6 BU messages. The movement of MNs can be predicted by observing the variation of MN's position in a fixed period. In Figure 1, a new flag C is added in HMIPv6's BU message format, and it provides the movement recording of MNs for the calculation of the movement patterns. The M flag is defined in HMIPv6, and it indicates MAP registration. When an MN registers with the MAP, the M and A flags must be set to distinguish this registration from a BU being sent to the HA or a CN (Correspondent Node). An optional flag N

indicates a lower hierarchical MAP registration in the mobile networks. When C is set, M and N should be set in the MAP. The lower hierarchy MAPs will cover many ARs (Access Routers) that located far from the default MAP. When an MAP receives a BU from an MN, it will look up its binding cache at first. If there is no record, it will inform other MAPs. If there are no records in all MAPs, the call is identified as a new call. Because the IPv6 supports piggyback, the above procedure can use data messages to reduce the overhead of IPv6 headers.

The operation procedure of the MAP for the BU registration of MN is shown in Figure 2. When an MAP receives a BU with C flag set, it records the current registration time (t_{i-2}), the registration time (t_{i-1}) for the next times, and the registration time (t_i) for the next two times. The MAP also calculates $T_1 = t_i - t_{i-1}$, $T_2 = t_{i-1} - t_{i-2}$. The value of T_2 and T_1 represents MN's cell residency time in the current and next handoff cells. We define T_{th} as the critical threshold residency time. If both T_1 and T_2 are smaller than T_{th}, this call is recognized as a high-speed MN. The MAP uses MN' LCoA (on-link Care of Address) to identify which AR serves the MN and calculates the number of high-speed MNs and all MNs. The above procedure can reveal the MN density in the ARs and mobility patterns.

The mobility information can be combined with GCP, FGCP, and LFGCP as three mobility-based CAC schemes. It is evident that a high-speed MN needs much more capacity. When the number of high-speed MN is larger than a certain

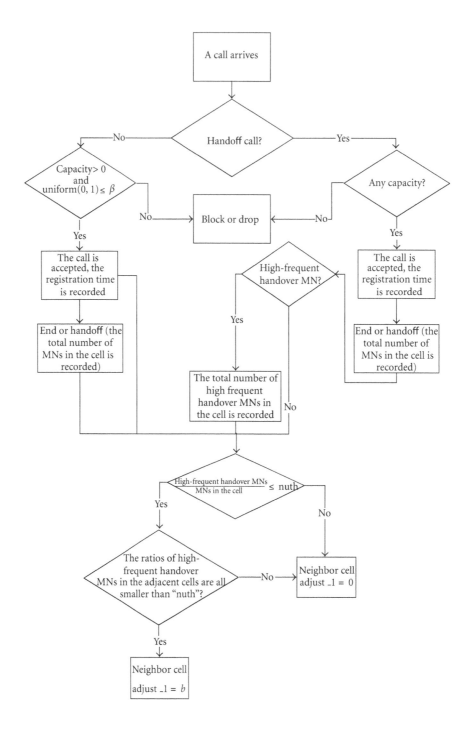

$$\beta = (1 - ((\text{adjust\_1/capacity}) \times (\text{capacity–residual capacity})))$$

FIGURE 3: The MBLFGCP CAC scheme.

ratio, the capacity of the cell will be exhausted. The ratio of high-speed MNs (Rhm) is defined to be

The ratio of high-speed MNs

$$= \frac{\text{(the total number of high-speed MNs in the cell)}}{\text{(the total number of MNs in the cell)}}. \quad (1)$$

The parameter "nuth" is defined as the threshold of the ratio of high-speed MNs, the parameter "adjust" as the reserved capacity, and the parameter "adjust_1" as a random adjustable value. The description of MBLFGCP (Mobility-Based LFGCP) CAC scheme is shown in Figure 3. The MBLFGCP combines MBGCP (Mobility-Based GCP) and MBLGCP (Mobility-Based LGCP), as same as the LFGCP

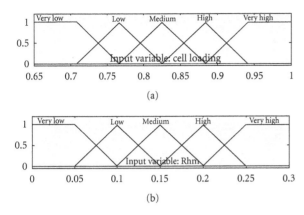

(a)

(b)

FIGURE 4: The membership functions of the input fuzzy variables.

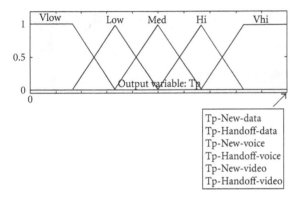

FIGURE 5: The membership functions of the output fuzzy variables.

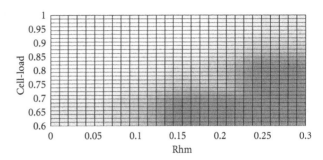

FIGURE 6: The value of the output variable.

3. The Proposed Admission Control Algorithm

Because the packet-based traffic exhibits highly burst and nonstationary properties, the previous CAC schemes cannot handle the drastic changes of traffic. Fuzzy logic is suitable to dynamicly control the thresholds for multiple traffic in the CAC schemes. We assume that there is one BS or several BSs under an AR. For the decision of the threshold values, the cell loading of the candidate BS and the ratio of high-speed nodes in the candidate BS are the input variables of the FIS, and the values of the threshold are the output variables of the FIS.

3.1. Dynamic Fuzzy Control of the Threshold Values for Multiple Traffic. Fuzzy logic, used to explain how to make suitable decision from imprecise and dissimilar information, is a good candidate to deal with the CAC threshold problem because it is able to simplify a large state space of resolution by means of reasonable rules. According to the understanding of the dynamic fuzzy control of the CAC threshold, the objective of the problem is to select the most appropriate threshold values taking into account different inputs.

For the decision of the threshold values, two criteria are used: the cell loading of the candidate BS and the ratio of high-speed nodes in the candidate BS. The cell loading of the candidate BS is defined to be

cell loading

$$= \frac{\text{(the total bandwidth of all traffic used in the cell)}}{\text{(the total bandwidth capacity in the cell)}}. \quad (2)$$

These values of threshold parameter (Tp) could be dynamically changed depending on the system requirements. We define the output parameters as follows.

(A) Tp-New-data (T_{da}): the threshold parameter for admission control of new generated data traffic, where T_{da} depends on the total number of the voice and video traffic (N_{vo}, N_{vi}).

(B) Tp-New-voice (T_{vo}): the threshold parameter for admission control of new generated voice traffic, where T_{vo} depends on the total number of the data and video traffic (N_{da}, N_{vi}).

(C) Tp-New-video (T_{vi}): the threshold parameter for admission control of new generated video traffic,

combines GCP and LGCP. The MBGCP will reject any new call when the parameter "adjust" equals "gc" (the number of free channels). The MBFGCP uses β to do admission control of new call. If the ratio of higher-mobility MNs in the adjacent cells is all smaller than "nuth", the parameter "adjust_1" of the center cell will change to b $(0 < b < 1)$. Then β will be set according to the residual capacity of the cell. If it is a new call, the capacity of the service cell should be checked at first. If there is enough capacity, we use probability of β to accept a call or reject a call. The MBLFGCP uses β to do admission control when the "adjust_1" equals b.

The detailed mobility-based CAC schemes and the performance comparison of these CAC schemes have been shown in our previous works [13, 14]. These CAC schemes only distinguish the priority between new call and handoff call and reserve fixed amount of bandwidth for high-priority traffic. These CAC schemes cannot satisfy the requirements of the present network environment which contains several types of service [15, 16]. On the other hand, reserving fixed amount of bandwidth will result in worse usage of BS (Base Station) bandwidth [16, 17]. Therefore, we propose a CAC scheme which incorporates multiple traffic types and adjusts the admission threshold dynamically using FIS (Fuzzy Inference System) to achieve better usage of resources.

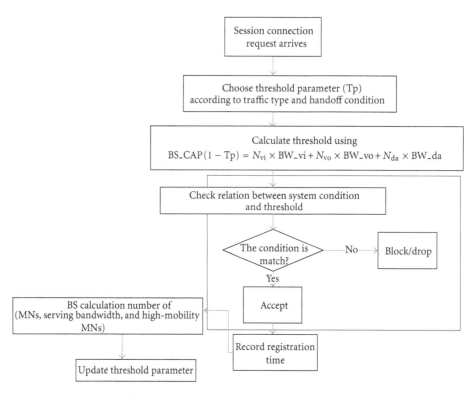

FIGURE 7: The main operation procedure of the proposed algorithm.

where T_{vi} depends on the total number of the voice and data traffic (N_{vo}, N_{da}).

(D) Tp-Handoff-data (T_{h_da}): the threshold parameter for admission control of handoff data traffic, where T_{h_da} depends on the total number of the voice and video traffic (N_{vo}, N_{vi}).

(E) Tp-Handoff-voice (T_{h_vo}): the threshold parameter for admission control of handoff voice traffic, where T_{h_vo} depends on the total number of the data and video traffic (N_{da}, N_{vi}).

(F) Tp-Handoff-video (T_{h_vi}): the threshold parameter for admission control of Handoff video traffic, where T_{vi} depends on the total number of the voice and data traffic (N_{vo}, N_{da}).

The FIS decision procedures operate in three steps, namely, fuzzification, inference engine, and defuzzification [18, 19]. The objective of the fuzzification process is to assign, for each input linguistic variable, a value between 0 and 1 corresponding to the degree of membership of the input to a given fuzzy set. The degree of membership values is obtained through membership functions. These input and output variables have five fuzzy sets: "very high" (VHi), "high" (Hi), "medium" (Med), "low", and "very low" (VLow). The membership functions of the input fuzzy variables are shown in Figure 4, and the membership functions of the output fuzzy variables are shown in Figure 5.

For each combination of fuzzy set from the fuzzification step, the inference engine makes use of some predefined fuzzy rules to indicate the suitability of selecting outputs.

TABLE 1: The fuzzy logic rules used in the FIS.

Rhm Cell-Load	VLow	Low	Med	Hi	VHi
VHi	VLow	VLow	VLow	Low	Med
Hi	VLow	Low	Low	Med	Hi
Med	VLow	Low	Med	Hi	VHi
Low	Low	Med	Hi	Hi	VHi
VLow	Med	Hi	VHi	VHi	VHi

Fuzzy rules were defined as a set of possible scenario utilizing a series of If-Then rules. For example, if the cell loading is "high," and Rhm is "high," the output variable is "medium". The fuzzy logic rules used in the FIS are shown in Table 1. Finally, the defuzzification converts the outputs of the inference engine into a crisp value, that is, a number ranging between 0 and 1. The other operation methods of the FIS [20] are shown in Table 2. The value of the output fuzzy variable is shown in Figure 6. The relationship between the input and output fuzzy variable has different style for different traffic types. The small value of the output variable, defined as the colored ranges, indicates that the call is easy to be accepted.

3.2. The Main Operation Procedure of the Proposed Admission Control Algorithm. The main operation procedure of the proposed algorithm is shown in Figure 7. The algorithm is described in the following.

When a new or handoff session enters the cell range of a BS, the BS should check the available bandwidth and decides

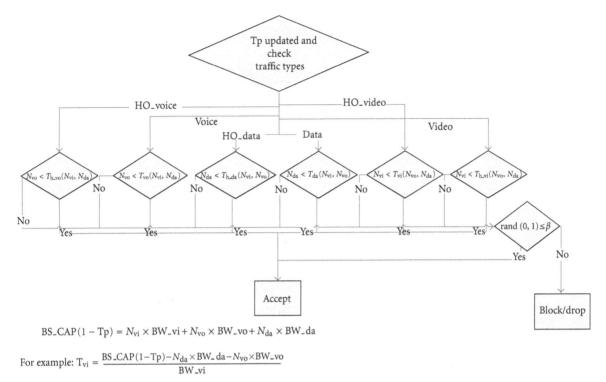

$$BS\_CAP(1 - Tp) = N_{vi} \times BW\_vi + N_{vo} \times BW\_vo + N_{da} \times BW\_da$$

$$\text{For example: } T_{vi} = \frac{BS\_CAP(1-Tp) - N_{da} \times BW\_da - N_{vo} \times BW\_vo}{BW\_vi}$$

FIGURE 8: The scheme used to check the relationship between the system status and the threshold values.

TABLE 2: The operation methods of the FIS.

Operation	Method	Mathematical formula
Intersection	Standard intersection	$t(p,q) = \min(p,q)$
Union	Standard union	$s(p,q) = \max(p,q)$
Implication	Mamdani product implication	$B'(y) = \max_{l=1}^{m}[\max_{x \in X}(A'(x) \wedge A_1^l(x_1) \wedge A_2^l(x_2) \wedge B(y))]$
Aggregation	Max	
Defuzzification	Center of gravity defuzzification	$y^* = \dfrac{\sum_{i=1}^{k} y_i B(y_i)}{\sum_{i=1}^{k} B(y_i)}$

to accept or block this session. If there is available residual bandwidth, the BS should select the suitable threshold parameter according to the traffic type (voice or data or video) and call type (new or handoff). Then the BS uses the selected threshold parameter to do admission control. If the system capacity is enough, this session is to be accepted. Otherwise, the BS uses the probability of β to do admission control as MBLFGCP. The other procedures are same as that of the MBLFGCP.

Because the BS should reserve a fraction of bandwidth to accept high-priority sessions, the summation of the bandwidth that occupied by all current traffic sessions should be equal to a part of the total bandwidth. Here, we used the following equation to calculate the value of the selected threshold parameter.

$$BS\_CAP(1 - Tp)$$
$$= N_{vi} \times BW\_vi + N_{vo} \times BW\_vo + N_{da} \times BW\_da, \quad (3)$$

where N_{vi}, N_{vo}, and N_{da} represent the session number of video, voice, and data sessions in a BS, respectively. BW_vi, BW_vo, and BW_da represent the required bandwidth of video, voice, and data sessions in a BS, respectively, and BS_CAP is the total bandwidth of a BS.

The detailed scheme, the region enclosed by the red line in Figure 7, used to compare the system status and the threshold values is shown in Figure 8. For example, the meaning of $N_{vo} < T_{vo}(N_{vi}, N_{da})$ can be explained as follows: if the number of the new voice is smaller than the selected threshold parameter, the session will be accepted, otherwise, the BS uses β to do admission control as in MBLFGCP.

4. Simulation Description

We use a self-made C++ simulator to compare the performance of the following schemes: no CAC (uncontrolled), LFGCP, MBLFGCP, and the proposed FIS-based CAC algorithm in the Hierarchical Mobile IPv6 networks.

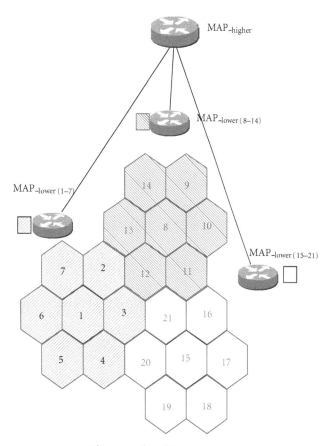

FIGURE 9: The network architecture in the simulation.

TABLE 3: The simulation parameters.

	Voice	Data	Video
Duration	180 s	40 s	300 s
Data rate	25 kbps	75 kbps	400 kbps
Percentage	40%	58%	2%
Velocity	10 km/hr~55 km/hr (random walk)		
Arrival rate	0.4~1.1 sessions/second, Poisson distribution		
Cell capacity	10 Mbps		
Cell Radius	250 m		

TABLE 4: The maximum values of the threshold parameters and the range of β.

Maximum value of Tp	Set-1	Set-2	Set-3	Set-4
Tp-New-data	0.12	0.139	0.139	0.15
Tp-Handoff-data	0.085	0.115	0.115	0.102
Tp-New-voice	0.086	0.06	0.06	0.072
Tp-Handoff-voice	0	0	0	0
Tp-New-Video	0.102	0.108	0.108	0.108
Tp-Handoff-video	0	0	0	0
Range of β	0.17~0.8	0.25~0.65	0.3~0.75	0.25~0.65

Three performance indicators are defined in the following:

$$Pd = \frac{\text{handoff dropping sessions}}{\text{all sessions in an AR}},$$

$$Pb = \frac{\text{new blocking sessions}}{\text{all sessions in an AR}}, \quad (4)$$

$$Pb \,\&\, d = \frac{\text{dropping or blocking sessions}}{\text{all sessions in an AR}}.$$

5. Performance Evaluation

We use four different fuzzy sets for the performance comparison. The maximum values of the threshold parameters are shown in Table 4. The maximum values of the threshold parameters are mapped to "very high" (VHi). Because the voice and video handoff traffic have the first priority, Tp-Handoff-voice and Tp-Handoff-video are both equal to zero.

The LFGCP and the MBLGCP use the β value to identify the acceptance probability of a new call or a handoff call. The value curves β with respect to the occupied capacity are shown in Figure 10. We set the parameter adjust_1 to be 0.3 and the reserved bandwidth (guard channel) to be 400 kbps (4% of BS_CAP). For example, the acceptable probability of a new call or a handoff call is 1 when the occupied capacity is smaller than the reserved bandwidth and the acceptable probability of a new call or a handoff call is decreased to 0.7 as shown in Figure 10(a).

The comparison of blocking probability of all traffic types is shown in Figure 11, and the comparison of dropping probability of all traffic types is shown in Figure 12. We have compared no CAC (uncontrolled), LFGCP, MBLFGCP, and the proposed FIS-based CAC schemes in the Hierarchical

The network architecture of the simulation is shown in Figure 9. There are 7 ARs under a MAP (MAP is also an AR), and there are 3 MAP_lower (Lower Hierarchy MAPs) under a MAP_higher (Higher Hierarchy MAP). When an MN registers with the MAP_higher, the M flag must be set. When an MN registers with the different MAP_lower, the N and M flag must be set. If the movement is in the same MAP_lower, the N flag must be set. When a BU message with M and N flag is sent to MAP_lower, this BU message will be forwarded to MAP_higher. We assume that AR1-7 are under MAP_lower1, AR8-14 are under MAP_lower2, and AR15-21 are under MAP_lower3.

The simulation parameters are shown in Table 3. Here the video traffic includes only real-time video conference applications. The average session duration of voice, data, and video traffics are 180, 40, and 300 seconds, separately. The percentage of voice, data, and video traffics are 40%, 58%, and 2%, separately. We assume that the connection level arrival rate in the AR follows Poisson distribution, and the mean arrival rate varies from 0.4 to 1.1 sessions per second. The average velocities of mobile nodes are from 10 km/hour to 55 km/hour with random walk mobility model. To model the movement of the MNs in the system, we assume that the time is slotted, and that the MN can make at most one move during a slot. The movements are assumed to be stochastic and independent from one MN or another. The numerical results take the average of 10 independent simulation runs.

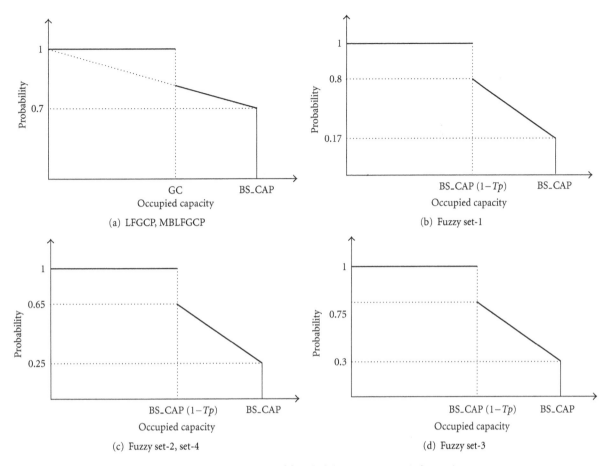

FIGURE 10: The value curve of β probability versus occupied capacity.

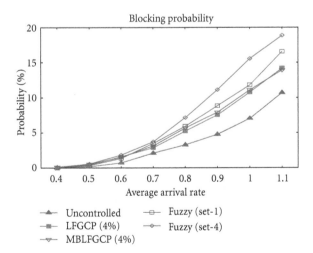

FIGURE 11: The comparison of blocking probability of all traffic types.

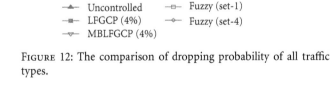

FIGURE 12: The comparison of dropping probability of all traffic types.

Mobile IPv6 networks. For simplicity, set-1 and set-4 are used as representatives of the four fuzzy sets. The proposed schemes have higher blocking probability and lower dropping probability. There is a tradeoff between increased Pb and decreased Pd according to the different values of the threshold parameters. For example, the set-4 reserves more bandwidth to the higher-priority traffic; the reserved bandwidth increased more than other schemes when the arrival rate increases. Owing to the same reason, the set-4 provides the highest blocking probability and the lowest dropping probability.

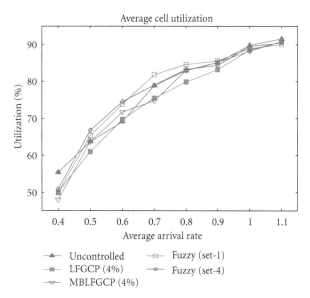

FIGURE 13: The average cell utilization.

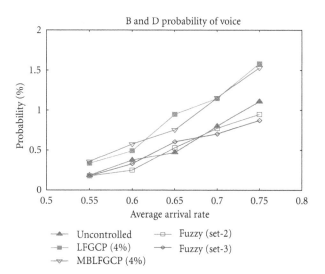

FIGURE 14: The blocking and dropping probability of voice traffic.

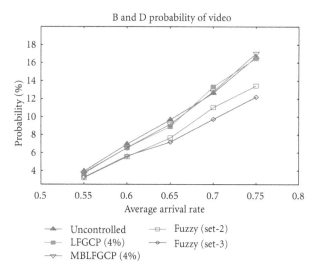

FIGURE 15: The blocking and dropping probability of video traffic.

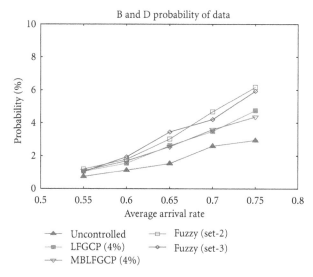

FIGURE 16: The blocking and dropping probability of data traffic.

The average cell utilization, the ratio of used capacity with the total capacity in a cell, among no CAC (uncontrolled), LFGCP, MBLFGCP, and the proposed FLS-based CAC algorithm (set-1, set-4) are shown in Figure 13. Because the proposed scheme makes dynamical fuzzy decision of the threshold values, it is obvious that the proposed algorithm provides higher cell utilization than the others. The comparison of the blocking and dropping probability of voice traffic is shown in Figure 14, where the proposed algorithm provides much lower Pb&d than MBLFGCP and LFGCP and also has a little better performance than the "uncontrolled" scheme. Because the video traffic needs much more bandwidth than other traffic, the video traffic is easier to be blocked or dropped. From the comparison of the blocking and dropping probability of video traffic that is shown in Figure 15, it is obvious that the proposed scheme has the best performance among all these CAC schemes.

The comparison of the blocking and dropping probability of data traffic is shown in Figure 16. Because the purpose of the proposed scheme tries to accept the real-time traffic at first, the proposed scheme has the worst performance for data traffic. The proposed scheme makes good performance for voice and video traffic with a sacrifice of the performance of data traffic.

6. Conclusions

We extend HMIPv6 Binding Update message to support CAC schemes. These CAC schemes can reduce the probability of the handoff dropping and cell overload and limit the new call blocking probability. We also propose a CAC scheme which incorporates multiple traffic types and adjusts the admission threshold dynamically using FIS to achieve better usage of resources. According to the simulation results, the proposed scheme presents good performance of voice and video traffic at the expenses of poor performance on data traffic. In future work, we will try to use genetic algorithm or adaptive neuron-fuzzy inference system (ANFIS) to make more complex and effective admission control schemes in HMIPv6 networks.

References

[1] D. Johnson, C. Perkins, and J. Arkko, "Mobility Support in IPv6," IETF RFC3775, pp.1–165, 2004.

[2] H. Soliman, C. Castelluccia, K. El Malki, and L. Bellier, "Hierarchical Mobile IPv6 Mobility Management (HMIPv6)," IETF RFC 5380, pp. 1–25, October 2008.

[3] I. F. Akyildiz, J. Xie, and S. Mohanty, "A survey of mobility management in next-generation all-IP-based wireless systems," *IEEE Wireless Communications*, vol. 11, no. 4, pp. 16–28, 2004.

[4] A. K. M. M. Hossain and K. Kanchanasut, "A handover management scheme for mobile IPv6 networks," in *Proceedings of the 14th International Conference on Computer Communications and Networks (ICCCN '05)*, pp. 43–48, San Diego, Calif, USA, October 2005.

[5] D. Bruneo, L. Paladina, M. Paone, A. Puliafito, C. Papardo, and S. Sperone, "Call admission control in hierarchical mobile networks," in *Proceedings of the 10th IEEE Symposium on Computers and Communications (ISCC '05)*, pp. 780–785, La Manga del Mar Menor, Cartagena, Spain, 2005.

[6] M. Ahmed, "Call admission control in wireless networks: a comprehensive survey," *IEEE Communications Surveys & Tutorials*, vol. 7, pp. 49–68, 2005.

[7] G. le Grand and E. Horlait, "A predictive end-to-end QoS scheme in a mobile environment," in *Proceedings of the 6th IEEE Symposium on Computers Communications (ISCC '01)*, pp. 534–539, Hammamet, Tunisia, July 2001.

[8] J. M. Moon, M. Y. Yun, G. S. Park, K. I. Kim, Y. J. Kim, and S. H. Kim, "QoS provisioning in domain based mobile IP networks," in *Proceedings of the 57th IEEE Semiannual Vehicular Technology Conference*, pp. 447–451, Jeju, Republic of Korea, April 2003.

[9] K. I. Kim, S. H. Kim, J. M. Moon, and Y. J. Kim, "Hierarchical admission control scheme for supporting mobility in mobile IP," in *Proceedings of the IEEE Military Communications Conference (MILCOM '02)*, pp. 431–435, Anaheim, Calif, USA, October 2002.

[10] J. Hou and Y. Fang, "Mobility-based call admission control schemes for wireless mobile networks," *Wireless Communications and Mobile Computing*, vol. 1, no. 3, pp. 269–282, 2001.

[11] D. Hong and S. S. Rappaport, "Traffic model and performance analysis for cellular mobile radio telephone systems with prioritized and nonprioritized handoff procedures," *IEEE Transactions on Vehicular Technology*, vol. 35, no. 3, pp. 77–92, 1986.

[12] R. Ramjee, R. Nagarajan, and D. Towsley, "On optimal call admission control in cellular networks," in *Proceedings of the IEEE Conference on Computer Communications (INFOCOM '96)*, pp. 43–50, San Francisco, Calif, USA, 1996.

[13] S. F. Yang and J. S. Wu, "Mobility based call admission control in hierarchical mobile IPv6 networks," in *Proceedings of the 4th IASTED Asian Conference on Communication Systems and Networks (AsiaCSN '07)*, pp. 271–276, Phuket, Thailand, 2007.

[14] J. S. Wu, W. Y. Lin, and S. F. Yang, "Hierarchical mobile IPv6 mobility management in integrated Wi-Fi and WiMAX networks," *Journal of Internet Technology*, vol. 8, no. 3, pp. 253–260, 2007.

[15] T. C. Chau, K. Y. M. Wong, and B. Li, "Optimal call admission control with QoS guarantee in a voice/data integrated cellular network," *IEEE Transactions on Wireless Communications*, vol. 5, no. 5, pp. 1133–1141, 2006.

[16] B. J. Hwang, I. S. Hwang, and L. F. Ku, "Adaptive bandwidth management and reservation scheme in heterogeneous wireless networks," *Journal of Internet Technology*, vol. 10, no. 3, pp. 237–244, 2009.

[17] S. Rito, P. Carvalho, and V. Freitas, "Admission control in multiservice IP networks: architectural issues and trends," *IEEE Communications Magazine*, vol. 45, no. 4, pp. 114–121, 2007.

[18] B. J. Hwang, I. S. Hwang, and S. C. Chang, "Adaptive resource management with fuzzy bandwidth control for multi-services in two-tier wireless networks," *Journal of the Chinese Institute of Engineers*, vol. 33, no. 2, 2010.

[19] J. M. Mendel, "Fuzzy logic systems for engineering: a tutorial," *Proceedings of the IEEE*, vol. 83, no. 3, pp. 345–377, 1995.

[20] W. Pedrycz, *Fuzzy Control and Fuzzy Systems*, John Wiley & Sons, New York, NY, USA, 1993.

3

A Retroactive-Burst Framework for Automated Intrusion Response System

Alireza Shameli-Sendi, Julien Desfossez, Michel Dagenais, and Masoume Jabbarifar

Départment de Genie Informatique et Génie Logiciel, École Polytechnique de Montréal, P.O. Box 6079, Succ. Downtown, Montreal, QC, Canada H3C 3A7

Correspondence should be addressed to Alireza Shameli-Sendi; alireza.shameli-sendi@polymtl.ca

Academic Editor: Rui Zhang

The aim of this paper is to present an adaptive and cost-sensitive model to prevent security intrusions. In most automated intrusion response systems, response selection is performed locally based on current threat without using the knowledge of attacks history. Another challenge is that a group of responses are applied without any feedback mechanism to measure the response effect. We address these problems through retroactive-burst execution of responses and a Response Coordinator (RC) mechanism, the main contributions of this work. The retroactive-burst execution consists of several burst executions of responses with, at the end of each burst, a mechanism for measuring the effectiveness of the applied responses by the risk assessment component. The appropriate combination of responses must be considered for each burst execution to mitigate the progress of the attack without necessarily running the next round of responses, because of the impact on legitimate users. In the proposed model, there is a multilevel response mechanism. To indicate which level is appropriate to apply based on the retroactive-burst execution, we get help from a Response Coordinator mechanism. The applied responses can improve the health of Applications, Kernel, Local Services, Network Services, and Physical Status. Based on these indexes, the RC gives a general overview of an attacker's goal in a distributed environment.

1. Introduction

Multisteps cyberattacks are common problems in distributed systems. Many security tools or system loggers may be installed in distributed systems and monitor all events in the network. Security managers often have to process huge numbers of alerts per day produced by such tools [1].

The Linux Trace Toolkit next generation (LTTng) [2] is a powerful software tool that provides a detailed execution trace of the Linux operating system with low impact. Its counterpart, the User Space Tracer (UST) library, provides the same trace information from user mode for middle-ware and applications [3]. The Target Communication Framework (TCF) agent collects traces from multiple systems. After collecting all traces, we need a powerful tool to monitor the health of a large system continuously such that system anomalies can be promptly detected and handled appropriately.

Intrusion Detection Systems (IDSs) are tools that monitor systems against malicious activities. We use network-based IDS (NIDS) to monitor the network and host-based IDS (HIDS) to locally monitor the health of a system. IDSs are divided into two categories: *Anomaly-based* and *Signature-based* [4, 5] techniques. Anomaly-based detection is interesting to detect unknown attack patterns and does not need predefined signatures. On the other hand, it suffers from the fact that it is difficult to define normal behavior and that malicious activity may look like normal usage pattern [6, 7]. In signature-based techniques, we compare captured data with well-defined attack patterns. Because of the pattern matching, this technique has the advantage of being deterministic and can be customized for each system we want to protect. Moreover, signature-based techniques are stateless; once an attack matches a signature, an alert is emitted and the detection component does not record it as a state change.

One solution, to tackle the limitation of detection based only on stateless signatures, is to use a finite state machine (FSM) to track the evolution of an attack. That way, while an attack is in progress, the state changes and we can trigger appropriate responses based on a confidence level threshold, which leads to a lower false positive rate. Based on the previous discussion about the advantages and disadvantages between anomaly-based and signature-based techniques, and since LTTng produces accurate traces, we decided to develop our framework with the FSM approach in order to track multistep attacks.

The main contributions of this work are the following. The proposed framework has a novel response execution organization named *retroactive-burst*. The term retroactive refers to the fact that we have a mechanism for measuring the effectiveness of the applied responses. The term burst refers to the fact that each retroactive execution consists of several bursts each consisting in relevant responses to apply. The idea is that each burst mode execution of responses in each retroactive execution must mitigate the progress of attack and avoid the need to run another burst. In contrast to previous models, this model is round-based. The online risk assessment measures the risk index of an applied round of responses instead of one applied response. Also, a multilevel response selection mechanism is implemented in our model. The higher level corresponds to strong responses. This helps to control the cost in performance and increases the intelligence of the Intrusion Response System (IRS). A Response Coordinator helps to select the appropriate level based on a global overview of past history of applied responses and attacks.

The paper is organized as follows. First, we investigate earlier work and several existing methods for intrusion response. The proposed model is discussed in Section 3. Experimental results are given in Section 4. Finally, we conclude and future work is discussed.

2. Related Work

Automated response systems try to be fully automated using decision-making processes without human intervention. The major problem in this approach is the possibility of executing an improper response in case of problem [8]. It can be classified according to the following characteristics.

Response Selection. There are three response selection models. (a) static model maps an alert to a predefined response. This model is easy to build, but the major weakness is that the response measures are predictable [9]. (b) Dynamic model responses are based on multiple factors such as system state, attack metrics (frequency, severity, confidence, etc.) and network policy. In other words, the response to an attack may not be the same depending for instance on the targeted host. One drawback of this model is that it does not consider intrusion damage [10, 11]. (c) Cost-sensitive model is an interesting technique that tries to attune intrusion damage and response cost. To measure intrusion damage, a risk assessment component is needed [8].

Adjustment Ability. There are two types of adjustment ability. (a) The first is non-adaptive: In this model, response selection mechanism remains the same during the attack period. It does not use the response history to order responses. (b) The second is daptive. In these approaches, the system has an appropriate ability to automatically adjust the response selection based on success or failure of response in the past [12].

Response Execution. There are two types of response execution [13]. (a) The first is burst: In this model, there is no mechanism to measure the risk index of the host/network once the response has been applied. The major weakness in this model is the cost in performance caused by applying all responses, while a subset of the responses may be enough to mitigate the attack. (b) The second is retroactive: in these approaches, there is a feedback mechanism which has the ability to measure the response effect based on the result of the last applied response. There are some challenges in adaptive approaches. For example, how can we measure the success of the last applied response and how multiple concurrent malicious activities can be handled [12]?

Foo et al. [12] proposed a graph-based approach called ADEPTS. The responses for the affected nodes are based on some parameters such as confidence level of attack and previous measurements of responses in similar cases. Thus, ADEPTS uses a feedback mechanism to estimate the success or failure of an applied response.

In [14], Stakhanova et al. proposed a cost-sensitive preemptive intrusion response system. It monitors system behavior in terms of system calls. The authors presented a response system which is automated, cost-sensitive, preemptive, and adaptive. The response is triggered before the attack completes. There is a mapping between system resources, response actions, and intrusion patterns which has to be defined in advance. Whenever a sequence of system calls matches a prefix in a predefined abnormal graph, the response algorithm, based on confidence level threshold, decides whether to repel the attack or not. If the selected response succeeds in mitigating the attack, its success factor is increased by one, while on the contrary, it is decreased by one.

In [15], Lee et al. proposed a cost-sensitive model based on three factors: damage cost that characterizes the amount of damage that could potentially be caused by the attacker, operational cost that illustrates the effort for monitoring and detecting the attacks by an IDS, and response cost that is the cost of acting against attacks.

Retroactive approach was first proposed by Mu and Li [8]. They presented a hierarchical task network planning to repel intrusions. This model is able to avoid unnecessary responses and reduce the risk of false positive response by adjusting risk thresholds of subtasks. The interesting idea in this paper is response time decision-making. It can estimate the execution time of each response. Each response has a static risk threshold associated. The permission for running each response is the current risk index of the network.

In case of response execution, our technique closely relates to [8]. They try to measure the risk index after running each response. Our experience shows that this measure is not enough to make the decision of running the next response and cannot be applied in a production environment. To tackle this issue, we have defined a retroactive-burst execution mechanism. For adjustment ability, our technique closely relates to [14], but there are many distinguishing features. They used a static damage cost for each node in abnormal graph. In other words, their risk assessment is static. By contrast, we have implemented a dynamic (online) risk assessment component that helps our response component to attune intrusion damage and response cost over time. Another distinguishing feature that separates our model from previous models is that the majority of the proposed response selection mechanisms focus on the local view of threats and responses to select a set of responses and do not have a general view of the network status. In the proposed model, we designed a novel approach named response coordinator to tackle this weakness.

3. Proposed Model

To design a strong intrusion response system, we should have a flexible response mechanism to handle different malicious activities. Figure 1 illustrates the proposed structure for such an intrusion response system. The proposed IRS framework consists of five modules.

3.1. Module (1) Manager. Manager is responsible for getting alerts from the detection and online risk assessment components and eventually run the appropriate responses on the attacked machine. Online risk assessment (ORA) component guarantees that our model is cost-sensitive. ORA measures the risk index of an applied round of responses (R_{index}). The detection component has all the detailed information about the malicious activity such as the severity, the confidence level (C_{level}), and the type of resource targeted. It sends an alert after each state change in the FSM. In our FSM, a weight is associated to each state, and the sum of all weights is 100. The confidence level related to each raised alert is equal to the sum of all weights of all previous states. The confidence level guarantees that our model is preemptive. The `Activator` process gets all alerts from all the components. Once the following condition (1) is true, it starts the `Establish_Remote_Connection` and `Select_Response` processes:

$$R_{index} \times C_{level} > \text{Threshold.} \tag{1}$$

The `Establish_Remote_Connection` part generates a connection string and sends it to the `Open_Channel` process. The `Open_Channel` tries to connect to a remote agent running in the target host. Since TCF [16] is a lightweight and extensible communication daemon, we chose it as remote agent. After establishing a channel to the TCF remote agent, `Run_Plans` process applies responses on the target computer as Figure 1 illustrates.

The `Run_Plans` process is the core of our response framework. Unlike usual response systems, it considers the time factor and applies responses using a multistep reaction procedure. Mu and Li [8], tried to measure the risk index

after running each response. Our experience shows that this measure is not enough to make the decision of running the next response.

To tackle this issue, we have defined a round-based response mechanism. Figure 2 illustrates six responses for a specific malicious activity which are ready in pending queue in the `Run_Plans` process before starting the first round. Sending the next round of responses is based on (1). Upon running a round of responses, new risk index of network has to be measured from the Online Risk Assessment component after a specific time. As shown in Figure 2, each response has a `Response_Effect` that defines how the selected responses are ordered in the pending queue. Figure 3 shows two possible scenarios after launching the first round of responses. In the first situation, since the risk index of the network is decreasing, the next round is not required. This intelligence prevents overly impacting the network. By contrast, in the second situation, in spite of the application of the first round, the risk index shows that malicious activity is still progressing. Thus, the second round of responses has to be applied.

3.2. Module (2) Strategy. An intrusion can be defined as any set of actions that threaten the Confidentiality (C), Integrity (I), Availability (A), and Performance (P) of host/network resources such as files, kernel, or user accounts. To react against attacks, we have designed four strategies to evaluate all responses.

(1) *MAX-Confidentiality* ensures that any authorized user can have access only to the limited subset of resources required.

(2) *MAX-Integrity* verifies that any authorized user can only modify the resources in a conform manner.

(3) *Availability* means that the resources are always available to the authorized users.

(4) *Performance* means that the system responds within the time expected.

3.3. Module (3) Responses. This module is responsible for managing the set of responses available. A database connects the Strategy and Responses modules. This connection is a structure to measure each response effect. Our evaluation relies on the positive effect and negative impact of responses to the strategies (C, I, A, and P).

3.4. Module (4) Response Coordinator (RC). Most of proposed response mechanisms focus on the local view of threats and responses and do not have a general view of the network status. Thus, they suffer from not having global information about the attacker's goal. To tackle this issue, we introduce the RC module. We divide the system status in five general categories: Applications, Kernel, Local Services, Network Services, and Physical Status. The purpose of RC is to improve the quality of responses over time. Let us briefly describe the RC categories.

Application Status. There are many applications installed in the system like Web applications, desktop applications,

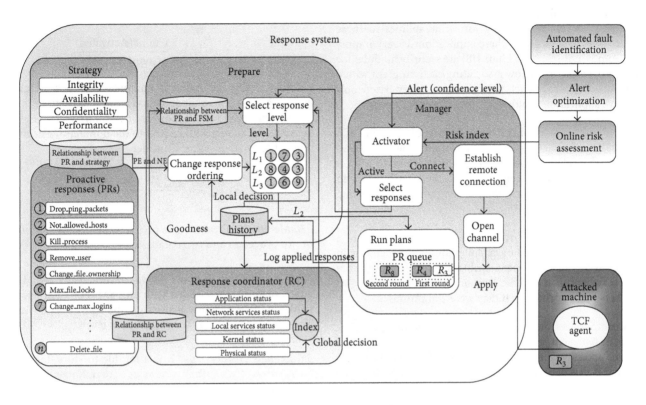

FIGURE 1: Proposed architecture for automated response system.

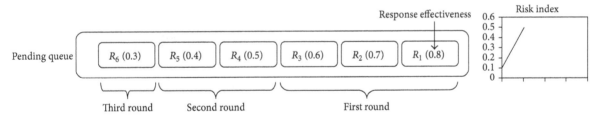

FIGURE 2: Pending queue in *Run_plans* process before starting the first round of responses.

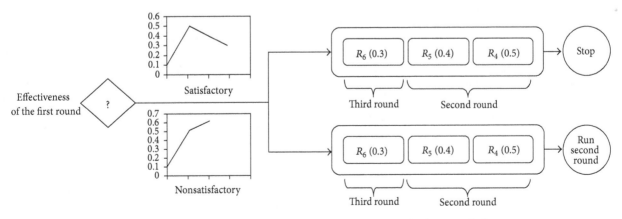

FIGURE 3: Two possible outcomes for decision-making after running the first round of responses.

programming tools, DBMS, OpenOffice, and web browsers. Malicious hackers are looking for vulnerabilities in these applications. The health of these applications is very important. AppArmor [17] or SELinux [18] are security modules for the Linux kernel that allow associating each program with a security policy that restricts its capabilities. Policy-based tools improve application health.

Kernel Status. It represents the higher level of criticality of a local system. In modern operating systems, the kernel and the kernel modules have access to any resource of a local machine. If an attacker gains access to the kernel, it can do anything on the local machine with very little chance of being detected.

Local Services Status. Virtually, each service represents a security threat that could be exploited by an intruder to gain further access to the system. Unlike local applications, the local services run at a higher level of privilege and could give attackers higher privileges if they were compromised.

Network Services Status. Like the local services, network services represent a security risk that could be exploited to gain access to a system. The major difference with local services is that they can be exploited from outside.

Physical Status. It represents the status of the physical devices of the machine in terms of usage and performance. For example, when a machine is under a network flood attack, the network interface health is considered critical. Over time, we gather statistics about how many responses are applied in each category. These statistics help to discover major health problems of each host, detect major health problems of the whole network, help administrator to chose a policy suited for the organization, and it can help the `select_response_level` process to select the more appropriate levels of responses.

3.5. Relationship between Responses and RC DB. Table 1 shows the relationship between responses and RC categories. RC process updates Table 1 based on the `plans_history` database. Each response (R_i) is associated with one or more RC category (Application, Kernel, ...). For example, in Table 1, response R_1 is related to Application, Local Services, and Network Services (Linked). Each RC category has a weight (W_i) which represents the importance of the category for the organization ($W_A, W_K, W_{LS}, W_{NS}, W_P$). In the online risk assessment component, we associate each host (H_i) with a value (V_{Hi}), representing the priority of this host for the organization. In Table 1, *Applied* indicates that a response has been applied and on which hosts. We activate the categories associated with a response when the sum of the values of the hosts which applied this response is greater than a threshold based on the following (n is a subset of hosts that a specific response has been applied on them).

$$\sum_{i=1}^{n} V_{H_i} > \text{Threshold.} \tag{2}$$

The status of each category of RC is computed using

$$\text{Status}(W_i) = \frac{\text{Count (Activated)}}{\text{Count (Linked)}}. \tag{3}$$

Finally, the RC index is computed using a weighted average by (4). The result of Status and RC calculations is one of the values: *Zero (0), L (Low), M (Medium),* or *H (High). k* is five in our model with respect to the number of categories defined for system status. Consider

$$RC_{\text{index}} = \frac{\sum_{i=1}^{k} W_i \times \text{Status}(W_i)}{k}. \tag{4}$$

3.6. Module (5) Prepare. The prepared module is composed of two processes and two databases.

3.6.1. Relationship between Responses and FSM DB. Each attack pattern is associated with an FSM. For each defined FSM, multiple response actions can be defined in advance. These response actions are organized in levels.

3.6.2. Plans_History DB. It is a log file to store *Target IP, User_Name, Date, Time, Resource, Alert_Name, Level_Id, Round_Responses,* and *Round_Success.* As explained in the Manager module, it is possible that all responses are not applied by the *Run_Plans* process; so at the end of each round, it will update the *plans_history* to store the status of the round.

3.6.3. Change_Response_Ordering Process. After selecting the appropriate level of responses required to repel the attack (using the `Select_Response_Level`), we need to order the responses of the selected level. This process guarantees that our model is adaptive. The ordering operation has to be done using

$$\text{RE} = \left[(\text{Positive\_effect}) - (\text{Negative\_impact}) \right] \times \text{Goodness.} \tag{5}$$

Positive_effect and *Negative_impact* are static parameters. Goodness is a dynamic parameter that represents the history of success (S) or failure (F) of each response for a specific type of host. The goodness parameter guarantees that our model is dynamic in case of response effectiveness and helps IRS component to prepare the best set of response over time. To measure the success or failure of a round of responses, we use the result of the online risk assessment component. As mentioned in Figure 3, if the risk index of the network is decreasing, the next round is not required and the status of the previous applied round is set to success. By contrast, in the second situation, in spite of the application of the first round, the risk index shows that malicious activity is still progressing. Thus, the second round of responses has to be applied, and the status of the previous applied round is set to failure.

3.6.4. Select_Response_Level Process. Information coming from the plans_history database and the RC process are used

TABLE 1: Relationship between Responses and RC.

Response name	RC					Hosts					
	Application	Kernel	Local Services	Network Services	Physical	H_1	H_2	H_3	H_4	...	H_n
	w_A	w_K	w_{LS}	w_{NS}	w_P	VH_1	VH_2	VH_3	VH_4	...	VH_n
R_1	Linked		Linked	Linked				Applied			
R_2	Activated	Activated		Linked		Applied	Applied	Applied			
R_3	Activated	Activated		Activated	Activated	Applied		Applied			Applied
R_4	Linked		Linked	Linked	Linked		Applied		Applied		
⋮											
Status	Medium	High	Zero	Low	Medium						
Index	Low										

TABLE 2: Policies for dynamic response level selection.

Policy	RC.index	Selected Level
P1 = There is not any information in plans_history	low	1
	Medium	1
	High	2
P2 = (There is related information in plans_history) and (Previous status was successful) and (Time of previous run is far to current time)	Low	current_level
	Medium	current_level
	High	current_level + 1
P3 = (There is related information in plans_history) and (Previous status was successful) and (Time of previous run is near to current time)	Low	current_level
	Medium	current_level + 1
	High	current_level + 2
P4 = (There is related information in plans_history) and (Previous status was not successful) and (Time of previous run is far to current time)	Low	current_level + 1
	Medium	current_level + 2
	High	current_level + 3
P5 = (There is related information in plans_history) and (Previous status was not successful) and (Time of previous run is near to current time)	Low	current_level + 2
	Medium	last_level
	High	last_level

to select the best response level to repel an intrusion in progress. When it receives a message from the Manager module, it tries to find related information in the plans_history database. Depending on the existing knowledge about a similar attack and on the RC index, it selects the appropriate level. Table 2 describes the different policies available to select dynamically a response level.

4. Experimental Results

The Linux Trace Toolkit next generation (LTTng) is a powerful software tool that provides a detailed execution trace of the Linux operating system with a low impact on performance. Using traces, LTTng records computer activities as seen by the kernel and eventually the userspace applications if they are instrumented with UST [7].

Although execution trace contains important and valuable information to detect system faults and network attacks, this information is usually behind the large number of events. Trace-based detection systems usually need a preliminary step to alleviate this problem. Trace abstraction is one possible solution that is used in the literature to reduce the trace size [19], to generate high level synthetic information [20], and to extract complete statistics of system resources usage [21]. This high level information can then be used easily in the detection phase.

In our experiments, Automated Fault Identification (our IDS) [20] and our framework were developed on IP xxx.xxx.72.12; the TCF agent and the attacked machine were developed on IP xxx.xxx.72.131 but in a virtual machine. We have considered the Escaping a chroot jail attack. Chrooting changes the root directory of a process. As Figure 4 illustrates, when a process is in a chroot, it can only access a subdirectory of the file hierarchy and does not have access to higher level directories. If an attacker can exploit a vulnerability in the chroot system, it can access higher level directories.

LTTng traces contain the related events and system calls; the Automated Fault Identification component can detect the attack using the appropriate FSM. It sends an alarm in the IDMEF [22] format to the automated intrusion

TABLE 3: Plans_history database, after applying the first round of $level_1$.

Target IP	User_Name	Date	Time	Resource	Alert_Name	Level_Id	Round_Responses	Response_success
xxx.xxx.72.131	Smith	2012/10/02	10:05:06	Filesystem Root	Chroot	$level_1$	RS_1, RS_2, RS_4	S

TABLE 4: Plans_history database, after applying the first round of $level_2$.

Target IP	User_Name	Date	Time	Resource	Alert_Name	Level_Id	Round_Responses	Response_success
xxx.xxx.72.131	Smith	2012/10/02	10:05:06	Filesystem Root	Chroot	$level_1$	RS_1, RS_2, RS_4	S
xxx.xxx.72.131	Peter	2012/10/02	10:10:23	Filesystem Root	Chroot	$level_2$	RS_1, RS_3, RS_4	S

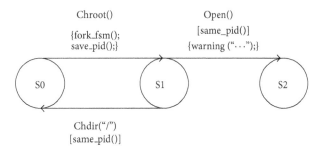

FIGURE 4: Escaping the chroot jail.

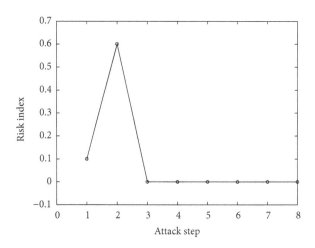

FIGURE 5: The online risk assessment result for escaping the chroot jail.

response framework. While this attack is in progress, the state changes and we can trigger appropriate responses based on a confidence level threshold. Our threshold value for (1) is 0.5. If state S1 sends an alert, since its confidence level is 0.5 and risk index (output of online risk assessment component) is 0.1, the rule of (1) is not triggered. If state S2 sends an alert, since the confidence level of S2 is 1 and the value of risk index is 0.6, the IRS component creates a channel to the target computer (xxx.xxx.72.131) and applies a first round of responses through the TCF agent. Sending the next round of responses is based on the new risk index and calculating (1). Our framework has two response levels for this attack:

List of Responses = {

RS1: KILL_PROCESS, RS2: LOCK_USER,

RS3: REMOVE_ALL_USERS, RS4: LOGOUT,

RS5: RESET}

Level1 = {Round1 (RS1, RS2, RS4), Round2 (RS5)}

Level2 = {Round1 (RS1, RS3, RS4), Round2 (RS5)}

4.1. First Scenario. Since the `plans_history` database does not have any information about this type of alarm, `select_response_level` process selects $level_1$ (Policy = P_1, RC.index = Low). RS_1 is the first response applied by the `Run_Plans` process. It kills the problematic processes. Then, RS_2 is executed to change the current user's password. RS_4 is then executed to logout the problematic user. From this moment, the user cannot login anymore to the machine using its system account. Table 3 illustrates the content of the plan_history database after these actions have been applied. Since $round_1$ causes that risk index to decrease, $round_2$ is not applied and this framework keeps the impact on service

availability to a minimum. The risk curve caused by Escaping the chroot jail is shown in Figure 5. As seen, this attack has two steps. The risk index of the first and second step is 0.1 and 0.6, respectively. Since the IRS component will control this attack, the risk index will be zero after the second step.

4.2. Second Scenario. If other accounts are available on the victim machine, the attacker may login with another account. Suppose, at this time, that the RC index is *Medium*. The next time the same attack pattern reappears, the system will adapt its response and $level_2$ is selected (Policy = P_3, RC.index = Medium). Once again the problematic process is killed and, this time, all users on the system are removed. Table 4 illustrates the updated `plan_history` database after applying $level_2$. At this point, all users of the system have been removed and logged out.

5. Conclusion

Network services are becoming larger and increasingly complex to manage. It is extremely important to maintain the users QoS, the response time of applications, and critical services in high demand. On the other hand, we see impressive changes in the ways in which attackers gain access to systems and infect computers. An intrusion response system has to accurately assess the value of the loss incurred by a compromised resource and has an accurate evaluation of the responses cost. The aim of this paper is introducing a novel framework for automated intrusion response system. In our model, unnecessary responses are controlled by an online risk assessment component. Each response is put in a multilevel mechanism for each FSM and run in a retroactive-burst mode execution. This is the main contribution of this paper. The response coordinator named RC enables us to have a general view of applied responses history. Taking control of the network status by RC leads us to have a reliable IRS which keeps the network quality of service.

Acknowledgments

The support of the Natural Sciences and Engineering Research Council of Canada (NSERC), Ericsson Software Research, and Defence Research and Development Canada (DRDC) is gratefully acknowledged.

References

[1] F. Xiao, S. Jin, and X. Li, "A novel data mining-based method for alert reduction and analysis," *Journal of Networks*, vol. 5, no. 1, pp. 88–97, 2010.

[2] M. Desnoyers and M. Dagenais, "LTTng: tracing across execution layers, from the hypervisor to user-space," in *Proceedings of the Linux Symposium*, Ottawa, Canada, 2008.

[3] J. Blunck, M. Desnoyers, and P. M. Fournier, "Userspace application tracing with markers and tracepoints," in *Proceedings of the Linux Kongress*, October 2009.

[4] N. B. Anuar, H. Sallehudin, A. Gani, and O. Zakari, "Identifying false alarm fornetwork intrusion detection system using hybrid data mining and decision tree," *Malaysian Journal of Computer Science*, vol. 21, no. 2, pp. 101–115, 2008.

[5] A. Lazarevic, L. Ertz, V. Kumar, A. Ozgur, and J. Srivastava, "A comparative study of anomaly detection schemes in network intrusion detection," in *Proceedings of the 3rd SIAM International Conference on Data Mining*, 2003.

[6] Yusof, *Automated Signature Generation of Network Attacks [B.S. thesis]*, University Teknologi Malasia, 2009.

[7] "Difference between signature based and anomaly based detection in IDS," http://www.secguru.com/forum/difference.

[8] C. P. Mu and Y. Li, "An intrusion response decision-making model based on hierarchical task network planning," *Expert Systems with Applications*, vol. 37, no. 3, pp. 2465–2472, 2010.

[9] Y. M. Chen and Y. Yang, "Policy management for network-based intrusion detection and prevention," in *Proceedings of the IEEE/IFIP Network Operations and Management Symposium, Application Sessions (NOMS '04)*, pp. 219–232, Seoul, South Korea, April 2004.

[10] G. B. White, E. A. Fisch, and U. W. Pooch, "Cooperating security managers: a peer-based intrusion detection system," *IEEE Network*, vol. 10, no. 1, pp. 20–23, 1996.

[11] P. Porras and P. Neumann, "EMERALD: event monitoring enenabling responses to anomalous live disturbances," in *Proceedings of the National Information Systems Security Conference*, 1997.

[12] B. Foo, Y. S. Wu, Y. C. Mao, S. Bagchi, and E. Spafford, "ADEPTS: adaptive intrusion response using attack graphs in an e-commerce environment," in *Proceedings of the International Conference on Dependable Systems and Networks*, pp. 508–517, July 2005.

[13] A. Shameli-Sendi, N. Ezzati-Jivan, M. Jabbarifar, and M. Dagenais, "Intrusion response systems: survey and taxonomy," *International Journal of Computer Science and Network Security*, vol. 12, no. 1, pp. 1–14, 2012.

[14] N. Stakhanova, S. Basu, and J. Wong, "A cost-sensitive model for preemptive intrusion response systems," in *Proceedings of the 21st International Conference on Advanced Information Networking and Applications (AINA '07)*, pp. 428–435, Washington, DC, USA, May 2007.

[15] W. Lee, W. Fan, M. Miller, S. J. Stolfo, and E. Zadok, "Toward cost-sensitive modeling for intrusion detection and response," *Journal of Computer Security*, vol. 10, no. 1-2, pp. 5–22, 2002.

[16] http://wiki.eclipse.org/DSDP/TCF.

[17] https://help.ubuntu.com/community/AppArmor/.

[18] http://www.nsa.gov/research/selinux/.

[19] N. Ezzati-Jivan and M. Dagenais, "A stateful approach to generate synthetic events from kernel traces," *Advances in Software Engineering*, vol. 2012, Article ID 140368, 12 pages, 2012.

[20] H. Waly and B. Ktari, "A complete framework for kernel trace analysis," in *Proceedings of the 24th Canadian Cference on Electrical and Computer Engineering (CCECE '11)*, pp. 1426–1430, Niagara Falls, ON, Canada, May 2011.

[21] N. Ezzati-Jivan and M. Dagenais, "A framework to compute statistics of system parameters from very large trace files," *ACM SIGOPS Operating Systems Review*, vol. 47, no. 1, pp. 43–54, 2013.

[22] H. Debar, D. Curry, and B. Feinstein, "The intrusion detection message exchange format," http://www.ietf.org/rfc/rfc4765.txt.

4

ECOPS: Energy-Efficient Collaborative Opportunistic Positioning for Heterogeneous Mobile Devices

Kaustubh Dhondge,[1] Hyungbae Park,[1] Baek-Young Choi,[1] and Sejun Song[2]

[1] *University of Missouri-Kansas City, 546 Flarsheim Hall, 5110 Rockhill Road, Kansas City, MO 64110, USA*
[2] *Texas A&M University, Fermier Hall 008, 3367 TAMU, College Station, TX 77843, USA*

Correspondence should be addressed to Kaustubh Dhondge; kaustubh.dhondge@mail.umkc.edu

Academic Editor: Lingjia Liu

The fast growing popularity of smartphones and tablets enables us to use various intelligent mobile applications. As many of those applications require position information, smart mobile devices provide positioning methods such as Global Positioning System (GPS), WiFi-based positioning system (WPS), or Cell-ID-based positioning service. However, those positioning methods have different characteristics of energy-efficiency, accuracy, and service availability. In this paper, we present an Energy-Efficient Collaborative and Opportunistic Positioning System (ECOPS) for heterogeneous mobile devices. ECOPS facilitates a collaborative environment where many mobile devices can opportunistically receive position information over energy-efficient and prevalent WiFi, broadcasted from a few other devices in the communication range. The position-broadcasting devices in ECOPS have sufficient battery power and up-to-date location information obtained from accurate but energy-inefficient GPS. A position receiver in ECOPS estimates its location using a combination of methods including received signal strength indicators and 2D trilateration. Our field experiments show that ECOPS significantly reduces the total energy consumption of devices while achieving an acceptable level of location accuracy. ECOPS can be especially useful for unique resource scarce, infrastructureless, and mission critical scenarios such as battlefields, border patrol, mountaineering expeditions, and disaster area assistance.

1. Introduction

Smart mobile devices such as smartphones and tablets are rapidly becoming prevalent in our lives. They have spurred a paradigm shift from traditional restricted phone applications to intelligent mobile applications such as location-based, context-aware, and situation-aware services. For example, a social-network-based traffic information system [1] allows each mobile user to report and use real-time traffic information, in addition to the archived traffic information from the US Department of Transportation.

As many of those application services require position information, smart mobile devices provide various positioning services via Global Positioning System (GPS) [2], WiFi-based positioning system (WPS) [3], or Cell-ID Positioning [4]. Being dedicated equipment for positioning, GPS becomes available for many smart devices as an additional feature and is considered to be an accurate and preferred method for location-based services (LBSs) [5, 6]. However,

its high energy consumption, due to the Time To First Fix (TTFF), becomes a significant drawback. WPS approximates a position from the location information of a nearby wireless access point (AP) that is stored in the database. Its energy efficiency is much better than GPS, and the accuracy is moderate. As WiFi is a de facto standard in wireless local area network (WLAN) communication, it is broadly available on most smart devices. However, the service is limited to indoor or urban areas where the access points are densely populated. Cell-ID Positioning provides an approximate location from the serving cell tower, where a cell area range is around $100 \sim 500$ m in urban areas, but it can span up to 10 Km for rural areas. Although this is the most power saving approach, due to a large error range caused by the coarse cell tower density, Cell-ID Positioning cannot offer the utility of most LBS applications. In addition, mobile devices such as the WiFi version of tablets are not fully equipped with 3G/4G data chips at the present time even though 3G and 4G wireless networks provide enough bandwidth to enable

TABLE 1: Characterization of various positioning methods.

Positioning method	Accuracy	Energy efficiency	Equipment availability	Service limitations
GPS	High (within 10 m)	Low	Low	Indoor and canyon
WPS	Moderate (within 50 m)	Moderate	High	Coarse AP density area
Cell-ID Positioning	Low (within 5 Km)	High	Moderate	Rural area

explicit support for real-time LBS. We have summarized the characteristics of positioning methods ([7]) in Table 1.

Energy efficiency while maintaining required accuracy for the given service limitations is one of the most critical issues in mobile devices, due to limited battery life and the high energy consumption of applications. As different positioning methods available on a mobile device have different characteristics with respect to accuracy, energy-efficiency, and service availability, there have been several proposals for dynamic selection of a positioning method on an individual device. For example, [8] uses an accelerometer for movement detection to power cycle GPS, if the device is not mobile. However, the effectiveness of most of the existing heuristics is limited by equipment constraints or service availability, as the applications choose a preferred positioning method that is available within an individual device.

In this paper, we propose ECOPS to facilitate a WiFi hotspot mode [9] or WiFi Direct mode [10] based approximation in collaboration with a few available GPS broadcasting devices under budget constraints. ECOPS is a collaborative positioning method between WiFi and GPS mobile devices, in addition to a positioning method selection heuristic within a mobile device. It can achieve moderate accuracy with low energy usage. Although there is a previous collaborative work [8] that pairs two devices via Bluetooth to save GPS power cycle, the approach needs both GPS and Bluetooth on both devices. Instead, ECOPS supports heterogeneous methods among mobile devices. There are many mobile devices including the majority of current tablets that only support a basic wireless communication method which is WiFi. The WiFi-only device can obtain position information from a GPS device with ECOPS. This proposed system can operate opportunistically, where each device can resolve the location via various available methods including trilateration [11] with three GPS broadcasting devices and a received signal strength indicator (RSSI) [12] or approximation with geomagnetic sensors [13] and a single GPS device without requiring any WiFi AP.

We implemented ECOPS using Android-powered mobile devices such as smartphones and tablets. The evaluation results show that ECOPS significantly saves the total energy consumption of the devices while achieving a good level of location accuracy. In addition, it enables constrained devices to enjoy location-based services that would otherwise not be possible.

The rest of the paper is organized as follows. Potential application scenarios are described in Section 2. Section 3 discusses the existing and state-of-the-art techniques. A detailed explanation of the proposed system is presented in Section 4. The performance evaluations and experimental scenarios are explained in Section 5. Finally, we conclude the paper in Section 6.

2. Application Scenarios

While security and social incentive issues are not in the scope of this paper, the proposed opportunistic and collaborative positioning scheme can be especially useful for unique resource scarce and mission critical applications. Such examples include border patrol, battlefields, mountaineering expeditions, and disaster area assistance.

For example, suppose a team of border patrol officers is searching for an illegal immigrant in the border area. In some areas of rigid terrain, GPS and cellular signals can be lost in a canyon. Some projects [14] employ a low-altitude tethered aerostat to set up a temporary WiFi hotspot. To help with positioning, a few officers stay at the top of the valley to relay their GPS position information to the officers searching down in the valley. Such a collaborative positioning is a natural application scenario of ECOPS.

In a battlefield scenario, when a platoon is air-dropped into a war zone, it is nearly impossible to find WPS services in the surroundings. Even with the availability of technology like LANdroids [15] to provide a network in such conditions, it is not a simple task. Also, it is crucial for soldiers to have accurate location information in the battlefield. In such a scenario, the capabilities of ECOPS can be exploited to maintain accurate location information while reducing overall energy consumption. Although one may not have a strong incentive to take a lead and offer location information for others, such concerns are lifted immediately if a leadership hierarchy preexists in the application scenario. For instance, when a platoon is being deployed in a battlefield, the platoon leader chooses to be the primary location broadcaster using ECOPS along with a few others at the top of the hierarchy. The other soldiers in the unit are able to estimate their location information based on the geocoordinates they receive from their unit's command. This will result in fewer devices from the unit querying satellites for location information and reduce the overall energy consumption. Extending the lifetime of devices during the operation is a mission critical parameter as the duration of an operation is not fixed and often tends to be longer than expected. Under the Battlefield Air Targeting Man Aided Knowledge (BATMAN) [16] project, the United States Air Force is actively seeking to equip their soldiers with modern Android-powered smartphones to obtain accurate location information with high energy efficiency. Modified versions of Android [17, 18] enable the desired level of security for military use. Such projects can benefit greatly by ECOPS.

Another scenario where ECOPS can be extremely useful is during natural calamities. In such cases, emergency

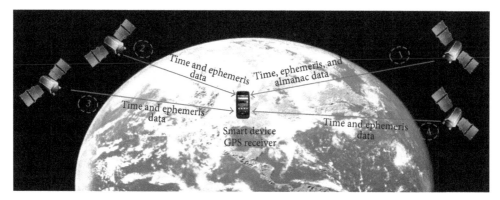

FIGURE 1: Illustration of Global Positioning System.

responders who are involved in search and rescue missions can host an ECOPS-based location broadcasting service over WiFi Direct. As they move around the area, victims can use their smart devices to either request assistance or transmit their locations.

3. Related Work

Positioning schemes on mobile devices have been a long standing topic of exploration. This resulted in three main positioning techniques using either the information provided by the GPS, WPS, or Cell-ID Positioning. Also, there have been several research proposals for specific environments.

3.1. Global Positioning System (GPS). The Global Positioning System (GPS) is a satellite navigation system that provides location and time information anywhere on earth with four or more GPS satellite signals. It is originally deployed and maintained by the United States government and is now freely accessible to anyone [2]. The GPS provides very high level of accuracy, but suffers from a high TTFF due to the large distance between the GPS receiver and serving satellites. This problem has been somewhat addressed by the use of assisted GPS (aGPS) that relies on the cellular or internet infrastructure to get a faster lock on the serving satellites while obtaining precise time information from the network.

Within the navigation message continuously broadcasted by each of the satellites in the constellation, the GPS receiver looks for three important pieces of data as illustrated in Figure 1. The first piece of data consists of the GPS date and time information. It additionally also consists of the health statistics of the satellite. The ephemeris data forms the second important piece and allows the GPS receiver to calculate the position of the satellite and is broadcasted every 30 seconds. The ephemeris data is valid for no longer than four hours. The third important piece is the almanac data which provides approximate information concerning the rest of the satellites. This data is transmitted over 12.5 minutes and is valid for a maximum of 180 days. The almanac data can be obtained from any satellite, and it enables the GPS receiver to determine which particular satellite to search for next. As the signal from the selected satellite becomes directly available, the GPS receiver then downloads the second important data,

that is, the ephemeris data. It is absolutely necessary that the GPS receiver has the satellite's complete copy of the ephemeris data to determine its position. In case the signal is lost in the middle of acquiring this data, the GPS receiver will have to discard whatever data was downloaded and start searching for a new satellite signal.

Once the GPS receiver has ephemeris data directly from three or more satellites, it can carry out various methods to accurately determine its own location. These methods involve and are not restricted to 3D trilateration, Bancroft's method, and multidimensional Newton-Raphson calculations. Due to the high propagation delays, getting the ephemeris and almanac data can take up to 15 minutes for a device just out of the factory, and then around ~20 seconds after the initial configuration. To expedite this process, some GPS receivers can use multiple channels for faster fixes. Another strategy is to obtain the ephemeris and almanac data from a faster network like the cellular network or the internet as in the case of a GPS.

3.2. WiFi-Based Positioning System (WPS). WPS maintains an extensive database of WiFi access points (APs) along with their geographic locations [19, 20]. This information has to be collected painstakingly over a large duration of time and is vulnerable to changes in the location of APs or the discontinuation of their service. The information of APs-SSID and geographic location can be collected manually or in a more automated way by retrieving the GPS location of smart devices connected to the AP and associating that information with the AP. Once such a large and dedicated database is ready and a device is in the vicinity of an AP, or several APs, it can provide the RSSI values and the SSID of the APs to the WPS servers. The WPS servers, based on proprietary techniques, apply filtering approaches and trilateration techniques to this data and determine the accurate location of the smart device. This geographic location information is then relayed back to the smart device which can exploit it for various LBSs. The illustration of WPS is depicted in Figure 2.

While the WPS service approaches work well in terms of energy efficiency [21–23], they are not globally available for users. A solution leveraging the existing infrastructure, such as APs without requiring any specialized infrastructures for localization, has been proposed in [24]. However, since this

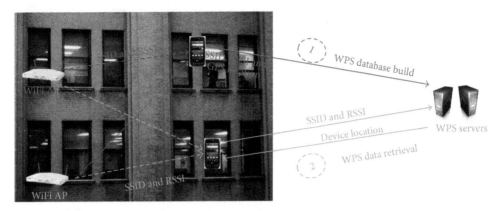

FIGURE 2: Illustration of WiFi positioning system.

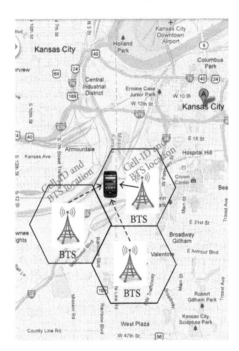

FIGURE 3: Illustration of Cell-ID Positioning.

localization scheme is limited to the indoors and still relies on infrastructure, such as APs, it cannot be useful outdoors where the WiFi signals are neither dense enough nor covered.

3.3. Cell-ID Positioning. In Cell-ID Positioning, a mobile device obtains its position from the geographic location of its associated base transreceiver station (BTS), with an error range proportional to the signal strength within a cell. The mobile device can estimate its location as the BTS periodically broadcasts its Cell-ID along with its location. Once this information is available to the mobile device, it can use the location of the BTS as its own location with the error calculated using the propagation model. Another technique that may be used for cell phones to estimate their location is to observe the delay in receiving a special message broadcasted by the BTS from the time it was transmitted. This information is used by the mobile device to estimate its distance from the BTS.

Note that a cell size can be very large especially in rural areas and highways where the density of cellular towers is very low. One cellular tower is often capable for serving up to 5 Km radius. As this large cell size leads to a significant error range, other nearby cell tower signals may be used in order to improve the accuracy [4, 25]. Such approaches also exploit the fading phenomenon independently or along with predictive techniques to improve the accuracy of Cell-ID Positioning. However, the accuracy is still limited as the propagation model needed for the trilateration does not work well, due to complex signal fading behavior over long distances. The illustration of Cell-ID Positioning is depicted in Figure 3.

3.4. Recent Research Proposals. While most of commercial approaches heavily depend on infrastructures [3, 26], or use extra high-end sensors and exploit the available information from an *individual* device [26–28], research proposals mostly aim to improve the positioning accuracy or energy efficiency through algorithmic approaches [8, 23, 24, 29–33].

The work in [31–33] attempt to learn a known location from a training phase for a better location accuracy.

```
1: check the residual power (p_r);
2: if GPS-equipped device & p_r ≥ p_min then
3:     device becomes PB and activates WiFi hotspot;
4:     executes CollaborativePB();
5: else if non-GPS device || p_r < p_min then
6:     device becomes PR and executes CollaborativePR();
7: end if
```

ALGORITHM 1: ECOPS: Initial procedure deciding whether a device becomes either a PB or a PR.

The authors of [33] employ indoor positioning, and perform fingerprinting and training of the known space using multiple sensors in a smartphone such as WiFi radio, cellular communications radio, accelerometer, and magnetometer. In order to improve Cell-ID location accuracy in low-end cell phones where neighboring cell tower information is not available, [32] uses RSSI from only the associated cell tower and leverages the signal strength history to estimate the location. The Cell-ID Aided Positioning System (CAPS) [31] relies on the continuous mobility and position history of a user to obtain better location accuracy over a basic cell tower-based approach. It uses Cell-ID sequence matching to estimate current position based on the history of Cell-ID and GPS position sequences that match the current Cell-ID sequence. CAPS assumes that the user moves on the same routes repeatedly and has the same cellular chip and infrastructure availability.

A few studies address energy efficiency of smartphones using power duty cycling techniques [7, 8, 31] that use a combination of the basic positioning techniques in a smartphone. The authors of [7] use different positioning schemes depending on the condition, for the purpose of target tracking. In the scheme, energy-efficient but inaccurate Cell-ID Positioning or WPS is used when the target is distant, while accurate but energy-inefficient GPS is used when the target is close. The rate-adaptive positioning system (RAPS) [8] uses built-in sensors in a smartphone to determine if the phone has moved beyond a certain threshold and decides whether to turn on the GPS or not. RAPS also stores the space-time history of the user's movements to estimate how to yield high energy efficiency. Another idea presented by the authors involves a Bluetooth-based position synchronization (BPS) in which devices share their location information over a Bluetooth connection. While a Bluetooth connection consumes less power as compared to a WiFi ad hoc, it also limits the range of communication to less than 10 m. Our work has advantages over the basic BPS technique in several aspects. Not only does a WiFi ad hoc mode give us a better range, but we have also taken into account the heterogeneity amongst the devices in terms of availability of a GPS chip or cellular connection. We expect all the devices to have at least a WiFi module present onboard. In BPS, once location information is obtained from a neighboring device, only a fixed error range of 10 m (e.g., same as the range of a typical Bluetooth) is associated with that information. However, in ECOPS we exploit the RSSI values of the connection to determine the accurate distance between the two devices, and when three or more location

transmitting devices are available, the trilateration technique achieves pinpoint locating capabilities.

The work in [34] proposed to use minimal auxiliary sound hardware for acoustic ranging in order to improve the accuracy. The acoustic ranging technique estimates the distance among peer phones, then maps their locations jointly against a WiFi signature map subject to ranging constraints. It is a WPS augmentation technique to improve the accuracy over a pure WPS.

Our approach is unique in that we use a collaborative approach rather than focusing on the information in an individual device and do not rely on any special hardware or infrastructure such as WPS or Cell-ID Positioning. Note that we only use a small amount of GPS information and the WiFi ad hoc mode of mobile nodes. ECOPS is specifically aimed at resource constrained environments such as battlefields where GPS is the only available positioning infrastructure, and WiFi ad hoc mode is readily available in most mobile devices while allowing good network range (up to 100 m). Beside controlling energy usage and location accuracy, we allow to use heterogeneous mobile device types.

4. ECOPS Approach

In this section, we discuss ECOPS algorithms in detail. Figure 4 shows an ECOPS deployment example. It consists of mobile devices with heterogeneous positioning methods available such as GPS, WiFi, and Cell-ID. These devices virtually establish an ad hoc network using WiFi to build a collaborative positioning environment. In the established ECOPS ad hoc network, a device may function as either a position broadcaster (PB) or a position receiver (PR). A GPS-equipped device with sufficient battery life and up-to-date location information becomes a candidate for a PB. Other devices with no GPS that need current location information will become PRs.

Three algorithms are presented for the overall operation of the ECOPS. Algorithm 1 describes the initial procedure deciding whether a device becomes a PB or a PR. After the initial decision, Algorithms 2 and 3 depict how the devices in ECOPS collaboratively maintain their most updated location information as a PB or a PR, respectively. For GPS-equipped devices, the role of the devices can be changed during their operation according to their residual energy level (i.e., PB ↔ PR). As illustrated in Algorithm 1, a device, once it starts ECOPS operation, will check the time elapsed since the device got the location information (t_e) and residual power

```
1: while p_r ≥ p_min do
2:     listen to connection request from a PR;
3:     wait for location request from a PR;
4:     if PR requests then
5:         check the time elapsed since the device got location
              information (t_e)
6:         calculate I_decay;
7:         if I_decay < α then
8:             update its GPS location information;
9:             t_e = 0;
10:        end if
11:    end if
12:    broadcast current GPS location information;
13:    check the residual power (p_r);
14: end while
15: execute CollaborativePR();
```

ALGORITHM 2: ECOPS: *CollaborativePB()*.

```
1: while non-GPS device || (GPS-equipped device & p_r < p_min) do
2:     sleep until the device needs to update location information
3:     numofPBs = 0;
4:     check the list of available PBs;
5:     make connection to each PB and request GPS location
          information sequentially;
6:     calculate the distance to each PB using the obtained
          RSSI value;
7:     set numofPBs to the number of the detected PBs
8:     if numofPBs == 1|| one of PBs is within the near field
          threshold (β meters) then
9:     use the received GPS location information immediately
          without trilateration;
10:    continue;
11:    end if
12:    if numofPBs == 2 then
13:    calculate two possible locations (PR) and get the
          middle location between the two possible locations;
14:    end if
15:    if numofPBs >= 3 then
16:    select three PBs randomly and calculate the its cur-
          rent location (PR) with the GPS coordinates and
          distance information of the selected PBs;
17:    end if
18:    if GPS-equipped device then
19:        check the residual power (p_r);
20:    end if
21: end while
22: execute CollaborativePB();
```

ALGORITHM 3: ECOPS: *CollaborativePR()*.

(p_r) to see if it is qualified for being a PB. Since we are looking for the devices that have the most recent location information with enough residual power, the device with the conditions such as $p_r \geq p_{\min}$ and $I_{\text{decay}} \geq \alpha$ can be a PB, where $p_{\min}$ is the minimum residual energy that a PB has to maintain and I_{decay} is the level of the validity with respect to time for the location information, defined by

$$I_{\text{decay}} = 100 \times \left(1 - \frac{t_e}{t_d} \right), \qquad (1)$$

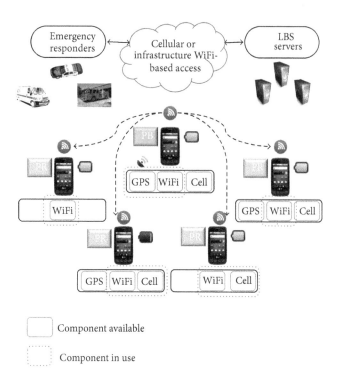

FIGURE 4: ECOPS deployment example.

where t_d is the maximum time in which the location information is considered to be valid.

If a device is equipped with a GPS receiver and satisfies the p_{min}, it can be a PB. Once it becomes a PB, it will start its WiFi hotspot mode and serve the most up-to-date location information to a PR when a PR requests the location information. An Android device cannot use the WiFi Internet service while it is in the WiFi hotspot mode. However, with (Android 4.0), WiFi Direct technology can be used for PBs. In a PB mode with WiFi Direct, the users can enjoy their WiFi Internet service and provide the most up-to-date location information simultaneously. The device without a GPS receiver will automatically be a PR once it enters ECOPS, and then search for PBs around it.

As shown in Algorithm 2, once the device enters the PB mode, it plays a role of the PB while it satisfies the p_{min} constraint. The threshold α is a system parameter that can be varied according to the requirement of applications. The tradeoff between location accuracy and energy consumption can be adjustable using α. An application requiring high accuracy will select a small amount of α, but a high value of α is used for applications requiring low energy consumption. The PB will check I_{decay} to see if the current location information is adequate (e.g., $I_{decay} \geq \alpha$) before broadcasting it.

In Algorithm 3, a PR will collect the possible number of GPS coordinates and corresponding RSSI values and apply opportunistic localization as illustrated in Figure 5. If a PR finds a PB within the threshold distance (β meters), then a PR uses the GPS coordinate from a PB as is. The parameter β is controllable and users of ECOPS can set it according to their preference. Once a PR estimates its location, it can become a PB. However, we do not use those cases in our experiments

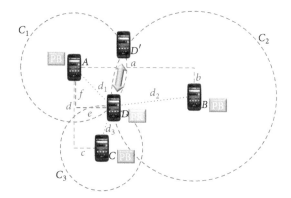

FIGURE 5: 2D trilateration.

to avoid the additional errors that will be induced from PBs and focus on the PR's accuracy.

ECOPS is opportunistic, meaning that getting the most updated location via trilateration is not limited by the number of available PBs. Supposing that there is only one GPS broadcaster in Figure 5, say node C, then the center of an error range of the circle C_3 will become the PR's approximated position. Another possible situation is when there are two PBs, say nodes A and B; then the middle point of two possible points, D and D', is selected as an approximated PR location. The accuracy of the estimated location will range from one point where the two circles intersect in the best case to the diameter of the smaller circle in the worst case, respectively. In order to get the most accurate location information for a PR, we need at least three PBs to provide their location information obtained from the GPS receiver along with the RSSI values, so that we can build an absolute coordinate system from the relative coordinate system. For example, in Figure 5, we calculate the distance parameters a, b, c, and d using the algorithm described in [35] in order to obtain the values of e and f. We convert the obtained distances e and f into the unit of the GPS coordinates to get the final calculated GPS coordinate. The distance between two GPS coordinates, (lat_1, lng_1) of e and (lat_2, lng_2) of f, is computed using the haversine formula that gives a spherical distance between two points from their longitudes and latitudes [35, 36]. The formula is described in (2) and the formula for the value of dist is shown in (3):

$$F_{dist}\left(lat_1, lng_1, lat_2, lng_2\right)$$
$$= \text{rad 2 deg}\left(a\cos\left(\text{dist}\right)\right) \times 60 \times 1.1515 \qquad (2)$$
$$\times 1.609344,$$

$$\text{dist} = \sin\left(\text{deg 2 rad}\left(lat_1\right)\right) \times \sin\left(\text{deg 2 rad}\left(lat_2\right)\right)$$
$$+ \cos\left(\text{deg 2 rad}\left(lat_1\right)\right) \times \cos\left(\text{deg 2 rad}\left(lat_2\right)\right) \qquad (3)$$
$$\times \cos\left(\text{deg 2 rad}\left(lng_1 - lng_2\right)\right).$$

Thus, we can calculate relative coordinates (a, b, c, and d) as follows:

$$a = F_{dist}\left(A_{lat}, A_{lng}, B_{lat}, A_{lng}\right),$$
$$b = F_{dist}\left(A_{lat}, A_{lng}, A_{lat}, B_{lng}\right),$$

$$c = F_{\text{dist}}\left(A_{\text{lat}}, A_{\text{lng}}, C_{\text{lat}}, A_{\text{lng}}\right),$$
$$d = F_{\text{dist}}\left(A_{\text{lat}}, A_{\text{lng}}, A_{\text{lat}}, C_{\text{lng}}\right). \tag{4}$$

The distances (d_1, d_2, and d_3) between node D and other nodes (A, B, and C) can be derived from the measured RSSI values of node D, using the formula from the path loss propagation model [37]:

$$\text{RSSI} = -\left(10n \cdot \log_{10} d + \mathscr{L}\right), \tag{5}$$

where RSSI is the received power which is a function of the distance between the transmitter and the receiver (T-R), n is the signal propagation constant (also called propagation exponent), d is the T-R separation distance in meters, and $\mathscr{L}$ is the system loss factor. Based on (5), we derived the distance (d) between two devices using the average RSSI value as follows:

$$d = 10^{(-\text{RSSI}-\mathscr{L})/10n}. \tag{6}$$

Now, the three circles in Figure 5 can be represented by the following, respectively:

$$C_1 : X^2 + Y^2 = d_1{}^2, \tag{7}$$

$$C_2 : (X - a)^2 + (Y - b)^2 = d_2{}^2, \tag{8}$$

$$C_3 : (X - c)^2 + (Y - d)^2 = d_3{}^2, \tag{9}$$

where the location of node A is set to $(0, 0)$.

We obtain the relative coordinate of PR node D from node A, (e, f), by calculating the point where these three circles intersect. In other words, we want to calculate the coordinate values of X and Y that simultaneously satisfy (7), (8), and (9). We first extend (8) and (9) as follows:

$$\begin{aligned} C_2 &: X^2 - 2aX + a^2 + Y^2 - 2bY + b^2 = d_2{}^2, \\ C_3 &: X^2 - 2cX + c^2 + Y^2 - 2dY + d^2 = d_3{}^2. \end{aligned} \tag{10}$$

By applying (7) into (10), the circles C_2 and C_3 can be written as

$$\begin{aligned} C_2 &: d_1{}^2 - 2aX + a^2 - 2bY + b^2 = d_2{}^2, \\ C_3 &: d_1{}^2 - 2cX + c^2 - 2dY + d^2 = d_3{}^2. \end{aligned} \tag{11}$$

Finally, the node D's coordinate that satisfies the three circles is attained by replacing X and Y with e and f, respectively, in (11). We can formulate the equations in terms of e and f as follows:

$$\begin{aligned} e &= \frac{d\left(D_{\text{vec}\,1}\right) - b\left(D_{\text{vec}\,2}\right)}{2\left(bc - ad\right)}, \\ f &= \frac{c\left(D_{\text{vec}\,1}\right) - a\left(D_{\text{vec}\,2}\right)}{2\left(ad - bc\right)}, \end{aligned} \tag{12}$$

where $D_{\text{vec}\,1} = d_2{}^2 - d_1{}^2 - a^2 - b^2$ and $D_{\text{vec}\,2} = d_3{}^2 - d_1{}^2 - c^2 - d^2$.

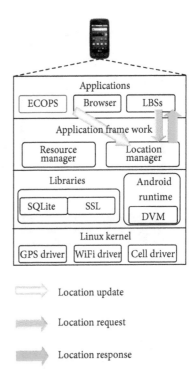

FIGURE 6: Android module architecture.

We have implemented ECOPS as an Android application for a feasibility test and analysis. Figure 7 shows the screenshots of the ECOPS application. Figure 7(a) displays the main screen that allows users to manually select an ECOPS device option either in PB mode or PR mode, or to request the selection automatically based on various parameters such as the remaining energy and sensor availabilities. Figure 7(b) presents a PB screen that lists the broadcasting location information. Figure 7(c) shows a PR screen that lists the received information and measured distance using the RSSI value. Although the current implementation is on an application level, as illustrated in Figure 6, it is still capable of making the received location information available to other application services. It will eventually be implemented within the application framework so that other applications can use the ECOPS services via APIs.

5. Experiments

In this section, we present the evaluation results of ECOPS in terms of energy efficiency and location accuracy. We have implemented an ECOPS Android application and used several Android smartphones including Samsung Galaxy Nexus S running Android version 2.3.6 and two LG Optimus V running Android version 2.2.2. We have turned the GPS off on some of the devices to mimic heterogeneous devices.

5.1. Validation of Smartphone GPS Accuracy and Propagation Model. As a first step, we test the accuracy of commodity GPS receivers on smartphones since they are not dedicated devices like the navigation devices for positioning. We have measured the accuracy of smartphones' GPS, by walking around

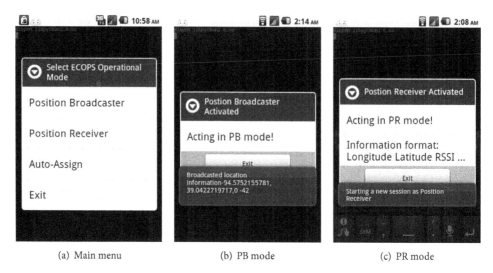

(a) Main menu   (b) PB mode   (c) PR mode

FIGURE 7: ECOPS screenshots.

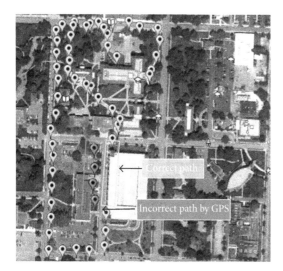

FIGURE 8: GPS trace obtained by smartphone.

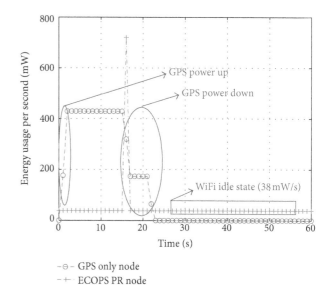

FIGURE 9: Energy usage: GPS versus ECOPS PR.

the Kansas City area while carrying three smartphones. As shown in Figure 8, the GPS collected locations are presented accurately except for a little error between tall buildings (~10 m).

Next, we validate the *path* loss model for correlation of the distance between a WiFi signal emitter and receiver with the measured RSSI values at the signal receiver for both indoor and outdoor environments. We compared the measured RSSI value with the theoretical RSSI value from the *path* loss model. As RSSI values often vary at each time of measurement for a given location, we used an averaged RSSI value with multiple samples (e.g., 1,000 samples within a few seconds). In Figures 10 and 11 we compare the measured RSSI with the theoretical RSSI while varying the distance between PB and PR; both inside a building and in outdoor environments are shown, respectively. The theoretical RSSI values are derived from (5). The dotted blue line shows the measured average RSSI values, and the solid green line represents the theoretical RSSI values at the corresponding distances. The system loss

factor value (A) is set to 30. For the indoor environment, since we measured the RSSI between two devices while they were in the line-of-sight, we set the system loss factor (n) to 0.6. For the outdoor environment, we used $n = 1.9$. As evidenced in the figures, we observe that the *path* loss model works well for us in estimating the distance.

5.2. Energy Consumption. We now compare the total energy consumption of ECOPS devices to that of devices with GPS only scheme in various settings. First, we compare the energy consumption of a node that is ECOPS PR with a node using only GPS at per second granularity as illustrated in Figure 9. This power consumption profiling was done using PowerTutor [38]. The GPS uses 429 mW/s continuously once it is powered up and takes several seconds to power down which adds up to the energy consumption. Meanwhile, the WiFi module once powered up uses 720 mW/s in an

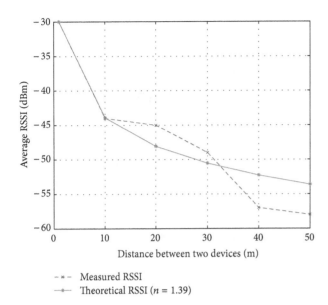

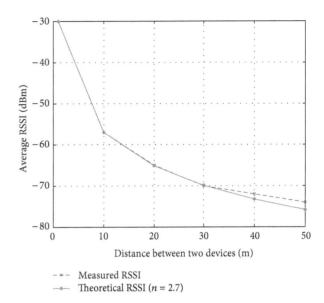

FIGURE 10: Measured RSSI (avg. of 1,000 samples) at various indoor spots.

FIGURE 11: Measured RSSI (avg. of 1,000 samples) at various outdoor spots.

active state and 38 mW/s when in an idle state. During the experiment, for the same operational time of one minute, an ECOPS PR node uses only 3000 mW of energy in total whereas the GPS-only node uses 7432 mW of total energy. This clearly shows that an ECOPS PR is more energy efficient than a GPS-only node. These values are for an LG Optimus V model in particular, and similar for most smartphones.

Next, we contrast the energy consumption of a node that is ECOPS PR with a node using only GPS while varying the operational time with 1 minute increments as illustrated in Figure 12. We do this experiment to analyze the effectiveness of ECOPS over a duration of time. It shows that ECOPS is increasingly energy efficient with the elapsed time over the GPS only scheme.

In Figure 13, we compare the energy consumption of nodes that are ECOPS PR with nodes using only GPS while varying the number of devices in the network. We do this experiment to analyze the energy efficiency of ECOPS as the number of devices in the network scales. Note that for the ECOPS PR scheme, the PRs receive GPS data from three PBs and their energy consumption is accounted for in the results. The energy efficiency of ECOPS compared with the GPS only scheme is clear from Figure 13 and becomes increased substantially as the number of devices in the network scales.

5.3. *Location Accuracy*. In this section, we evaluate the location accuracy of ECOPS as compared to that of GPS, WPS, and Cell-ID Positioning. We tested ECOPS in a soccer field using four smartphones for the accuracy measurements. The soccer field was chosen, so that we have a clear and unhindered view of the sky, and in turn the experimental results are not influenced by the GPS position errors, and the ECOPS errors are precisely measured. We turned on GPS for three devices and turned it off for a device that acted as the PR. In order to measure the location accuracy, as illustrated in

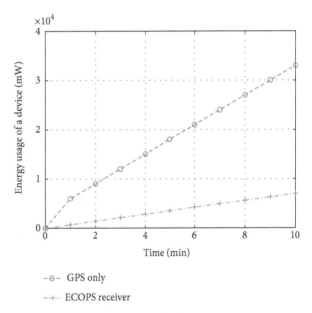

FIGURE 12: Comparison of individual node energy consumption: GPS versus ECOPS PR.

Figure 14, we placed the PR device at the center of the area and moved the other PB devices around multiple locations within the soccer field. The PR device computed its location using the measured RSSI values, and GPS coordinates from the PBs, and the trilateration technique described in Section 4.

We have moved the PBs to various places around the PR and recorded the PR's computed locations. As shown in Figure 15, we observed that ECOPS achieves a minimum error range of 2.32 m and a maximum error range of 33.31 m. While from Figure 16 we can observe that nearly 60% of these locations are within a 10 m error range and less than 10% have an error range greater than 15 m. The results represent that

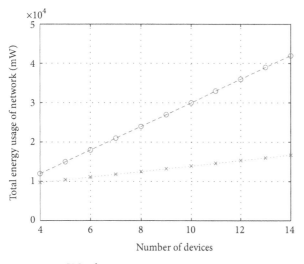

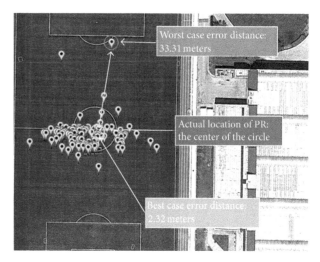

FIGURE 15: Experiment results: points calculated with three GPS coordinates and RSSI values.

FIGURE 13: Comparison of total energy consumption of nodes (1 min): GPS versus ECOPS.

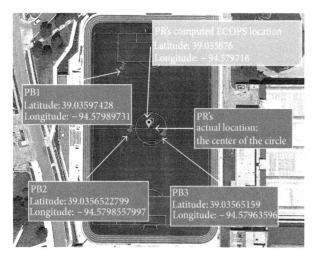

FIGURE 14: An example of field experiments.

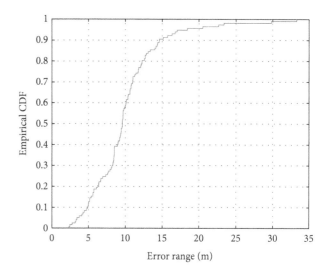

FIGURE 16: Distribution in error range for location estimated by PR.

ECOPS can achieve a higher location accuracy than WPS while using less energy than GPS receivers. Also, note that the error ranges we observe here are an amalgamation of the general GPS receiver error from the PBs and the distance measurement error from the RSSI values.

Finally, we compare the errors of different positioning methods in Figure 17. As before, a smartphone that needs positioning is located at the center of soccer field. The network positioning API in Android obtains the location information either from WPS or Cell-ID Positioning. In order to ensure the Cell-ID Positioning in Android, the smartphone acquired the location from network positioning API while turning off the WiFi signal. The location information received was off by almost 300 m. Together with the location, it also suggested its own estimated error range of 1,280 m associated with it. Clearly, such information is too

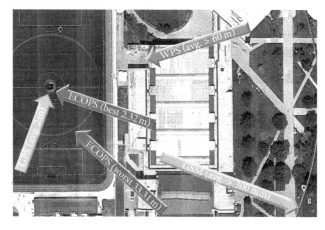

FIGURE 17: Accuracy comparison: ECOPS, GPS, WPS, and GSM-based positioning.

inaccurate to be used in most of LBS application scenarios. As for WPS, the smartphone obtained the location from Android network positioning API while turning off cellular signal. Note that WPS is not typically available in outdoor environment. Thus, we used an average WPS error from what we experimented at multiple locations in Kansas City area where WPS is available and found it to be 60 m. It is the dotted blue line in Figure 17. While the GPS-based location information proved to be the most accurate with an error range of about 2 m, ECOPS achieved the accuracy ranging from 2.32 m to 33.31 m. This is better than the performance of a WPS and fairly close to GPS accuracy while saving energy costs. This encourages us to comment that even when WPS service might be available, using ECOPS will facilitate a smartphone to receive more accurate location information at the same energy cost.

6. Conclusion

We have presented an Energy Efficient Collaborative Opportunistic Positioning System (ECOPS) for heterogeneous mobile devices. Unlike existing approaches that are seeking the best available positioning method from an individual device, ECOPS facilitates collaborative environments among a set of mobile devices, and thus mobile devices benefit from their neighboring devices. ECOPS supports heterogeneous devices to maximize energy-efficiency, as a device with only WiFi can collaborate with a few available GPS broadcasting devices via WiFi hotspot mode or WiFi Direct-based approximation. A beneficiary device may use one or more locations' information from neighbors opportunistically, depending on their availability. Furthermore, each device improves the received location accuracy via various available methods including trilateration or approximation with geomagnetic sensors. We have implemented an ECOPS prototype application on Android 2.3.6 and 2.2.2 and have tested it with various types of Android mobile devices. The results show that ECOPS provides accuracy within 10 m for nearly 60% of the location estimates, and within 15 m for more than 90% of them. ECOPS also offers significantly more energy efficiency than a GPS-only scheme, while overcoming various service limitations.

Future work includes fine-tuning the accuracy by opportunistically exploiting other available sensors on mobile devices. We also plan to consider strategies for various types of LBSs to improve their utility and energy efficiency.

References

[1] E. Kwon, S. Song, D. Seo, and I. Jung, "Agent-based on-line traffic condition and information analysis system for wireless V2I communication," in *Proceedings of the 2nd International Conference on Ubiquitous and Future Networks (ICUFN '10)*, pp. 360–365, Jeju Island, Republic of Korea, June 2010.

[2] "Global positioning system standard positioning service performance standard," http://www.gps.gov/technical/ps/2008-SPS-performance-standard.pdf.

[3] "Skyhook wireless," http://www.skyhookwireless.com/.

[4] E. Trevisani and A. Vitaletti, "Cell-ID location technique, limits and benefits: an experimental study," in *6th IEEE Workshop on Mobile Computing Systems and Applications (WMCSA '04)*, pp. 51–60, December 2004.

[5] "Google latitude," 2012, http://www.google.com/latitude.

[6] "Foursquare," https://foursquare.com/.

[7] U. Bareth and A. Kupper, "Energy-efficient position tracking in proactive location-based services for smartphone environments," in *Proceedings of the 35th IEEE Annual Computer Software and Applications Conference (COMPSAC '11)*, pp. 516–521, Munich, Germany, July 2011.

[8] J. Paek, J. Kim, and R. Govindan, "Energy-efficient rate-adaptive GPS-based Positioning for smartphones," in *Proceedings of the 8th Annual International Conference on Mobile Systems, Applications and Services (MobiSys '10)*, pp. 299–314, New York, NY, USA, June 2010.

[9] "Android 2. 2 platform highlights—portable hotspot," http://developer.android.com/about/versions/android-2.2-highlights.html.

[10] "Wi-Fi direct," http://developer.android.com/guide/topics/wireless/wifip2p.html.

[11] Y. Zhang, L. Yang, and J. Chen, *RFID and Sensor Networks: Architectures, Protocols, Security and Integrations*, CRC Press, New York, NY, USA, 2009.

[12] T. Rappaport, *Wireless Communications Principles and Practice*, Prentice Hall, New York, NY, USA, 1996.

[13] "3-Axis geomagnetic sensor for electronic compass," http://developer.android.com/guide/topics/connectivity/wifip2p.html.

[14] M. Mohorcic, D. Grace, G. Kandus, and T. Tozer, "Broadband communications from aerial platform networks," in *Proceedings of the 13th IST Mobile and Wireless Communications Summit*, pp. 257–261, 2004.

[15] "LANdroids robot," 2012, http://www.irobot.com/gi/research/AdvancedPlatforms/LANdroidsRobot.

[16] "The air force has its own batman," 2012, http://money.cnn.com/video/technology/2012/05/18/t-ts-wpafb-batman.cnnmoney/.

[17] "U.S. government, military to get secure Android phones," 2012, http://www.cnn.com/2012/02/03/tech/mobile/government-android-phones/index.html.

[18] National Security Agency(NSA), "Nsa-grade security enhanced android source released," 2012, http://www.androidauthority.com/nsa-grade-securityenhanced-android-source-released-45532/.

[19] "Google maps location based services," http://support.google.com/maps/bin/answer.py?hl=en&answer=1725632.

[20] "Apple location based services," http://www.apple.com/privacy/.

[21] B. N. Schilit, A. LaMarca, G. Borriello et al., "Challenge: ubiquitous location-aware computing and the "place lab" initiative," in *Proceedings of the 1st ACM International Workshop on Wireless Mobile Applications and Services on WLAN Hotspots (WMASH '03)*, pp. 29–35, September 2003.

[22] W. Ho, A. Smailagic, D. P. Siewiorek, and C. Faloutsos, "An adaptive two-phase approach to WiFi location sensing," in *Proceedings of the 4th Annual IEEE International Conference on Pervasive Computing and Communications Workshops (PerCom Workshops '06)*, pp. 452–456, Pisa, Italy, March 2006.

[23] D. Kelly, R. Behant, R. Villingt, and S. McLoone, "Computationally tractable location estimation on WiFi enabled mobile

phones," in *Proceedings of the IET Irish Signals and Systems Conference (ISSC)*, 2009.

[24] K. Chintalapudi, A. P. Iyer, and V. N. Padmanabhan, "Indoor localization without the pain," in *Proceedings of the Mobile Computing and Networking (MobiCom '10)*, pp. 173–184, 2010.

[25] "Blackberry locate service," https://developer.blackberry.com/devzone/develop/platform_services/platform_locate.html.

[26] "Ekahau real time location system (RTLS)," http://www.ekahau.com/products/real-time-location-system/overview.html.

[27] "Cisco AeroScout location-based services solution," http://www.cisco.com/web/strategy/docs/manufacturing/Aeroscout--Cisco-Brochure.pdf.

[28] "Broadcom: new location architecture with BCM4752," http://www.broadcom.com/products/features/GNSS.php.

[29] F. Schrooyen, I. Baert, S. Truijen et al., "Real time location system over WiFi in a healthcare environment," *Journal on Information Technology in Healthcare*, vol. 4, no. 6, pp. 401–416, 2006.

[30] A. Ofstad, E. Nicholas, R. Szcodronski, and R. R. Choudhury, "AAMPL: accelerometer augmented mobile phone localization," in *Proceedings of the 1st ACM International Workshop on Mobile Entity Localization and Tracking in GPS-Less Environments (MELT '08)*, pp. 13–18, New York, NY, USA, September 2008.

[31] J. Paek, K. H. Kim, J. P. Singh, and R. Govindan, "Energy-efficient positioning for smartphones using cell-ID sequence matching," in *Proceedings of the 9th International Conference on Mobile Systems, Applications, and Services (MobiSys '11)*, pp. 293–306, New York, NY, USA, July 2011.

[32] M. Ibrahim and M. Youssef, "A hidden Markov model for localization using low-end GSM cell phones," in *IEEE International Conference on Communications (ICC '11)*, pp. 1–5, Kyoto, Japan, 2011.

[33] E. Martin, O. Vinyals, G. Friedland, and R. Bajcsy, "Precise indoor localization using smart phones," in *Proceedings of the 18th ACM International Conference on Multimedia ACM Multimedia 2010 (MM '10)*, pp. 787–790, October 2010.

[34] H. Liu, Y. Guan, J. Yang et al., "Push the Limit of WiFi based Localization for Smartphones," in *Proceedings of the 18th Annual International Conference on Mobile Computing and Networking (Mobicom '12)*, pp. 305–316, 2012.

[35] "Calculating distance between two points given longitude/latitude," http://www.freevbcode.com/ShowCode.asp?ID=5532.

[36] R. W. Sinnott, "Virtues of the Haversine," *Sky and Telescope*, vol. 68, no. 2, article 158, 1984.

[37] K. Aamodt, "Applicationnote AN042 (Rev.1.0)," pp. 7-8, 2006.

[38] "PowerTutor," http://ziyang.eecs.umich.edu/projects/powertutor/.

5

Response Time Analysis of Messages in Controller Area Network: A Review

Gerardine Immaculate Mary,[1] **Z. C. Alex,**[1] **and Lawrence Jenkins**[2]

[1] *School of Electronics Engineering, VIT University, Vellore, Tamilnadu 632014, India*
[2] *Department of Electrical Engineering, IISc, Bangalore, Karnataka 560012, India*

Correspondence should be addressed to Gerardine Immaculate Mary; gerardine@yahoo.com

Academic Editor: Zhiyong Xu

This paper reviews the research work done on the response time analysis of messages in controller area network (CAN) from the time CAN specification was submitted for standardization (1990) and became a standard (1993) up to the present (2012). Such research includes the worst-case response time analysis which is deterministic and probabilistic response time analysis which is stochastic. A detailed view on both types of analyses is presented here. In addition to these analyses, there has been research on statistical analysis of controller area network message response times.

1. Introduction

The arbitration mechanism employed by CAN means that messages are sent as if all the nodes on the network share a single global priority-based queue. In effect, messages are sent on the bus according to fixed priority nonpreemptive scheduling [1]. In the early 1990s, a common misconception was that although the protocol was very good at transmitting the highest priority messages with low latency, it was not possible to guarantee that the less urgent signals carried in lower priority messages would meet their deadlines [1]. In 1994, Tindell et al. [2–5] showed how research into fixed priority preemptive scheduling for single processor systems could be applied to the scheduling of messages on CAN. This analysis provided a method of calculating the worst-case response times of all CAN messages. Using this analysis it became possible to engineer CAN-based systems for timing correctness, providing guarantees that all messages and the signals that they carry would meet their deadlines. In 2007, Davis et al. [1] refuted this analysis and showed that multiple instances of CAN messages within a busy period (this period begins with a critical instant) need to be considered in order to guarantee that the message and the signals that they carry would meet their deadlines, since

CAN effectively implements fixed priority nonpreemptive scheduling of messages.

Real-time researchers have extended schedulability analysis to a mature technique which for non-trivial systems can be used to determine whether a set of tasks executing on a single CPU or in a distributed system will meet their deadlines or not [1, 2, 4, 5]. The essence of this analysis is to investigate if deadlines are met in a worst-case scenario. Whether this worst case actually will occur during execution, or if it is likely to occur, is not normally considered [6].

In contrast with schedulability analysis, reliability modelling involves the study of fault models, the characterization of distribution functions of faults, and the development of methods and tools for composing these distributions and models in estimating an overall reliability figure for the system [6].

This separation of deterministic (0/1) schedulability analysis and stochastic reliability analysis is a natural simplification of the total analysis. This is because the deterministic schedulability analysis is quite pessimistic, since it assumes that a missed deadline in the worst case is equivalent to always missing the deadline, whereas the stochastic analysis extends the knowledge of the system by computing how often a deadline is violated [7].

There are many other sources of pessimism in the analysis, including considering worst-case execution times and worst-case phasings of executions, as well as the usage of pessimistic fault models. In a related work [8], a model for calculating worst-case latencies of controller area network (CAN) frames (messages) under error assumptions is proposed. This model is pessimistic, in the sense that there are systems that the analysis determines to be unschedulable, even though deadlines will be missed only in extremely rare situations with pathological combinations of errors.

In [9, 10] the level of pessimism is reduced by introducing a better fault model, and in [9] variable phasings between message queuing are also considered, in order to make the model more realistic. In [11] the pessimism introduced by the worst-case analysis of CAN message response times is reduced by using bit-stuffing distributions in the place of the traditional worst-case frame sizes which are referred to in [6, 7].

The organization of the paper is as follows: in Section 2, the review of the research on Worst Case Response Time Analysis of CAN messages is presented, and in Section 3, the review of the research on Probabilistic Response Time Analysis of CAN messages is presented. In both sections, the method of bit stuffing is reviewed.

2. Worst-Case Response Time Analysis of CAN Messages

In automotive applications, the *messages* sent on CAN are used to communicate state information, referred to as *signals*, between different ECUs. Examples of signals include wheel speeds, oil and water temperature, engine rpm, gear selection, accelerator position, dashboard switch positions, climate control settings, window switch positions, fault codes, and diagnostic information. In a high-end vehicle there can be more than 2500 distinct signals, each effectively replacing what would have been a separate wire in a traditional point-to-point wiring loom.

Many of these signals have real-time constraints associated with them. For example, an ECU reads the position of a switch attached to the brake pedal. This ECU must send a signal, carrying information that the brakes have been applied, over the CAN network so that the ECU responsible for the rear light clusters can recognise the change in the value of the signal and switch the brake lights on. All this must happen within a few tens of milliseconds of the brake pedal being pressed. Engine, transmission, and stability control systems typically place even tighter time constraints on signals, which may need to be sent as frequently as once every 5 milliseconds to meet their time constraints [1]. Hence it is essential that CAN messages meet their deadlines.

2.1. Related Work. CAN is a serial data bus that supports priority-based message arbitration and non-pre-emptive message transmission. The schedulability analysis for CAN builds on previous research into fixed priority scheduling of tasks on single processor systems [12].

In 1990, Lehoczky [13] introduced the concept of a busy period and showed that if tasks have deadlines greater than their periods (referred to as *arbitrary deadlines*) then it is necessary to examine the response times of all invocations of a task falling within a busy period in order to determine the worst-case response time. In 1991, Harbour et al. [14] showed that if deadlines are less than or equal to periods, but priorities vary during execution, then again multiple invocations must be inspected to determine the worst-case response time. We note that non-pre-emptive scheduling is effectively a special case of pre-emptive scheduling with varying execution priority—as soon as a task starts to execute, its priority is raised to the highest level. In 1994, Tindell et al. [12] improved upon the work of Lehoczky [13], providing a formulation for arbitrary deadline analysis based on a recurrence relation.

Building upon these earlier results, comprehensive schedulability analysis of non-pre-emptive fixed priority scheduling for single processor systems was given by George et al. in 1996 [15]. In 2006, Bril [16] refuted the analysis of fixed priority systems with deferred pre-emption given by Burns in [17], showing that this analysis may result in computed worst-case response times that are optimistic. The schedulability analysis for CAN given by Tindell et al. in [2–5] builds upon [17] and suffers from essentially the same flaw. A similar issue with work on pre-emption thresholds [18] was first identified and corrected by Regehr [19] in 2002. A technical report [20] and a workshop paper [21] highlight the problem for CAN but do not provide a specific in-depth solution.

The revised schedulability analysis presented in [1] aims to provide an evolutionary improvement upon the analysis of CAN given by Tindell et al. in [2–5]. To do so, it draws upon the analysis of Tindell et al. [12] for fixed priority pre-emptive scheduling of systems with arbitrary deadlines, and the analysis of George et al. [15] for fixed priority non-pre-emptive systems, and also presents a sufficient but not necessary schedulability tests, to overcome the complexities involved in calculating the response times of multiple instances of CAN messages within the busy period.

2.2. Bit Stuffing in CAN Messages. CAN was designed as a robust and reliable form of communication for short messages. Each data frame carries between 0 and 8 bytes of payload data and has a 15-bit Cyclic Redundancy Check (CRC). The CRC is used by receiving nodes to check for errors in the transmitted message. If a node detects an error in the transmitted message, which may be a bit-stuffing error, a CRC error, a form error in the fixed part of the message or an acknowledgement error, then it transmits an error flag [22]. The error flag consists of 6 bits of the same polarity: "000000" if the node is in the error active state and "111111" if it is error passive. Transmission of an error flag typically causes other nodes to also detect an error, leading to transmission of further error flags.

Figure 1 illustrates CAN error frames, reproduced from [1]. The length of an error frame is between 17 and 31 bits. Hence each message transmission that is signalled as an error

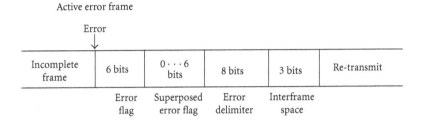

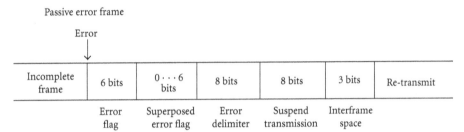

FIGURE 1: CAN error frames.

can lead to a maximum of 31 additional bits of error recovery overhead plus retransmission of the message itself [22].

One characteristic of Nonreturn-to-Zero code that is adopted in CAN bus is that the signal provides no edges that can be used for resynchronization if transmitting a large number of consecutive bits with the same polarity. Therefore bit stuffing is used to ensure synchronization of all bus nodes. This means that during the transmission of a message, a maximum of five consecutive bits may have the same polarity. The bit-stuffing area in a CAN bus frame includes the SOF, Arbitration field, Control field, Data field, and CRC field. Since bit stuffing is used, six consecutive bits of the same type (111111 or 000000) are considered an error.

As the bit patterns "000000" and "111111" are used to signal errors, it is essential that these bit patterns are avoided in the variable part of a transmitted message (refer to Figure 3). The CAN protocol therefore requires that a bit of the opposite polarity is inserted by the transmitter whenever 5 bits of the same polarity are transmitted. This process referred to as bit stuffing, is reversed by the receiver. The worst-case scenario for bit stuffing is shown in Figure 2 [1]. Note that each stuff bit begins a sequence of 5 bits that is itself subject to bit stuffing.

Stuff bits increase the maximum transmission time of CAN messages. After including stuff bits and the interframe space, the maximum transmission time C_m of a CAN message containing s_m data bytes is given by

$$C_m = \left(g + 8s_m + 13 + \left\lfloor \frac{g + 8s_m - 1}{4} \right\rfloor \right) \tau_{\text{bit}}, \qquad (1)$$

where g is 34 for standard format (11-bit identifiers) or 54 for extended format (29-bit identifiers), $\lfloor a/b \rfloor$ is notation for the *floor* function, which returns the largest integer less than or equal to a/b, and τ_{bit} is the transmission time for a single bit.

The formula given in (1) simplifies to

$$C_m = (55 + 10s_m) \tau_{\text{bit}} \qquad (2)$$

for 11-bit identifiers and

$$C_m = (80 + 10s_m) \tau_{\text{bit}} \qquad (3)$$

for 29-bit identifiers.

2.3. Scheduling Model. The system is assumed to comprise a number of nodes (microprocessors) connected via CAN. Each node is assumed to be capable of ensuring that at any given time when arbitration starts, the highest priority message queued at that node is entered into arbitration [1].

The system is assumed to contain a static set of hard real-time messages each statically assigned to a node on the network. Each message m has a fixed identifier and hence a unique priority. As priority uniquely identifies each message, in the remainder of this paper we will overload m to mean either message m or priority m as appropriate. Each message has a maximum number of data bytes s_m and a maximum transmission time C_m, given by (1).

Each message is assumed to be queued by a software task, process or interrupt handler executing on the host microprocessor. This task is either invoked by, or polls for, the event and takes a bounded amount of time between 0 and J_m to queue the message ready for transmission. J_m is referred to as the *queuing jitter* of the message and is inherited from the overall response time of the task, including any polling delay.

The event that triggers queuing of the message is assumed to occur with a minimum interarrival time of T_m, referred to as the message *period*. This model supports events that occur strictly periodically with a period of T_m, events that occur sporadically with a minimum separation of T_m, and events that occur only once before the system is reset, in which case T_m is infinite.

Each message has a hard deadline D_m, corresponding to the maximum permitted time from occurrence of the initiating event to the end of successful transmission of

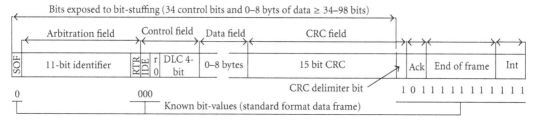

Before stuffing   1 1 1 1 1 0 0 0 0 1 1 1 1 0 0 0 0 1 1 1 1 . . .

After stuffing   1 1 1 1 1 0 0 0 0 0 1 1 1 1 1 0 0 0 0 0 1 1 1 1 1 0 . . .

Stuff bits

FIGURE 2: Worst-case bit stuffing.

Bits exposed to bit-stuffing (34 control bits and 0–8 byts of data ≥ 34–98 bits)

| Arbitration field | | Control field | Data field | CRC field | | | | |

| SOF | 11-bit identifier | RTR IDE | r 0 | DLC 4-bit | 0–8 bytes | 15 bit CRC | Ack | End of frame | Int |

CRC delimiter bit

0   000   1 0 1 1 1 1 1 1 1 1 1 1 1

Known bit-values (standard format data frame)

FIGURE 3: CAN frame layout (standard format data frame).

the message, at which time the message data is assumed to be available on the receiving nodes that require it. Tasks on the receiving nodes may place different timing requirements on the data; however in such cases we assume that D_m is the tightest of such time constraints.

The *worst-case response time* R_m of a message is defined as the longest time from the initiating event occurring to the message being received by the nodes that require it.

A message is said to be *schedulable* if and only if its worst-case response time is less than or equal to its deadline ($R_m \leq D_m$). The system is schedulable if and only if all of the messages in the system are schedulable [1].

2.4. Response Time Analysis. Response time analysis for CAN aims to provide a method of calculating the worst-case response time of each message. These values can then be compared to the message deadlines to determine if the system is schedulable.

For systems complying with the scheduling model given in Section 2.3, the CAN has effectively implemented fixed priority non-pre-emptive scheduling of messages. Following the analysis in [2–5] the worst-case response time of a message can be viewed as being made up of three elements:

(i) the queuing jitter J_m, corresponding to the longest time between the initiating event and the message being queued, ready for transmission on the bus,

(ii) the queuing delay W_m, corresponding to the longest time that the message can remain in the CAN controller slot or device driver queue before commencing successful transmission on the bus,

(iii) the transmission time C_m, corresponding to the longest time that the message can take to be transmitted.

The worst-case response time of message m is given by

$$R_m = J_m + W_m + C_m. \tag{4}$$

The queuing delay comprises *blocking* B_m, due to lower priority messages which may be in the process of being transmitted when message m is queued and *interference* due to higher priority messages which may win arbitration and be transmitted in preference to message m.

The maximum amount of blocking occurs when a lower priority message starts transmission immediately before message m is queued. Message m must wait until the bus is idle before it can be entered into arbitration. The maximum blocking time B_m is given by

$$B_m = \max_{k \in \mathrm{lp}(m)} (C_k), \tag{5}$$

where $\mathrm{lp}(m)$ is the set of messages with lower priority than m.

The concept of a *busy period*, introduced by Lehoczky [13], is fundamental in analysing worst-case response times. Modifying the definition of a busy period given in [14] to apply to CAN messages, a priority level-m busy period is defined as follows

(i) It starts at some time t^s when a message of priority m or higher is queued ready for transmission, and there are no messages of priority m or higher waiting to be transmitted that were queued strictly before time t^s.

(ii) It is a contiguous interval of time during which any message of priority lower than m is unable to start transmission and win arbitration.

(iii) It ends at the earliest time t^e when the bus becomes idle, ready for the next round of transmission and arbitration, yet there are no messages of priority m or higher waiting to be transmitted that were queued strictly before time t^e.

The key characteristic of a busy period is that all messages of priority m or higher queued strictly before the end of the busy period are transmitted during the busy period. These messages cannot therefore cause any interference on a subsequent instance of message m queued at or after the end of the busy period.

In mathematical terminology, busy periods can be viewed as right half-open intervals: $[t^s, t^e)$ where t^s is the start of the busy period and t^e the end. Thus the end of one busy period may correspond to the start of another separate busy period. This is in contrast to the simpler definition given in [13], which unifies two adjacent busy periods as we have defined them, and therefore sometimes results in analysis of more message instances than is strictly necessary. For example, in the extreme case of 100% utilisation, the busy period defined in [13] never ends, and an infinite number of message instances would need to be considered.

The worst-case queuing delay for message m occurs for some instances of message m queued within a priority level-m busy period that starts immediately after the longest lower priority message begins transmission. This *maximal* busy period begins with a so-called *critical instant* [1] where message m is queued simultaneously with all higher priority messages, and then each of these messages is subsequently queued again after the shortest possible time intervals. In the remainder of this paper a busy period means this maximum length busy period.

If more than one instance of message m is transmitted during a priority level-m busy period, then it is necessary to determine the response time of each instance in order to find the overall worst-case response time of the message.

In [2–5], Tindell gives the following equation for the worst-case queuing delay:

$$W_m = B_m + \sum_{\forall k \in hp(m)} \left\lceil \frac{W_m + J_k + \tau_{bit}}{T_k} \right\rceil C_k, \qquad (6)$$

where $hp(m)$ is the set of messages with priorities higher than m and $\lceil a/b \rceil$ is notation for the *ceiling* function which returns the smallest integer greater than or equal to a/b.

Although W_m appears on both sides of (6), as the right hand side is a monotonic nondecreasing function of W_m, the equation may be solved using the following recurrence relation:

$$W_m^n = B_m + \sum_{\forall k \in hp(m)} \left\lceil \frac{W_m^{n+1} + J_k + \tau_{bit}}{T_k} \right\rceil C_k. \qquad (7)$$

A suitable starting value is $W_m^0 = B_m$. The relation iterates until either $J_m + W_m^{n+1} + C_m > D_m$, in which case the message is not schedulable or $W_m^{n+1} = W_m^n$, in which case the worst-case response time of the *first instance of the message in the busy period* is given by $J_m + W_m^{n+1} + C_m$.

The flaw in the previous analysis is that, given the constraint $D_m \leq T_m$, it implicitly assumes that if message m is schedulable, then the priority level-m busy period will end at or before T_m. We observe that with fixed priority pre-emptive scheduling this would always be the case, as on completion of transmission of message m, no higher priority message could be awaiting transmission. However, with fixed priority non-pre-emptive scheduling, a higher priority message can be awaiting transmission when message m completes transmission, and thus the busy period can extend beyond T_m [1].

The length t_m of the priority level-m busy period is given by the following recurrence relation, starting with an initial value of $t_m^0 = C_m$ and finishing when $t_m^{n+1} = t_m^n$:

$$t_m^{n+1} = B_m + \sum_{\forall k \in hp(m) \cup m} \left\lceil \frac{t_m^n + J_k}{T_k} \right\rceil C_k, \qquad (8)$$

where $hp(m) \cup m$ is the set of messages with priority m or higher. As the right hand side is a monotonic nondecreasing function of t_m, the recurrence relation is guaranteed to converge provided that the bus utilisation U_m, for messages of priority m and higher, is less than 1:

$$U_m = \sum_{\forall k \in hp(m) \cup m} \frac{C_k}{T_k}. \qquad (9)$$

If $t_m \leq T_m - J_m$, then the busy period ends at or before the time at which the second instance of message m is queued. This means that only the first instance of the message is transmitted during the busy period. The existing analysis calculates the worst-case queuing time for this instance via (7) and hence provides the correct worst-case response time in this case.

If $t_m > T_m - J_m$, then the existing analysis may give an optimistic worst-case response time depending upon whether the first or some subsequent instance of message m in the busy period has the longest response time.

The analysis presented in Appendix A.2 of [15] suggests that t_m is the smallest value that is a solution to (8); however this is not strictly correct [1]. For the lowest priority message, $B_m = 0$ and so $t_m = 0$ is trivially the smallest solution. This problem can be avoided by using an initial value of $t_m^0 = C_m$ [1].

The number of instances Q_m of message m that become ready for transmission before the end of the busy period is given by

$$Q_m = \left\lceil \frac{t_m + J_m}{T_m} \right\rceil. \qquad (10)$$

To determine the worst-case response time of message m, it is necessary to calculate the response time of each of the Q_m instances and then take the maximum of these values.

In the following analysis, the index variable q is used to represent an instance of message m. The first instance in the busy period corresponds to $q = 0$ and the final instance to $q = Q_m - 1$. The longest time from the start of the busy period to the instance at q beginning successful transmission is given by

$$W_m^{n+1}(q) = B_m + qC_m + \sum_{\forall k \in hp(m)} \left\lceil \frac{W_m^n + J_k + \tau_{bit}}{T_k} \right\rceil C_k. \qquad (11)$$

The recurrence relation starts with a value of $W_m^0(q) = B_m + qC_m$ and ends when $W_m^{n+1}(q) = W_m^n(q)$ or when $J_m + W_m^{n+1}(q) - qT_m + C_m > D_m$ in which case the message is unschedulable. For values of $q > 0$ an efficient starting value is given by $W_m^0(q) = W_m(q-1) + C_m$. The event of initiating instance q of the message occurs at time $qT_m - J_m$ relative to the start of the busy period, so the response time of instance q is given by

$$R_m(q) = J_m + W_m(q) - qT_m + C_m. \qquad (12)$$

The worst-case response time of message m is therefore

$$R_m = \max_{q=0 \cdots Q_m - 1} (R_m(q)). \qquad (13)$$

The analysis presented previously is also applicable when messages have deadlines that are greater than their periods, so-called arbitrary deadlines [1]. However, if such timing characteristics are specified, then the software device drivers or CAN controller hardware may need to be capable of buffering more than one instance of a message. The number of instances of each message that need to be buffered is bounded by

$$N_m = \left\lceil \frac{R_m}{T_m} \right\rceil. \qquad (14)$$

The analysis presented in [15] effectively uses $Q_m = \lfloor t_m/T_m \rfloor + 1$ rather than $Q_m = \lceil t_m/T_m \rceil$. This yields a value which is one too large when the length of the busy period plus jitter is an integer multiple of the message period. Although this does not give rise to problems, the more efficient formulation given by (10) is preferred [1].

The analysis given in this section as per Davis et al. [1] corrects a significant flaw in the previous schedulability analysis for CAN, given by Tindell et al. [2–5]. However, this schedulability test presented is more complex, potentially requiring the computation of multiple response times.

An upper bound on the queuing delay of the second and subsequent instances of message m within the busy period is therefore given by

$$W_m^{n+1} = C_m + \sum_{\forall k \in hp(m)} \left\lceil \frac{W_m^n + J_k + \tau_{bit}}{T_k} \right\rceil C_k. \qquad (15)$$

This result suggests a simple but pessimistic schedulability test. An instance of message m can either be subject to blocking due to lower priority messages or to push through interference of at most C_m due to the previous instance of the same message, but not both. Hence we can modify (7) to provide a correct sufficient but not necessary schedulability test:

$$W_m^{n+1} = \max(B_m, C_m) + \sum_{\forall k \in hp(m)} \left\lceil \frac{W_m^n + J_k + \tau_{bit}}{T_k} \right\rceil C_k. \qquad (16)$$

A further simplification is to assume that the blocking factor always takes its maximum possible value:

$$W_m^{n+1} = B^{max} + \sum_{\forall k \in hp(m)} \left\lceil \frac{W_m^n + J_k + \tau_{bit}}{T_k} \right\rceil C_k, \qquad (17)$$

where B^{max} corresponds to the transmission time of the longest possible CAN message (8 data bytes) irrespective of the characteristics and priorities of the messages in the system. So far we have assumed that no errors occur on the CAN bus. However as originally shown in [2–5], schedulability analysis of CAN may be extended to include an appropriate error model.

In [1] it is assumed that the maximum number of errors present on the bus in some time interval $[0, t]$ is given by the function $F(t)$. No specific detail about this function is assumed, save that it is a monotonic non-decreasing function of t. The schedulability equations are modified to account for the error recovery overhead. The worst-case impact of a single bit error is to cause transmission of an additional 31 bits of error recovery overhead plus retransmission of the affected message. Only errors affecting message m or higher priority messages can delay message m from being successfully transmitted. The maximum additional delay caused by the error recovery mechanism is therefore given by

$$E_m(t) = \left(31\tau_{bit} + \max_{k \in hp(m)u_m} (C_k) \right) F(t). \qquad (18)$$

Revising (8) to compute the length of the busy period we have

$$t_m^{n+1} = E_m(t_m^n) + B_m + \sum_{\forall k \in hp(m)u_m} \left\lceil \frac{t_m^n + J_k}{T_k} \right\rceil C_k. \qquad (19)$$

Again an appropriate initial value is $t_m^0 = C_m$. Equation (19) is guaranteed to converge, provided that the utilisation U_m including error recovery overhead is less than 1.

As before, (10) can be used to compute the number of message instances that need to be examined to find the worst-case response time:

$$W_m^{n+1}(q) = E_m(W_m^n + C_m) + B_m + qC_m$$
$$+ \sum_{\forall k \in hp(m)} \left\lceil \frac{W_m^n + J_k + \tau_{bit}}{T_k} \right\rceil C_k. \qquad (20)$$

Equation (20) extends (11) to account for the error recovery overhead. Note that as errors can impact the transmission of message m itself, the time interval considered in calculating the error recovery overhead includes the transmission time of message m as well as the queuing delay. Equations (20), (12), and (13) can be used together to compute the response time of each message instance q and hence find the worst-case response time of each message in the presence of errors at the maximum rate specified by the error model.

The sufficient schedulability tests given earlier in this section can be similarly modified via the addition of the term $E_m(W_m^n + C_m)$ to account for the error recovery overhead [1].

3. Probabilistic Response Time Analysis of CAN Messages

3.1. Probabilistic Bit-Stuffing Distributions. When performing worst-case response-time analysis, the worst-case number of stuff bits is traditionally used. In [7], Nolte et al. introduce a worst-case response time analysis method which uses distributions of stuff bits instead of the worst-case values. This makes the analysis less pessimistic, in the sense that we obtain a distribution of worst-case response times corresponding to all possible combinations of stuff bits of all message frames involved in the response time analysis. Using a distribution rather than a fixed value makes it possible to select a worst-case response time based on a desired probability p of violation; that is, the selected worst-case response time is such that the probability of a response-time exceeding it is $\leq p$. The main motivation for calculating such probabilistic response-times is that they allow us to reason about tradeoffs between reliability and timeliness.

The number of bits, apart from the data part in the frame, which are exposed to the bit-stuffing mechanism, is defined as g which is in the range $\{34, 54\}$. This is because we have either 34 (CAN standard format) or 54 (CAN extended format) bits which are exposed to the bit-stuffing mechanism. 10 bits in the CAN frame are not exposed to the bit-stuffing mechanism (refer to Figure 3). The number of bytes of data in CAN message frame i is defined as L_i which is in the range $[0, 8]$.

Recall that a CAN message frame can contain 0 to 8 bytes of data. According to the CAN standard [22], the total number of bits in a CAN frame before bit stuffing is therefore

$$8L_i + g + 10, \tag{21}$$

where 10 is the number of bits in the CAN frame not exposed to the bit-stuffing mechanism. Since only $g + 8L_i$ bits in the CAN frame are subject to bit stuffing, the total number of bits after bit stuffing can be no more than

$$8L_i + g + 10 + \left\lfloor \frac{g + 8L_i - 1}{4} \right\rfloor. \tag{22}$$

Intuitively the above formula captures the number of stuffed bits in the worst case scenario, shown in Figure 2.

The expression (22) describes the length of a CAN frame in the worst case. In [6], the number of stuff bits is represented as a distribution. By using a distribution of stuff bits instead of the worst-case number of stuff bits, it is possible to obtain a distribution of response times that allow to calculate less pessimistic (compared to traditional worst-case) response times based on probability.

Firstly, let us define γ as the distribution of stuff bits in a CAN message frame. We express γ as a set of pairs containing the number of stuff bits with corresponding probability of occurrence. Each pair is defined as $(x, P(x)) \varepsilon \gamma$, where $P(x)$ is the probability of exactly x stuff bits in the CAN frame. Note that $\sum_{x=0}^{\infty} P(x) = 1$.

As shown in [6], we can extract 9 different distributions of stuff bits depending on the number of bytes of data in the CAN message frame. We define γ_{L_i} as the distribution representing a CAN frame containing L_i bytes of data. Recall

that L_i is the number of bytes of data (0 to 8) in a message frame i.

We define $n = \gamma(p)$ as the worst-case number of stuff bits, n, to expect with a probability P based on the stuff-bit distribution γ, that is, $\sum_{x=n+1}^{\infty} P(x) \leq p$, or to express it in another way, the probability of finding more than n stuff bits, based on the stuff-bit distribution γ, is $\leq p$.

Note that the selection of a probability P should be done based on the requirements of the application. With a proper value for p, the worst case mean time to failure should sufficiently exceed what is required. Finally, by assuming (as in [6]) that CAN message frames are independent in the sense of number of stuff bits, we can define $\prod_n \gamma$ as the joint distribution corresponding to the combination of n distributions of stuff bits; that is, the number of stuff bits caused by a sequence of n messages sent on the bus is described by $\prod_n \gamma = \gamma x \gamma x \gamma \cdots x \gamma$,

where x denotes multiplicative combination of discrete distributions. If the distributions happen to be equal, $\prod_n^- \gamma$ is defined as the joint distribution of n *equal* distributions of stuff bits; that is, the number of data bytes is the same for all messages considered by the expression.

In order to include the bit-stuffing distributions in (12), we need to redefine C_i and B_i as $C_i(p)$ and $B_i(p)$, where

$$C_i(p) = c_i + \gamma_{L_i}(p) \tau_{bit}, \tag{23}$$

where γ_{L_i} is the distribution of stuff-bits in the message and C_i is the transmission time of message i excluding stuff-bits:

$$C_i = (8L_i + g + 10) \tau_{bit},$$

$$B_i(p) = b_i + \gamma_{\max_{k \in lp(i)}(L_k)}(p) \tau_{bit},$$

$$b_i = \max_{k \in lp(i)} (C_k) + 3\tau_{bit},$$

$$\begin{aligned} R_i^n(p) = {} & J_i + b_i + C_i \\ & + \sum_{j \in hp(i)} I_j \left(R_i^{n-1}(p) - J_i - C_i \right) \left(C_j + 3\tau_{bit} \right) \\ & + \psi_i(p) \tau_{bit}, \end{aligned} \tag{24}$$

where ψ_i is defined as the distribution of the total number of stuff-bits of all messages involved in the response time analysis for message i.

This approach obtains the maximum stuffed bits under a given probability P, to reduce pessimism of the worst-case response time and busload value.

Anyu Cheng et al. in [23] extend this work in [7] and gives the probability distribution curves of stuffed bits in message's different lengths by introducing the probability model of stuffed bits. They design and develop scheduling analysis software on fixed priority message scheduling. Then they use the software to analyses the schedulability for the messages in a hybrid electric vehicle. Furthermore, a simulation experiment based on CANoe was made to test the design. By comparing the results, it shows that algorithm based on the probability model of stuffed bits is right, and the designed software is accurate and reliable.

3.2. Probabilistic Error Model. The analysis as presented does not cover the effect of transmission errors. Obviously, detected errors trigger the transmission of an error frame as well as a retransmission which increases the busy window and therefore the response time. On the other hand a longer busy window might increase the probability that successive errors might affect the busy window [24]. In order to include effects of errors (e.g., retransmission overhead) different approaches were introduced.

3.2.1. Related Work. A method to analyse worst-case real-time behaviour of a CAN bus was developed by Tindell et al. [5]. By applying processor scheduling analysis to the CAN bus, they showed that in the absence of faults the worst-case response time of any message is bounded and can be accurately predicted. Moreover, the analysis can be extended in order to handle the effect of errors in the channel.

The error recovery mechanism of CAN involves the retransmission at any corrupted messages. An additional term can be introduced into their analysis, called the error recovery overhead function, which is the upper bound of the overhead caused by such retransmissions in a time interval. A very simple fault model is used [5], to show how the schedulability analysis is performed in the presence of errors in the channel. The model is based on a minimum interarrival time between faults. The authors note that the error recovery function can be more accurately determined either from observation of the behaviour of CAN under high noise conditions or by building a statistical model.

Punnekkat et al. [8] extend the work of Tindell et al. by providing a more general fault model which can deal with interference caused by several sources. Punnekkat's model assumes that every source of interference has a specific pattern, consisting of an initial burst of errors and then a distribution of faults with a known minimum interarrival time. Except for the more general fault model, the rest of the schedulability analysis is performed like [5].

Both Tindell and Punnekkat use models based on a minimum interarrival time between faults and therefore assume that the number of faults that can occur in an interval is bounded. In the environment where CAN is used, faults are caused mainly by Electromagnetic Interference (EMI) which is often observed as a random pulse train with a Poisson distribution [24]. Therefore the assumption made by the bounded model may not be appropriate for many systems because there is a realistic probability of faults occurring closer than the minimum interarrival time.

Unlike Tindell and Punnekkat, Navet et al. [25] propose a probabilistic fault model, which incorporates the uncertainty of faults caused by EMI. The fault model suggested by Navet uses a stochastic process which considers both the frequency of the faults and their gravity. In that model, faults in the channel occur according to a Poisson law and can be either single-bit faults or burst errors (which have a duration of more than one bit) according to a random distribution. This allows the interference caused by faults in the channel to be modeled as a generalised Poisson process. Note that if the occurrence of faults in the channel follows a Poisson law, the maximum number of transmission errors suffered by the

system in a given interval is not bounded, so the probability of having sufficient interference to prevent a message from meeting its deadline is always nonzero; therefore every system is inherently unschedulable.

Hence Navet's analysis does not try to determine whether a system is schedulable (as [5, 8]), but it calculates the probability that a message does not meet its deadline. Obtaining such a probability, named Worst Case Deadline Failure Probability (WCDFP), gives a measure of the system reliability, because a lower value of the WCDFP implies a high resilience to interference.

Navet's analysis uses the scheduling analysis of Tindell to calculate the maximum number of faults that can be tolerated for each message before the deadline is reached. This number is called K_m and only depends on the characteristics (length, priority, period, etc.) of the message set. The worst-case response time that K_m faults would generate is called $R_{m\,max}$. Once K_m and $R_{m\,max}$ are obtained, they are used with the fault model to find the probability that a message may miss its deadline. Navet defines the WCDFP of a message m as the probability that more than K_m errors occur during $R_{m\,max}$. This probability can be analytically calculated as the fault model assumed by Navet is a generalized Poisson process.

The main drawback of the analysis is that it includes two inaccuracies which increase the pessimism in the estimation of the WCDFP. The first source of pessimism is implicit in the definition of WCDFP. The definition of WCDFP does not properly reflect the conditions in which a message can miss its deadline. In order for a message to miss a deadline, faults in the channel is required to occur while the message is queued or in transmission; a fault occurring after the message has been received cannot delay the message. This condition is more restrictive than the condition used in [25], which is that K_m errors occur at any time during the maximum response time of the message, independently of whether the message has already been received.

The second source of pessimism is an overly pessimistic assumption about the nature of burst errors where a fault causes a sequence of bits to be corrupted. In Navel's analysis, a burst error of duration "u" bits is treated as a sequence of u single bit faults [25, Equation (7)], each causing a maximal error overhead (an error frame and the retransmission of a frame of higher or equal priority). This assumption is inconsistent with the CAN protocol specification [22] since in reality a burst error can cause retransmission of only one frame, because no message is sent again until the effect of the burst is finished. This causes pessimism of several orders of magnitude.

A different method to calculate probability of deadline failure in CAN under fault conditions is proposed in [9]. This work points out that errors happening during bus idle do not cause any message retransmission, and therefore those errors cause interference lower than the interference typically considered in scheduling analysis. To avoid this source of pessimism when performing scheduling analysis, the effect of errors is modelled with a fixed pattern of interference; this is a simplification of the fault model presented in [8]. Due to this determinism, interactions between messages and errors can be analysed through simulation, and then the probability of having a message that misses its deadline can be determined. Nevertheless, this method has important drawbacks. First, an interference pattern for every possible error source is hard to be determined. And second, combination of several error sources increases the complexity of the analysis to such an extent that it becomes infeasible, so random sampling is used.

Modelling arrivals of errors with a random distribution, as done in [10], allow a more generalized solution. Broster et al. [26] propose an analysis that provides an accurate probability of deadline failure without excess pessimism, based on the assumption that faults are randomly distributed.

In [27], an approach is presented to tightly bound the reliability for periodic, synchronized messages. Therefore, a reliability metric $R(t)$ is defined which denotes the probability that CAN communication survives time t without a deadline miss. The reliability is calculated based on the hyperperiod, which is the time when the activation pattern of a periodic message set repeats itself. It is defined by the least common multiple over all periods. Hence, the complexity of the algorithm depends on the amount of activations in the hyperperiod. This algorithm is suitable for automotive message sets in which periods are typically multiples of 10 ms. However, if messages are not synchronized, or the relative phasing is unknown, the approach is not applicable. In [26], the busy-window approach is used, and a tree-based approach is presented, where different error scenarios are evaluated iteratively. In a second step, these scenarios are translated to probabilities and a worst-case deadline failure probability is calculated. The approach was extended in [28], and the tree-based was superseded by a simpler, more accurate approach. However, both methods [26, 28] allow only deadlines smaller than the periods, which is a limit for practical use since bursty CAN traffic is not supported. In [24], existing methods are generalized to support arbitrary deadlines and derive a probabilistic response time bound.

3.2.2. Error Model. In [24, 26] the occurrence of errors is modeled by using a Poisson model. Practically, a Poisson process models independent single bit errors (without bursts), where λ specifies the bit error rate. The probability for the occurrence of m error-events in the time window λt is

$$p(m, \Delta t) n = \frac{e^{-\lambda \Delta t}(\lambda \Delta t)^m}{m!}. \quad (25)$$

It is possible that a message of length C is hit by multiple error events and only one retransmission occurs (e.g., after reception when the CRC is checked), but it is assumed that in the worst-case condition, each error event will lead to exactly one retransmission. Thus, we can directly use (25) to obtain the probability that K error events occur during a given time window, and the probability for the error-free case is

$$P(w_{i|0}) = p(0, w_{i|0}) = e^{-\lambda w_{i|0}}. \quad (26)$$

For $K > 0$, it is not enough to just calculate $p(K, w_{i|K})$, because error events have to occur in certain segments of the busy window, and more efficient technique was used in [27], which can be applied for the general case in which a busy-window includes multiple queued activations which can be affected by errors. The approach works as follows: one error-event in the entire busy window $w_{i|1}$ can happen in two ways. The error may actually lead to an $w_{i|1}$ busy window with the probability $P(w_{i|1})$. Or, we face a busy window of length $w_{i|0}$ and the error event occurs in the interval $(w_{i|0}, w_{i|1})$:

$$p(1, w_{i|1}) = P(w_{i|1}) + P(w_{i|0}) p(1, w_{i|1} - w_{i|0}). \quad (27)$$

The value of $P(w_{i|1})$ can then be obtained by rearranging the equation. Similarly we can apply this idea to $K = 2$. Two errors in the time window $w_{i|2}$ may occur in the following mutually exclusive ways. (i) A busy window of length $w_{i|2}$ actually occurs assuming two error events with the probability $P(w_{i|2})$. (ii) $w_{i|1}$, occurred which implies exactly one error in $w_{i|1}$ and the second error must then happen in the interval $(w_{i|1}; w_{i|2})$. (iii) $w_{i|0}$ occurred which implies no error in $w_{i|0}$. And exactly two errors must be in the interval $(w_{i|0}, w_{i|2})$:

$$p(2, w_{i|2}) = P(w_{i|2}) + P(w_{i|1}) p(1, w_{i|2} - w_{i|1})$$
$$+ P(w_{i|0}) p(2, w_{i|2} - w_{i|0}). \quad (28)$$

By rearranging the equation for $P(w_{i|2})$, we get the probability for a $K = 2$ busy window. The same argument is valid for the following K-error busy windows, and (28) is generalized into the following form:

$$P(w_{i|K}) = p(K, w_{i|K})$$
$$- \sum_{j=0}^{K-1} P(w_{i|j}) p(K - j, w_{i|K} - w_{i|j}). \quad (29)$$

The worst-case response time exceedance function can be calculated as

$$P^+[R_i > r] = 1 - \sum_{\forall K | R_{i|K} < r} P(w_{i|K}). \quad (30)$$

Practically, this function denotes a bound for the probability that a response time exceeds a certain threshold, and the probability that a deadline is exceeded can be bounded to $P^+[R_i > D_i]$.

4. Conclusion

In this review paper, the worst case response time analysis of messages in controller area network and the probabilistic response time analysis of CAN messages are reviewed. The worst-case response time analysis includes the worst-case response time analysis presented in early 1990s by Tindell et al. [2–5] and the worst case response time analysis by Davis et al. [1] in 2007. Davis et al. in [1] have pointed out the flaw in the earlier analysis by Tindel et al. and showed that multiple instances of the CAN messages should be analysed to determine the response time and hence the schedulability of the CAN messages. The worst-case response time analysis leads to excessive level of pessimism; we may choose a pessimistic approach but with as little pessimism as possible, since worst case does not always occur. The probabilistic response time analysis of CAN messages is recommended; here two approaches are considered [6, 7], namely, instead of using the worst-case bit-stuffing pattern, we can consider a distribution of possible bit stuffing according to the application and select one most probable bit-stuffing pattern, thereby we are less pessimistic; another probabilistic approach is considering the probability of occurrence of errors [24–26]. In worst-case analysis, it is assumed that every error flag transmitted has a retransmission associated, whereas this is not true, since the same error can cause many error flags and only one retransmission. This assumption causes some level of pessimism. There are different methods presented in [6] whereby we can reduce the number of stuff bits, either by using XOR operation on the messages before transmission (encoding) and redoing the XOR after reception (decoding), thus avoiding having continuous bits of zeros or ones, thereby avoiding bit stuffing. The other method presented in [6] is to choose the priorities such that the identifier bits do not have continuous ones or zeros, thereby avoiding bit stuffing. Of course in this method the number of priorities that can be used is reduced.

Another approach in making the best usage of the bandwidth is to schedule the messages with offsets, which leads to a desynchronization of the message streams. This "traffic shaping" strategy is very beneficial in terms of worst-case response times [29, 30]. The Worst-Case Response Time (WCRT) for a frame corresponds to the scenario where all higher priority CAN messages are released synchronously. Avoiding this situation and thus reducing WCRT can be achieved by scheduling stream of messages with offsets. Precisely, the first instance of a stream of periodic frames is released with a delay, called the offset, in regard to a reference point which is the first time at which the station is ready to transmit. Subsequent frames of the streams are then sent periodically, with the first transmission as time origin. The choice made for the offset values has an influence on the WCRT, and the challenge is to set the offsets in such a way so as to minimize the WCRT, which involves spreading the workload over time as much as possible. The future work is to present the review of statistical approach to response time analysis. It is proposed that a fusion of methods may be adopted to cater to the requirement of the application; for safety critical application like automotive and industrial application, the worst-case response time analysis is recommended, and for noncritical applications where we can introduce some tolerance we may apply the probabilistic response time analysis.

References

[1] R. I. Davis, A. Burns, R. J. Bril, and J. J. Lukkien, "Controller area network (CAN) schedulability analysis: refuted, revisited and revised," *Real-Time Systems*, vol. 35, no. 3, pp. 239–272, 2007.

[2] K. W. Tindell, H. Hansson, and A. J. Wellings, "Analysing real-time communications: controller area network (CAN)," in *Proceedings of the 15th IEEE Real-Time Systems Symposium (RTSS '94)*, pp. 259–263, IEEE Computer Society Press, 1994.

[3] K. Tindell and J. Clark, "Holistic schedulability analysis for distributed hard real-time systems," *Microprocessing and Microprogramming*, vol. 40, no. 2-3, pp. 117–134, 1994.

[4] K. Tindell and A. Burns, "Guaranteeing message latencies on control area network (can)," in *Proceedings of the 1st International CAN Conference*, Citeseer, 1994.

[5] K. Tindell, A. Burns, and A. J. Wellings, "Calculating controller area network (can) message response times," *Control Engineering Practice*, vol. 3, no. 8, pp. 1163–1169, 1995.

[6] T. Nolte, H. Hansson, and C. Norstrom, "Minimizing CAN response-time analysis jitter by message manipulation," in *Proceedings of the 8th IEEE Real-Time and Embedded Technology and Applications Symposium (RTAS '02)*, pp. 197–206, September 2002.

[7] T. Nolte, H. Hansson, and C. Norstrom, "Probabilistic worst-case response-time analysis for the controller area network," in *Proceedings of the 9th IEEE Real-Time and Embedded Technology and Applications Symposium (RTAS '03)*, pp. 200–207, May 2003.

[8] S. Punnekkat, H. Hansson, and C. Norstrom, "Response time analysis under errors for CAN," in *Proceedings of the 6th IEEE Real-Time Technology and Applications Symposium (RTAS '00)*, pp. 258–265, June 2000.

[9] H. Hansson, C. Norström, and S. Punnekkat, "Integrating reliability and timing analysis of CAN-based systems," in *Proceedings of the IEEE International Workshop on Factory Communication Systems (WFCS '00)*, IEEE Industrial Electronics Society, Porto, Portugal, September 2000.

[10] H. Hansson, C. Norström, and S. Punnekkat, "Reliability modelling of time-critical distributed systems," in *Proceedings of the 6th International Symposium on Formal Techniques in Real-Time and Fault-Tolerant Systems (FTRTFT '00)*, M. Joseph, Ed., vol. 1926 of *Lecture Notes in Computer Science*, Springer, Pune, India, September 2000.

[11] T. Nolte, H. Hansson, C. Norström, and S. Punnekkat, "Using bit-stuffing distributions in CAN analysis," in *Proceedings of the IEEE/IEE Real-Time Embedded Systems Workshop (RTES '01)*, December 2001.

[12] K. W. Tindell, A. Burns, and A. J. Wellings, "An extendible approach for analyzing fixed priority hard real-time tasks," *Real-Time Systems*, vol. 6, no. 2, pp. 133–151, 1994.

[13] J. Lehoczky, "Fixed priority scheduling of periodic task sets with arbitrary deadlines," in *Proceedings of the 11th IEEE Real-Time Systems Symposium (RTSS '90)*, pp. 201–209, IEEE Computer Society Press, December 1990.

[14] M. G. Harbour, M. H. Klein, and J. P. Lehoczky, "Fixed priority scheduling periodic tasks with varying execution priority," in *Proceedings of the 12th IEEE Real-Time Systems Symposium (RTSS '91)*, pp. 116–128, IEEE Computer Society Press, December 1991.

[15] L. George, N. Rivierre, and M. Spuri, "Pre-emptive and non-pre-emptive real-time uni-processor scheduling," Tech. Rep. 2966, Institut National de Recherche et Informatique et en Automatique, Versailles, France, 1996.

[16] R. J. Bril, "Existing worst-case response time analysis of real-time tasks under fixed-priority scheduling with deferred preemption is too optimistic," CS-Report 06-05, Technische Universiteit, Eindhoven, The Netherlands, 2006.

[17] A. Burns, "Pre-emptive priority based scheduling: an appropriate engineering approach," in *Advances in Real-Time Systems*, S. Son, Ed., pp. 225–248, Prentice-Hall, 1994.

[18] Y. Wang and M. Saksena, "Scheduling fixed priority tasks with pre-emption threshold," in *Proceedings of the 6th International Workshop on Real-Time Computing Systems and Applications (RTCSA '99)*, pp. 328–335, December 1999.

[19] J. Regehr, "Scheduling tasks with mixed pre-emption relations for robustness to timing faults," in *Proceedings of the 23rd IEEE Real-Time Systems Symposium (RTSS '02)*, pp. 315–326, IEEE Computer Society Press, December 2002.

[20] R. J. Bril, J. J. Lukkien, R. I. Davis, and A. Burns, "Message response time analysis for ideal controller area network (CAN) refuted," CS-Report 06-19, Technische Universiteit Eindhoven, Eindhoven, The Netherlands, 2006.

[21] R. J. Bril, J. J. Lukkien, R. I. Davis, and A. Burns, "Message response time analysis for ideal controller area network (CAN) refuted," in *Proceedings of the 5th International Workshop on Real-Time Networks (RTN '06)*, 2006.

[22] International Standards Organisation, *ISO 11898. Road Vehicles—Interchange of Digital Information—Controller Area Network (CAN) for High-Speed Communication*, 1993.

[23] A. Cheng, L. Zhang, and T. Zheng, "The schedulability analysis and software design for networked control systems of vehicle based on CAN," in *Proceedings of the IEEE 2nd International Conference on Computing, Control and Industrial Engineering (CCIE '11)*, vol. 2, pp. 274–278, Wuhan, China, August 2011.

[24] P. Axer, M. Sebastian, and R. Ernst, "Probabilistic response time bound for CAN messages with arbitrary deadlines," in *Proceedings of the Design, Automation & Test in Europe Conference & Exhibition (DATE '12)*, pp. 1114–1117, Dresden, Germany, March 2012.

[25] N. Navet, Y. Q. Song, and F. Simonot, "Worst-case deadline failure probability in real-time applications distributed over controller area network," *Journal of Systems Architecture*, vol. 46, no. 7, pp. 607–617, 2000.

[26] I. Broster, A. Burns, and G. Rodriguez-Navas, "Probabilistic analysis of can with faults," in *Proceedings of the 23rd IEEE Real-Time Systems Symposium (RTSS '02)*, pp. 269–278, 2002.

[27] M. Sebastian and R. Ernst, "Reliability analysis of single bus communication with real-time requirements," in *Proceedings of the 15th IEEE Pacific Rim International Symposium on Dependable Computing (PRDC '09)*, pp. 3–10, November 2009.

[28] I. Broster and A. Burns, "Comparing real-time communication under electromagnetic interference," in *Proceedings of the 16th Euromicro Conference on Real-Time Systems (ECRTS '04)*, pp. 45–52, July 2004.

[29] M. Grenier, L. Havet, and N. Navet, "Pushing the limits of CAN—scheduling frames with offsets provides a major performance boost," in *Proceedings of the 4th European Congress on Embedded Real Time Software*, Toulouse, France, 2008.

[30] L. Du and G. Xu, "Worst case response time analysis for CAN messages with offsets," in *Proceedings of the IEEE International Conference on Vehicular Electronics and Safety (ICVES '09)*, pp. 41–45, Pune, India, November 2009.

6

System Health Monitoring Using a Novel Method: Security Unified Process

Alireza Shameli-Sendi,[1] Masoume Jabbarifar,[1] Michel Dagenais,[1] and Mehdi Shajari[2]

[1] *Départment de Genie Informatique et Génie Logiciel, École Polytechnique de Montréal, P.O. Box 6079, Succ. Downtown, Montreal, QC, Canada H3C 3A7*
[2] *Department of Computer Engineering & Information Technology, Amirkabir University of Technology, 424 Hafez Avenue, Tehran, Iran*

Correspondence should be addressed to Alireza Shameli-Sendi, alireza.shameli-sendi@polymtl.ca

Academic Editor: Lixin Gao

Iterative and incremental mechanisms are not usually considered in existing approaches for information security management System (ISMS). In this paper, we propose SUP (security unified process) as a unified process to implement a successful and high-quality ISMS. A disciplined approach can be provided by SUP to assign tasks and responsibilities within an organization. The SUP architecture comprises static and dynamic dimensions; the static dimension, or disciplines, includes business modeling, assets, security policy, implementation, configuration and change management, and project management. The dynamic dimension, or phases, contains inception, analysis and design, construction, and monitoring. Risk assessment is a major part of the ISMS process. In SUP, we present a risk assessment model, which uses a fuzzy expert system to assess risks in organization. Since, the classification of assets is an important aspect of risk management and ensures that effective protection occurs, a Security Cube is proposed to identify organization assets as an asset classification model. The proposed model leads us to have an offline system health monitoring tool that is really a critical need in any organization.

1. Introduction

Information security is a primary requirement in today's communication world. These requirements are driven either by business need or by regulations. Many organizations find it difficult to derive a framework to define those requirements. In most cases, information has become the vital "asset" of businesses and is called "information asset" or "intellectual asset" [1]. It is essential to protect this asset so as to ensure its confidentiality, integrity, and availability [2]. While preserving these essential protections, the right information should be available to the right people, at the right place and at the right time. It is expected to make the information secure to guarantee that it is correct and available.

Also, it can be guaranteed that information is not jeopardized by misuse, which could lead to the loss of business and low performance of regulations. Obviously, information security management plays a very important and crucial role in each organization. The organization is expected to follow certain security compliance regulations and standards, together with the implementation of an information security management infrastructure. Therefore, an appropriate information security infrastructure, which is a vital need for most organizations, must be provided and implemented. Information security standards are helping organizations at this stage. There are many standards available for deriving a framework to define and structure the organization's requirements. As an example, one of the most applicable standards is ISO27001, which is an ISO accredited standard for information security management [2]. There are several reasons why an organization should implement the ISO27001 standard and the primary one will be the business demand [3].

Many organizations have introduced an ISMS to improve their security information management but always have big challenges to align goals of ISMS with their native security structure [4]. There are different ways of implementing an ISMS, but they are unable to implement it effectively and cannot keep it continuously within the organization. In this paper, a framework is proposed to cover ISO27001 and ISO17799 in such a manner that roles for all of the personnel in the organization are defined and each role has been assigned to predefined tasks. Also, each role has a specific workflow which is also defined in the framework. On the other hand and contrary to the ISO27001 standard which uses a waterfall model of implementation, in this proposed framework we will explore incremental and iterative mechanisms to implement an ISMS. Also, while implementing the ISMS, the proposed framework can figure out the status of the executed sections that makes the implementation effective.

This paper is organized as follows: first, we discuss related work and several existing methods. The proposed model is illustrated in Section 3. In Section 4, experimental results are presented. Conclusion and future work will be discussed in Section 5.

2. Related Work

2.1. Information Security Management System. Information security means protecting information and information systems [5]. Protection concept refers to the unauthorized access, disruption or, etc. Usually, the attacker exploits security goals (CIA): data confidentiality (C), data integrity (I), and service availability (A) using vulnerabilities that are a flaw or weak point in system security procedure, design, or implementation. Data confidentiality ensures that any authorized user can have access to only certain resources such as "information in database," "system configuration," and "network topology" which are needed to be protected against inappropriate disclosures. Integrity verifies that any authorized user can modify resources in an acceptable manner. Availability means that the assets are always accessible by the authorized users. An information security management system consists of some policies concerned with information security management. ISO/IEC 27001 standard gives overview of information security management systems. The key point in implementing ISMS is that it must remain effective and efficient over time. Thus, ISO/IEC 27001 standard incorporates *Plan-Do-Check-Act* (PDCA) cycle to keep long-term effectiveness and efficiency and adopt information systems changes [2]. PDCA is an iterative four-step management method. Unfortunately, a problem still occurs in the implementation of ISMS with PDCA; all activities scheduled in the *Plan* phase are only performed later in the *Do* phase. ISMS implementation experiences in the past few years indicate that the proposed method has still not reached full maturity and could not ensure that ISMS remains effective and stable over time. Indeed, it emerged as a nonincremental method. The proposed algorithm not only keeps the iterative nature of the PDCA model but also manages all activities incrementally.

2.2. Risk Assessment. Risk assessment is a major part of the ISMS Process. There are two types of risk assessment: (1) online: online risk assessment is a real-time process of evaluation and provides a risk index related to the host or network. Online risk assessment is very important in terms of minimizing the performance cost incurred. In the dynamic model, we can dynamically evaluate attack cost by propagating the impact of confidentiality, integrity and availability through dependencies model or attack graph [6–12]. (2) Offline: in Information security management system we use offline risk assessment. The information security management system standards specify guidelines and a general framework for risk assessment. In many existing standards, such as NIST and ISO27001, risk assessment is described. However, while these standards present some guidelines, there are no details on how to implement it in an organization. In a complex organization, risk assessment is a complicated process which involves many assets.

Guan et al. [13] assessed information security risks according to the likelihood and impact factors of each. In this method, risk factors are determined according to standard ISO17799 categorization. Then, it is assumed that determining the likelihood of each risk is similar to determining the weights in pairwise comparisons in the AHP method. Based on this view, the likelihood or weight of each risk factor is being determined using experts' opinions. On the other hand, the vulnerability of each information asset for each risk factor is considered equal to its impact severity, which takes its relative value from experts through linguistic variables.

Wang and Elhag [14] proposed a fuzzy TOPSIS method based on alpha level sets and applied it in bridge risk assessment. In this example, the likelihood and impact of different threats are being determined in linguistic variable forms and then are applied in bridge risk assessment by multiplying their related fuzzy values. Likewise, four effective criteri on impact severity are introduced. Experts express their opinion in the form of these four criterion, with which the severity impact is then calculated.

Kondakci [15] presented a composite system used for quantitative network security assessment. The idea is preventing the evaluation of each asset separately by applying repetitive attacks. The proposed model (composite system) generates and executes attacks once, composes risk data, and uses the risk data for the entire network in order to perform the overall assessment.

We agree with the arguments presented in [15, 16] that existing risk assessment models are often difficult to implement and handle in real world contexts without using appropriate software, because of their computational complexity. We are interested as [15, 16] to offer a model that not only tries to represent risk effect with a quantitative value but also can be easily implemented by any organization in the SUP model. Another important point is that all of the steps of proposed risk assessment are managed in SUP structure incrementally and iteratively.

2.3. Contribution. The main contributions of this paper can be summarized as (1) contrary to the ISO27001 standard which uses a waterfall model of implementation, in this proposed framework we will explore incremental and iterative mechanisms to implement an information security management system. The iterative approach can prevent project failure and cause robust implementation of security goals in the last iteration. (2) Role segregation has not been considered in ISO27001 standard and other security models properly. SUP proposes an appropriate role segregation and makes sure that we establish a framework where we can easily segregate security roles, and responsibilities. Roles have been segregated into about 20 roles and in each phase of SUP, it is clear which activities have to be done by each role and which artifacts have to be generated. (3) Since the proposed model is incremental and iterative, one of the important features of SUP is monitoring. Monitoring ensures that we established a framework to monitor roles, responsibilities, new assets, security policies and continuity of the executive committee of the organization. (4) In SUP, we present the FEMRA (fuzzy expert model for risk assessment) model, which uses a fuzzy expert system for risk assessment in organizations. Many risk assessment models have been proposed during the last decade. The distinguishing feature that separates our model from previous models is that all the steps to assess risk are done incrementally and iteratively based on the SUP structure. (5) To determine the risk, effective criterions are considered, and experts present their opinion with respect to these criterions. It leads us to increased accuracy and reliability of the results. (6) Asset classification plays a very important role in information security management. In the proposed risk assessment, we have designed a security cube (an asset classification), which is a combination of the valuable and important assets of the organization from a security perspective.

3. Proposed Model

SUP is an iterative and incremental approach that can help design, implement, monitor, and manage information security management system. This approach provides any organization with a predictable life-cycle security process for the development, adoption, and continual improvement of the information security solution [17]. Several fundamental principles which support successful iterative development are laid at the core of the SUP and represent the essential structure of the SUP [18, 19].

(i) Classify the assets with the proposed security cube.

(ii) Identify high risks early and manage continuously.

(iii) Work as a team.

(iv) Improve quality of implementation over time.

(v) Implement a modular ISMS with components.

3.1. Why Develop Iteratively and Incrementally? In the waterfall method, the biggest problem is that risk management will be reduced whenever the business model, assets identification, threats, and/or vulnerabilities are not perfectly known. Another problem of the waterfall method for the implementation of an ISMS is that the strategies of future phases are not considered before they are started. The initial idea behind developing an ISMS iteratively is that, in contrast with the waterfall implementation, the developer is allowed to take advantage of what was learned during the development of earlier, incremental, deliverable versions of security levels within the organization. Learning comes from both the development and reaching the security levels, where possible. Risks are mitigated earlier, because elements are integrated progressively. We can accommodate changing the requirements in this method. We can facilitate the ISMS improvement and refinement which results in more robust ISMS. An iterative approach is generally superior to a linear or waterfall approach for many different reasons [20].

In the security unified process, iterations are planned in number, duration, and objective. A proper assessment of objectives enables the move to the next iteration successfully. The iterative approach can prevent project failure and cause robust implementation of security goals in the last iteration.

3.2. Structure of the SUP. As seen in Figure 1, the proposed information security management model includes two dimensions: static, which are disciplines, and dynamic, which are phases. In this architecture, the static dimension comprises six disciplines that are represented by business modeling, asset, security policy, implementation, configuration and change management, and project management. The dynamic dimension contains four life-cycle phases that are illustrated by inception, analysis and design, construction, and monitoring. Also, each phase can iterate. The area under the curve that is associated with each discipline shows the relative amount of effort and activity required to perform it over time. Along the vertical axis are the disciplines, which are a collection of workflows related to a major *area* of concern within the overall project [17, 18]. Figure 2 presents asset discipline.

A workflow consists of some activities that produce a result of observable value. Figure 3 presents, identifies and analyzes risk workflow. As seen in Figure 3, in each workflow, we have some roles, activities, and artifacts that are integrated to provide the goal of workflow. Table 1 explains each concept of elements in workflows. As mentioned, role segregation has not been considered in ISO27001 standard and other security models properly. SUP proposes an appropriate role segregation and makes sure that we establish a framework where we can easily segregate security roles and responsibilities. As mentioned, Figure 3 illustrates one of the SUP model workflow, that are relevant to the asset discipline. Roles segregation is clearly shown in this workflow that includes eleven roles: *threat evaluator, network specialist, network security specialist, communication specialist, computer specialist, network designer specialist, vulnerabilities evaluator, software specialist, information security specialist, physical security specialist, and human resource analyzer.* Six activities have been specified, and in fact each role is responsible to perform the related subactivities. Also, all the artifacts (output of activities) should be updated, and each role has to keep updated the related sections of each artifact. Fifteen

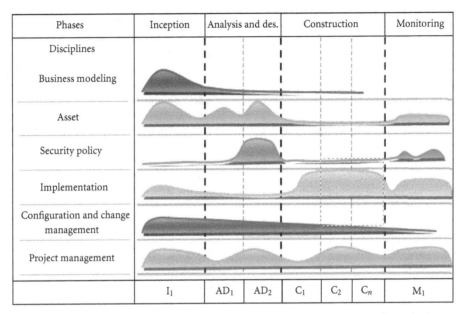

Phases	Inception	Analysis and des.	Construction			Monitoring
Disciplines						
Business modeling						
Asset						
Security policy						
Implementation						
Configuration and change management						
Project management						
	I$_1$	AD$_1$	AD$_2$	C$_1$	C$_2$	C$_n$	M$_1$

FIGURE 1: SUP architecture (phases: dynamic dimension; disciplines: static dimension).

artifacts are shown as the input artifacts that are generated in the previous workflows.

3.3. Milestones. From a security management perspective, all security life cycles of SUP are decomposed into four phases, and each phase is concluded by a major milestone. These milestones are represented by inception objectives, risk management, security level, and monitoring milestones. In each milestone, there are some major criteria that must be evaluated to determine whether the objectives of the phase have been met or not. These criteria are the phases objectives that must be reached. For instance, at the security-level milestone, the primary evaluation criteria for the construction phase involves the answers to these questions.

(i) Is the security level acceptable?

(ii) Are the identified risks reduced?

The construction phase may be started again if it fails to reach this milestone. A positive assessment shows that the project can be moved to the next phase successfully. Figure 4 shows the phases and milestones of a security management project at each phase end.

3.4. Phases, Objectives, and Activities. The inception phase is the first security project phase. In this phase, an accurate identification of the organization's business model as well as an asset identification is performed. The most important objectives in this phase that must be met and evaluated are.

(i) agreement that the cost/schedule estimates are appropriate.

(ii) agreement that the right set of security requirements have been obtained and that there is a common understanding of these requirements.

(iii) agreement that the identified assets are acceptable.

(iv) agreement that the defined risk assessment and management methodology is appropriate.

(v) formation of the executive committee of the organization.

Table 2 describes the activities during the inception phase of the SUP. During the analysis and Design phase, the analysis of assets to identify vulnerability points, threat points, and eventually risks is a vital step. During this phase, the most important objectives which need to be evaluated are as follows.

Activities of the Inception Phase

(i) Agreement that the classified assets are acceptable.

(ii) All risks have been identified, and a mitigation strategy exists for each.

(iii) Risks have been identified in accordance with the risk assessment and management methodology.

(iv) The designed system is in accordance with the identified risks.

(v) Agreement that the designed system reduces risks.

(vi) Writing the security policy.

Table 3 describes the activities of the analysis and design phase of the SUP. The construction phase focuses on implementing the designs resulting in risks reduction within an organization. Implementing the designs is based on a workflow that is extracted from the analysis and design phase. This workflow shows that a design can be started based on design priority. If we treat the base on design priority, the risks are reduced to an acceptable level. In SUP, security levels based on design priority are divided in five levels. On the other hand, the construction phase consists of five iterations. At the end of each iteration, the organization will reach a new security level. During this phase, the most important objectives that must be evaluated are as follows.

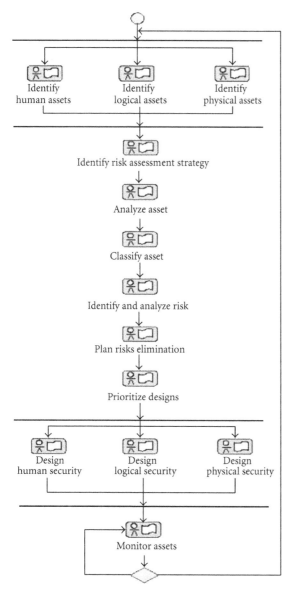

FIGURE 2: Asset discipline.

(i) Is the security level acceptable?

(ii) Are the identified risks reduced?

(iii) Agreement that the security level is acceptable.

Table 4 illustrates the activities of the SUP construction phase. During the monitoring phase, a monitoring program should be planned. The monitoring scope is the identification of new assets, vulnerabilities, and threats in asset discipline, reviewing the security policies in the security policy discipline and testing the implementations in the implementation discipline. The project manager must organize specific roles to ensure the ISMS effectiveness. During this phase, the most important objectives that must be evaluated are as follows.

(i) testing the implementation to keep the security at an acceptable level,

(ii) agreement that major risks do not exist.

Table 5 represents the activities of the SUP monitoring phase. ISO17799 includes eleven sections with 134 controls. Afterwards, ISO27001 has been developed as a wrapper to be put around ISO17799 to manage it with a PDCA model. By contrast, the SUP model comprises disciplines, workflows, and activities. Based on our structure, ISO17799 is mapped to the activities of the six disciplines and ISO27001 is mapped to the workflows of the six disciplines. Therefore, the percentage of project progress can easily be measured based on these two standards for each stage of the ISMS implementation project when using the SUP framework.

3.5. Risk Assessment. In SUP, we present the FEMRA (fuzzy expert model for risk assessment) model [21], which uses a fuzzy expert system for risk assessment in organizations. The risk assessment varies considerably with the context, the metrics used as dependent variables, and the opinions of the persons involved. Fuzzy logic thus represents an excellent model for this application. Organizations can use FEMRA as a tool to improve the ISMS implementation. One of the interesting characteristics of FEMRA is that it can represent each risk with a numerical value. The managers can detect higher risks by comparing these values and develop a good strategy to reduce them [22]. The relevant knowledge from human experts is stored as rule database in order to apply fuzzy logic and infer an overall numerical value [23]. There are three steps in the fuzzy model: fuzzification, inference engine, and defuzzification. The input and output of the fuzzy model is a number. In the inference engine, we define fuzzy rules. The first step in fuzzy logic processing involves a domain transformation called fuzzification. To transform crisp input into fuzzy input, membership functions must first be defined.

The next step is to apply if-then rules. The final step is defuzzification. This step is used to convert the fuzzy output set to a crisp number. We define three membership functions for input and output: low, medium, and high. Figure 5 illustrates the dependencies among some of the most important notions in the risk assessment terminology. There are three steps in the risk assessment model.

Step 1. The goal of the first step is to identify the assets and the potential threats applicable to the IT system. Three main bases of security known as the security golden triangle (confidentiality, integrity and availability) are used to evaluate assets, and calculate threat effects. Therefore, in this step, we have the CIA triad evaluated by experts.

Step 2. The goal of this step is to generate a list of asset vulnerabilities. We can then calculate asset values, vulnerability effects and threat effects.

Step 3. The goal of the final step is to calculate the risks. To calculate these effects, we use the fuzzy model that will be explained.

Algorithm 1 illustrates the proposed risk assessment pseudocode.

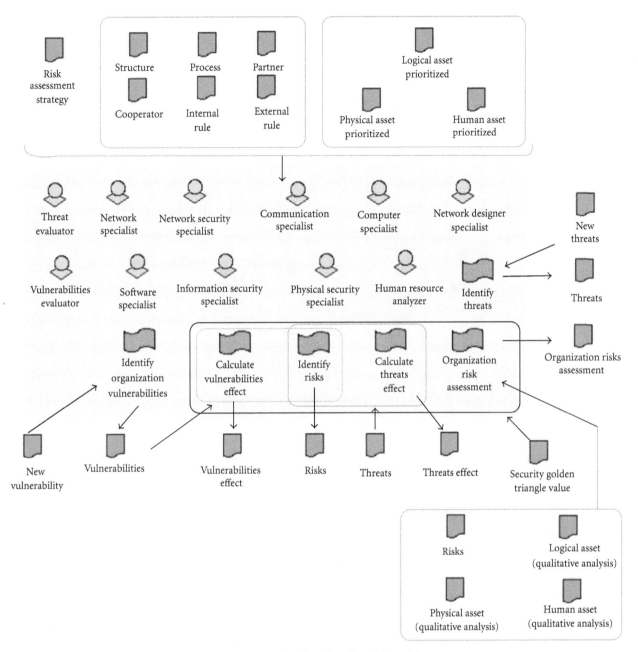

FIGURE 3: Identify and analyze risk workflow.

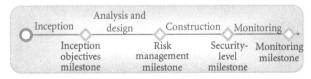

FIGURE 4: The phases and milestones of SUP.

3.5.1. Asset Classification and Identification. Asset classification plays a very important role in information security management. So far, some methods have been proposed to classify the assets in organizations. If we can classify assets properly, it will help us achieve effective asset protection. In the proposed asset classification, we have designed a security cube, which is a combination of the valuable and important assets of the organization from a security perspective, and the Zachman model [24]. Assets are classified according to three views.

(i) *Business View.* The business view consists of the three views of the Zachman framework (WHY-HOW-WHO), which includes value, policy, vision, mission, strategy, structure, process, partner, cooperator, internal rule, external rule, role, and human. There are also some empty fields that illustrate the flexibility of the model; some other parameters can be added to the cube.

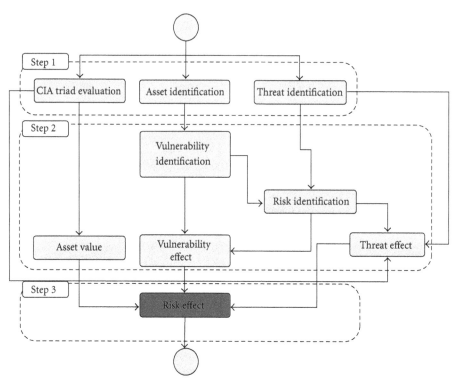

FIGURE 5: FEMRA risk assessment structure.

(ii) *Logical View.* The logical view is divided into three sections that are software, data, and logical infrastructure of networks. The data section is the WHAT view of the Zachman framework. The software section also is divided into foreign, country, and organization parts. Each part includes network tools, web application, application, programming, utility, DBMS, OS, and office. The data section is divided into personal and organizational parts, and each part comprises DB, file, paper, and brain storage. In the network section, the six parts are platform, application, strategy, protocol, communication, and design. Each part also includes different parameters that are illustrated in Figure 6.

(iii) *Physical View.* The physical view consists of four sections: media, storage, WHERE, and hardware components. The WHERE section is used as the WHERE view of the Zachman framework.

Each item in the cube should be evaluated with the four disciplines of SUP. This means that, when we are in the business modeling discipline, our view of each item is different than that from other disciplines. Additionally, in each discipline, each item should be evaluated with a *C-I-A* triad. Table 6 presents some examples of assets based on the security cube.

3.5.2. Threat Identification. A threat is something which may happen. When a threat materializes, it may result in

unwanted events which could damage the system or organization [2]. Threats can adversely affect assets. Table 7 shows some examples of threats.

3.5.3. CIA Triad Evaluation. Evaluating the *CIA* triad is key to calculate the organization's risks, and we can determine which one of these three complimentary goals is more important to an organization. The weight of confidentiality (C), integrity (I), and availability (A) are denoted as w_C, w_I, and w_A, respectively. We use n experts (e) to evaluate the *CIA* triad. $\{C_e, I_e, A_e\} \in [0, 1]$. This illustrates the expert opinion in confidentiality, integrity, and availability respectively. Obviously, a higher number of experts would give a better risk assessment. Finally, the base of the *CIA* triad can be calculated with the following formula:

$$\{C_e, I_e, A_e\} \in [0, 1],$$
$$w_C = \frac{\sum_{e=1}^{n} C_e}{n},$$
$$w_I = \frac{\sum_{e=1}^{n} I_e}{n}, \tag{1}$$
$$w_A = \frac{\sum_{e=1}^{n} A_e}{n}.$$

Table 8 illustrates the opinion of n experts about the *CIA* triad for a hypothetical organization.

3.5.4. Vulnerability Identification. A vulnerability is a flaw or weak point in system security procedures, design, or implementation. It could be exploited by an attacker or may

Require: SGT = $[C, I, A]$ {Security-golden-triangle}

Require: $E = [e_1, e_2, e_3, \ldots, e_n]$ {Experts}

1: Cube = [Business, Logical, Physical] {Security Cube}

2: Business = [Human]

3: Logical = [Foreign, Country, Organization, Personal, Organizational, Platform, Application, Strategy, Protocol, Communication, Design]

4: Physical = [Media, Storage, Where, Hardware Component]

5: **for** each $d \in$ Cube **do**

6:     **for** each $s \in d$ **do**

7:         A = AssetIdentification(d, s) {d: domains, s: sections}

8:     **end for**

9: **end for**

10: T = ThreatIdentification() {Threat Identification $T = [t_1, t_1, \ldots, t_n]$}

11: Evaluation(E, SGT) {*CIA* Triad Evaluation}

12: **for** each $a \in A$ **do**

13:     $V[a]$ = VulnerabilityIdentification(a) {Vulnerability Identification $V = [v_1, v_2 \ldots, v_n]$}

14: **end for**

15: R = RiskIdentification(A, V) {Risk Identification $R = [r_1, r_2, \ldots, r_n]$}

16: **for** each $a \in A$ **do**

17:     AV[a] = AssetValue(E, a) {Asset value}

18: **end for**

19: **for** each $v \in V$ **do**

20:     VE[v] = VulnerabilityEffect(E, v) {Vulnerability Effect}

21: **end for**

22: **for** each $t \in T$ **do**

23:     TE[t] = ThreatEffect(E, t) {Threat Effect}

24: **end for**

25: **for** each $r \in R$ **do**

26:     FRA = Fuzzification($r \cdot a$) {related asset}

27:     FRV = Fuzzification($r \cdot v$) {related vulnerability}

28:     FRT = Fuzzification($r \cdot t$) {related threat}

29:     RE[r] = defuzzification(FRA, FRV, FRT)

30: **end for**

31: **Return** SRE = Sort(RE)

ALGORITHM 1: Risk assessment ().

TABLE 1: Workflow elements.

Symbol	Name	Description
	Role	A role describes the responsibilities of person or a team in SUP. Role uses artifacts to perform activities and also generates some artifacts.
	Activity	Activity identifies the work that roles do to obtain meaningful results. Activity has input and output artifacts.
	Artifact	Artifact is a either final or intermediate product that is generated during the project. Artifact may be: (1) A document such as list of threats or vulnerabilities. (2) A model such as Risk Assessment Strategy

affect the security goals of the *CIA* triad. Vulnerability identification can be achieved by different means such as software tools in networks, questionnaire forms, and so forth [23]. Table 9 presents some examples of asset vulnerabilities.

3.5.5. Risk Identification. The objective of risk identification is to identify all possible risks to the assets. In the previous sections, we exposed all the vulnerabilities of each asset. We also exposed all threats to the organization's assets. In this

TABLE 2: Activities of the inception phase.

Discipline	Workflow	Activity
Business Modeling	Assess Business Status	Identify Organization Security Vision-Identify Organization Security Mission-Identify Organization Security Strategy-Identify Organization Security Policy-Identify Organization Security Value
	Identify Business Processes	Identify Business Structure-Identify Business Process-Identify Internal Rule-Identify External Rule-Identify Partner-Identify Cooperator
	Identify Roles and Responsibilities	Identify Human-Identify Role
Asset	Identify Human Asset	Identify Human
	Identify Logical Asset	Identify Organization Data-Identify Personal Data-Identify Organization Software-Identify Country Software-Identify Foreign Software-Identify Platform-Identify Network Services-Identify Network Design-Identify Protocol-Identify Communication Services
	Identify Physical Asset	Identify Media-Identify Storages-Identify Organization Map and Position-Identify Organization Hardware Components (Printer, Scanner, Fax, Modem, Antenna, Receiver, Sender, Camera, Fire Control, Access Control, Server Room, Server, Earthing Hole, Manhole, Duct, Riser, UPS, Mobile Computer, PC, USB, CD/DVD Writer, CD/DVD Reader, Flash Reader, FDD, Firewall, IDS, Switch, Router,...)
Security Policy	Indicate team members	Establish Management Team
	Indicate Scope of Implementation	Indicate Scope of Implementation
Implementation	Indicate Team Members	Establish Management Team-Establish Executive Team-Establish Advisor team
	Indicate Security Tools	Identify Organization Current Tools-Identify Security Tools-Identify Permitted tools-Indicate Buy Requirements
Configuration and Change Management	Plan Project Configuration and Change Control	Establish Configuration Management Policies-Establish Change Control Process
	Create Project Configuration Management Environment	Set up Configuration Management Environment
Project Management	Conceive New Project	Initiate Project-Develop Business Case-Identify and Assess Project Risks
	Create Security Plan	Define Project Organization and Staffing-Define Monitoring and Control Processes-Plan Phases and Iterations-Make Security Development Plan
	Monitor and Control Project	Monitor Project Status-Schedule and Assign Work-Report Status-Handle Exceptions and Problems
	Manage Iteration	Acquire Staff-Initiate Iteration-Assess Iteration
	Evaluate Project Scope and Risk	Identify and Assess Risks-Develop Business Case
	Close-Out Phase	Prepare for Phase Close-Out
	Plan for Next Iteration	Develop Iteration Plan-Develop Business Case

TABLE 3: Activities of the analysis and design phase.

Discipline	Workflow	Activity
	Identify Risk Assessment Strategy	Identify Risk Assessment Strategy
	Analyze Asset	Identify Asset Lifecycle-Identify Asset condition-Identify Asset Qualitative Analysis-Acceptable Use of Asset-Give Value to the Security Golden Triangle
Asset	Classify Asset	Label Asset-Prioritize Asset
	Identify And Analyze Risk	Identify Threats-Identify Organization Vulnerabilities-Calculate Vulnerabilities Effect-Calculate Threats Effect-Identify Risks-Organization Risks Assessment
	Plan Risks Elimination	Assign Risks to Designs
	Prioritize Designs	Identify Organization Security Levels-Prioritize Designs into Security Levels
	Design Human Security	Design Training Program-Segregation Security Role-Design Human events Procedure
	Design Physical Security	Design Earthing Hole-Design Physical Access Control-Design Fire Control-Design UPS-Design Camera-Design Wireless-Design Hardware Security Tools-Design Cabling-Design 2 and 3 Layer Tools-Design Server Room-Design Server Side-Design Client Side
	Design Logical Security	Design Availability-Design Reliability-Design Redundancy-Design Software Security Tools-Design Network Topology-Design Backup-Design Protocol-Design Switching-Design Logical Access Control-Design Zoning-Design Naming-Design Domain-Design Network Services-Design Platform-Design Communication Services-Design Software Framework Security-Design Source Security
	Document Human Information Security Policy	Human Access Control Procedure-Human events Procedure-Training Program Procedure-Security Use of Data Procedure-Human Confidentiality Agreement Procedure-Exchange Agreement Procedure-Prior Employment Procedure-During Employment Procedure-Termination Employment Procedure-punishes Employment Procedure-Probable Events Procedure
Security Policy	Document Logical Information Security Policy	Policy Cryptographic Procedure-Regulation Cryptographic Procedure-Information Handling Procedure-Data Exchange Procedure-Logical events Procedure-Logical Asset removal procedure-Logical Separation of Development Procedure-Logical Disposal and Reuse Procedure-User Registration Procedure-Mobile Computing-Teleworking-Monitoring System Procedure-Input Validation Procedure-Output Validation Procedure-Control Internal Processing Procedure-Restriction Change Package Procedure-Control Installation Package Procedure-Sensitive System Isolation Procedure-Out Sourcing Procedure-Internal Producing Procedure-Availability Procedure-Reliability Procedure-Redundancy Procedure-Software Security Tools Procedure-Network Topology Procedure-Backup Procedure-Protocol Procedure-Switching Procedure-Logical Access Control Procedure-Zoning Procedure-Naming Procedure-Domain Procedure-Network Services Procedure-Platform Procedure-Communication Services Procedure-Software Framework Security Procedure-Source Security Procedure

TABLE 3: Continued.

Discipline	Workflow	Activity
	Document physical Information Security Policy	Physical Asset Removal Procedure-Physical Separation of Development Procedure-Sitting and Protection Procedure-Supporting Utilities Procedure-Equipment Maintenance Procedure-Clean Environment procedure-mobile computer procedure-Physical Disposal and Reuse Procedure-Human events Procedure-Earthing Hole procedure-Physical Access Control procedure-Fire Control procedure-UPS procedure-Camera procedure-Wireless procedure-Hardware Security Tools procedure-Cabling procedure-2 and 3 Layer Tools procedure-Server Room procedure-Server Side procedure-Client Side procedure
Implementation	Buy Security Tools	Prioritize Need Tools
Configuration and Change Management	Manage Change Requests	Submit Change Request-Update Change Request-Review Change Request-Confirm Duplicate or Rejected CR
	Monitor and Control Project	Monitor Project Status-Schedule and Assign Work-Report Status-Handle Exceptions and Problems
Project Management	Manage Iteration	Acquire Staff-Initiate Iteration-Assess Iteration
	Evaluate Project Scope and Risk	Identify and Assess Risks-Develop Business Case
	Close-Out Phase	Prepare for Phase Close-Out
	Plan for Next Iteration	Develop Iteration Plan-Develop Business Case

TABLE 4: Activities of the construction phase.

Discipline	Workflow	Activity
Implementation	Implement Physical Design	Prioritize Physical Design-Schedule Physical Design-Implement Earthing Hole-Implement Physical Access Control-Implement Fire Control-Implement UPS-Implement Camera-Implement Wireless-Implement Hardware Security Tools-Implement Cabling-Implement 2 and 3 Layer Tools-Implement Server Room-Implement Server Side-Implement Client Side
	Implement Logical Design	Prioritize Logical Design-Schedule Logical Design-Implement Availability-Implement Reliability-Implement Redundancy-Implement Software Security Tools-Implement Network Topology-Implement Backup-Implement Protocol-Implement Switching-Implement Logical Access Control-Implement Zoning-Implement Naming-Implement Domain-Implement Network Services-Implement Platform-Implement Communication Services-Implement Software Framework Security-Implement Source Security
	Implement Human Design	Prioritize Human Design-Schedule Human Design-Implement Training Program-Implement Human events Procedure
Configuration and Change Management	Manage Change Requests	Submit Change Request-Update Change Request-Review Change Request-Confirm Duplicate or Rejected CR
Project Management	Monitor and Control Project	Monitor Project Status-Schedule and Assign Work-Report Status-Handle Exceptions and Problems
	Manage Iteration	Acquire Staff-Initiate Iteration-Assess Iteration
	Evaluate Project Scope and Risk	Identify and Assess Risks-Develop Business Case
	CloseOut Phase	Prepare for Phase Close-Out
	Plan for Next Iteration	Develop Iteration Plan-Develop Business Case

TABLE 5: Activities of the monitoring phase.

Discipline	Workflow	Activity
Asset	Monitor Asset	Identify New Asset-Identify New Treats-Identify New Vulnerabilities
Security Policy	Review Human Information Security Policy	Review All Procedure (monthly-seasonally-semesterly-yearly)
	Review Logical Information Security Policy	Review All Procedure (monthly-seasonally-semesterly-yearly)
	Review physical Information Security Policy	Review All Procedure (monthly-seasonally-semesterly-yearly)
Implementation	Monitor Physical Implementation	Test Earthing Hole-Test Physical Access Control-Test Fire Control-Test UPS-Test Camera-Test Wireless-Test Hardware Security Tools-Test Cabling-Test 2 and 3 Layer Tools-Test Server Room-Test Server Side-Test Client Side
	Monitor Logical Implementation	Test Availability-Test Reliability-Test Redundancy-Test Software Security Tools-Test Network Topology-Test Backup-Test Protocol-Test Switching-Test Logical Access Control-Test Zoning-Test Naming-Test Domain-Test Network Services-Test Platform-Test Communication Services-Test Software Framework Security-Test Source Security
	Monitor Human Implementation	Test Training Program-Test Human events Procedure
	Report Physical Implementation Monitoring	Report All Monitoring (monthly-seasonally-semesterly-yearly)
	Report Logical Implementation Monitoring	Report All Monitoring (monthly-seasonally-semesterly-yearly)
	Report Human Implementation Monitoring	Report All Monitoring (monthly-seasonally-semesterly-yearly)
Configuration and Change Management	Manage Change Requests	Submit Change Request-Update Change Request-Review Change Request-Confirm Duplicate or Rejected CR
	Monitor and Control Project	Monitor Project Status-Schedule and Assign Work-Report Status-Handle Exceptions and Problems
Project Management	Manage Iteration	Acquire Staff-Initiate Iteration-Assess Iteration
	Evaluate Project Scope and Risk	Identify and Assess Risks-Develop Business Case
	Close-Out Project	Prepare for Project Close-Out
	Plan for Next Iteration	Develop Iteration Plan-Develop Business Case

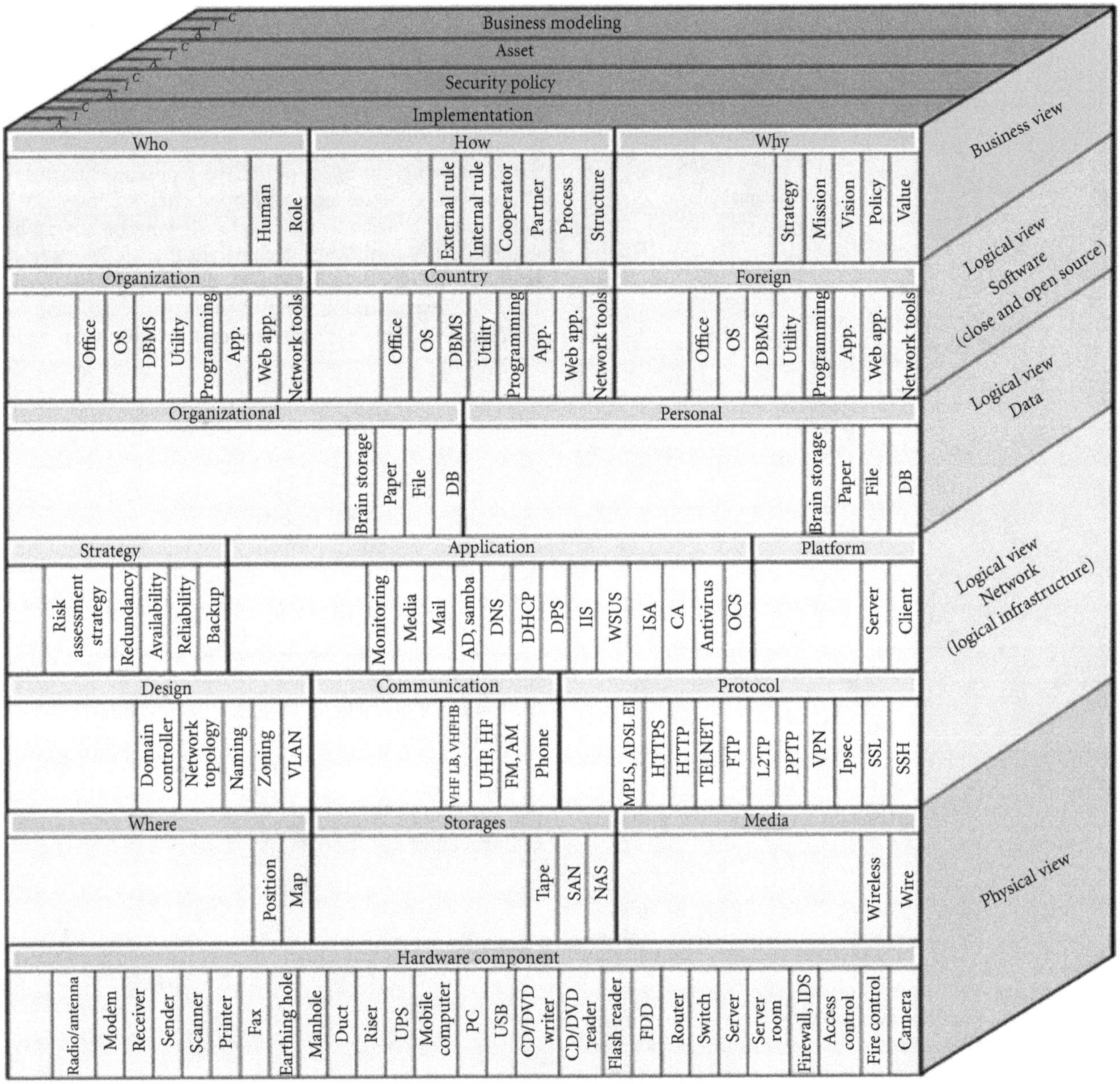

FIGURE 6: SUP cube.

TABLE 6: Assets.

ID	Domain	Section (sub)	Asset
A1	Business view	Who (human)	John Smith
A2	Logical view (software)	Organizational (app.)	Human Resource Application
A3	Logical View (Data)	Organizational (DB)	SQL_Server_1
A4	Logical view (network)	Application (DNS)	DNS_1
A5	Logical view (network)	Design (VLAN)	VLAN_1
A6	Physical view	Hardware component (server room)	Server_Room_1

TABLE 7: Threats.

ID	Threat
T1	Cache poisoning attacks
T2	Data deletion
T3	SQL injection
T4	VLAN hopping attacks
T5	Earthquake
T6	Data theft
T7	Directory traversal
T8	Data discovery
T9	Physical theft

TABLE 8: CIA triad evaluation.

Expert	Confidentiality (C)	Integrity (I)	Availability (A)
E_1	c_1	i_1	a_1
E_2	c_2	i_2	a_2
E_3	c_3	i_3	a_3
$\vdots$	$\vdots$	$\vdots$	$\vdots$
E_n	c_n	i_n	a_n
Weight	w_C	w_I	w_A

section, we determine which threats are related to which vulnerability. The relationship between each vulnerability and threat is a risk. Table 10 illustrates some risks within an organization.

3.5.6. Asset Value (AV). The *CIA* triad should be used to calculate the value of each asset. We use n experts to evaluate each asset. To get better results, we should get help from different experts for each group of assets in the security cube. For example, network experts should evaluate network assets such as servers, clients, and firewalls, software experts should evaluate software assets such as web applications. Each expert assigns a value from one to nine to each part of *CIA* triad based on Table 12. For example, a value of nine for confidentiality means that this asset's privacy is very high and a value of one for availability means that the availability of the asset is not important. Finally, the asset's value could be calculated with formula (2). AV_C, AV_I, and AV_A illustrates the calculation of asset value in confidentiality, integrity, and availability, respectively. Table 11 shows the calculation of asset value by n experts:

$$\{C_e, I_e, A_e\} \in [1, 9],$$

$$AV_C = w_C \cdot \left(\frac{\sum_{e=1}^{n} C_e}{n} \right),$$

$$AV_I = w_I \cdot \left(\frac{\sum_{e=1}^{n} I_e}{n} \right),$$

$$AV_A = w_A \cdot \left(\frac{\sum_{e=1}^{n} A_e}{n} \right),$$

$$AV = AV_C + AV_I + AV_A. \tag{2}$$

3.5.7. Vulnerability Effect (VE). We represent vulnerability effects with a percentage, and, for better accuracy, we get help from n experts. For example, 90% means a very high vulnerability percentage, which means that all threats related to this vulnerability have a high probability of occurring. Finally, the vulnerability effect could be calculated with formula (3). Table 13 shows experts' opinions for a given vulnerability

$$VE = \frac{\sum_{e=1}^{n} \text{effect}}{n}. \tag{3}$$

3.5.8. Threat Effect (TE). We used the *CIA* triad to calculate threat effects. We use n experts to calculate those effects. For each threat, we should get help from relevant experts to get better results. The calculation method of threats is similar to the one for assets. Each expert assigns a value from one to nine to each part of the *CIA* triad based on Table 11. For example, a value of nine in confidentiality means that this threat in the confidentiality area is very dangerous. Similarly, the value one in availability means that this threat cannot be dangerous for the availability. Finally, the threat effects could be calculated with formula (4). TE_C, TE_I, and TE_A illustrates the calculation of threat effect in confidentiality, integrity, and availability, respectively. Table 14 shows the calculation of threat effect by n experts:

$$\{C_e, I_e, A_e\} \in [1, 9],$$

$$TE_C = w_C \cdot \left(\frac{\sum_{e=1}^{n} C_e}{n} \right),$$

$$TE_I = w_I \cdot \left(\frac{\sum_{e=1}^{n} I_e}{n} \right), \tag{4}$$

$$TE_A = w_A \cdot \left(\frac{\sum_{e=1}^{n} A_e}{n} \right),$$

$$TE = TE_C + TE_I + TE_A.$$

3.5.9. Risk Effect (RE). Risk effects are modeled using three parameters: asset values, vulnerability effects, and threat effects. The following subsections will show how the risk effect can be calculated with the fuzzy model:

$$AV \in [1, 9],$$

$$VE \in [1, 100],$$

$$TE \in [1, 9], \tag{5}$$

$$RE = \text{defuzz} \cdot (\text{fuzz} \cdot (AV), \text{fuzz} \cdot (VE), \text{fuzz} \cdot (TE)).$$

TABLE 9: Asset vulnerabilities.

ID	Asset	Vulnerability
V1	A1 (John Smith)	No knowledge of file encoding using public keys
V2	A2 (Human Resource Application)	Unchecked user input
V3	A3 (SQL_Server_1)	Not using a mixed authentication mode
V4	A4 (DNS_1)	Insufficient transaction ID space
V5	A5 (VLAN_1)	Not properly configured
V6	A6 (Serve_Room_1)	Unsuitable location

TABLE 10: Some risks in an organization.

Asset ID	Vulnerability ID	Threat ID	Risk ID
A1	V1	T9	R1
A2	V2	T3	R2
A2	V2	T7	R3
A3	V3	T2	R4
A3	V3	T6	R5
A3	V3	T8	R6
A4	V4	T1	R7
A5	V5	T4	R8
A6	V6	T5	R9
A6	V6	T9	R10

TABLE 11: Asset value.

Expert	Confidentiality (C)	Integrity (I)	Availability (A)
E_1	c_1	i_1	a_1
E_2	c_2	i_2	a_2
E_3	c_3	i_3	a_3
$\vdots$	$\vdots$	$\vdots$	$\vdots$
E_n	c_n	i_n	a_n
Value	AV_C	AV_I	AV_A

TABLE 12: Range.

Level	Level	Effect
High	High	9
High	Medium	8
High	Low	7
Medium	High	6
Medium	Medium	5
Medium	Low	4
Low	High	3
Low	Medium	2
Low	Low	1

TABLE 13: Vulnerability Effect.

Expert	Effect
E_1	$P_1\%$
E_2	$P_2\%$
E_3	$P_3\%$
$\vdots$	$\vdots$
E_n	$P_n\%$
Effect	VE

TABLE 14: Threat effect.

Expert	Confidentiality (C)	Integrity (I)	Availability (A)
E_1	c_1	i_1	a_1
E_2	c_2	i_2	a_2
E_3	c_3	i_3	a_3
$\vdots$	$\vdots$	$\vdots$	$\vdots$
E_n	c_n	i_n	a_n
Effect	TE_C	TE_I	TE_A

(i) *Fuzzification.* Three membership functions are used for the three inputs, as can be seen in Figures 7(a), 7(b), and 7(c).

(ii) *Inference Engine.* The inference engine is fuzzy rule-based and is used to map an input space to an output space. The required rules for risk assessment are created as:

Rule 1:
if (Threat_Effect = Low)
then Risk_Effect = Low

Rule 2:
if (Threat_Effect = Medium and Vulnerability_Effect = Low)
then Risk_Effect = Low

Rule 3:
if (Threat_Effect = Medium and Vulnerability_Effect = Medium)
then Risk_Effect = Low

Rule 4:
if (Threat_Effect = Medium and Vulnerability_Effect = High)

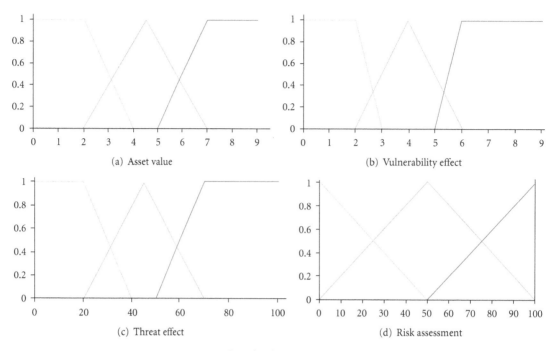

FIGURE 7: Three-level membership function.

then Risk_Effect = Medium

Rule 5:

if (Threat_Effect = High and Asset_Value = Low)
then Risk_Effect = Medium

Rule 6:

if (Threat_Effect = High and Vulnerability_Effect
= Low and
Asset_Value = Medium)
then Risk_Effect = Medium

Rule 7:

if (Threat_Effect = High and Vulnerability_Effect
= Medium and
Asset_Value = Medium)
then Risk_Effect = Medium

Rule 8:

if (Threat_Effect = High and Vulnerability_Effect
= High and Asset_Value = Medium)
then Risk_Effect = High

Rule 9:

if (Threat_Effect = High and Vulnerability_Effect
= Low and Asset_Value = High)
then Risk_Effect = Medium

Rule 10:

if (Threat_Effect = High and Vulnerability_Effect
= Medium and Asset_Value = High)
then Risk_Effect = High

Rule 11:

if (Threat_Effect = High and Vulnerability_Effect
= High and Asset_Value = High)

then Risk_Effect = High

(iii) *Defuzzification.* Finally, we build another member-ship function to represent the different possibilities identified by the risk assessment, as displayed in Figure 7(d). This process is called defuzzification. Two of the most common techniques are the centroid method and maximum method. In the centroid method, the crisp value of the output variable is computed by finding the center of gravity of the membership function. In the maximum method, the crisp value of the output variable is the maximum truth value (membership weight) of the fuzzy subset. The defuzzification technique that is used for this model is the centroid method.

4. Results

4.1. Risk Assessment. Table 15 shows the results of the risk assessment method for some risks (which were extracted based on Table 10). In this table, the asset values, vulnerability effects, and threat effects were calculated with formulas (2), (3) and (4) and the risk effects were calculated based on these three previous values and the fuzzy model.

4.2. SUP Framework. To verify the efficiency of the proposed model, it has been implemented in two industrial organizations. They both had implemented ISMS based on ISO27001 three years ago but lost its continuity after seven months. The goal was to reimplement ISMS in these organizations but using the SUP method instead. After waiting seven months, it was possible to make a meaningful comparison between the status of this implementation and the one they had

TABLE 15: Risk assessment results.

Risk ID	Asset Value (0–9)	Vulnerability effect (0–100)	Threat effect (0–9)	Risk effect (0–100)
R1	6.92	91.66	6.92	83.6
R2	9	46.66	7.56	83.6
R3	9	46.66	4.8	18.3
R4	9	50	3.08	18.8
R5	9	50	5	19.2
R6	9	60	5	45.6
R7	5.44	63.33	5.48	57.1
R8	5	73.33	2.68	46
R9	9	80	2.92	49.7
R10	9	80	6.92	83.7

TABLE 16: The comparison between the two methods.

Index no.	Index name	Organization 1		Organization 2	
		ISO 27001	SUP	ISO 27001	SUP
1	Monitoring	27	81	36	63
2	Maintenance and continuity	15	61	18	71
3	Reporting	43	60	51	70
4	Customer confidence	50	82	60	73
5	Risk assessment	50	93	50	80
6	Business continuity	48	66	56	49
7	Role segregation	10	96	11	98
8	Configuration and change management	10	40	12	36
	Results	%32	%72	%37	%67

with ISO27001. The results of these two implementations are presented in Table 16. The comparison between the two methods is based on 8 parameters, which are the most important aspects of the ISMS implementation.

(i) *Monitoring.* This aspect ensures that we established a framework to monitor roles, responsibilities, new assets, security policies and continuity of the executive committee of the organization.

(ii) *Maintenance and Continuity.* This aspect ensures that our Information Security Management System will not lose its stability over time. Continuity is one of the biggest challenges that all security managers deal with, because we have to consider security in all business processes, and it needs perfect risk assessment and management over time.

(iii) *Reporting.* This aspect ensures that we established a framework for easy and continuous reporting.

(iv) *Customer Confidence.* customers expect their information to be secure and private. If we implement a powerful ISMS mechanism, we can improve customer confidence. For this purpose, we have to determine some indicators.

(v) *Risk Assessment.* This aspect makes sure that our risk assessment model identifies high risks and prioritizes them properly. Obviously, it helps us more accurately reduce risks in the risk management step. Also, it makes sure that we have good asset classification. As mentioned, asset classification plays a very important role in information security management. If we can classify assets properly, it will help us to achieve an effective asset protection.

(vi) *Business Continuity.* It makes sure that our business continuity management process prevents business disruptions and security failures and ensure that essential operations are restored as quickly as possible [2].

(vii) *Role Segregation.* It makes sure that we establish a framework where we can easily segregate security roles and responsibilities. Proper segregation helps other aspects of the ISMS implementation.

(viii) *Configuration and Change Management.* This aspect ensures that adapting to change, controlling change, and effecting change are under control. In ISMS, we have many security documents or policies that are related to each other, and changing a document is a challenge.

Each value in the aspect columns indicates the average of the top managers' opinions that have been gathered (all values are rounded up). Results show that SUP improves the ISMS implementation. The most impressive part of the results was shown in maintenance and continuity, role segregation, and risk assessment, because there is rarely success without iterative and incremental mechanisms. Also, significant improvements in other parameters cannot be ignored.

5. Conclusion

ISO27001 is the best framework to implement and maintain an organization's security. The most important point in this standard is that external certification of ISO27001 does not mean that you are really secure; it only means that you are managing security in line with the standard. On the other hand, ISO27001 points out methods for risk assessment and choosing controls and policies, but it never addresses the relations between all these parts as a well-designed integrated structure for security specialists. The results obtained clearly demonstrate the benefits of implementing the SUP framework to implement an ISMS. SUP has effectively improved the ISO27001 implementation process. Using the SUP framework within an organization leads to a better and higher-quality ISMS implementation. Effective management, increased success of the ISMS implementation, and well-defined tasks for each person who has a role in the ISMS implementation are precisely identified. One of the most important parts to ensure an effective ISMS implementation is the classification of assets, for which the security cube is proposed in the SUP method. To bring the organization to a certain security level, an incremental and iterative process has been designed. Therefore, security levels are divided into N levels, and by achieving each one, the organization will reach the desired security. For each of these levels, or iteration, there is a workflow of designs. SUP have been implemented in two industrial organizations, and its results have been compared with the previous implementation status of ISMS. The results show the significant improvement in evaluation indicators.

Acknowledgments

The authors would like to thank Alexandre Montplaisir of the DORSAL laboratory at École Polytechnique de Montréal for interesting discussions and helpful feedback. The support of the Natural Sciences and Engineering Research Council of Canada (NSERC), the Defence Research and Development Canada (DRDC), and the Ericsson Software Research is gratefully acknowledged.

References

[1] M. Dey, "Information security management—a practical approach," in *Proceedings of the IEEE AFRICON*, pp. 1–6, September 2007.

[2] ISO, "Information technology Security techniques Information security management systems Requirements," ISO/IEC 27001, 2005.

[3] J. Eloff and M. Eloff, "Information security management—a new paradigm," in *Proceedings of the SAICSIT*, pp. 130–136, 2003.

[4] J. S. Broderick, "ISMS, security standards and security regulations," *Information Security Technical Report*, vol. 11, no. 1, pp. 26–31, 2006.

[5] L. Chung, "Dealing with security requirements during the development of information systems," in *Proceedings of the 5th International Conference on Advanced Information Systems Engineering (CAiSE '93)*, pp. 234–251, Paris, France, 1993.

[6] S. Kondakci, "A new assessment and improvement model of risk propagation in information security," *International Journal of Information and Computer Security*, vol. 1, no. 3, pp. 341–366, 2007.

[7] S. Kondakci, "A causal model for information security risk assessment," in *Proceedings of the 6th International Conference on Information Assurance and Security*, pp. 143–148, IEEE Computer Society, 2010.

[8] S. Kondakci, "Network security risk assessment using bayesian belief networks," in *Proceedings of the 2nd IEEE International Conference on Social Computing, IEEE International Conference on Privacy, Security, Risk and Trust*, pp. 952–960, IEEE Computer Society, August 2010.

[9] S. Kondakci, "A recursive method for validating and improving network security solutions," in *Proceedings of the International Conference on Security of Information and Networks (SIN '07)*, pp. 74–83, Trafford Publishing, 2007.

[10] C. Pak, "The near real time statistical asset priority driven (NRTSAPD) risk assessment methodology," in *Proceedings of the 9th ACM SIG-Information Technology Education Conference (SIGITE '08)*, pp. 105–112, ACM, October 2008, New York, NY, USA.

[11] C. Pak and J. Cannady, "Asset priority risk assessment using hidden Markov models," in *Proceedings of the 10th ACM Special Interest Group for Information Technology Education (SIGITE '09)*, pp. 65–73, Fairfax, Va, USA, October 2009.

[12] C. Xiaolin, T. Xiaobin, Z. Yong, and X. Hongsheng, "A markov game theory-based risk assessment model for network information system," in *Proceedings of the International Conference on Computer Science and Software Engineering (CSSE '08)*, pp. 1057–1061, December 2008.

[13] B. C. Guan, C. C. Lo, P. Wang, and J. S. Hwang, "Evaluation of information security related risks of an organization—the application of the multi-criteria decision-making method," in *Proceedings of the 37th IEEE Annual International Carnahan Conference on Security Technology*, pp. 168–175, October 2003.

[14] Y. M. Wang and T. M. S. Elhag, "Fuzzy TOPSIS method based on alpha level sets with an application to bridge risk assessment," *Expert Systems with Applications*, vol. 31, no. 2, pp. 309–319, 2006.

[15] S. Kondakci, "A composite network security assessment," in *Proceedings of the 4th International Conference on Information Assurance and Security*, pp. 249–254, IEEE Computer Society, 2008.

[16] M. Hamdi and N. Boudriga, "Algebraic specification of network security risk management," in *Proceedings of the ACM Workshop on Formal Methods in Security Engineering (FMSE '03)*, pp. 52–60, October 2003.

[17] L. Muller, M. Magee, P. Marounek, and A. Philipson, "IBM IT governance approach-business performance through IT

execution," 2008, http://www.redbooks.ibm.com/abstracts/sg247517.html.

[18] IBM Rational Unified Process (RUP), http://www-01.ibm.com/software/awdtools/rup.

[19] P. Kroll and P. Kruchten, *Rational Unified Process Made Easy: A Practitioner's Guide to the RUP*, Addison-Wesley, Boston, Mass, USA, 2003.

[20] C. Larman and V. R. Basili, "Iterative and incremental development: a brief history," *Computer*, vol. 36, no. 6, pp. 47–56, 2003.

[21] A. Shameli-Sendi, M. Jabbarifar, M. Shajari, and M. Dagenais, "FEMRA: fuzzy expert model for risk assessment," in *Proceedings of the 5th International Conference on Internet Monitoring and Protection*, pp. 48–53, Barcelona, Spain, 2010.

[22] K. Haslum, A. Abraham, and S. Knapskog, "Fuzzy online risk assessment for distributed intrusion prediction and prevention systems," in *Proceedings of the 10th International Conference on Computer Modeling and Simulation*, pp. 216–223, IEEE Computer Society Press, Cambridge, UK, 2008.

[23] G. Stoneburner, A. Goguen, and A. Feringa, "Risk management guide for information technology systems," http://csrc.nist.gov/publications/nistpubs/800-30/sp800-30.pdf.

[24] J. A. Zachman, "The Zachman framework," http://www.zachmaninternational.com/.

7

Highly Accurate Timestamping for Ethernet-Based Clock Synchronization

Patrick Loschmidt, Reinhard Exel, and Georg Gaderer

Institute for Integrated Sensor Systems, Austrian Academy of Sciences, 2700 Wiener Neustadt, Austria

Correspondence should be addressed to Patrick Loschmidt, patrick.loschmidt@oeaw.ac.at

Academic Editor: Liansheng Tan

It is not only for test and measurement of great importance to synchronize clocks of networked devices to timely coordinate data acquisition. In this context the seek for high accuracy in Ethernet-based clock synchronization has been significantly supported by enhancements to the Network Time Protocol (NTP) and the introduction of the Precision Time Protocol (PTP). The latter was even applied to instrumentation and measurement applications through the introduction of LXI. These protocols are usually implemented in software; however, the synchronization accuracy can only substantially be improved by hardware which supports drawing of precise event timestamps. Especially, the quality of the timestamps for ingress and egress synchronization packets has a major influence on the achievable performance of a distributed measurement or control system. This paper analyzes the influence of jitter sources remaining despite hardware support and proposes enhanced methods for up to now unmatched timestamping accuracy in Ethernet-based synchronization protocols. The methods shown in this paper reach sub-nanosecond accuracy, which is proven in theory and practice.

1. Introduction

In instrumentation and measurement, the General Purpose Interface Bus (GPIB) was for a long time *the* system for data collection and networking of equipment. This bus system has a dedicated wiring for triggering devices and to simultaneously start measurements. The reason for the continuous usage of this relatively old technology is the excellent tool and driver support and the simplicity of the system. Despite these arguments, GPIB has several drawbacks in the handling (connectors, cable) and generality of the approach. First of all GPIB is limited in terms of cable length and number of bus devices. The parallel data transfer and strict arbitration scheme also limit the achievable data rate and make handling and configuration quite complicated for the user. Second, GPIB is also limited in terms of its functionality and does not comply to modern networked systems.

A solution for the test and measurement industry to tackle the drawbacks of GPIB can be found in the LAN extensions for instrument (LXI) [1] approach. This de facto standard uses the well-established Ethernet technology to network measurement devices. The advantage is clearly that one can embed such a system seamlessly into office and lab networks having all advantages of a full network functionality. The application in test and measurement is however only feasible if it can be ensured that the devices are properly triggered. The approach of LXI is to use synchronized clocks for this: a device which detects a trigger condition sends out the time of the trigger condition causing all other devices to a-posteriori save the data at that previous instant of time. This requires that all devices keep some backlog of historic data. It is clear that the precision and the usability of the data highly depend on the accuracy of the clocks in such systems and therefore the synchronization technology. For synchronizing computer clocks, the most prominent approach is the Network Time Protocol (NTP) [2]. This protocol, which is widely used in the Internet, manages accuracies of several milliseconds, with certain extensions even microseconds [3]. As this accuracy is not sufficient for high-precision measurements, the need for a new protocol arose: the Precision Time Protocol (PTP) [4].

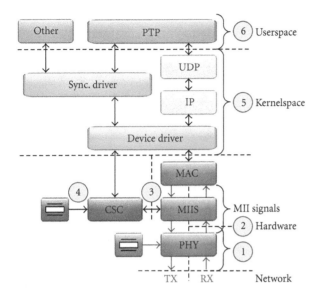

FIGURE 1: Synchronization node overview and possible internal sources of jitter.

The PTP periodically transmits synchronization messages to update the time on a master-slave basis. For that an algorithm for master election, management, and delay compensation is set on one of the upper layers of the communication stack. In the LXI case, this is the application layer where PTP communicates over User Datagram Protocol (UDP). The standard itself, however, is independent of the communication technology. Although the protocol can be implemented in software, high-precision timestamping has to be done in hardware in order to cancel out protocol stack jitter. This paper outlines the possibilities, analyzes different jitter sources, and proposes new approaches for this highly accurate timestamping. For that, first the state of the art in Ethernet-based clock synchronization is summarized. The motivation points out the reasons for seeking higher precision of timestamps. The following chapters show the influence of the different parameters and required components of a timestamping network interface. Existing accurate methods are given in Section 5 together with their pros and cons in Table 1. Section 6 then presents our new method for highly accurate timestamping, which is then proven to be working in reality by measurements shown in Section 7. The paper is finally rounded up by a conclusion.

2. State of the Art

Figure 1 shows the typical software and hardware structure of an Ethernet-based clock synchronization node. The protocol stack, for example, NTP or PTP, is typically implemented in userspace; see Figure 1(6). Thus, event detection (timestamping) on that level [5] suffers from the jitter induced by all operations required to detect an external asynchronous hardware event (reception of a packet) at or below this layer. The main sources are typically the scheduling behavior of the operating system, data-(length-) dependent processing, or variable execution times, for example, due to caching. Similar

reasons are also valid for the kernelspace Figure 1(5) usually hosting the network, for example, Internet Protocol (IP), and transport layer, for example, UDP of the protocol stack [3].

Due to the timely uncertainties in software (except for specially designed real-time systems), almost all high-accuracy synchronization systems rely on event detection close to the physical layer. Since in Ethernet even the datalink layer, that is, Media Access Control (MAC), has variable processing time on the transmit path due to the Carrier Sense Multiple Access (CSMA) mechanism and a possible back-off delay [6], accurate solutions rely on timestamping on the Media Independent Interface (MII). The necessary data scanner, that is, the Media-Independent Interface Scanner (MIIS) block, can be attached to the MII as a separate device [7] or integrated within the functionality of the MAC.

The advantage of the MII is that all receive signals are already in the digital domain but are still source synchronous with respect to the analog data on the line. This gives the synchronization node the possibility to determine timestamps with high precision as the interface is phase-locked to the opposite transmitter. In contrast, interfaces synchronous to the local oscillator, for example, R(G)MII, introduce additional jitter as indicated by (2) of Figure 1 because elastic buffering is required to compensate for clock frequency offsets.

All effects that can deteriorate the performance via the physical layer (see Section 4.3) are summarized by Figure 1(1). These mainly include the analog properties of the physical layer entity (PHY), the cable, and the transmission standard. Timestamping can also be done directly at the physical layer, as shown in [8].

Beside the event detection itself, Figure 1 also outlines the integration of necessary synchronization functions in hardware with the Clock Synchronization Cell (CSC). This element is responsible for timekeeping and timestamping. It is driven by an oscillator which itself is again subject to instabilities indicated by Figure 1(4). In this case, due to the separate oscillator (e.g., for higher stability), an additional clock transition, Figure 1(3), is introduced which again adds jitter. This issue can be solved by using a single oscillator for media transmission as well as timekeeping.

To build a complete Ethernet networks, one element is essential: the switch. In principle Ethernet switches use the same PHY and MAC as ordinary nodes. Concerning clock synchronization, the residential time of a packet on a switch has to be measured to compensate for varying switching decision or queuing times. However, it can be said that the principles and influences are similar to a node, and therefore the results of this paper can be applied accordingly.

3. Motivation

As outlined in the introduction, synchronization is, among other areas, mandatory for test and measurement applications. Precise timestamping is required, because accurate synchronization over packet-oriented depends on a common event that can be detected by the synchronizing nodes. Such events are special messages, regularly sent out by PTP

TABLE 1: Comparison of the different approaches.

Approach	Type	Advantage	Disadvantage	Complexity	Impl. effort	Accuracy
HSC	Single shot	Linearity	High-speed clocks	Low	Low	Medium
PSC	Single shot	No high-speed clocks	Linearity issues	Low	Low	Medium
TDL	Single shot	Single-event capturing	Temperature dependency	High	High	High–very high
TSA	Single shot avg.	Simplicity	Leakage effects	Low	Low	Low–medium
DPE	Phase estimator	High freq. range	Analog parts req.	High	Medium	High
PFE	**Phase estimator**	**Purely digital, size**	**Narrow freq. range**	**Medium**	**Low**	**Medium–very high**
PFE + TSA	**Phase estimator avg.**	**At least PFE perf.**	**Correlation dependency**	**Medium**	**Low**	**Very high**

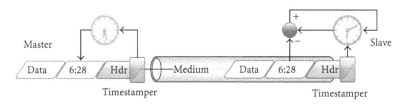

FIGURE 2: Basic method for clock synchronization in packet-based networks and the necessity of event detection (timestamping).

together with the absolute time of the event. Moreover, PTP uses a master-slave approach, where one clock master synchronizes several slaves. The basic principle of timestamping is indicated in Figure 2. For packet-oriented networks, the synchronization protocols define the occurrence of a packet (mostly, the start of the data frame) on the medium as the common event. As shown in the figure, the master node catches the transmission time and copies it into the synchronization packet. On the other end, the slave detects the reception and compares the event time with the information contained in the packet and adjusts its clock. The remaining offset between the clocks, which is due to the transmission delay on the network, can be compensated by round-trip delay measurements. The latter use the same timestamping techniques by sending a packet from slave to master or vice versa. Assuming that the delay on one link is symmetrical; that is, it takes the same time to transmit a message from node A to B as from node B to A, the line delay can be calculated by using the time difference between send and receive event, reducing it by the residential time at the remote side, and taking the half of the result as the delay of the link.

The alternative to precise timestamping—long-term averaging to enhance the precision—cannot be applied due to nonstationary jitter of several elements within the synchronization loop, in particular the oscillator. Thus, accurate timestamping is the key for any high-accuracy clock synchronization method. This paper focuses on the influence factors affecting the system precision despite the usage of hardware timestamping in Ethernet to develop methods able to acquire precise timestamps. Further, tradeoffs are identified that allow to tune different parameters to achieve a predefined accuracy boundary efficiently.

4. Sources for Inaccuracy

Since timestamping at a certain network layer avoids timely influences on the accuracy of all layers above, hardware timestamping cancels out software dependencies. Still, also for hardware implementations, certain limitations due to remaining jitter sources exist that influence the achievable accuracy [9]. As the first two of the following aspects are influenced by a wide range of parameters, the impact is summarized in this section while more detail is presented in the appendix.

4.1. Oscillator. An ideal oscillator serving as a timebase for a node would require only a single synchronization at startup to compensate for the initial offset. Due to the fact that every oscillator is subject to a number of physical phenomena, the progress of time is not constant; even worse, the accuracy is dependent on the considered hold-over time, which is the interval between two synchronization events. Periodic resynchronization is therefore indispensable. Several short-time noise phenomena, for example, phase noise, additionally complicate precise timestamping.

4.2. Synchronization Interval. Considering only the stability characteristics of a selected oscillator, an optimal synchronization interval can be chosen. Usually the longest interval with the lowest absolute clock jitter is chosen to minimize necessary network traffic between the nodes. However, as inaccuracies in timestamping cannot be distinguished from oscillator jitter, both have to be as low as possible. While the timestamp inaccuracy is independent on the synchronization interval, the timebase error caused by the oscillator instability increases with time. Hence, depending on the interval either the oscillator or the timestamping can be identified as the limiting factor.

4.3. Physical Layer Properties. Since it is not (cost) efficient to replace commercial off-the-shelf (COTS) PHYs with a proprietary solution supporting timestamping, the most reasonable way to add high-precision timestamping to a system is to use the interface of the PHY to the MAC. Thus, the delay behavior of the PHY still has influence on the achievable performance of the timestamping method.

The most important properties are the line coding, the translation to MII, and the internal phase-locked loop (PLL). Since Ethernet is designed as an asynchronous network, the receive side of the physical layer has to recover the transmission clock in order to correctly decode the data. The other direction, the data transmission can be performed with the locally available clock. This does not introduce a clock transition and therefore does not increase the jitter (The reason why clock transitions add jitter is given in Section 4.4).

Beside dynamic link delay changes, also the absolute delay of the PHY-to-PHY system can vary each time the link is newly established. This is due to the fact that, for example, in Fast Ethernet, the 125 MBaud on the line have to be translated to four bit symbols on the 25 MHz MII, which allows five different locking positions [10].

The delay behavior for the three most popular copper-based Ethernet transmission standards is illustrated in Figure 3 using two Marvell 88E1111 PHYs over a 3 m direct connection. Since 10 Base-T keeps the line idle when there is no data to be transmitted, the PLL of the receiver has to resynchronize to the transmission clock with each packet. If the packet rate is low, the behavior is similar to a link reestablishment since the PLL can take any of the possible locking positions, that is, two different, 100 ns apart for Figure 3. On high packet rates, the drift of the receive PLL between two packets is small and thus the PHY can stay synchronized, which then results only in the jitter of the clock recovering process.

Compared to the original Ethernet, Fast Ethernet introduced 4B/5B line encoding and the *Idle* code-group (clause 24.2.2.1.2 of [6]). The coding replaces four bit by five bit groups, which are coded in a way that long constant bit sequences are avoided to ease clock recovery. Additionally, it is possible to insert control codes, for example, to denote the start of a transmission (/J/, /K/). Hence, the synchronization can be maintained continuously, independent of the data transfer, which results in significantly lower standard deviation of the transmission delay.

In contrast to the enhancement from the original 10 Base-T to 100 Base-T, Gigabit Ethernet does not give a performance boost for clock synchronization. Resulting from the fact that the physical layer uses a single clock for both directions, there is a master and a slave PHY.

Thus, there is a clock transition on the receiver side to the local clock. Due to the 125 MHz clock rate, this gives an equally distributed communication delay over a window of eight nanoseconds on the slave side, while the master only

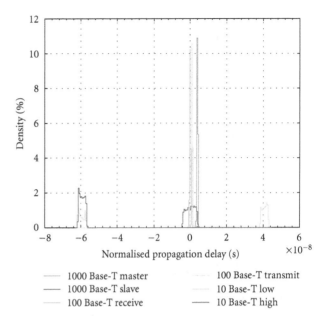

FIGURE 3: Comparison of various Ethernet physical layer transmission standards.

shows PLL and oscillator phase noise. Also the assumption that the problem of asymmetric delays of Ethernet can be solved with Gigabit Ethernet due to the bidirectional usage of all copper-lines does not turn out to be true, as shown in this figure.

Summarizing the findings, it can be said that apart from the initial locking with a specific absolute delay, the communication jitter for Fast Ethernet is by far the lowest (with a standard deviation $\sigma = 0.286$ ns compared to 1.387 ns for 10 Base-T and theoretic 2.309 ns for 1000 Base-T).

4.4. Timestamp Resolution. The resolution of the timestamp basically influences the quality of the timebase comparison for the control loop of the synchronization system. While in general it is no problem to gain enough resolution in hardware, the difficulty arises from the fact that the timestamp has to be transferred through various network layers to the application [11]. Linux, for example, started supporting timestamps with nanosecond resolution from version 2.6.22 on. The necessary structure to transfer hardware timestamps to the applications were added in version 2.6.30. Currently, the resolution is limited to one nanosecond, which makes it difficult to safely achieve synchronization accuracies below the nanosecond.

Figure 4 illustrates the main problem for highly accurate timestamping. Since Ethernet is an asynchronous network, the ingress packets are asynchronous to the local clock of the timebase. Thus, the issue boils down to detecting the occurrence of a packet, that is, frame active signal, with high precision. In synchronous digital designs, the asynchronous activation of a single event between two clock edges can be detected at the earliest with the next edge. Highly accurate solutions therefore have to measure/estimate

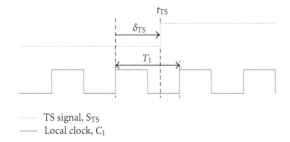

FIGURE 4: Timestamping error due to phase/frequency shift.

the exact occurrence of the event with respect to the local clock [12].

5. Existing Single-Shot Methods

Single-shot methods are one solution to the problem of accurate timestamping and measure δ_{TS} directly. That is done by determining how long after the rising edge of the local clock the timestamp signal $\mathcal{S}_{TS}$ has been asserted. For that purpose, a clock cycle T_l is divided into $n \in \mathbb{N}^+$ equally spaced fractions, which reduce the timestamping variance (the variance of a uniform distribution) to $\sigma_{TS}^2 = T_l^2/(12n^2)$. The main advantage is that the timestamp signal is not required to occur in regular intervals. Events can be detected without any further reference even on their first occurrence.

5.1. High-Speed Counter (HSC).
This approach divides T_l by a short-width high-frequency counter with a period $T_h = T_l/n$. The counter is reset at every rising edge of the local clock, and its value is frozen when $\mathcal{S}_{TS}$ is active. The sampled counter value divided by n then describes the relative phase offset δ_{TS}. Since the period of the local clock is exactly a multiple of T_h, the clock transition between these two clocks can be designed without any additional jitter, and consequently the timestamping variance reduces by n^2. The result is similar to a design completely clocked with $1/T_h$ with the advantage that only a few logic elements have to run at a high frequency.

With very low additional effort, n can be doubled using registers sampling with the opposite edge of the clock. Such register pairs using both edges, called Double Data Rate (DDR) registers, are available in many devices to be used for communication links. The additional improvement by a factor of two is achieved without change in the clock rate and is a special case of the next option requiring only an inverter.

5.2. Phase-Shifted Clocks (PSCs).
The use of phase-shifted clocks is another method to partition T_l. For this technique, $n - 1$ additional clocks are generated, which are phase shifted by $2\pi/k$ with $k = 0, 1, \ldots, n - 1$ with respect to C_l. The timestamp signal is registered into n registers, each with a different generated clock. If the $\mathcal{S}_{TS}$ gets active, the first i registers still sample the old state. This generates a so-called thermometer code, which is converted to a binary code and used in the same manner as the HSC. Since $\mathcal{S}_{TS}$ drives

n registers, special care has to be taken that the clock at the registers has the designed phase shift (i.e., the registers are timely equally spaced), since otherwise the thermometer code becomes nonlinear. This effect and the number of output clocks per PLL limit n to a value of about 10 in state-of-the-art Field Programmable Gate Array (FPGA) devices (e.g., Altera Stratix III family [13]).

5.3. Tapped Delay Lines (TDLs).
TDLs are a common approach for digitizing times with sub-nanosecond accuracy. The basic configuration of a TDL consists of a serial chain of n latches having a delay τ_L, a second chain of noninverting buffers with delay $\tau_B < \tau_L$, and an output logic as described in [14]. The signal to be timestamped is then fed through all latches, which freeze its current state at the rising edge of a second signal (clock). The resulting thermometer code can then be evaluated after the next clock edge.

Nevertheless, it has to be considered that such a design uses asynchronous logic, and therefore the delays τ_L and τ_B are not only placement but also temperature dependent. The linearity of a TDL may be compromised by these effects, and special calibration logic may be required. The possible precision depends on the intrinsic switching speed of the latches and is typically in the range of 100 ps [15].

5.4. Proposed Phase-Estimating Solution.
Phase-estimating methods do not measure δ_{TS} directly, but rather estimate it using the fact that $\mathcal{S}_{TS}$ is asserted synchronously to the communication clock. The relatively new approach for highly accurate time interval measurements is described in [16] for a active clock skew compensation in VLSI designs using analog components. The authors of [17] present a similar method using a 10 MHz atomic clock source sampled by an analog to digital converter (ADC) driven by the communication clock. The resulting waveform is used to perform a phase estimation by a 1024 pt Fast Fourier Transform (FFT). While the results show a very low timestamping standard deviation of about 10 ps, this approach requires one ADC per timestamper and an atomic clock to achieve the mentioned performance.

5.5. Approach.
As with analog single-shot methods, for the targeted application area, timestamping in Ethernet, additional components (especially analog ones) are rather impractical. Consequently, a technique to implement the scheme using pure digital function blocks is presented by us in [12].

In this approach, the frequencies of the involved clocks have to fulfill several requirements in order to benefit from the method of phase estimation. First of all, the rising edge of the local clock T_l should occur equally distributed within the clock cycles of T_c averaged over a given time span (i.e., the rising edge of the local clock should cover all phases of the communication clock with equal probability). This includes that T_c must not match T_l or multiples thereof because in this case the rising edge would always coincide with a certain phase of T_c and the necessary averaging time span would be infinite. It is known from estimation and detection theory that applying a randomization function may help [18]. However, such a randomization function (e.g., a clock with very high clock jitter) is an impractical solution as the clock jitter reduces the maximum attainable clock frequency in the same way.

In order to be able to sample T_c (or signals synchronous to it) at a number of different phase states, the local clock has to be a nonmultiple of the communication clock. To represent this criteria, the nominal local clock period T_l is given by

$$T_l = T_c \frac{1 - \beta}{n}, \quad 0 < \beta \ll 1, \qquad (1)$$

with the design parameter β as the relative frequency offset factor and n as the nominal oversampling factor. A cycle slip (i.e., when the rising edge of two clocks pass each other) occurs, if the difference in the periods sums up to T_l as given by

$$
\begin{aligned}
T_l &= \frac{1}{\varepsilon} \left[\frac{T_c}{n} - T_l \right] \\
&= \frac{1}{\varepsilon} \left[\frac{T_l}{1 - \beta} - T_l \right],
\end{aligned}
\qquad (2)
$$

$$\varepsilon = \frac{\beta}{1 - \beta}. \qquad (3)$$

Using (3) cycle slips will happen after every $1/\varepsilon$ local clock periods. This implies that $\mathcal{C}_c$ has been sampled at $\lceil 1/\varepsilon \rceil + 1$ different phase points over one cycle slip period and the maximal attainable precision is nominal βT_l. Selecting a very small β results in a small frequency offset and great resolution, but this can cause $T_c \leq n T_l$ due to instabilities of the two involved oscillators during the long theoretical cycle slip period. Consequently, cycle slips might not happen at all, or even worse, reverse cycle slips can occur, resulting in possible data loss.

Furthermore, small frequency differences are unusable since the rising edge instance is only equally distributed within T_c over a long averaging window, and for short averaging windows the leakage effect [19] becomes dominant.

5.6. Timestamp Averaging (TSA). Timestamping a frame m times by means of the communication clock is one option to estimate the phase at the timestamping event based on the assumption that δ_{TS} averages to 0.5. Given that the timestamps are centered before and after the assertion of δ_{TS} (i.e., $(m - 1)/2$ timestamps before and after the event) and that the clock rate is not changed during the timestamping period, the final timestamp TS is calculated by a weighted average over the timestamps TS_i following

$$TS = \sum_{i=(1-m)/2}^{(m-1)/2} \alpha_i TS_i, \quad \sum_i \alpha_i = 1. \qquad (4)$$

This Finite Impulse Response (FIR) filter can be simplified to a window integrator with $\alpha_i = 1/m$ with some limitations,

namely, leakage effects. The timestamping window should cover one cycle slip period or multiples thereof to get the timestamps equally distributed over one T_c period. Since the cycle slip period is dependent on the current frequency offset, it varies with the oscillator drift between the communication and local clock. One solution to this problem is to adjust m to cover always a multiple of the cycle slip periods or by capturing a big number of such periods and using a windowing function to minimize leakage effects. The leakage can also be reduced by selecting a rather large ε with the drawback of reduced resolution.

In the optimal case the resulting timestamping variance reduces to $\sigma_{TS}^2 = T_l^2/(12m)$. For example, a typical IEEE 1588 frame with about 80 bytes frame length may create $m = 160$ timestamps on the 4-bit-wide MII. Given that T_l equals 10 ns and all timestamps can be considered uncorrelated, the standard deviation becomes 228 ps.

5.7. Digital Phase Estimation (DPE). The phase of the communication clock can be also directly estimated by phase detectors. Such a detector can be, for instance, based on a mixer, which shifts the spectrum of the clock to a low frequency similar to common superheterodyne receivers. The output of the mixer is low-pass filtered to remove aliases at multiples of the input frequency and is conducted into a phase estimator. Given that the duty cycle of the clock input signal is constant, the low frequency part of the downmixed signal then is a measure for the phase difference at the inputs. Nevertheless, real filters with a low bandwidth introduce significant group delay, which has to be taken into account for the calculation of the timestamp. In order to allow for a digital implementation, the mixer can be replaced by an XOR gate and the output can be filtered in the same way. A further solution would be to use an external analog antialiasing filter in combination with an ADC and only perform the second filtering digitally, similar to Zhu's method [17].

A pure digital implementation without requiring external parts can be achieved, but in such a processing scheme undersampling occurs. As the XORed signal is not bandwidth-limited, sampling results in alias frequencies that can dominate the signal (e.g., if the "1 bit" sampler is sourced from a clock correlated with $\mathcal{C}_l$). One feasible solution is to sample the mixed signal by a clock which is uncorrelated to both inputs and apply the sampled signal to a low-pass filter with very low relative bandwidth. Such filters are typically Infinite Impulse Response (IIR) type since comparable FIR filters would need a big number of filter taps. IIR filters on the other hand have a frequency-dependent group delay, which means that the frequency offset between $\mathcal{C}_l$ and $\mathcal{C}_c$ must be estimated in order to compensate for the filter's group delay.

5.8. Combined Phase/Frequency Estimation (PFE). Rather than estimating δ_{TS} directly, it is also possible to estimate the phase by its derivative, the frequency offset, together with a reference point. In the following, the hat notation (e.g., $\hat{x}$ for an estimation of x) is used to differentiate between the true value and its estimation.

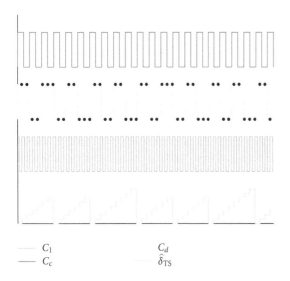

$$\begin{array}{ll} \text{—— } C_\mathrm{l} & C_d \\ \text{—— } C_c & \hat{\delta}_\mathrm{TS} \end{array}$$

FIGURE 5: Phase estimation between cycle slips.

The principle of our phase estimation by frequency estimation approach can be implemented as follows. Whenever the communication clock is phase aligned to the local clock (i.e., when a cycle slip occurs), the phase estimation $\hat{\delta}_\mathrm{TS}$ is set to zero. In every subsequent clock cycle $\hat{\delta}_\mathrm{TS}$ is incremented by the estimated inverse cycle slip period $\hat{\epsilon}$. In other words, $\hat{\delta}_\mathrm{TS}$ is the sampled integral of $\hat{\epsilon}$ over one cycle slip period. Given that the frequency is stable in the averaging interval, $\hat{\delta}_\mathrm{TS}$ ideally would reach 1.0 at the next cycle slip as depicted in Figure 5 for $n = 2$. For the reason of better visibility, a relative high value of 0.13 was chosen for β resulting in a (rather short) cycle slip period of 6.7 local clock cycles.

The accurate detection of the cycle slip instant is critical for the start of the integration of the frequency offset to get $\hat{\delta}_\mathrm{TS}$. To make the method independent of the communication clock duty cycle, a derived clock C_d with the period $2T_c$ is generated digitally. C_d is fed into a shift register with $5 + n$ taps clocked with the local clock. Further, this clock is used for cycle slip checking and performing edge detection. While the first two shift taps are used for buffering, the middle taps ($2 + n$ down to 2) are used for cycle slip detection. If all $n + 1$ middle taps contain the same binary value, a cycle slip must have happened. The last two taps (1 down to 0) are used to detect rising and falling edges of C_d at which the buffered timestamp signal δ_TS is checked for a high level.

The dots on the derived communication clock, C_d, mark the sampling points of this signal by the local clock, C_l. Each time the signal is sampled three times with the same value, a cycle slip must have occurred and the phase is reset.

Due to the fact that the cycle slip period is in general not an integer number, the phase estimation cumulates an error with each reset. Thus, higher orders of the cycle slip period exist. In picture this can be seen; that, every third time, the cycle slip is detected one period (of C_c) later in order to compensate for early detection at the previous two reset events. The higher order can be calculated by taking the remainder, which is $0.7 \cdot T_\mathrm{l}$ and summing it up to one period of C_c: $3 \times 0.7 \times T_\mathrm{l} \approx T_c$. Obviously, there is again a remainder, $0.1 \cdot T_\mathrm{l}$, which again causes a higher order periodicity. Note that these higher orders can only be used to refine the timestamp if the remainder of the cycle slip period does not wrap over. Even for selected frequencies, this is only applicable for a very narrow frequency range. Considering the oscillator tolerance for Ethernet (50 ppm), the method is not feasible. However, even if the higher-order periodicities are neglected, TSA can be used to improve the accuracy. The relative frequency offset $\hat{\beta}$ can be calculated by monitoring the number of rising edges of C_c with respect to C_l. In average, every $1/\hat{\epsilon}$ local clock cycles, a cycle slip will occur, which results in a missing rising edge with respect to the local clock. To achieve a continuous value of $\hat{\epsilon}$, a low-pass filter is used. The bandwidth of the filter must be narrow enough to track frequency changes of the oscillator while removing the cycle slip frequency. In general, IIR filters which have poles close to one are ideally suited for this application. Alternatively, the frequency offset $\hat{\epsilon}$ can be calculated by the cycle slip rate $1/\hat{\epsilon}$, but this requires a division block, which consumes a significant amount of logic resources. In any case, the calculation of the final timestamp involves summing up the last value of the rate-controlled timebase plus $\hat{\delta}_\mathrm{TS}$ times the clock rate.

5.9. Summary. The selection of the cycle slip rate not only has to consider the accuracy requirements of the application but also the behavior of the physical layer. As mentioned, for example, 10 Base-T does not provide a continuous clock supply that can be measured by the phase/frequency estimation. Therefore, the factor β has to be chosen in a way that the measurement can be done within the reception/transmission time of a single packet, which is rather stringent. Alternatively, the precision can be enhanced by keeping the carrier active via the transmission of several (arbitrary) packets to allow the phase/frequency estimation to settle. The last packet of such a burst can then be timestamped with relatively high precision. Obviously, the provision of a continuous link implies much higher potential for accurate timestamping due to the permanent tracking of phase and frequency.

6. Implementation and Evaluation

One major advantage of the presented phase estimating method over single-shot techniques is the fact that the measured signal only passes one digital processing path. Unless for the latter techniques, only one sampling register is directly connected to the δ_TS or the respective synchronous clock signal. Therefore, linearity problems due to unequal signal propagation delays to registers or between other logic elements, for example, buffers in TDLs, cannot occur. This makes the mentioned method also robust against temperature and other effects, which have direct influence on the signal propagation properties within an integrated circuit. Nevertheless, there might be a small (asymmetric) delay between the receive and the transmit path since two

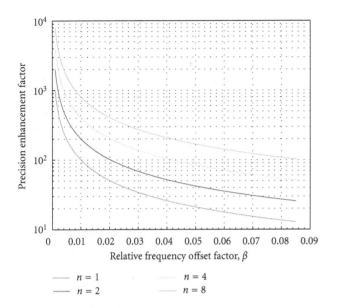

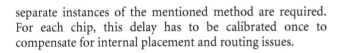

FIGURE 6: Dependency of the theoretical and the effective precision enhancement on the relative frequency offset.

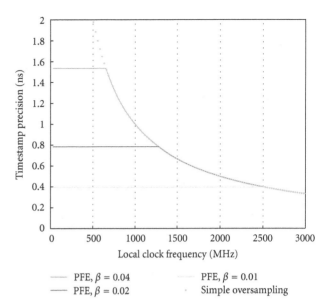

FIGURE 7: Timestamp precision with a 25 MHz communication clock for the PFE approach and simple oversampling.

separate instances of the mentioned method are required. For each chip, this delay has to be calibrated once to compensate for internal placement and routing issues.

6.1. Precision. Mathematically, the maximal attainable precision is given by $\beta T_1 = T_c(\beta - \beta^2)/n$. Using (1) the enhancement over the period of the communication clock results in a factor of $n/(\beta - \beta^2)$. Figure 6 shows the shape of this function and the possible improvement due to oversampling. Unfortunately, the results for $n > 1$ are only theoretical values.

As the phase estimation is reset at every cycle slip, cycle slips and the interpolated phase value are correlated. Oversampling increases the number of interpolation steps for δ, yet, the number of reachable values within one cycle slip period stays the same. It can be shown that with an oversampling ratio n only every nth value can be reached by the rising edge of $\mathcal{C}_c$. Hence, the effective precision is only $T_c(\beta - \beta^2)$, independent of n, and only scales with the duration of the cycle slip period.

Still, if n is set anything below $1/\beta$, the combined phase-frequency estimation method offers improved precision. Figure 7 depicts an example for a 25 MHz communication clock with three frequency offset factors β. For simple oversampling with a high-speed clock, the timestamp precision is exactly the period of the clock. If PFE is used, the precision improves to βT_1 until the frequency (or the oversampling factor n resp.) is highly increased. For $1 < n/\beta$, the PFE method degrades to the standard oversampling method. Frequencies in the range of multiple GHz cannot be reached with simple circuits, yet, the PFE method offers the same precision with design frequencies in the range of 50 MHz only.

6.2. Physical Limits. One critical parameter for the PFE method or in general for any form of highly precise timestamping is the phase noise of the clock. If the phase noise is low with respect to the calculated precision, then the considerations taken up to this point are directly applicable. However, measurements on PHY revealed that the phase noise is in the range of 100–250 ps RMS, 124 ps for the setup in [9]. While the phase noise does not alter the frequency estimation due to its long-term averaging, it causes the phase estimation circuit to see cycle slips too early or too late causing a timestamp jitter similar to the clock jitter. The clock can be cleaned by means of clock conditioners or the PLL inside the FPGA. The latter is readily available in FPGA-based solutions, but itself has a relatively high self-noise (around 200 ps RMS jitter) [13].

As discussed in Section 6, a randomization function is beneficial to remove clock correlation and leakage. Considering that the local clock frequency $1/T_1$ is typically around 50–300 MHz, the randomization by the clock jitter is far too low as it should cover one clock cycle uniformly distributed. For PFE with a high value of β (and therefore low precision), the randomization caused by the clock jitter can reduce the correlation between the timestamps. Hence, if multiple timestamps are averaged, the jitter may actually improve the precision of a packet's timestamp.

As already outlined, timestamping a frame multiple times can increase the precision, if the timestamps are not totally correlated. Since every Ethernet packet is at least 64 bytes long [6], a timestamper attached to the MII can draw 128 timestamps starting at beginning of the frame. These timestamps can then be fed into a minimum mean square error (MMSE) estimator calculating one timestamp for the frame using the least squares method. This combination of two methods PFE and TSA can guarantee at least the

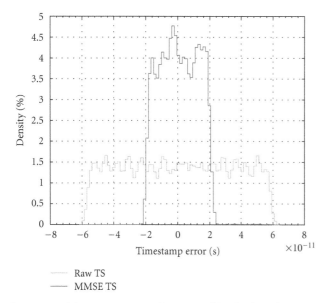

FIGURE 8: Timestamp error for a combined phase/frequency estimation ($\beta = 0 : 002$; $n = 2$) with linear MMSE estimator using 128 samples. The histogram shows a total of 50 kTS in 75 bins, giving a standard deviation of 12.036 ps.

performance of PFE only and offers improved precision for timestamps with lower correlation.

Measurement results of an FPGA-based implementation showing the feasibility of the described method are given in Figure 8. Both, communication and local clock, are sourced from a frequency generator with a rubidium clock as reference. The communication clock was set to 25 MHz and the local clock to 50.1 MHz resulting in $\beta = 0.002$ and $n = 2$. Every millisecond the generation of a timestamp set consisting of 128 timestamps within the communication clock domain is triggered. The captured timestamps in the local clock domain are then compared with the ideal ones, and the error is shown in the figure. The calculated precision for this setup should have a uniform distribution with $T_c(\beta - \beta^2) = 8$ ps width. The measured graph shows that it is actually about 120 ps wide. With MMSE averaging the timestamp precision improves to a width 40 ps or 12.036 ps standard deviation, respectively. The results can be interpreted in the following way. For precisions in the low picosecond range physical effects (e.g., clock jitter, thermal noise) dominate the timestamping. For larger values of β, for instance, $\beta = 0.0045$, as shown in [12], the calculated precision can be achieved even with the FPGA's PLLs.

7. Conclusion

A comparison of the methods analyzed within this paper is given in Table 1. Single shot is the method of choice if the event is not aligned to a clock. For events that appear synchronous to a clock, like the case for Ethernet with MII, phase estimation methods offer a similar or even superior performance with respect to, for example, a TDL, while requiring only low complexity and slow logic. The advantage

of the purely digital design of the PFE overwhelms the restriction to a low-frequency range in particular for the intended timestamping application.

In conclusion it can be said that highly accurate clock synchronization is of utmost importance for test and measurement applications where a perse non-real-time network is used to sample/collect data as in the LXI approach. The latter uses PTP to achieve that functionality by distributing absolute time information to attached network nodes. The used messages have to be supplied with the actual ingress or egress time at the synchronizing nodes. Providing a precise value for that event was shown to be again an issue of timestamping.

It is further shown that there are several different possibilities to timestamp, and various jitter sources exist within a Ethernet IP/UDP node. It can be stated as a rule of thumb that, the closer one gets to the physical layer, the lower the jitter and therefore the influence on the precision of a timestamp.

As a further conclusion of this paper, it can be said that timestamping is a crucial issue for highly accurate clock synchronization: several methods like HSCs, PSC, TDLs, or the phase-estimating methods as DPE are limited in terms of their reachable accuracy. It was shown that this limitation is however a bound, which is much lower than previously published results in terms of accuracy. Finally, timestamping using a MMSE estimator together with PFE can bring the accuracy down to an equal distribution with a standard deviation of only 12 ps.

Appendix

A. Timebase Issues

A.1. Oscillator. The physical properties of oscillators are an essential parameter for the accuracy of a clock synchronization node. In general, the stability of oscillators is dependent on the sampling period and thus defines the criteria to select the right synchronization interval, the hold-over time, respectively.

The Allan variance [20], which is defined by the expectation value, $\langle \cdot \rangle$, of the normalized frequency y over a sampling period τ, that is,

$$\sigma_y^2(\tau) = \frac{1}{2} \left\langle (y_{n+1} - y_n)^2 \right\rangle, \qquad (A.1)$$

is used to characterize oscillators. A low Allan variance means good stability over a certain measurement period τ. As the fractional frequency error can be also calculated by $y_n = 1/\tau(x_{n+1} - x_n)$, with x_n as the time error, at sample number n, an estimator of the Allan deviation can also be derived in the time domain by offset measurements from an ideal clock. A typical graph in double logarithmic scale for the Allan variance is shown in Figure 9. For short periods it will decrease by 100, if the sample time is increased by a factor 10. For large periods, long-term physical effects (e.g., temperature changes, aging) increase the value. One interesting area of sampling time for the case of clock synchronization is the minimum around 1 s. As

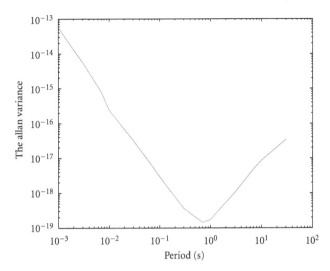

FIGURE 9: Typical Allan variance of an uncompensated crystal oscillator.

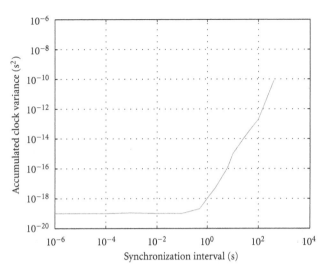

FIGURE 10: Absolute variance representing the accuracy with respect to the synchronization interval.

shown in the figure, the lowest values of the Allan variance can be observed. This so-called Allan-Floor results from a minimum in the sum of several different contributing noise contributions (white noise, flicker phase noise, white frequency noise, flicker frequency noise, and random walk frequency noise) of the oscillator. The individual power spectral density shapes add up in a way that, at a specific observation interval, a minimum as in Figure 9 can be observed.

Since clock synchronization seeks for a stable progress of time, the sample interval with the lowest deviation is of interest. The next section gives insight on how the synchronization interval should be chosen if a certain oscillator, that is, Allan deviation curve, is used.

A.2. Synchronization Interval. The most interesting and easiest changeable parameter in a synchronization system is the equidistant interval T_{sI} for exchanging synchronization messages. For further investigation of the influence, it is assumed that both, the master and the slave, are equipped with an oscillator that has a drift $D(t)$. The presence of varying drift of the oscillators will increase the offset between the nodes with the progression of time. If it is assumed that two oscillators were perfectly synchronous at the begining of a synchronization interval, the offset α after T_{sI} is [9]

$$\alpha = \int_{T_{sI}} (D_M(t) + D_S(t)) dt. \tag{A.2}$$

If the Allan variance of the oscillator is known, the standard variance of α can be estimated. The two-sample Allan variance can be interpreted as a variance of the frequency change rate. Therefore, the frequency variance is the integral of the Allan variance over T_{sI} plus a frequency offset, the standard variance σ_D^2 for the drift. Another integration results in the time variance plus a time offset. If we assume that the frequency and time offsets are compensated in the

synchronization system's servo, the variance of the time error is just the denormalised Allan variance (the normalized Allan variance multiplied by T_{sI}^2). Since the master and the slave oscillators are statistically independent, the resulting variance of α is the sum of the standard variances of both nodes.

For a typical oscillator, the accumulated clock variance remains constant for short intervals (as depicted in Figure 10). Thus, just from the oscillator's point of view, one gains in the first step no additional accuracy if the system synchronizes more often. For long synchronization intervals, the standard deviation rises significantly, which is mainly due to long-term effects like temperature changes. Consequently, the synchronization period should be selected as the maximum value that is available before the flicker floor of the Allan deviation is reached. This is equal to the end of the zero slope part of the accumulated clock variance at about 0.2 s. From the oscillator's point of view, there is no difference on which point of the zero slope part the synchronization period is chosen, which means that there is no direct further accuracy gain by exchanging more timing messages than necessary. Nevertheless it has to be mentioned that in principle an improvement of the resolution by averaging samples can be done where an increased synchronization rate has a positive influence due to that fact that the number of samples is increased.

PTP version 1 [21] has a default synchronization interval of 2 s and allows synchronization intervals between one and 16 s, incrementing by a factor of two. As pointed out by Figure 10, even the shortest possible period, according to the IEEE 1588 standard, of one second is rendered nonoptimal for the tested oscillator resulting in a degradation of accuracy.

A closer look at the basic data for the diagrams reveals that a synchronization interval of 0.5 s or even better 0.2 s can significantly reduce the jitter introduced by the clock source sampling. If PTP version 2 [4] is used in order to allow for the mentioned values of T_{sI}, the control loop is supplied with a higher quality of timestamps in slightly shorter intervals, while the network load is still within a reasonable range of about five packets per second.

Acknowledgments

This project was partly financed by the province of Lower Austria, the European Regional Development Fund, the FIT-IT project ε-WiFi under contract 813319 in cooperation with Oregano Systems, and the EU under the FP7 STREP flexWARE Contract number 224350. Due to availability reasons, PHYs from Marvell were used in our measurements.

References

[1] LAN eXtensions for Instrumentation (LXI), LXI Standard, 2008. http://www.lxistandard.org.

[2] D. L. Mills, "Internet time synchronization: the network time protocol," *IEEE Transactions on Communications*, vol. 39, no. 10, pp. 1482–1493, 1991.

[3] J. Ridoux and D. Veitch, "Ten microseconds over LAN, for free (extended)," *IEEE Transactions on Instrumentation and Measurement*, vol. 58, no. 6, pp. 1841–1848, 2009.

[4] "IEEE standard for a precision clock synchronization protocol for networked measurement and control systems," in *Proceedings of the IEEE Standards Interpretations for IEEE Std 1588–2008 (Revision of IEEE Std 1588-2002)*, pp. c1–c269, Piscataway, NJ, USA, July 2008.

[5] A. Marco, R. Casas, J. L. S. Ramos, V. Coarasa, A. Asensio, and M. Obaidat, "Synchronization of multihop wireless sensor networks at the application layer," *IEEE Wireless Communications*, vol. 18, no. 1, pp. 82–88, 2011.

[6] "Specific requirements part 3: carrier sense multiple access with collision detection (CSMA/CD) access method and physical layer specifications," in *Proceedings of the IEEE Standard for Information Technology—Telecommunications and information exchange between systems—Local and metropolitan area networks*, IEEE Computer Society, New York, NY, USA, December 2008.

[7] P. Ferrari, A. Flammini, D. Marioli, and A. Taroni, "A distributed instrument for performance analysis of real-time ethernet networks," *IEEE Transactions on Industrial Informatics*, vol. 4, no. 1, Article ID 4475682, pp. 16–25, 2008.

[8] R. Ben-El-Kezadri and G. Pau, "TimeRemap: stable and accurate time in vehicular networks," *IEEE Communications Magazine*, vol. 48, no. 12, Article ID 5673072, pp. 52–57, 2010.

[9] P. Loschmidt, R. Exel, A. Nagy, and G. Gaderer, "Limits of synchronization accuracy using hardware support in IEEE 1588," in *Proceedings of the IEEE International Symposium on Precision Clock Synchronization for Measurement, Control and Communication (ISPCS '08)*, pp. 12–16, Ann Arbor, Mich, USA, 2008.

[10] D. Rosselot, "Application Note: DP83848 and DP83849 100Mb Data Latency," Tech. Rep. 1507, National Semiconductor, Santa Clara, Calif, USA, 2006.

[11] P. Loschmidt, *On enhanced clock synchronization performance through dedicated ethernet hardware support*, Ph.D. dissertation, Vienna University of Technology, Vienna, Austria, 2010.

[12] R. Exel and P. Loschmidt, "High accurate timestamping by phase and frequency estimation," in *Proceedings of the International IEEE Symposium on Precision Clock Synchronization for Measurement, Control and Communication (ISPCS '09)*, pp. 126–131, Brescia, Italy, October 2009.

[13] (2011, Mar) PLL Clock Management Features in Altera FPGAs. Altera Corporation, http://www.altera.com/support/devices/pll_clock/pll-overview.html.

[14] J. Kalisz, R. Szplet, J. Pasierbinski, and A. Poniecki, "Field-programmable-gate-array-based time-to-digital converter with 200-ps resolution," *IEEE Transactions on Instrumentation and Measurement*, vol. 46, no. 1, pp. 51–55, 1997.

[15] R. Szplet, J. Kalisz, and R. Szymanowski, "Interpolating time counter with 100 ps resolution on a single FPGA device," *IEEE Transactions on Instrumentation and Measurement*, vol. 49, no. 4, pp. 879–883, 2000.

[16] B. Amrutur, P. K. Das, and R. Vasudevamurthy, "0.84 ps Resolution clock skew measurement via subsampling," *IEEE Transactions on Very Large Scale Integration (VLSI) Systems*, pp. 1–9, 2010.

[17] X. Zhu, G. Sun, S. Yong, and Z. Zhuang, "A high-precision time interval measurement method using phase-estimation algorithm," *IEEE Transactions on Instrumentation and Measurement*, vol. 57, no. 11, pp. 2670–2676, 2008.

[18] S. M. Kay, *Fundamentals of Statistical Signal Processing*, vol. 1 of *Estimation Theory*, Prentice Hall, New York, NY, USA, 1993.

[19] X. Dai and I. H. R. Gretsch, "Quasi-synchronous sampling algorithm and its applications," *IEEE Transactions on Instrumentation and Measurement*, vol. 43, no. 2, pp. 204–209, 1994.

[20] D. W. Allan, "Time and frequency (time-domain) characterization, estimation, and prediction of precision clocks and oscillators," *IEEE Transactions on Ultrasonics, Ferroelectrics, and Frequency Control*, vol. 34, no. 6, pp. 647–654, 1988.

[21] "IEEE Std. 1588–2002 IEEE standard for a precision clock synchronization protocol for networked measurement and control systems," in *Proceedings of the IEEE Standards Interpretations for IEEE Std 1588–2002*, pp. i–144, Piscataway, NJ, USA, November 2002, replaced by 61588-2004.

8

Cognitive Scout Node for Communication in Disaster Scenarios

Rajesh K. Sharma,[1] Anastasia Lavrenko,[1] Dirk Kolb,[2] and Reiner S. Thomä[1]

[1] International Graduate School on Mobile Communications, Ilmenau University of Technology, Helmholtzplatz 2,
 98684 Ilmenau, Germany
[2] Reconnaissance Research & Development (RRD) Division, MEDAV GmbH, Gräfenberger Straße 32-34, 91080 Uttenreuth, Germany

Correspondence should be addressed to Rajesh K. Sharma, rajesh-kumar.sharma@tu-ilmenau.de

Academic Editor: Enrico Del Re

The cognitive radio (CR) concept has appeared as a promising technology to cope with the spectrum scarcity caused by increased spectrum demand due to the emergence of new applications. CR can be an appropriate mean to establish self-organization and situation awareness at the radio interface, which is highly desired to manage unexpected situations that may happen in a disaster scenario. The scout node proposed in this paper is an extended concept based on a powerful CR node in a heterogeneous nodes environment which takes a leading role for highly flexible, fast, and robust establishment of cooperative wireless links in a disaster situation. This node should have two components: one is a passive sensor unit that collects and stores the technical knowledge about the electromagnetic environment in a data processing unit so-called "radio environment map" in the form of a dynamically updated database, and other is an active transceiver unit which can automatically be configured either as a secondary node for opportunistic communication or as a cooperative base station or access point for primary network in emergency communications. Scout solution can be viable by taking advantage of the technologies used by existing radio surveillance systems in the context of CR.

1. Introduction

Communication has been an indispensable part of everyday life in the present days. Apart from making the general life better, modern communications should also be applicable for relief and support to the victims of exceptional adverse situations which include disaster scenarios like earthquakes, floods, cyclones, forest fires and terrorist attacks. Such scenarios impose new requirements on the communication systems. Some of the tasks of a cognitive radio network for emergency situations may be (1) to support specific service requests (higher traffic, coverage, localization, emergency messages, etc.), (2) to re-establish communications in a short time, and (3) to assist rescue forces communications and provide interoperability among them and also among rescue forces and public network.

One of the first tasks in disaster is to organize rescue operations in a quick and efficient manner which as well requires rescue forces to be provided with reliable and stable communication facilities. One of the common problems here is providing interoperability among rescue responders originally using different communication standards [1, 2]. In terms of public communication systems, obvious problems in such scenarios are capacity overload with the resulting service denial and absence of coverage in some areas. Whereas the communication capabilities are in higher demand both for rescue responders and public users, the situation gets worse since the communication infrastructure may be fully or partially destroyed. Repairing the original network in a conventional way is time consuming and is not a correct measure in an exceptional situation. In such scenarios actual needs and requirements for communications can vary significantly depending on the scale of the disaster, place, and time elapsed since the beginning of the event. Therefore, a flexible and intelligent communication system which is aware of the situation and gets self-organized and adapted to the current operational demands is highly beneficial to deal with an unpredictable and time-varying situation. Naturally, cognitive radio (CR) capabilities seem to be highly potential for these purposes.

Cognitive radio (CR) has been considered as a technology for increasing spectral efficiency in wireless communications systems, by having sophisticated radios that can sense and take advantage of spectral opportunities [3]. Unlicensed CR users adaptively adjust radio parameters to the network environment, resulting in improved spectral efficiency. Cognitive radios (referred to as secondary users) may temporarily use spectrum as long as they do not interfere with primary users (PUs) that own the license to that spectrum. Although CR is often considered solely in terms of the use of temporary "white spaces" in the given frequency range detected by a secondary system, its capabilities can be useful for many other applications. Recently, several additional applications of CR have been investigated. For example, in [1], the application of CR for public safety along with other emerging applications has been discussed. The authors have also raised the related standardization issues for a CR technology to support such emerging applications. In [2], CR has been considered as an appropriate solution to the problems of public safety and emergency case communications, especially those related to interoperability issues.

If we consider exploiting CR in the disaster situation we need to address, however, a much broader and more exceptional problem area where the postdisaster unpredictable situation and its solution is needed to be taken into account. This includes analysis of the situation and reaction according to the current needs and priorities. Different levels of possible support should be envisaged: from providing additional services for local groups of users to establishing cooperation between the secondary and the primary system [4, 5]. This results in a very broad range of requirements for the CR node. Therefore, the secondary node must be equipped with strong cognitive abilities to explore the situation, identify the available resources, and act according to the current need.

To utilize CR capabilities efficiently for an adequate and timely assistance in disaster situation, there is a need for obtaining relevant information on the service or system which requires support. For instance, to provide interoperability to the various emergency responders information on their modes of operation must be available which is not always a case especially in the presence of the forces subordinate to the different departments. In case of partial damage of the existing system infrastructure, there might be a need of support for its re-establishment which as well requires information on the system's operational parameters, capabilities, and current needs which demands increased cost and complexity. Here, the advantage can be taken from the current developments in the radio surveillance systems which basically solve similar problems but for different goals. Although the increased cost and complexity for advanced capabilities may not be justifiable for all of the secondary nodes, this can be justifiable for a single powerful node in the network which can assist other nodes for the improved performance.

In this paper, we propose a concept of a powerful cognitive node having extended capabilities which coexists in a network, where heterogeneous primary as well as secondary cognitive radios are in operation. This proposed node is different from other nodes in its features and missions. Firstly, it has more advanced sensing, signal processing capabilities, and additional flexibility in terms of mobility which are not available in normal cognitive nodes. Secondly, in the case of exceptional situation it gets self-organized in the system which needs support and provides some emergency services or reinforce affected services. Thirdly, during normal operation scenario it works as a secondary user (SU) in CR system making the cognitive communication more efficient and reliable avoiding interference to the primary system. The requirements of such node, its operating modes, its application scenarios, and research components for its design and development are discussed in this paper. The proposed system is found to have remarkable similarities with radio surveillance system; therefore, it can take the advantage of the later in several aspects. Note that the principal goal of such a node is an altruistic (cooperative) support in the disaster scenario rather than spectrum efficiency and throughput as it is considered in normal situations. Due to its foremost function of reconnaissance and observation in the radio environment, this node will be termed "scout" in this paper.

The remainder of the paper is organized as follows. Section 2 provides the general concept overview of the scout including its applications, operating scenarios and modes, and requirements. Section 3 discusses several issues and solutions for the most important task, the resource estimation and awareness, of the scout. Scout design and implementation issues are discussed in Section 4. Section 5 discusses briefly the current developments and operational issues in radio surveillance system from which scout can take advantage in terms of signal intelligence for its viability. Finally, the concluding remarks are given in Section 6.

2. Scout System Concept

Since one of the main aims of the cognitive radio node with extended capabilities is scouting-related radio resources, it is proposed here to call it "scout." The resources consist of radio spectrum resources that may be available in several dimensions like frequency, time, code, space, direction, polarization as well as the radio network infrastructure. The scout needs global information about radio resources for centralized decision to be taken by it and to act globally in the network. Some of the important global information related to radio resources include information about the primary systems and their modes of operation, unused frequency bands, the spatial and temporal statistics of its use, the distribution of the available nodes of the primary and secondary (CR) network, propagation characteristics in the primary and secondary network, and so forth. Although the need for knowing so many details about the primary system is unusual form the viewpoint of conventional (opportunistic) CR, it is important for scout since the "cooperative CR" vision is to be addressed by it. All the collected information must be stored in a database which in the literature is commonly referred to as a radio environment map (REM) [6].

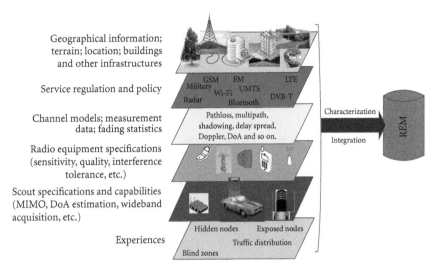

Geographical information;
terrain; location; buildings
and other infrastructures

Service regulation and policy

Channel models; measurement
data; fading statistics

Radio equipment specifications
(sensitivity, quality, interference
tolerance, etc.)

Scout specifications and capabilities
(MIMO, DoA estimation, wideband
acquisition, etc.)

Experiences

FIGURE 1: A REM obtained by integrating various databases (modified from [6]).

Radio environment map (REM) is an abstraction of real-world radio scenarios. It is an integrated spatiotemporal database which characterizes the radio environment of cognitive radios in multiple domains. It can be exploited to support cognitive functionality of the user equipment, even if the subscriber unit is relatively simple [6]. The illustration of how a REM is obtained from various information sources is shown in Figure 1. REM is assigned a central role in scout because different classes of collected sensor data (e.g., from the spectrum analysis and the physical layer analysis) and a priori knowledge are kept updated in it. It means that it consists of static and dynamic as well as temporally and spatially varying information in a well-managed form.

The cognitive engine is the brain of the CR system which executes a set of nested loops constituting a cognition cycle, drawing on experience and stored knowledge in REM to optimize a set of user-chosen quality-of-service measures [7]. Naturally, the scout must also be equipped with a more powerful cognitive engine than other CR nodes because it may need higher processing power for sensor signal data reduction or compression using relatively large database from the REM as well as real observation during its operation. Since it should be a more strategic database-supported planning tool having situation awareness, it is something more than a simple cognitive engine and we can better term it as "cognitive planning tool."

The scout needs to take cognitive decision for its "act" phase which may be either a cooperation to the primary system or secondary communication according to its mission plan. Based on the sensing data, the a priori knowledge to the environment, the situation based on REM analysis, and agreed requirements the cognitive planning tool of the mobile scout provides the local decision as well as the decision based on the global (network-based) data processing in the heterogeneous nodes environment. Cognitive planning tool, which employs artificial intelligent (AI) techniques for cognitive mission control [8], has well defined cognitive control and decision rules, with the prioritization, classification, and consideration of various application requirements (disaster or mass event scenarios, etc.). It implements the duties of a mission control for the scout and also interacts with sensing and detection unit for learning.

During the operation of the network, the tasks (mission) of the scout could change and adapt according to the network status. While its first mission will be dominated by the simple exploration of the environment for supporting network establishment, the scout in later stages can switch to either altruistic or opportunistic communication mode in the network operation. A simple functional architecture of scout is shown in Figure 2(a), which is also expressed in the form of a scout cycle as shown in Figure 2(b) derived from a classical cognitive radio cycle [3].

Since scouts are envisaged to be powerful and versatile nodes working in a partially destroyed infrastructure primary network as well as a centralized/distributed secondary network, they should be able to estimate the resource, support the primary communication as an altruistic node in the form of relay nodes as well as communicate as secondary cognitive nodes in an opportunistic manner. The operation of the scout consists of two parts: one is the "observation and awareness" which is the task of collecting information from radio environment and storing it in REM. This can be also termed the scout mode of operation. The another operation is the "planning, deciding, and acting" by the scout which further results in two different roles to be played by it, based on which this operation can be classified into two modes: (1) altruistic support for primary communication as a relay node and (2) secondary opportunistic communication. These two operating modes can be seen in Figures 3(a) and 3(b), respectively. It is apparent that the node requires to possess high level of reconfigurability in order to be able to operate in both of these modes.

In the altruistic communication mode, scout communicates to the primary network based on the collected information by it. It discovers the network status and

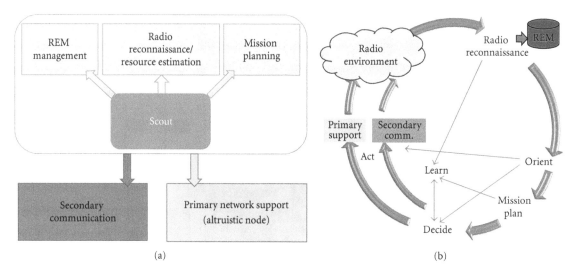

FIGURE 2: (a) A functional architecture of the scout and (b) a simple scout cycle of operation.

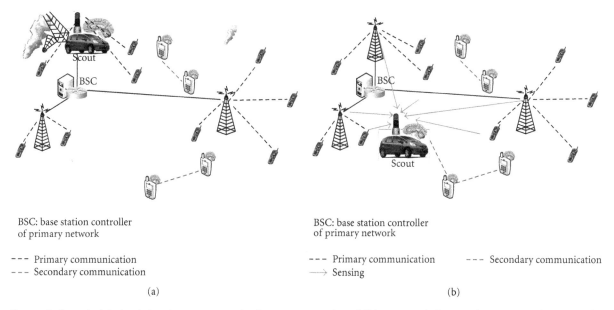

FIGURE 3: Scout in (a) altruistic primary communication support mode and (b) opportunistic secondary communication mode.

identifies the location of the failure. It gets self-organized itself in the primary network as a communication node and, even possibly, replaces the failed node and takes its role. This mode of operation requires signalling and synchronization issues to be resolved, and it poses highly sophisticated system requirements.

In the secondary opportunistic communication mode, the scout behaves simply as a CR node, but due to its extended capabilities it can contribute significantly more than other nodes for filling the REM whose information can be provided to other CR nodes in the network. Thus, it can support SU CR nodes which may have very limited sensing capabilities by giving valuable advice for radio resource access.

3. Resource Estimation Capabilities of Scout

Resource estimation is the first and the most important part of the scout task. Since the very exceptional operational conditions are considered, all the available equipment capabilities should be used in order to achieve the most robust and reliable estimation to ensure that resources would be fully and efficiently exploited in all the possible dimensions like spectrum, direction, location, and time. There may be different requirements for estimation depending upon the action to be taken by the scout. If the PU is observed for the purpose of secondary communication, the identification of white spaces may be sufficient. If the purpose of estimation is to help the victim users in primary system, the scout has

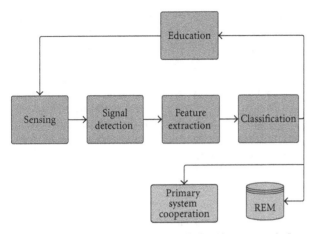

FIGURE 4: PHY mode identification and classification work-flow.

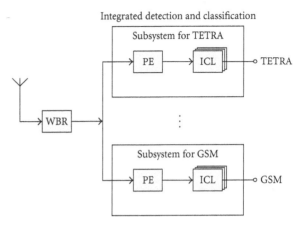

FIGURE 5: Processing chain with a common wideband receiver (WBR), transmission class-specific subsystems for pattern extraction (PE) and for integrated detection and classification (ICL).

to find out what the primary users need and what physical layer (PHY) signalling they can accept. PU PHY mode identification and classification (from finite sets) is, therefore, essentially required especially for the second purpose. This includes detection of primary and/or secondary users and identification of their operational parameters. Here, one of the core tasks to perform is signal classification which could be implemented on the basis of pattern recognition theory using specific signal features of the considered communication standard. Features could characterize frequency domain like central frequency, bandwidth of a signal, frequency hopping pattern and/or time domain like waveform, and signal duration. A simple block diagram showing the work-flow for PHY mode identification is shown in Figure 4.

Another possible estimation object is temporary statistics of primary and/or secondary users. To make the sensing and identification easy and reliable for the future events, the estimation of PU and SU statistics and storing the data in REM is important. It could involve time, frequency, and space domains as well as primary network state estimation, traffic estimation, and so forth. Some statistics is to be obtained from the measurements using the scout node itself. However, many background data including geographical information, terrain, buildings, service regulation, and so forth, provide additional valuable information for the estimation of primary user statistics. This information could be used as a base for prediction of the network status, choice of the secondary network PHY mode, and compiling higher level network protocols.

3.1. Advanced Spectrum Sensing. Some existing spectrum sensing techniques are matched filtering, waveform-based sensing [9], cyclostationary-based sensing [10–12], energy detection (ED) [13–16], autocorrelation-based sensing [17, 18], sample covariance-based detection [19], and cepstral-based detection [20, 21].

For scout, it is mandatory to select the most reliable combination of features to handle the current radio scenarios successfully and to decrease the probability of errors. Talking about the combination of spectrum sensing together with REM, the question whether it is a good idea to use the

information of the current radio environment to ease the processing always appears. If this information is used to support spectrum sensing, one should keep in mind that the radio scenario changes over time and location. Thus, it is mandatory that the spectrum sensing is updated automatically to fit to the current REM. Due to the fact that in some cases a priori information can be accessed and applied easily, however, in other cases the opposite happens as the current a priori information becomes irrelevant due to the new requirements. Nevertheless, for the operator of the scout, it is not obvious which kind of sensing technique is the best for a given radio scenario. So, the goal is to make the decision to choose the sensing features as automatically as possible.

If the scout starts in a new environment with noneducated sensing and PHY identification, it can later switch to educated sensing which not only makes the sensing easier but also enhance the sensing performance. This is actually the simple and straightforward application of cognitive principle which involves learning, cognition, and then educating other nodes.

In [21], a new sensing approach has been introduced where the main idea is to combine modern object detection techniques with new upcoming ideas from CR. By doing, this it was possible to combine different sensing approaches in such a way that a highly robust and real-time capable system for radio signal detection and classification emerged. The decision which sensing approach fits to the defined requirements was done automatically based on the current radio scenario or rather the current REM. Figure 5 shows the structure of the new system. It contains several subsystems for classification which are adapted to the radio standards of interest. This allows the operator of the scout to focus on updating the REM and not to spend too many efforts in trying to set up a spectrum sensing manually. In such case the sensing can be robust, fast, and reliable compared to the uneducated (blind) sensing. The neighbouring nodes with reduced sensing capabilities also can take advantage from the sensing decision of the scout.

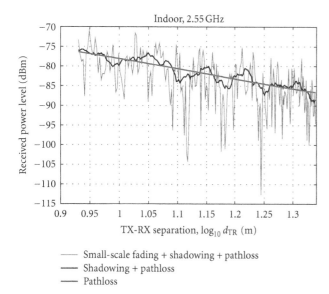

FIGURE 6: The received power in an indoor environment showing the effect of small-scale fading, shadowing, and pathloss.

3.2. Estimation of Channel Statistics.

Since the sensing and estimation procedures all rely on the signals obtained from the sources in the environment, the reliability of the estimation from the received signal parameter depends upon the accuracy in the predicted channel parameters at the given location. The channel parameters of high importance are pathloss, small-scale fading parameters, and large-scale fading (shadowing) statistics. These parameters are illustrated in Figure 6 which is based on the real measurement in an indoor environment. Apart from these parameters delay spread based on power delay profile, Doppler spread, angle of arrival, and so forth in the given environment are the parameters to be estimated and stored in REM. Since exceptional disaster scenario is to be considered, the channel statistics and models used in the normal situation may not be applicable in this situation. Therefore, a realistic assumption of the channel statistics in disaster scenario is needed especially for initial attempts of estimation. Later, estimation of channel statistics based on current measurement results and the resource estimation and identification based on those new statistics will make the system highly reliable.

A main challenge in spectrum sensing and estimation arises due to hidden node problem. The hidden node problem can be caused by many factors including severe multipath fading or shadowing that secondary users observe while scanning PU transmissions. Here, the CR device causes unwanted interference to the PU (receiver) as the primary transmitter's signal could not be detected because of the positioning of devices in space. Since the hidden node problem arises due to the channel fading, the correct statistics of the fading in the radio environment helps to identify the hidden nodes. Channel statistics should be estimated by using PU and SU nodes as excitation signal sources.

It is important to note that fading goes along with other channel statistics, for example, angular spread and effective channel rank. So although knowledge about fading may be enough to explain the hidden node problem and to decide about channel availability for secondary communication, it will be not enough to assess the antennas influence and decide the optimum transmission mode including MIMO multiplexing versus diversity, beamforming, coding, and so forth. The small-as well as large-scale statistics are essential for cognitive link adaptation. In distributed and heterogeneous network, a cooperative link statistics are needed for the effective link and relay node implementation. For fulfilling these requirements, we should know more parameters and statistics related to the channel for the scout operation.

3.3. Tracking and Data Fusion.

To use the information potential of the scout system in various decision tasks, the continuously collected data must not overwhelm the system. Instead, the data are to be condensed (fused) in such a way that high-quality information results serving as a basis for decision support in particular applications and on all levels of hierarchy [22].

Data fusion can also help to combine heterogeneous information having different types, sources, qualities, and so forth. It can help weight the quality and importance of information and help to handle incomplete and unreliable information. Data fusion is a very well-known method for the improvement of sensing performance. There might be different levels or layers of data fusion: from decision level that combines measured values(sensor decisions) [23] up to level where mostly data are retrieved, categorized, combined, and so forth [24].

Knowledge-based systems (KBS) can interpret the fusion results by considering and analysing issues such as the context in which the data are observed, the relationship among observed entitles, hierarchical groupings of targets or objects, and predictions of future actions of targets or entities [24]. Key issues for developing such a system include the creation of the knowledge base. Since the scout is a cognitive node equipped with a dynamically updated database (REM) and cognitive mission control unit, it can perform the knowledge-based data fusion for the better performance.

Fusion of sensor data may be utilized in different cases: data produced at different instants of time (i.e., target tracking), data being collected from different sensor sources, data with background information on the sensor performance as well as data with nonsensor context information [22]. Since scout is a single node, it can perform data fusion based on the information it collects at different instants of its movement (different locations) with a proper source tracking. If distributed nodes provide their local sensing results to the scout, it can also perform decision fusion based on the sensing results of the distributed nodes and its own sequential observations. And, as a consequence, the scout can plan its mission, which includes not only the choice of the track, to maximize its performance.

3.4. Information Compression (Compressive Sensing).

It is a known fact from the success of lossy compression that most of the data we acquire are not important and do not cause the

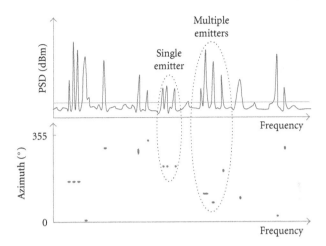

FIGURE 7: An example of data fusion between spectral and DoA information.

loss in information when they are discarded. If the sensing is performed just to acquire the important information, it makes the system efficient in the management of data. Practically, that might be the only possibility to handle the sensing process and to handle the huge amount of data.

There has been a significant research in the field of compressed sensing in the last few years. Compressed data acquisition protocols directly acquiring just the important information about the compressible signals have been proposed [25]. This sensing principle might enhance the sensing performance dramatically with reduced measurement time, reduced sampling rates, or reduced analog-to-digital (ADC) converter resources requirements [25].

A compressive sensing method capturing and representing compressible signals at a rate significantly below the Nyquist rate has been proposed in [26]. This method employs nonadaptive linear projections that preserve the structure of the signal. The signal is reconstructed from these projections using an optimization process. In [27], a Bayesian formalism has been employed for estimating the underlying signal based on compressive-sensing measurements. This framework has been utilized for CR primary user detection in [28], achieving the sampling reduction advantage with significantly less computational complexity.

Information compression using compressed sensing can play a significant role in scout performance by making the sensing more efficient and effective, whereas the REM remains efficient by storing compressed sensing data. Compression seems to be a solution to better exploit the limited hardware capabilities in terms of spectral coverage and speed, and also in terms of the required capacity of the data link to the fusion center.

4. Scout Design and Implementation Issues

The first task of the scout is to explore the spectral environment. The node should be compact enough for field operations on a mobile platform, for instance, a car.

Accordingly, the requirements include the selection of appropriate algorithms for signal analysis and signal estimation, appropriate platforms and approaches for implementation procedures. The appropriate methods of information fusion and database programming are to be used to establish the REM.

The important requirements in the implementation of scout include coherent multichannel receivers with wideband fast sensing capabilities. The antenna and bandwidth requirements are some of the key issues to be considered. Quality of service (QoS) and security issues are also important. Some of these issues are discussed here.

4.1. Antenna Requirements. From implementation point of view one of the important system parts required to perform estimation tasks discussed in Section 3 is wideband and/or tunable directional antennas which can gather information about spectrum resource in different directions for the given geographic location. Antenna arrays having direction-of-arrival (DoA) estimation capability makes the scout much more powerful than having a single antenna for both altruistic and opportunistic modes of operation. Direction finding is important for scout because it provides a bearing for a detected signal allowing to focus on a target area rather than random detection under the unknown resource distribution. It may be considered as a prerequisite for localization of a node. It makes possibility of tracking the target and allows intelligence fusion with other sensor data. By jointly exploiting spectrum and azimuth information, a more reliable automated emitter detection in dense scenarios becomes possible. For example, the spectral information combined with DoA information can distinguish between single emitter and multiple emitters along with their directions over a given frequency band as illustrated in Figure 7. It also provides SNR gain for the detection of weak signals. Separation of multiple stations for certain signal types is possible by direction finding. Additionally, high-resolution direction finding algorithms allow separation of multiple cochannel signals in the radio environment. Location and direction finding methods have been studied for long time [29, 30]; however robust, fast, simple, and highly accurate algorithms are still interesting topics for today's research [31].

Although both beamforming and high-resolution DoA estimation are important for scout, they are different from each other. The beamforming gain in the former is strictly coupled to the size of the array. The latter can achieve high resolution performance in case of high SNR and precise antenna calibration. The requirements (and pitfalls) are described in [32].

The DoA estimation is possible with wideband array capability which makes scout more expensive and heavy. DoA estimation makes possibility of exploiting spatial dimension (direction) as an additional radio resource. Larger bandwidth, big antenna arrays, and multichannel receivers are needed for this purpose, which is a considerable effort in terms of cost and complexity. Adaptive beamforming [33], which requires also antenna arrays can be used by the node to control and avoid interference so that coexistence of primary and secondary network can be possible. Opportunistic antenna selection using orthogonal radiation patterns and/or polarization can be possible with small antenna arrays, but they have limited direction finding capability. Although such wideband array equipment may cost more than a base station today, there have already been many efforts to get cheaper equipment in radio surveillance community with a fast technological progress. Since the scout concept is for tomorrow's technology, its use in exceptional situations will be certainly feasible both technically and economically.

4.2. Frequency and Bandwidth Related Issues. Bandwidth requirement of antennas depends upon the specific task to be performed by the scout. During the sensing and reconnaissance phase, very wideband antenna or multiband antennas which consist of several antennas for the different frequency bands to scan the whole available bands may be highly desirable. However, for the communication phase, narrower band antenna to filter unwanted signals may be required. Reconfigurable antenna seems to be highly useful whose radiation pattern (direction; beamwidth) and bandwidth versus gain characteristics play an important role in the performance of the device.

The size of the antenna needed for scout operation depends upon the frequency band it is used for. Sometimes the antennas look large physically, but are small electrically. For example, if we talk about a wideband antenna in 60 GHz band, the size will be small making the scout simple to implement. However, when lower VHF/UHF bands are considered, physically large antennas will be required, and obtaining same bandwidth will be also more difficult. Designing wideband antennas in these bands need more weight and space for scout device.

In general, the lowest frequency of operation determines the antenna size. Sometimes we can use antennas that are electrically small, for example, for DoA resolution, which might work reasonably, but price that we have to pay is the reduced gain. This is a typical option for lower frequency. Fortunately, in this case the gain disadvantage can be partly compensated by lower free space attenuation. But there is always a compromise between gain, DoA resolution, and antenna array size which is influenced by platform size. Since the application of scout is broad, the use of narrowband and wideband as well as small and large antennas should be considered while designing the system.

4.3. Quality-of-Service Issues. For the application scenarios discussed in Section 2, different quality-of-service (QoS) requirements are to be satisfied by the scout node. In opportunistic communication mode, the scout working as a conventional CR must satisfy the interference constraint to the primary users. It must be able to serve for both real-time and best-effort traffic with the desired data rate and delay. Since there are different applications demanding large variation of capacity and delay requirements, cognitive engine should be able to make optimal transmission decision for the opportunistic communication.

The QoS requirements for altruistic communication mode are even more wider. For example, in one case, the scout acting as an altruistic node may need to establish a backbone connection to a local network of some users to get them connected to the public network. In the other extreme case, there may be a situation where it is necessary to reach a single user in a large distance. So, depending upon the user distribution and the radio environment there will be a much wider scope of QoS requirements to be fulfilled as compared to the regular networks. This requires high flexibility in the capability of scout node in terms of coverage, throughput, latency, reliability, and so forth. Since the QoS requirements may be interdependent, the choice of optimal parameters for the communication is important, which is to be performed by the cognitive planning tool. For example, choice of a frequency band will have influence on coverage (e.g., lower frequency can be used to reach distant users or to broadcast short messages, whereas higher frequencies are to be used to satisfy the high data rate demand in shorter distances). Beamforming versus multiplexing MIMO can be used to trade-off between coverage and capacity.

4.4. Security Issues. It is a well-known fact that there are malicious organizations that can attempt interception of the signals to and from the scout and make it to take incorrect decision in its mission. Any information flaw may result with harmful effect in the scene instead of fulfilling the desired goals. Therefore, it is crucial that the over the air information should be secure, which adds more challenge in the implementation. Although a detailed study on addressing the security issues on scout is important, it is not discussed here since it is beyond the scope of this paper.

5. Current Developments in Signal Intelligence and Scout Viability

Although the scout node discussed in this paper is a new concept, there are already technological achievements to serve a base for the scout development, especially in the radio surveillance applications. Also, the capabilities mentioned in Section 3 are expected to be achieved in the near future as many researches are focussed on these areas in cognitive radio perspectives.

Since to know what is on air has always been of strong interest, this noncivil market of radio surveillance can look back on a long development of several decades. A typical radio surveillance system consists of one or several wideband receivers, digital signal processing units, and some postprocessing systems. Dependent on the task of such a system, different capabilities, for example, radio signal detection and classification; direction or location finding, can be enabled. Ongoing developments show that especially the tactical systems for direction or location finding get smaller and consume less power which is ideal for vehicle-based missions. To fulfil a radio surveillance task, high flexibility of the applied system is necessary. It can happen that the mission details, for example, a priori information regarding occupied frequencies, radio services and networks,

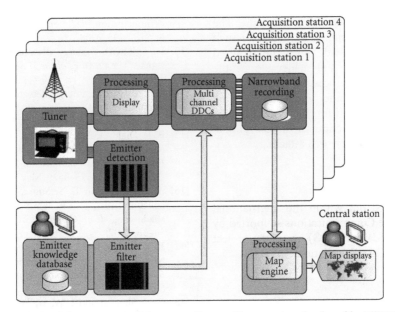

FIGURE 8: Multisensor setup of the new radio surveillance system developed by MEDAV.

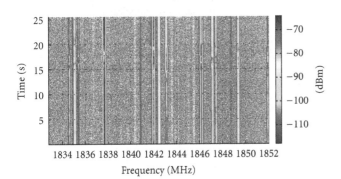

FIGURE 9: Spectrogram obtained by the wideband receiver IZT R3200 in GSM-1800 downlink.

and their assumed locations change over time, frequency, and especially over location. In case of a dislocation of a radio surveillance system, there is a high probability that new radio standards of interest appear. Thus, every stage of the processing chain, for example, the signal detection and classification, should be adaptable to new radio scenarios. It is obvious that the systems for radio surveillance are technically similar to the scout, which is proposed. In addition to the technical conformities, there are a lot of common aspects regarding the mission process itself. In sum, it would be a good idea to combine the knowledge gained from radio surveillance and the ideas of the research areas like cognitive radio in order to create smarter solutions.

As an example, a new system of MEDAV [34] for monitoring of fast changing radio scenarios contains tools for mission planning, sensor controlling, and real-time situation pictures. With this software it is possible to control and task not only the proposed direction finding (DF) system but also other sensor types. The modular concept allows to do most of the signal processing, for example, radio signal

detection and classification, within the scout and to gather the resulting information in the fusion center to combine it with information coming from other sensors. The focus of the system is on mobile sensors with robust data links and low data rates between the sensor and the fusion center. Thus, it is a perfect basis for the proposed scout concept. Figure 8 shows the structure of a multisensor setup.

Keeping most of the signal processing and analysis in the software, antenna and radio front-end characteristics, however, still play a key role imposing the strongest restrictions on the overall sensing capabilities of scout. Since the main objective of scout is the assessment of the radio environment, one of the important aspects for its viability is existence of appropriate receivers. Currently, there are already some solutions available on the market which could be suitable for the scout design. For instance, digital wideband receiver R3200 developed by IZT GmbH [35] can cover frequency range from 9 kHz to 18 GHz with the maximum real-time instantaneous bandwidth of 19.2 MHz for I/Q baseband data. As an example, a spectrogram which is obtained by this receiver in an indoor location is shown in Figure 9, which gives a clear picture of the instantaneous user activity in GSM-1800 downlink.

Since the radio surveillance systems for small-sized vehicular platform are already available in the market [34, 36, 37], scout can take advantage from the technology used by these systems with the addition or enhancement of the capabilities in resource estimation as discussed in Section 3, including a full-fledged REM, and also addressing the issues mentioned in Section 4.

6. Conclusion

In this paper, we have discussed an extended concept based on cognitive radio which can be used as a secondary communication as well as a cooperative (altruistic) node for partially destroyed primary network infrastructure. The different requirements and implementation issues for such a node (scout) have been discussed. Since the required functionalities are advanced but still achievable in the present day of very high speed processors as well as the storage devices, a special cognitive node with such advanced features can be a highly useful and feasible system for the communication support to the victims in the exceptional situations including disasters and terrorist attacks.

Acknowledgments

This work has been carried out within the International Graduate School on Mobile Communications supported by the German Research Foundation (DFG) under the project "GRK 1487," and the Carl-Zeiss Foundation.

References

[1] J. Wang, M. Ghosh, and K. Challapali, "Emerging cognitive radio applications: a survey," *IEEE Communications Magazine*, vol. 49, no. 3, pp. 74–81, 2011.

[2] A. Gorcin and H. Arslan, "Public safety and emergency case communications: opportunities from the aspect of cognitive radio," in *Proceedings of the 3rd IEEE Symposium on New Frontiers in Dynamic Spectrum Access Networks (DySPAN '08)*, pp. 1–10, October 2008.

[3] J. Mitola and G. Q. Maguire Jr., "Cognitive radio: making software radios more personal," *IEEE Personal Communications*, vol. 6, no. 4, pp. 13–18, 1999.

[4] Use Cases for Cognitive Applications in Public Safety Communications Systems—Volume 1: Review of the 7 July Bombing of the London Underground, Wireless Innovation Forum, 2007, http://groups.winnforum.org/d/do/1565.

[5] Use Cases for Cognitive Applications in Public Safety Communications Systems Volume 2, Chemical Plant Explosion Scenario, Wireless Innovation Forum, 2010, http://groups.winnforum.org/d/do/2325.

[6] Y. Zhao, J. H. Reed, S. Mao, and K. K. Bae, "Overhead analysis for radio environment mapenabled cognitive radio networks," in *Proceedings of the 1st IEEE Workshop on Networking Technologies for Software Defined Radio Networks (SDR '06)*, pp. 18–25, September 2006.

[7] B. Le, T. W. Rondeau, and C. W. Bostian, "Cognitive radio realities," *Wireless Communications and Mobile Computing*, vol. 7, no. 9, Article ID 129497, pp. 1037–1048, 2007.

[8] A. He, K. K. Bae, T. R. Newman et al., "A survey of artificial intelligence for cognitive radios," *IEEE Transactions on Vehicular Technology*, vol. 59, no. 4, pp. 1578–1592, 2010.

[9] A. Sahai, R. Tandra, S. M. Mishra, and N. Hoven, "Fundamental design tradeoffs in cognitive radio systems," in *Proceedings of the 1st International Workshop on Technology and Policy for Accessing Spectrum (TAPAS '06)*, August 2006.

[10] M. Öner and F. Jondral, "Cyclostationarity based air interface recognition for software radio systems," in *Proceedings of the IEEE Radio and Wireless Conference (RAWCON '04)*, pp. 263–266, September 2004.

[11] R. S. Roberts, W. A. Brown, and H. H. Loomis Jr., "Computationally efficient algorithms for cyclic spectral analysis," *IEEE SP Magazine*, vol. 8, no. 2, pp. 38–49, 1991.

[12] D. Cabric, "Addressing the feasibility of cognitive radios: using testbed implementation and experiments for exploration and demonstration," *IEEE Signal Processing Magazine*, vol. 25, no. 6, pp. 85–93, 2008.

[13] H. Urkowitz, "Energy detection of unknown deterministic signals," *Proceedings of the IEEE*, vol. 55, no. 4, pp. 523–531, 1967.

[14] V. I. Kostylev, "Energy detection of a signal with random amplitude," in *Proceedings of the International Conference on Communications (ICC '02)*, pp. 1606–1610, May 2002.

[15] F. F. Digham, M. S. Alouini, and M. K. Simon, "On the energy detection of unknown signals over fading channels," in *Proceedings of the International Conference on Communications (ICC '03)*, pp. 3575–3579, May 2003.

[16] A. Ghasemi and E. S. Sousa, "Asymptotic performance of collaborative spectrum sensing under correlated log-normal shadowing," *IEEE Communications Letters*, vol. 11, no. 1, pp. 34–36, 2007.

[17] R. K. Sharma and J. W. Wallace, "Improved spectrum sensing by utilizing signal autocorrelation," in *Proceedings of the IEEE 69th Vehicular Technology Conference*, pp. 1–5, Barcelona, Spain, April 2009.

[18] R. K. Sharma and J. W. Wallace, "Correlation-based sensing for cognitive radio networks: bounds and experimental assessment," *IEEE Sensors Journal*, vol. 11, no. 3, pp. 657–666, 2011.

[19] Y. Zeng and Y. C. Liang, "Spectrum-sensing algorithms for cognitive radio based on statistical covariances," *IEEE Transactions on Vehicular Technology*, vol. 58, no. 4, pp. 1804–1815, 2009.

[20] M. Li, V. Rozgić, G. Thatte et al., "Multimodal physical activity recognition by fusing temporal and cepstral information," *IEEE Transactions on Neural Systems and Rehabilitation Engineering*, vol. 18, no. 4, pp. 369–380, 2010.

[21] D. Kolb, U. Uebler, and E. N. Nöth, "A novel transmission scanner framework for real-time applications," in *Proceedings of the RTO-MPIST-092- Military Communications and Networks. NATO Research and Technology Organisations*, 2010.

[22] W. Koch, "On Bayesian tracking and data fusion: a tutorial introduction with examples," *IEEE Aerospace and Electronic Systems Magazine*, vol. 25, no. 7, pp. 29–51, 2010.

[23] Z. Chair and P. K. Varshney, "Optimal data fusion in multiple sensor detection systems," *IEEE Transactions on Aerospace and Electronic Systems*, vol. 22, no. 1, pp. 98–101, 1986.

[24] D. L. Hall and J. Llinas, "An introduction to multisensor data fusion," *Proceedings of the IEEE*, vol. 85, no. 1, pp. 6–23, 1997.

[25] D. L. Donoho, "Compressed sensing," *IEEE Transactions on Information Theory*, vol. 52, no. 4, pp. 1289–1306, 2006.

[26] R. G. Baraniuk, "Compressive sensing," *IEEE Signal Processing Magazine*, vol. 24, no. 4, pp. 118–121, 2007.

[27] S. Ji, Y. Xue, and L. Carin, "Bayesian compressive sensing," *IEEE Transactions on Signal Processing*, vol. 56, no. 6, pp. 2346–2356, 2008.

[28] S. Hong, "Multi-resolution bayesian compressive sensing for cognitive radio primary user detection," in *Proceedings of the 53rd IEEE Global Communications Conference (GLOBECOM '10)*, pp. 1–6, December 2010.

[29] A. J. Berni, "Angle-of-arrival estimation using an adaptive antenna array," *IEEE Transactions on Aerospace and Electronic Systems*, vol. 11, no. 2, pp. 278–284, 1975.

[30] S. S. Reddi, "Multiple source location-a digital approach," *IEEE Transactions on Aerospace and Electronic Systems*, vol. 15, no. 1, pp. 95–105, 1979.

[31] S. D. Blunt, T. Chan, and K. Gerlach, "Robust DOA estimation: the reiterative superresolution (RISR) algorithm," *IEEE Transactions on Aerospace and Electronic Systems*, vol. 47, no. 1, pp. 332–346, 2011.

[32] M. Landmann, M. K. Käske, and R. S. Thomä, "Impact of incomplete and inaccurate data models on high resolution parameter estimation in multidimensional channel sounding," *IEEE Transactions on Antennas and Propagation*, vol. 60, no. 2, pp. 557–573, 2012.

[33] R. M. Radaydeh and M.-S. Alouini, "Impact of co-channel interference on the performance of adaptive generalized transmit beamforming," *IEEE Transactions on Wireless Communications*, vol. 10, no. 8, pp. 2616–2629, 2011.

[34] Radio Monitoring and Surveillance Solutions, MEDAV, 2011, http://www.medav.de/.

[35] IZT R3200 Digital Wideband Receiver, IZT GmbH, 2012, http://www.izt-labs.de/en/products/kategorie/receivers/produkt/izt-r3200-1/.

[36] Radio Surveillance Overview, Synectics, 2011, http://www.synx.com/index.php/Products/radio-surveillance.html.

[37] Radio Surveillance and Intelligence, Morcom, 2011, http://www.morcom.com/.

9

An Approach for Network Outage Detection from Drive-Testing Databases

Jussi Turkka,[1,2] Fedor Chernogorov,[2] Kimmo Brigatti,[2] Tapani Ristaniemi,[2] and Jukka Lempiäinen[1]

[1] *Department of Communications Engineering, Tampere University of Technology, 33720 Tampere, Finland*
[2] *Department of Mathematical Information Technology, University of Jyväskylä, 40014 Jyväskylä, Finland*

Correspondence should be addressed to Jussi Turkka, jussi.turkka@tut.fi

Academic Editor: Sayandev Mukherjee

A data-mining framework for analyzing a cellular network drive testing database is described in this paper. The presented method is designed to detect sleeping base stations, network outage, and change of the dominance areas in a cognitive and self-organizing manner. The essence of the method is to find similarities between periodical network measurements and previously known outage data. For this purpose, diffusion maps dimensionality reduction and nearest neighbor data classification methods are utilized. The method is cognitive because it requires training data for the outage detection. In addition, the method is autonomous because it uses minimization of drive testing (MDT) functionality to gather the training and testing data. Motivation of classifying MDT measurement reports to periodical, handover, and outage categories is to detect areas where periodical reports start to become similar to the outage samples. Moreover, these areas are associated with estimated dominance areas to detected sleeping base stations. In the studied verification case, measurement classification results in an increase of the amount of samples which can be used for detection of performance degradations, and consequently, makes the outage detection faster and more reliable.

1. Introduction

Modern radio access networks (RAN) are complex infrastructures consisting of several overlaying and cooperating networks such as next-generation high-speed-packet-access (HSPA) and long-term evolution (LTE) networks and as such are prone to the impacts of uncertainty on system management and stability. Classical network management is based on a design principle which requires knowledge of the state of all existing entities within the network at all times. This approach has been successfully applied to networks of limited scale but it is foreseen to be insufficient in the management of future complex networks. In order to maintain a massive multivendor and multi-RAN infrastructure in a cost-efficient manner, operators have to employ automated solutions to optimize the most difficult and time-consuming network operation procedures. Self-organizing network concept [1] has emerged in the last years, with the goal to foster automation and to reduce human involvement in management tasks. It implies autonomous configuration, optimization, and healing actions which would result in a reduced operational burden and improve the experienced end user quality-of-service (QoS). One of the downsides of the SON concept is the necessity to gather larger amounts of operational data from user equipment (UE) and different network elements (NE).

To guarantee sufficient coverage and QoS for subscribers in indoor and outdoor environments, mobile operators need to carry out various radio coverage measurements. In the past, manual drive tests have been employed for this purpose. However, there are some challenges and limitations in manual drive testing that could be improved. Firstly, manual drive testing is a resource-consuming task requiring a lot of time, specialized equipment, and the involvement of highly qualified engineers. Secondly, it is impossible to capture the full coverage data from every geographical location by using manual drive testing, since most of the UE generated traffic comes from indoor locations, while drive testing is limited mainly to roads. The cost and reachability limitations of manual drive testing prompts the research towards automated UE-assisted data gathering solutions which can minimize the need for manual drive testing and allow gathering of more comprehensive databases. If UEs measure the radio coverage periodically and provide the measurements together with location and time information to the network, then large radio environment databases with user-perceived coverage experience can be built to support the RAN operation and optimization. However, essential problems with these large databases are the information overflow and a "curse" of dimensionality. Those problems need to be addressed while analyzing and transforming the raw measurement data in these huge operational databases into meaningful information. This paper describes an approach to the above-mentioned problems by proposing a data-mining framework for the analysis of the UE-reported radio measurements. This approach allows the detection of the coverage problems in a cellular network on the basis of learning the network's prior operational behavior. The proposed framework is validated with simulations by using *Renesas Mobile Europe's* state-of-art LTE system simulator to construct large MDT measurement databases.

The article is organized as follows: Section 2 describes the Minimization of Drive Tests concept which can be used to gather and build the UE measurement report databases for HSPA and LTE networks with the focus on coverage aspects. Section 3 describes the data-mining framework which is used for the analysis of the MDT databases, and finally, Section 4 describes simulation scenarios and the performance evaluation results of outage detection caused by a specific type of network failure known as "*sleeping cell.*"

2. Minimization of Drive Tests

Minimization of Drive Testing use cases for self-organizing networks were introduced by the operators alliance Next Generation Mobile Networks (NGMN) during 2008 [2] and at the time of writing this, the MDT solutions are researched by the network vendors and operators in the 3rd Generation Partnership Project (3GPP) [3, 4]. The goal of the MDT research in 3GPP is to define a set of measurements, measurement reporting principles and procedures which would help to collect coverage-related information from UEs. MDT feasibility study phase [3] started at late 2009 and during 2010 it focused on defining the reported measurement entities and MDT use cases for example, coverage optimization and QoS verification. Coverage optimization use case targets for the detection of such network problems as coverage holes, weak coverage, pilot pollution, overshoot coverage, and issues with uplink coverage, as described in [3]. After the feasibility study, the research focused on defining MDT measurement, reporting and configuration schemes for LTE release 10 during 2011 [4]. The MDT measurement and reporting schemes are *immediate MDT* and *logged MDT*. The immediate MDT scheme extends Radio Resource Control (RRC) measurement reporting to include the available location information to the measurement reports for UEs which are in connected mode [4]. In the logged MDT scheme, the UEs can be

configured to collect measurements in idle mode and report the logged data to the network later [4]. After the release 10, the main focus of MDT work will be on enhancements in the availability of the detailed location information and improvements in QoS verification [5].

2.1. MDT Measurement Configuration. MDT measurements can be configured in LTE either by using management based or signaling-based configuration procedures [4, 6]. In the *management-based configuration*, the base stations are responsible for configuring all selected UEs in a particular area to do the immediate or logged MDT measurements [4, 6]. The *signaling-based MDT* is an enhancement to a signaling-based *subscriber and equipment trace* functionality [6] where the MDT data is collected from one specific UE instead of a set of UEs in a particular area. Detailed signaling flows for activating MDT measurements are described in [6].

The MDT measurement functionality allows operators to collect measurements either periodically or at an instance of a trigger such as a network event [3, 4]. The measurement report consists of the available location, time, cell-identification data and radio-measurement data. There are different mechanisms for estimation of user locations. The most coarse location info is the serving Cell Global Identification (CGI) and in the best case the detailed location is obtained from the Global Navigation Satellite System (GNSS). The cell identification info consists of the serving-cell CGI or Physical Cell Identifications (PCI) of the detected neighboring cells. The radio measurements for the serving and neighboring cells include the reference signal received power (RSRP) and reference signal received quality (RSRQ) for LTE system and common pilot channel received signal code power (RSCP) and received signal quality (E_C/N_0) for HSPA system [3, 4].

2.2. Logged MDT. The logged MDT measurement and reporting scheme enables data gathering from the UEs which are camped normally in RRC idle state. The logged MDT configuration is provided to the UEs via RRC signaling while UEs are in RRC connected mode. Logged mode configuration parameters are listed and described with more details in [4]. When the UE moves to the RRC idle state, MDT measurement data that is, time, location info and radio measurements, are logged to UE memory. The network can ask UEs to report the logged data when UE returns back to RRC connected state. Currently there can be only one RAT specific logged MDT configuration per UE which is valid only for the RAN providing the configuration. If an earlier configuration exists it will be replaced by newer one [4]. Since the logged MDT mode is an optional feature for UEs, this paper focuses more on the immediate MDT which will be a tool for operators to gather the measurements from LTE release 10 and onwards.

2.3. Immediate MDT. Immediate MDT is based on the existing RRC measurement procedure with an extension to include the available location information to the measurement reports. LTE release 10 RRC specifications [7] allow

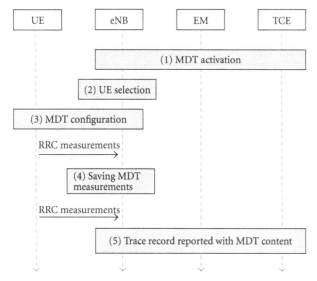

FIGURE 1: Immediate MDT reporting.

operators to configure RRC measurements in a way that RSRP and RSRQ measurements are reported periodically from the serving cell and intrafrequency, interfrequency and inter-RAT neighboring cells with the available location information. The immediate MDT measurement reporting principles are depicted in Figure 1 as described in [6].

Before the immediate MDT reporting can be started, a base station—E-UTRAN NodeB (eNB) is activated and configured to collect immediate MDT measurements. In step 1, an element manager (EM) sends a cell trace session activation request to the eNB including MDT configuration so that the eNB can later report the trace records back to the trace element (TCE). After the cell traffic trace activation, the eNB selects the UEs for MDT while taking into account the user consent that is, users permission for an operator to collect the MDT measurements. The eNB sends the RRC measurement configurations to the selected UEs for example, reporting triggers, intervals, and list of intrafrequency, interfrequency and inter-RAT measurements with a requirement that UEs include the available location information into the measurement reports as specified in the RRC specification information element (IE) *ReportConfigEUTRA* field [7].

When the RRC measurement condition is fulfilled for example, a periodical timer expires or a certain network event occurs, the UE sends available RSRP and RSRQ measurements to the eNB with the available *LocationInfo* IE added to the measurement report [7]. If detailed location information is available, then the latitude and the longitude are included into the measurement report. If the detailed location information is obtained by using GNSS positioning method then the UE shall attach time information to the report as well [4]. This GNSS time information is used to validate the detailed location information. Note that in case of the immediate MDT, the UE does not send the absolute time information as it does in case of logged MDT. The eNB is responsible for adding the time stamp to the received MDT

measurement reports when saving the measurements to the trace record.

2.4. MDT Database. The MDT database is constructed by collecting the MDT measurements from the network. In our study the MDT database consists of periodical measurements, as well as measurements collected at the time instance of A3 (A3 event is E-UTRAN RRC measurement event which triggers when neighboring cell becomes an offset better than the serving cell) events preceding successful intra-LTE handovers (HO) and radio link failures (RLF). It is assumed that each measurement sample in the analyzed database consists of 22 features as described in Table 1.

The MDT measurement samples consist of the latitude, longitude, serving cell, and neighboring cell radio measurements reported by the UE. In addition, time information, serving-cell wideband channel quality indicator (WCQI) and uplink power headroom report (PHR) values were added by the eNB. Moreover, a label of the report condition is always appended to a measurement sample, that is, eNB knows if the MDT data sample is a periodical, A3 event-triggered measurement report or UE RLF report [4]. Currently, the release 10 MDT specifications do not support the feature of collecting detailed location for A3 events. However, this feature is to be included to MDT in release 11. Therefore, the structure of the MDT measurement sample described in Table 1 is assumed to be common for all of these three types of MDT reports.

3. Outage Detection Data-Mining Framework

It is known that the SON framework includes three functionalities, namely self-configuration, self-optimization, and self-healing. Self-configuration is related to the initial steps of the network setup. Self-optimization is concentrated on monitoring the network state and automatic parameter tuning for achievement of the highest possible network performance without compromising the robustness of its operation. In case of a network failure or malfunction, the self-healing tries to autonomously detect problems, diagnose root causes, and compensate or recover from the malfunctioning state back to normal operation. A good example of self-healing is the cell-outage management [8, 9] use case in LTE networks, which aims to improve the offline coverage optimization process by detecting and mitigating outage situations automatically. For this purpose, the self-healing algorithm requires several key performance indicator (KPI) measurements from both eNBs and UEs. The KPIs such as cell load, RLF counters, handover failure rate or, UEs neighboring cell RSRP measurements may be used as indicators of the network outage [8]. In [9], the condition for the outage was based on predefined thresholds of received signal strength and quality. However, deployment of several self-organizing functionalities can increase significantly the number of measured and reported KPIs thus increasing the complexity of the network and SON architectures. This may result in new challenges for network engineers as well. Firstly, high-dimensional KPI databases of network measurements

TABLE 1: Structure of the MDT measurement.

Feature No.	Feature	Description
1	Time	Time stamp
2-3	Location	Latitude and longitude
4	Serving-cell info	CGI
5	RSRP	Serving-cell RSRP in dBm
6	RSRQ	Serving-cell RSRQ in dB
7–13	Three strongest intra-LTE neighbors	CGI and RSRP for each neighbor
14–20	Three best quality intra-LTE neighbors	CGI and RSRQ for each neighbor
21	Serving-cell wideband CQI	Indicator of wideband signal quality
22	Power headroom report	Available uplink transmission power

are created, making expert-driven manual data analysis for identifying the right KPI/fault-associations a complicated task. The KPI/fault-associations are needed for developing good algorithms. Secondly, since the networks are complex and dynamic in nature, it is not obvious which KPIs should be measured and how often. For example, how to select from among several performance indicators, those which are going to reveal a certain feature of the network behavior in the most meaningful and effective manner?

It is envisioned that the above-mentioned challenges can be solved with advanced machine learning and data-mining algorithms which rely on autonomous learning of network behavior and efficient processing of the high dimensional databases consisting of wide range of KPIs. The data-mining can be used for extracting interesting, previously unknown and potentially useful information patterns from the large databases [10]. Usually the data mining process consists of several phases such as data cleaning, database integration, task relevant data selection, data mining, and data-pattern evaluation [10]. Data cleaning, integration, and selection are data preprocessing phases where data is prepared for further analysis [10, 11]. The data mining itself can consist of several different functionalities such as classification of data, association of data, clustering of data, dimensionality reduction, and anomaly detection [10]. In the pattern evaluation phase, the information patterns are visualized and analyzed to see if novel and valid information can be extracted from them. Even if interesting information patterns are discovered, it does not mean that it is automatically usable or useful from the data mining problem point of view, and therefore, information patterns need to be validated.

Within the family of cell-outage use cases included into self-healing of cellular radio networks there is a specific problem called *sleeping cell*. The sleeping cell is a compound term, which includes erroneous network behavior ranging from performance degradation to complete service unavailability. A specific characteristic of sleeping cell is that the network performance is degraded but this degradation is not easily visible to network operators and thus detection of this problem with traditional alarming systems is a complicated and slow process as described in [12]. There is no definition of a certain network failure which would cause appearance of a sleeping cell, as there can be several reasons. One type of sleeping cell could be malfunction of eNB RF unit where the

eNB transmission and reception capabilities degrade slowly to a point where transmission, reception, or both are not working anymore. This results in an outage situation where eNB cannot provide service for the UEs in the coverage area of the sleeping cell. Indicators which could reveal sleeping cells are degradation in handover activity, low call setup rates and low cell loading. Different kinds of indicators are needed to detect sleeping cells in live networks since networks consist of several overlapping frequency layers and radio access technologies. In [13], a sleeping cell is detected by using statistical classification techniques for graphs constructed from UE reported neighboring cell patterns. Changes in the neighboring cell patterns are used as indicators of outage.

One of the main goals of the research into the minimization of drive test is the development of algorithms which make operation of the networks more robust and efficient, so we developed a data-mining framework which detects coverage problems, such as sleeping cells, by using the high-dimensional MDT measurement databases. The data-mining framework described in this paper relies on dimensionality reduction which allows simplifying the anomaly detection and data classification processes. Motivation of using the dimensionality reduction is to make the framework robust and easily extendable with new numerical KPIs. On the other hand, the motivation of classifying MDT measurement reports to periodical, handover, and outage categories is to detect areas where periodical reports collected from certain frequency layer starts to show assumptions of outage. It is worth of noting that periodical MDT measurements can be collected from intra- and interfrequency layers simultaneously [4]. Therefore, some measurements for classification are available even if UE is connected on different frequency layer than the sleeping cell. This can happen in live networks where operators have deployed several overlapping frequency layers for capacity and coverage. If UE starts to experience outage on one frequency layer then it is handed over to another frequency layer before radio link failure occurs.

3.1. Data Mining Framework. The data-mining framework consists of learning and problem-detection phases. In the learning phase, the MDT database is constructed by collecting UE reported measurements from the network as depicted in Figure 2.

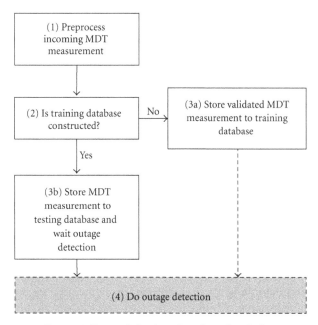

FIGURE 2: Data-mining learning phase description.

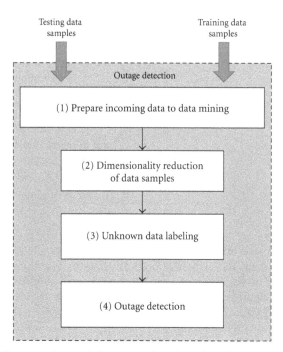

FIGURE 3: Data-mining outage detection-phase description.

The first step during the learning phase is preprocessing of the arriving MDT measurements which are labeled as periodical, HO-triggered, or RLF-triggered. Labeling is necessary because problem detection in step 4 relies on *supervised learning* from the labeled training samples. Labeling could be done at the eNB before the samples are sent to the TCE. The second step is to check whether or not a proper training database exists. In our case, the requirement is that a sufficient amount of periodical measurements and HO-triggered measurements are gathered from the network during its normal operation. In addition, some RLF samples from previous outage situations are gathered. A training database is created from the preprocessed MDT measurements which characterize normal network behavior without any outages. When the training database is constructed, all new measurement samples are put into the testing database. The operator needs to validate the training database and make sure it really resembles the needed network characteristics for example, the network behavior during its normal operation. The validation could be done by using anomaly detection and unsupervised learning techniques as described in [12].

In the problem-detection phase, recently received MDT measurements in the testing database are compared with the training data to detect anomalous behavior in the system, as depicted in Figure 3. The first step in the outage detection process is to prepare the data in the training and the testing set. Depending on the problem and the applied data mining algorithms, this preprocessing phase may contain several kinds of actions such as data cleaning, data integration, data transformation and data scaling. In our framework, each MDT measurement, as described in Table 1, is cleaned by splitting a single measurement to the header part and the data part. The header part contains information for postprocessing of the outage detection results, like visualization

and location correlation, but it is not used by the data-mining algorithm. The data part for ith measurement sample is a vector x_i consisting of 10 numerical features as follows:

$$x_i = \{\text{RSRP}_S, \text{RSRP}_{N1}, \ldots, \text{RSRP}_{N3}, \text{RSRQ}_S, \text{RSRQ}_{N1}, \ldots,$$
$$\text{RSRQ}_{N3}, \text{WCQI}, \text{PHR}\},$$

(1)

where RSRP_S and RSRQ_S are the serving cell measurements and RSRP_{Nj} and RSRQ_{Nj} are the jth strongest neighbor cell measurements, $j = \{1, 2, 3\}$. WCQI is the serving cell wideband CQI measurement and PHR is the serving cell power headroom report. RSRP and RSRQ measurements are given in a logarithmic scale as specified in [14]. Note that in our studies the WCQI and PHR measurements are not exactly the same as in 3GPP specifications. First of all, the CQI represents the downlink wideband signal-to-interference ratio and it is expressed using a dB scale. Moreover, the PHR metric is scaled by the allocation size resulting in a PHR per physical resource block metric as proposed in [15] since it was seen to improve the detection of uplink coverage problems and uplink power control parameterization problems. Thus, the high-dimensional data classifier consisted of 10 features. In addition, the performance of the 10-feature classifier was compared to an 8-feature classifier since the availability of the WCQI and PHR measurements depends on the eNB implementation. The 8-feature classifier uses only UE reported RSRP and RSRQ measurements.

3.2. Dimensionality Reduction. The next step in the outage detection framework is the dimensionality reduction step. The target of the dimensionality reduction is to represent high-dimensional data sets in a lower dimensional space making the data mining faster and less complicated. By having the dimensionality reduction step employed to the framework, the outage detection framework is more robust and can be extended easier with new numerical KPIs. Dimensionality reduction techniques, such as principal component analysis (PCA) are widely used in machine learning.

In our framework, the testing and training data set dimensionality is reduced by using a nonlinear diffusion maps methodology [16–19]. The diffusion maps method allows finding meaningful data patterns in the high-dimensional space and represents them in the lower dimensional space using diffusion coordinates and diffusion distances while preserving local structures in the data. The diffusion coordinates parameterize the high-dimensional data sets, and the diffusion distance provides a local preserving distance metric for the data. In the following, we shortly describe the used dimensionality reduction method originally proposed in [19]:

(i) The data set X is used to construct a unidirectional graph G, where the graph vertices are the data points x and the edges between the data points are defined by a kernel weight function w_ε.

(ii) The diffusion is created by doing a random walk on the graph. The random walk is done from the Markov transition matrix $\mathbf{P}$ which can be obtained by normalizing kernel weight matrix $\mathbf{W}$ with a diagonal matrix $\mathbf{D}$.

(iii) Finally, if $\mathbf{P}$ exists then the Eigen decomposition of the $\mathbf{P}$ can be used to derive the diffusion coordinates $\Psi_t(x_i)$ in the embedded space and the diffusion-distance metric $D_t(x_i, x_j)$.

The kernel weight matrix $\mathbf{W}$ measures the pairwise similarity of the data points in the graph and it must be symmetric, positive, and fast decaying [19]. One common choice for the kernel is:

$$W_{i,j} = w_\varepsilon\left(x_i, x_j\right) = \exp\left(\frac{-\left\|x_i - x_j\right\|}{\varepsilon}\right). \tag{2}$$

If the weight $w_\varepsilon(x_i, x_j)$ between sample x_i and x_j is small it means that points are similar. On the other hand, if the weight is large then the points are different in nature. Variable ε can be used to scale the kernel weight function which on the other hand scales the size of the local neighborhood. In principle, any weight function form of $f(\|x_i - x_j\|)$ fulfilling the above-mentioned criteria could be used to estimate the heat kernel and thus used with the diffusion process [19]. The Gaussian kernel in (2) is scalable and it decays fast, that is, faster than plain Euclidean distance, and therefore it was chosen. Next, the diagonal matrix $\mathbf{D}$ is derived from $\mathbf{W}$ according to

$$D_{i,i} = \sum_{j=1}^{n} w_\varepsilon\left(x_i, x_j\right). \tag{3}$$

If a proper kernel is used, then the matrix $\mathbf{W}$ can be multiplied from left with matrix $\mathbf{D}^{-1}$ to get the normalized Markov transition matrix $\mathbf{P}$:

$$\mathbf{P} = \mathbf{D}^{-1}\mathbf{W}. \tag{4}$$

In the Markov matrix, the $P_{i,j}$, describes the probability to move from sample x_i to sample x_j in the graph with one step. The random walk in the graph is obtained by raising the Markov transition matrix $\mathbf{P}$ to the tth power $\mathbf{P}^t$. This gives the probability to move from sample x_i to sample x_j in the graph with t steps. Finally, the eigen decomposition of $\mathbf{P}^t$ provides tools to define the high-dimensional data set in $\mathbb{R}^n$ in the embedded space $\mathbb{R}^k$ by constructing an estimate of $\mathbf{P}^t$ by using only k largest eigenvectors:

$$\mathbf{P}^t = \sum_{l=1}^{k} \lambda_l^t \psi_l \phi_l^T, \tag{5}$$

where the variables ψ_l and φ_l are right and left eigenvectors, and the variable λ_l is the eigenvalue of the lth eigenvector. Moreover, the diffusion distance D_t^2 and diffusion coordinates Ψ_t can be constructed by using the eigenvalues and the right eigenvectors as proven in [19]:

$$D_t^2\left(x_i, x_j\right) = \sum_{l=1}^{k} \lambda_l^{2t}\left(\psi_l(x_i) - \psi_l\left(x_j\right)\right)^2, \tag{6}$$

where the diffusion distance D_t^2 is the Euclidean distance between the measurement x_i and x_j in the embedded space by using the diffusion coordinates. The diffusion coordinates are constructed using k most significant right eigenvectors and eigenvalues as given in [19]:

$$\Psi_t(x_i) = \left[\lambda_1^t\psi_1(x_i), \lambda_2^t\psi_2(x_i), \ldots, \lambda_k^t\psi_k(x_i)\right], \tag{7}$$

where the diffusion coordinates $\Psi_t(x_i)$ for measurement x_i can be obtained from the m-by-k diffusion coordinate matrix Ψ_t. The column vectors of Ψ_t are the right eigenvectors of $\mathbf{P}^t$ multiplied by the corresponding eigenvalue term λ_l^t as shown in (7). Moreover, the diffusion coordinates for measurement x_i are found in the ith row vector of the diffusion coordinate matrix Ψ_t. As seen from (6) and (7), the diffusion distance for samples in the high-dimensional space corresponds to the Euclidean distance of the samples in the embedded space.

3.3. Data Classification.

The third step in our outage detection framework is data classification used to learn the characteristics of the testing data. In our earlier paper, we considered unsupervised learning techniques to detect sleeping cells [12] by incorporating k means clustering without taking into account the periodical MDT measurements. In this paper, we are describing the application of the supervised learning classification algorithm known as nearest neighbors search (NNS). Difference between the supervised learning and the unsupervised learning techniques is that in the supervised learning we know labeling for the training data and based on the training data characteristics we try to label unknown testing data samples. In our approach the training data consists of samples which belong to one of three class types, labeled as periodical, handover, or RLF samples, and the target is to classify all unknown testing data samples to those three known category types. Motivation of classifying testing data to these three class types is to detect periodical MDT measurements which have similarities with samples belonging to the outage category. By doing the classification, early outage detection can be done even in cases that only insufficient amount of RLF reports are available.

The fundamental idea of NNS is to find a set S_i of nearest neighbors from the training database for each unknown sample x_i in the testing database. One method of determining S_i is to calculate a distance from x_i to all points in the training database. Therefore, the complexity of the NSS depends on the size of training and testing sets as well as the dimensionality of the data samples. In our work, the nearest neighbors search is done in embedded low dimensional space based on the Euclidean distances. This is equally the same as classifying samples in high dimensional space according to the diffusion distances. The set S_i is used to define the labeling for all the unknown samples. There can be a wide range of vendor specific algorithms to determine the label for the unknown samples based on the S_i but here a simple algorithm was used and the class label is chosen based on the largest class in terms of number of samples present in the set S_i.

3.4. Anomaly Detection. The final step of the outage detection framework is anomaly detection. By this stage, the testing database is already labeled and this information is used to detect possible outage or sleeping-cell problems in the network. There are two different principles for detecting anomalous base-station behavior. On one hand, anomalies can be detected in time domain by comparing target base-station behavior in time to the behavior observed earlier. This requires long observation times and data-gathering periods per base station for creating reliable time domain profiles. On the other hand, anomalous base-station behavior can be detected in base station domain by comparing target base-station behavior to the neighboring base stations. In the latter case, more data is gathered in a shorter time period but the data can be biased if the neighboring base stations behave differently, that is, due to the different parameterization. In our framework, the common assumption for all base stations is that during normal operation the amount of RLF samples is small. Thus, the data classification should not result in many periodical MDT samples which are considered to belong to the RLF class. On the other hand, when the network is in outage, many periodical MDT measurements should be similar to the RLF samples. Since the anomaly detection criterion that is, increase of the number of periodical MDT measurements which have similar characteristics as the RLF samples, assumes similar behavior of the base stations during normal operation, the outage detection is based on the base-station domain analysis.

In our framework, the anomaly detection is done by counting the number MDT reports labeled as RLF samples for each eNB and comparing this with the network normal operation in time and base-station domain. The detection is based on the well-known standard score metric which describes how similar an observation of a particular eNB is compared with the normal behavior of a set of neighboring eNBs taking into account the normal deviation of the observations. Standard score z_e for eNB e is defined as,

$$z_e = \frac{|x_e - \mu_x|}{\sigma_x}, \tag{8}$$

where variable x_e is the number of RLF-labeled samples for eNB e and variables μ_x and σ_x are expected mean and standard deviation of the number of RLF-labeled samples in the eNBs local neighborhood. If z_e is much larger than one, then eNB e is probably an anomaly since the amount of RLF-labeled observations do not fit within the normal deviation of the RLF observations.

4. Simulation Results

4.1. Simulation Configuration. Our outage detection approach was verified with the dynamic LTE system simulator which was used to collect a large MDT measurement database. The simulator is capable to simulate E-UTRAN LTE release 8 and beyond in downlink and uplink with several radio resource management, scheduling, mobility, handover, and traffic-modeling functionalities. The simulation scenario consists of a regular hexagonal network layout of 19 sites and 57 base stations with inter site distance of 1750 meters. The 7 center sites are normal cells where the UEs are placed to gather MDT measurements and the outer tier of 12 sites are used only to generate interference. The users were moving in the scenario with velocity of 3 km/h and handover parameters were chosen in a way that the performance during normal operation was assumed to be good. On the other hand, the radio link monitoring values were chosen to trigger the RLF slightly faster than normally to ensure that some RLF samples are gathered during the normal operation of the network. The simulation assumptions are based on the 3GPP macro case 3 specifications [20] defining the used bandwidth, center frequency, network topology, and radio environment as listed in Table 4.

The simulation campaign consisted of a reference and problem simulations. The reference simulation was used to gather training data during the normal operation of the network and the simulated MDT database consisted of 148723 periodical measurement samples, 698 handover samples, and 138 RLF samples. The periodicity of sending MDT measurement reports was 0.5 seconds. In the problem scenario, one eNB was attenuated completely since the target was to model a sleeping cell where the uplink and the downlink are malfunctioning. The outage was created by adding 50 dBi antenna attenuation to the eNB 8. Since all sites were operating on the same band and overlaying interfrequency layer didn't exist, the eNB 8 was in outage. This enlarged the dominance areas of the neighboring cells as depicted in the Figure 4. The dominance area indicates the area where a particular cell is the strongest serving cell. In the left figure, the eNB 8 dominance area is shown with turquoise color, and the size of the area is similar to the other cells. In the right figure, the eNB 8 is sleeping and the area is served by the neighboring cells. Note that the eNB 8 covers less than 5% of the overall area where the UEs are distributed during the simulation.

The described dominance area problem is easy to understand, and therefore, it is interesting to see how our approach is able to detect the change in the dominance areas. The MDT database gathered from the reference simulation provides the basis of the training database which defines the statistical structure and the characteristics of three classes. Since the MDT database from the reference simulation was large only a fraction of this data was used in the actual training data set. The training data set was constructed from 3000 periodical samples using random undersampling [21], all HO samples, and all RLF samples. Moreover, the size of the RLF data set was oversampled by a factor of 4 in order to have roughly the same amount of HO and RLF samples in the training data set. Even though oversampling leads to a certain degree of overfitting, and consequently might lead to a degradation of classification accuracy [22], it can also enhance the classifier performance as shown in [11]. All MDT data gathered from the problem simulation is used to construct the unknown database, and each sample in this database is labeled as either periodical, handover, or RLF class as earlier explained in Section 3.

4.2. Simulation Data Mining Results. To be able to detect the anomalous network behavior, all MDT measurement samples in the unknown database was labeled by using the training data set classifier. Labeling of unknown samples was done based on 7 nearest neighbors since this was found to perform reasonably well. The nearest neighbors in the training set were always chosen based on the Euclidean distance in the embedded space which is the same as the diffusion distance in the original space. Classification accuracy of the NNS algorithm applied to MDT data is shown in Tables 2 and 3. The classification accuracy is evaluated with confusion matrices showing the probability of *true-positive* labeling and *false-positive* labeling. Different confusion matrices are shown for 10-feature and 8-feature classifiers. The 10-feature classifier uses all 10 features including WCQI and PHR for the dimensionality reduction as described in (1), whereas the 8-feature classifier uses only UE reported RSRP and RSRQ values. Diagonal cells of the confusion matrices show the true-positive probability indicating the likelihood that a sample is correctly labeled to the same class it belongs. The false-positive likelihood indicates the probability for the samples to be labeled to a wrong class. This kind of comparison is easy to do since we know the real labels of the data. The number inside the parenthesis of the real class column indicates the total amount of the different sample types in simulations and confusion matrices showing how these samples were labeled by the different classifiers.

Table 2 shows the reference simulation labeling accuracy for all MDT samples. It can be seen that the true-positive-labeling likelihood of the reference data is more than 80% for all class types regardless of the used classifier. The 10-feature classifier performs better but the performance of 8-feature classifier is not much worse either. One should note that we do not try to achieve 100% classification accuracy since it is quite likely that some of the periodical, handover, and radio link failure samples would have similar kind of characteristics in any case. Periodical samples are collected in a periodical manner, and therefore, the samples preceding a handover or a radio link failure event are assumed to have similar kind of characteristics. It is worth noting that handovers occur at the cell edge, and depending on the handover parameters and the slow fading conditions some handovers can have similarities with radio link failures.

Classification quality of the MDT samples from the problem and reference simulation is approximately the same as shown in Table 3. Classification accuracy of the 10-feature classifier remains better in the problem scenario as well. There is a small change of 0.8% in handover false-positive labeling but that is negligible since the number of handover samples is only 683 meaning 8 samples were classified differently. A small change in periodical sample false-positive-labeling probability is observed as well. In the problem simulation, the 10-feature classifier labels 0.9% of the periodical samples to radio link failures. This is almost two times higher than in the reference simulation. However, this small difference of 0.4% is significant since the number of periodical samples in the problem simulation MDT database is huge that is, 148693 samples. This means that 1338 additional RLF-like samples were found from the set of periodical MDT samples indicating outage. This is 537% more samples than the 210 true RLFs detected in the problem scenario. If the 8-feature classifier is used the difference is same. However, the classification accuracy is slightly lower, and therefore the total number of RLF-labeled samples is higher in the reference and the problem simulation. On the other hand, the 8-feature classifier can be applied to the interfrequency measurements directly, since it does not use CQI or PHR measurements for the outage detection.

The final goal in the outage detection is to associate RLF-labeled samples with base stations. Generally, MDT samples with detailed location information are reported with latitude and longitude values and rest of the samples can be located based on the RF fingerprint of the MDT measurement. Recall that if only GCI of the serving cell would be used, the detected samples in the dominance area of malfunctioning eNB would be associated with neighboring cells leading to misjudgments. Our assumption is that majority of samples can always be located at least with the accuracy of the dominance area for example, an estimate of the strongest serving cell is known for each sample based on the operators estimate of the dominance areas. In urban network deployments, the definition of dominance areas can become ambiguous due to buildings, street layout, and slow fading. However, since the MDT is used to enhance the network coverage maps, it is assumed that dominance area estimates can be improved in urban environment as well. Therefore, it is

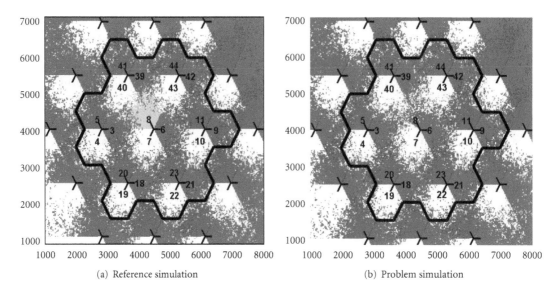

(a) Reference simulation   (b) Problem simulation

FIGURE 4: Network dominance areas.

TABLE 2: Reference simulation confusion matrices.

Real class	8 features (only RSRP and RSRQ)			10 features (with CQI and PHR)		
	Per.	HO	RLF	Per.	HO	RLF
Periodical (148723)	96.4%	2.9%	0.7%	96.6%	2.9%	0.5%
Handover (698)	11.9%	82.1%	6.0%	11.8%	83.0%	5.2%
Radio link failure (138)	0.0%	0.0%	100%	0.0%	0.0%	100%

assumed that if the MDT measurements bear the detailed location, the correlation with the dominance areas is not an issue. However, if one of the cells is missing, the positioning and correlation with the RF fingerprint databases could be challenging and even lead to wrong conclusions. In this paper, the inaccurate RF fingerprint positioning is not taken into account, and the results rely on the availability of the MDT reports with detailed location information, that is, latitude and longitude. In Figure 5, the normalized RLF-labeling results from the reference simulation are depicted for all base stations. The RLF-labeled samples are associated with the base stations according to the estimated dominance areas. Blue color refers to periodical samples, green color refers to handover samples, and red color refers to RLF samples which are labeled as radio link failures. The results are normalized with the total number of RLF-labeled samples in the reference scenario. There are a few radio link failures occurring in the reference scenario and only 3% of all RLF-like samples were detected to occur at the dominance area of the eNB 8. These RLFs in the reference scenario are due to the long intersite distances between the base stations and slow-fading effect especially in eNBs 6, 18, and 43.

Based on all RLF-labeled samples, a standard score for each base station is calculated by using (8). The standard score can be used as a simple indicator to detect if eNB behavior is normal or not since it takes into account the statistical variability of the RLF-labeled samples per base station during normal network operation. In Figure 6, standard-score distributions in reference scenario are shown

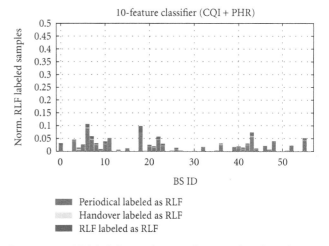

FIGURE 5: RLF-labeled samples per base station in reference simulation.

for 8-feature classifier with turquoise line and 10-feature classifiers with black-dashed line. Distributions are similar for both classifiers, and 95% of the eNBs have a standard score smaller than two.

The RLF-labeling results in the problem simulation are normalized in a same way as the reference simulation results. After triggering the sleeping-cell problem, the increase in the number of RLF-labeled samples is significant. Figure 7 shows that almost 40% of all RLF-labeled samples were associated

TABLE 3: Problem-simulation confusion matrices.

Real class	8 features (only RSRP and RSRQ)			10 features (with CQI and PHR)		
	Per.	HO	RLF	Per.	HO	RLF
Periodical (148693)	96.0%	2.9%	1.1%	96.2%	2.9%	0.9%
Handover (683)	13.3%	79.9%	6.8%	12.7%	81.4%	5.9%
Radio link failure (210)	3.3%	0.5%	96.2%	1.0%	1.0%	98.0%

TABLE 4: Simulator parameters.

Parameter	Notes	Value
3GPP macrocell scenario	Regular cell layout	57 sectors/19 BSs
Intersite distance		1.75 km
Distance-dependent path loss	Macro cell model [20]	$128.1 + 37.6 \log_{10}(R_{km})$
BS Tx power		46 dBm
Slow-fading standard deviation		8 dB
Slow-fading correlation		Site 0.5/Sector 1.0
Fast-fading profile		Typical Urban
UE velocity		3 km/h
UE placement	Uniformly distributed	7 centremost sites
RSRP/RSRQ Measurements	RSRP measurement period	40 ms
	L1 averaging window size	200 ms
	L3 filter coefficient	4
MDT reporting	Periodicity	500 ms
Handover parameters	A3 event threshold	3
	A3 event time to trigger	160 ms
	Handover preparation time	50 ms
Radio link failure monitoring	Qout threshold	−8 dB
	Qin threshold	−6 dB
	T310 timer	600 ms
Number of calls per simulation		4200
Base-stations loading	Full loading in all cells	100% RBs loaded
Diffusion parameter epsilon in (8)	Scales the size of local neighborhood	8
Embedded space dimension	Number of right eigenvectors	6

with the eNB 8 dominance area whereas it was only 3% in the reference scenario. Moreover, it was observed that the total number of RLF-labeled samples is higher for the 8-feature classifier since more periodical samples are labeled as RLFs due to slightly worse classification accuracy. Only 36% of the all RLF-labeled samples were associated with eNB 8 in this case. This indicates that both classifiers detect periodical measurements which are similar with the radio link failures. Moreover, eNB 8 standard score is 26.2 for the 10-feature classifier and 25.2 for the 8-feature classifier. This means that both classifiers detect anomalous network behavior since the standard score is much larger than two-indicating outage. However, the 10-feature classifier is able to isolate the problem from the reference simulation better since the standard score is larger and more RLF-labeled samples were associated with the malfunctioning eNB 8. This indicates that by using CQI and PHR metrics in the classification the

outage detection can be improved. On the other hand, the 8-feature classifier can also detect the problem but since it does not depend on the CQI and PHR it can be applied to the interfrequency measurements as well. However, the verification of the interfrequency layer outage is not done in this paper.

Note that UEs in the problem scenario would not detect the presence of the eNB 8. Hence, the existence of the location information and correlation with the dominance information helps to build a better understanding of the root cause and location of the problem. The locations of the RLF-labeled samples in the map grid are illustrated in Figure 8. The simulation area was divided to 42 × 48 meters rectangular map grid points. The number of the RLF-labeled samples were counted for each grid point, and a heat map was used to visualize the likelihoods of the RLF-labeled samples in the estimated dominance area

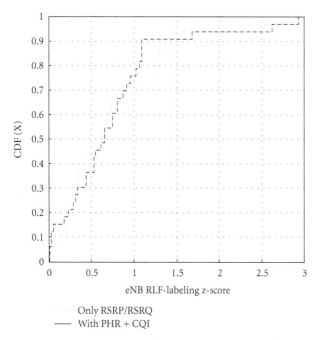

FIGURE 6: Standard-score distributions for reference simulation.

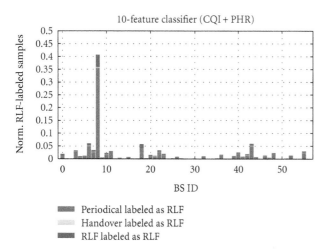

FIGURE 7: RLF-labeled samples per base station in problem simulation.

map. A gray color indicates areas in the heat map which might have some outage for example, when approaching a coverage hole, and a bright red color indicates areas where outage is detected. Figure 8(a) shows the heat map for the reference simulation together with estimated dominance areas, and it can be seen that some outage regions at the cell edges do exist due to the slow fading and large ISD between the sites. Figure 8(b) shows the heat map for problem simulation indicating clearly higher likelihood for the outage on the eNB 8 area compared with the reference simulation. It can be seen that the increased likelihood of RLF-labeled samples indicates the change on the dominance areas.

4.3. Anomaly Detection Time. Since anomaly detection is based on the increase in the number of periodical measurements classified as RLF samples, the detection time was analyzed by observing amount of reported samples instead of actual detection time. The amount of reported samples is a better metric, since time needed to gather a sufficient amount of samples for detection depends on the number of active users, user distribution, and MDT configuration, for example, periodicity of the measurements. Average base-station specific z-score metric before and after occurrence of the problem in eNB 8 is depicted in Figure 9.

In Figure 9, the colored curves depict how z-score metric behaves during system simulations in case 10-feature classifier is used. The x-axis indicates the average number of all received MDT reports per eNB, while the simulations advance. The y-axis indicates the eNB z-score as in (8). The z-score values were updated every five seconds but mean and standard deviation values were kept constant according to the reference simulation. Figure 9 indicates that if the observation window is too short, then anomalous base stations are not detected. In the reference simulation before the problem, approximately 3000 MDT samples per eNB are needed until some minor outage is detected. Solid green curve and dotted red curve indicate some outage in eNB 6 and eNB 18. The detection time in this case would depend on the average number of UEs per eNB, their movements in the eNB dominance area, and the periodicity of the MDT reports. For example, if 10 uniformly distributed UEs are sending MDT reports with periodicity of 0.5 second, then the detection for example, reception of 3000 samples, would take 2.5 minutes. The problem triggers after 4500 MDT reports per eNB are received. The eNB z-scores are cleared, and detection is restarted as well. Shortly after triggering the problem, eNB 8 starts to stand out from the statistics. Blue curve indicates that the z-score for eNB 8 is already more than 10 after reception of 1500 MDT reports per eNB. Moreover, purple curve shows that eNB 43 z-score increases from 2 to 3 due to the sleeping cell. This indicates that outage increases slightly in the dominance area of eNB 43 due to the problem in eNB 8. For the eNBs 6 and 18, the outage remains similar.

5. Conclusion

This paper described a data-mining framework which is capable of detecting network outage and sleeping cells in a cellular network by using drive testing databases. The framework is cognitive since it adapts to the deployed network configuration and topology by learning the network characteristics while gathering the training data for the problem classifier. In addition, the described outage detection framework works in a self-organizing manner since it uses the E-UTRAN minimization of drive testing functionality to gather the training and testing databases. The essence of the method is to label unknown data by finding similar characteristics from the previously known network data. For this purpose, diffusion maps dimensionality reduction and nearest neighbors data classification methods were utilized.

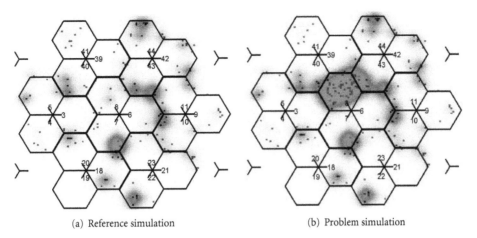

(a) Reference simulation   (b) Problem simulation

FIGURE 8: RLF-labeled samples on the map grid.

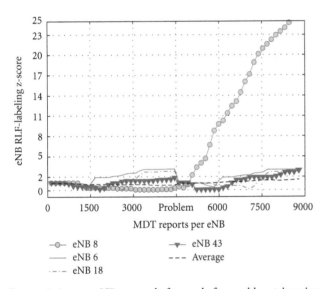

FIGURE 9: Average eNB z-score before and after problem triggering in eNB 8.

The presented approach is robust since the same principle utilized here can be used for a wide range of different network problems where the problem data can be isolated and used later as known problem classifiers.

In the case of the sleeping cell problem, the detection is based on finding periodical measurements which have similarities with the radio link failures. In the studied verification case, the algorithm gains 537% in the number of samples which can be used for the outage detection in addition to the real radio link failure reports. This makes detection more reliable and possibly faster compared with the algorithms which are based purely on the reported RLF events. Although our approach clearly helps to detect the outage situations by taking into account the periodical samples, there are still some drawbacks in this framework which needs to be solved in the practical deployments. First of all, our approach detects sleeping cells based on

the outage present in the dominance areas of the sleeping cell. However, in denser networks, the outage might be less severe and the neighboring base stations can serve the users in the dominance area of sleeping base station without a significant increase of the radio link failures. Moreover, since the typical live networks consist of several overlapping frequency layers, then radio link failures in one layer can be avoided by handing UEs over to another frequency layer. In such situations, the framework could be extended to take into account additional features such as loading level of the cells, the handover activity, or the interfrequency layer measurements. These features together with the change in dominance areas could eventually result in a more comprehensive solution to the sleeping-cell problem. However, one advantage of the presented framework is indeed the robustness due to the dimensionality reduction step. This is a stepping stone for future research allowing an easy inclusion of new features in case of different anomaly detection studies.

Acknowledgments

The authors would like to thank Amir Averbuch and Gil David from Tel Aviv University for their support with the knowledge mining. Moreover, they would like to thank *Renesas Mobile Europe* for use of their system simulator since the work could not have been done without it. In addition, constructive criticism, comments, and support from the colleagues at Magister Solutions Ltd., University of Jyväskyläm and the Radio Network Group at Tampere University of Technology were extremely valuable during the work.

References

[1] 3GPP TS 36.902, "Evolved Universal Terrestrial Radio Access Network (E-UTRAN), Self-Configuring and Self-Optimizing Network (SON) Use Cases and Solutions," v.9.3.1, March 2011.

[2] NGMN Alliance, "Next Generation Mobile Networks Use Cases related to Self Organising Network, Overall Description," v.2.02, December 2008.

[3] 3GPP TR 36.805, "Study on minimization of drive-tests in Next Generation Networks," v.9.0.0, December, 2009.

[4] 3GPP TS 37.320, "Radio measurement collection for Minimization of Drive Tests," v.0.7.0, June 2010.

[5] 3GPP RP-111361, "Enhancement of Minimization of Drive Tests for E-UTRAN and UTRAN—Core Part Approval," Nokia Siemens Networks, Nokia, MediaTek, 2011.

[6] 3GPP TS 32.422, "Subscriber and equipment trace, Trace control and configuration management," v.11.0.1, September 2011.

[7] 3GPP TS 36.331, "Evolved Universal Terrestrial Radio Access (E-UTRA), Radio Resource Control (RRC), Protocol specification," v.10.4.0, December 2011.

[8] M. Amirijoo, L. Jorguseski, T. Kürner et al., "Cell outage management in LTE networks," in *Proceedings of the 6th International Symposium on Wireless Communication Systems (ISWCS '09)*, pp. 600–604, Siena, Italy, September 2009.

[9] M. Amirijoo, L. Jorguseski, R. Litjens, and R. Nascimento, "Effectiveness of cell outage compensation in LTE networks," in *Proceedings of the IEEE Consumer Communications and Networking Conference (CCNC '11)*, pp. 642–647, Las Vegas, Nev, USA, January 2011.

[10] J. Han and M. Kamber, *Data Mining: Concepts and Techniques*, Morgan Kaufmann, 2000.

[11] S. B. Kotsiantis, D. Kanellopoulus, and P. E. Pintelas, "Data Preprocessing for Supervised Learning," *International Journal of Computer Science*, vol. 1, no. 2, pp. 111–117, 2006.

[12] F. Chernogorov, J. Turkka, T. Ristaniemi, and A. Averbuch, *Detection of Sleeping Cells in LTE Networks Using Diffusion Maps*, VTC Spring, Budapest, Hungary, 2011.

[13] C. M. Mueller, M. Kaschub, C. Blankenhorn, and S. Wanke, "A cell outage detection algorithm using neighbor cell list reports," in *Proceedings of the International Workshop on Self-Organizing Systems*, pp. 218–229, 2008.

[14] 3GPP TS 36.214, "Evolved Universal Terrestrial Radio Access (E-UTRA); Physical Layer; Measurements," v.10.1.0, March 2011.

[15] J. Turkka and J. Puttonen, "Using LTE power headroom report for coverage optimization," in *Proceedings of 74th IEEE Vehicular Technology Conference (VTC '11-Fall)*, San Francisco, Calif, USA, September 2011.

[16] R. R. Coifman, S. Lafon, A. B. Lee et al., "Geometric diffusions as a tool for harmonic analysis and structure definition of data: diffusion maps," *Proceedings of the National Academy of Sciences of the United States of America*, vol. 102, no. 21, pp. 7426–7431, 2005.

[17] R. R. Coifman and S. Lafon, "Diffusion maps," *Applied and Computational Harmonic Analysis*, vol. 21, no. 1, pp. 5–30, 2006.

[18] B. Nadler, S. Lafon, and R. R. Coifman, "Diffusion maps, spectral clustering and eigenfunctions of fokker-planck operators," in *Advances Neural Information Processing Systems*, vol. 18, pp. 955–962, 2005.

[19] A. Schclar, "A diffusion framework for dimensionality reduction," in *Soft Computing For Knowledge Discovery and Data Mining*, chapter IV, pp. 315–325, 2008.

[20] 3GPP TS 36.814, "Further advancements for E-UTRA physical layer aspects (Release 9)," v.9.0.0, March 2010.

[21] H. He and E. A. Garcia, "Learning from imbalanced data," *IEEE Transactions on Knowledge and Data Engineering*, vol. 21, no. 9, pp. 1263–1284, 2009.

[22] R. C. Holte, L. Acker, and B. W. Porter, "Concept learning and the problem of small disjuncts," in *Proceedings of the International Joint Conference on Artificial Intelligence*, pp. 813–818, 1989.

10

Survey and Challenges of QoE Management Issues in Wireless Networks

Sabina Baraković[1] and Lea Skorin-Kapov[2]

[1] Ministry of Security of Bosnia and Herzegovina, Trg BiH 1, 71000 Sarajevo, Bosnia and Herzegovina
[2] Faculty of Electrical Engineering and Computing, University of Zagreb, Unska 3, 10000 Zagreb, Croatia

Correspondence should be addressed to Lea Skorin-Kapov; lea.skorin-kapov@fer.hr

Academic Editor: Raimund Schatz

With the move towards converged all-IP wireless network environments, managing end-user Quality of Experience (QoE) poses a challenging task, aimed at meeting high user expectations and requirements regarding reliable and cost-effective communication, access to any service, anytime and anywhere, and across multiple operator domains. In this paper, we give a survey of state-of-the-art research activities addressing the field of QoE management, focusing in particular on the domain of wireless networks and addressing three management aspects: QoE modeling, monitoring and measurement, and adaptation and optimization. Furthermore, we identify and discuss the key aspects and challenges that need to be considered when conducting research in this area.

1. Introduction

Wireless mobile communications have experienced phenomenal growth throughout the last decades, going from support for circuit-switched voice services and messaging services to IP-based mobile broadband services using High Speed Packet Access (HSPA), Worldwide Interoperability for Microwave Access (WiMAX), and Long-Term Evolution (LTE) Radio Access networks [1]. Increasingly, mobile applications and services are being used in daily life activities in order to support the needs for information, communication, or leisure [2]. Mobile users are requiring access to a wide spectrum of various multimedia applications/services without being limited by constraints such as time, location, technology, device, and mobility restrictions. This represents the outcome of the currently leading trend and future aim in the telecommunications domain: the convergence between fixed and mobile networks, and the integration of existing and new wireless technologies. Such integrations aim to satisfy mobile users' requirements in terms of providing access to any service, along with reliable and cost-effective communication, anytime and anywhere, over any medium

and networking technology, and across multiple operator domains [3].

The ITU has specified the Next Generation Network (NGN) as a generic framework for enabling network convergence and realizing the aforementioned requirements [4]. The NGN concept is centered around a heterogeneous infrastructure of various access, transport, control, and service solutions, merged into a single multimedia-rich service provisioning environment. Today, an increasing number of mobile operators are migrating their networks in line with the 3GPP specified Evolved Packet System (EPS), consisting of a multiaccess IP-based core network referred to as the Evolved Packet Core (EPC), and a new LTE 4G radio access network based on Orthogonal Frequency Division Multiplexing (OFDM) [1, 5, 6]. While the network controlled and class-based Quality of Service (QoS) concept of the EPC are based on the 3GPP policy and charging control (PCC) framework [7–9] (discussed further in Section 4), intense recent research in the area of Quality of Experience (QoE) has shown that such QoS mechanisms may need to be complemented with more user-centric approaches in order to truly meet end-user requirements and expectations.

Today, humans are quality meters, and their expectations, perceptions, and needs with respect to a particular product, service, or application carry a great value [10]. While the ITU-T has defined QoE as the "*overall acceptability of an application or service, as perceived subjectively by the end user*" [11], ETSI defines QoE as "*a measure of user performance based on both objective and subjective psychological measures of using an ICT service or product*" [12] and extends QoE beyond subjective to include objective psychological measures.

QoE is therefore considered to be a multidimensional construct, encompassing both objective (e.g., performance related) and subjective (e.g., user related) aspects [13]. As such, QoE has been considered in relation to both QoS, which is primarily a technical, objective, and technology-oriented concept, as well as to User Experience (UX) [14] which is generally considered as a more user-oriented concept. The former focuses on the impact of network and application performance on user quality perception, while the latter primarily deals with the individual users' experiences derived from encounters with systems, impacted by expectations, prior experiences, feelings, thoughts, context, and so forth.

Various approaches such as [15–19] provide definitions of QoE that are closely related to technology-centric logic, not accounting for the subjective character of human experience, and lacking consideration of a broader definition of QoE [20]; that is, the consequence of the assumption that the optimization of QoS-related parameters will automatically result in increasing the overall QoE, leading to swift adoption of products and services on the consumption side. However, QoS is only a subset of the overall QoE scope. Higher QoS would probably result in higher QoE in many cases, but fulfilling all traffic-related QoS requirements will not necessarily guarantee high user QoE. Moreover, it is assumed that products and services that meet users' requirements and expectations and that allow them to have high QoE in their personal context will probably be more successful than products and services that have higher QoS but fail to meet users' high demands and expectations [21].

A recent definition that has emerged from the EU Qualinet community (COST Action IC1003: "European Network on Quality of Experience in Multimedia Systems and Services") encompasses the discussed aspects and defines QoE as "*the degree of delight or annoyance of the user of an application or service. It results from the fulfillment of his or her expectations with respect to the utility and/or enjoyment of the application or service in the light of the user's personality and current state. In the context of communication services, QoE is influenced by service, content, device, application, and context of use*" [22].

In the context of converged all-IP wireless networks, an important consideration is the impact of mobility on user QoE, further related to mechanisms for assuring session and connection continuity. Session establishment delays are impacted by authorization and authentication procedures, as well as session establishment signaling. Handover may impose additional delays and packet losses, resulting in potential loss of session-related content and awkward communication. Hence, mechanisms are necessary for achieving seamlessly session continuity and minimizing disruption time [21]. Besides the challenges that various types of mobility (terminal, session, user, service) and seamless handover between networks that use the same technology (horizontal handover) or networks that use different technologies (vertical handover) represent, the fast development of new and complex mobile multimedia services that can be delivered via various new mobile devices (smartphones, tablets, etc.) poses an additional challenge in the QoE provisioning process [3]. In the context of wireless systems, limitations arising from both device and transmission channel characteristics have a clear impact on user quality perception [23].

The overall goal of QoE management may be related to optimizing end-user QoE (end-user perspective), while making efficient (current and future) use of network resources and maintaining a satisfied customer base (provider perspective). In order to successfully manage QoE for a specific application, it is necessary to understand and identify multiple factors affecting it (subjective and objective) from the point of view of various actors in the service provisioning chain, and how they impact QoE. Resulting QoE models dictate the parameters to be monitored and measured, with the ultimate goal being effective QoE optimization strategies. Therefore, the overall process of QoE management may be broken down into three general steps: (1) QoE modeling, (2) QoE monitoring and measurements, and (3) QoE optimization and control [24].

With the implementation of successful QoE management, users will benefit with satisfied requirements/expectations and may be further inclined to adopt new complex services and support further technology development. Furthermore, QoE management is very important for all actors and stakeholders involved in the service provisioning chain: device manufacturers, network providers, service providers, content providers, cloud providers, and so forth. In today's highly competitive environment, where providers' price levels are decreasing and pricing schemes are becoming more similar [25], it is not enough to simply make services available to users, who further have the option of choosing from a spectrum of various providers. Actors involved in the process of service provisioning have identified the need to work towards meeting users' requirements and expectations by maximizing users' satisfaction with the overall perceived service quality, while at the same time minimizing their costs. Understanding and managing QoE is needed in order to react quickly to quality problems (preferably) before customers perceive them. Hence, successful QoE management offers stakeholders a competitive advantage in the fight to prevent customer churn and attract new customers.

Based on the previously mentioned, it may be concluded that QoE is a fast emerging multidisciplinary field based on social psychology, cognitive science, economics, and engineering science, focused on understanding overall human quality requirements [10]. Consequently, management of QoE as a highly complex issue requires an interdisciplinary view from user, technology, context, and business aspects, with flexible cooperation between all players and stakeholders involved in the service providing chain.

In this paper we give a survey of approaches and solutions related to QoE management, focusing in particular on wireless network environments. It is important to note that different QoE models and assessment methodologies are applicable for different types of services (e.g., conversational voice services, streaming audio-visual services, interactive data services, collaborative services). We do not focus on a particular service but rather give a general survey of approaches. The paper is organized as follows. Section 2 surveys the modeling of QoE by discussing the classification of a wide range of QoE influence factors into certain dimensions and describing existing general QoE models. The monitoring and measurement of QoE is described in Section 3, while Section 4 discusses the topic of QoE optimization and control. Finally, Section 5 concludes the paper by pointing out the challenges and open research issues in the field of QoE management.

2. QoE Modeling

As a prerequisite to successful QoE management, there is a need for a deep and comprehensive understanding of the influencing factors (IF) and multiple dimensions of human quality perception. QoE modeling aims to model the relationship between different measurable QoE IFs and quantifiable QoE dimensions (or features) for a given service scenario. Such models serve the purpose of making QoE estimations, given a set of conditions, corresponding as closely as possible to the QoE as perceived by end users. Based on a given QoE model specifying a weighted combination of QoE dimensions and a further mapping to IFs, a QoE management approach will then aim to derive Key Quality Indicators (KQIs) and their relation with measureable parameters, along with quality thresholds, for the purpose of fulfilling a set optimization goal (e.g., maximizing QoE to maximize profit, maximizing number of "satisfied" customers). An important issue to note is that different actors involved in the service provisioning chain will use a QoE model in different ways, focusing on those parameters over which a given actor has control (e.g., a network provider will consider how QoS-related performance parameters will impact QoE, while a content or service provider will be interested in how the service design or usability will impact QoE).

In this section we first discuss QoE IFs in general, and give an overview and comparison of general QoE modeling approaches, discussing in turn their applicability with respect to QoE management strategies. We then further consider more concretely QoE models targeted specifically towards wireless networks, highlighting the differences with respect to fixed networks. We end the section with a summary of QoE modeling challenges.

2.1. QoE Influence Factors. A QoE IF has been defined as "*any characteristic of a user, system, service, application, or context whose actual state or setting may have influence on the Quality of Experience for the user*" [22]. Figure 1 illustrates a multitude of different factors which may be considered in relation to QoE, making it clear that their grouping into categories aids in identifying such factors in a systematic way. Several existing approaches have addressed this issue and proposed classifications of QoE IFs into multiple dimensions.

It should be noted that specific IFs are relevant for different types of services and applications.

Stankiewicz and Jajszczyk [3] have classified the technology-oriented factors that impact QoE into three groups: QoS factors, Grade of Service (GoS) factors, and Quality of Resilience (QoR) factors, believing that provisioning of those at the appropriate level is crucial for achieving high QoE. Also, they take into consideration a number of additional factors (mostly nontechnology related) such as emotions, user profile, pricing policy, application specific features, terminals, codecs, type of content, and environmental, psychological, and sociological aspects, but they do not further group them. On the other hand, Baraković et al. [21] have categorized QoE influence factors into five dimensions: (1) technology performance on four levels: application/service, server, network, and device; (2) usability, referring to users' behavior when using the technology; (3) subjective evaluation; (4) expectations; and (5) context. Recently, Skorin-Kapov and Varela [26] have proposed the ARCU model that groups QoE factors into four multidimensional IF spaces: *Application* (application configuration-related factors), *Resource* (network/system related factors), *Context*, and *User* spaces.

Finally, a recent classification that has emerged from the EU Qualinet community in the form of a White Paper [22] groups QoE IFs into the following three categories (which are additionally divided into several subcategories as described in the referenced whitepaper).

(i) "Human IFs present any variant or invariant property or characteristic of a human user. The characteristic can describe the demographic and socioeconomic background, the physical and mental constitution, or the user's emotional state" (e.g., user's visual and auditory acuity, gender, age, motivation, education background, emotions).

(ii) "System IFs refer to properties and characteristics that determine the technically produced quality of an application or service. They are related to media capture, coding, transmission, storage, rendering, and reproduction/display, as well as to the communication of information itself from content production to user" (e.g., bandwidth, delay, jitter, loss, throughput, security, display size, resolution).

(iii) "Context IFs are defined as factors that embrace any situational property to describe the user's environment in terms of physical, temporal, social, economic, task, and technical characteristics" (e.g., location, movements, time of day, costs, subscription type, privacy).

2.1.1. Relationships between QoS and QoE. Among the wide scope of discussed IFs, a great deal of research has focused in particular on identifying the relationships between QoS parameters and QoE, whereby in many cases a user's perceived quality has been argued to mostly depend on QoS [27–29]. In studies focused on the mathematical interdependency of QoE and QoS, Reichl et al. [28, 30] have identified a

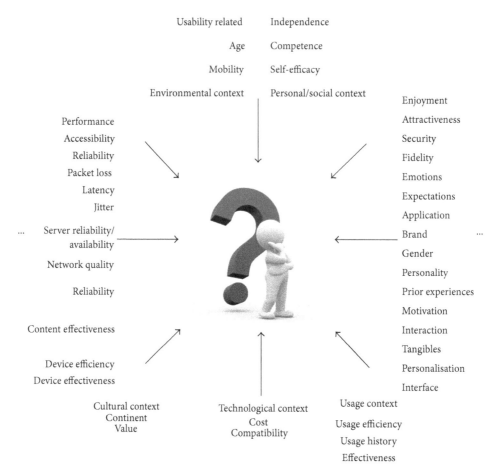

FIGURE 1: Different factors to be considered in relation to QoE.

logarithmic relationship between QoE and QoS. They argue that it can be explained on behalf of the Weber-Fechner Law (WFL) [31], which studies the perceptive abilities of the human sensory system to a physical stimulus in a quantitative fashion, and states that the *just noticeable difference* between two levels of certain stimulus is proportional to the magnitude of the stimuli. A logarithmic relationship formulates the sensitivity of QoE as a reciprocal function of QoS.

On the other hand, the IQX hypothesis presented and evaluated by Fiedler et al. in [29] formulates the sensitivity of QoE as an exponential function of a single QoS impairment factor. The underlying assumption is that the change of QoE depends on the actual level of QoE. Understanding the relationship between network-based QoS parameters and user-perceived QoE provides important input for the QoE management process, in particular to network providers with control over network resource planning and provisioning mechanisms.

2.2. From Subjective Quality Assessment to Objective Quality Estimation Models. When building a QoE model, quality assessment methodologies must be employed. While actual "ground-truth" user perceived quality may be obtained only via subjective assessment methodologies, the goal is to use subjective tests as a basis for building objective QoE models capable of estimating QoE based solely on objective quality

measurements. Hence, we shortly describe subjective quality assessment methodologies and different types of objective quality assessment methods and models.

2.2.1. Subjective QoE Assessment. Subjective quality assessments are based on psychoacoustic/visual experiments which represent the fundamental and most reliable way to assess users' QoE, although they are complex and costly. These methods have been investigated for many years and have enabled researchers to gain a deeper understanding of the subjective dimensions of QoE. Most commonly, the outcomes of any subjective experiment are quality ratings from users obtained during use of the service (in-service) or after service use (out-of-service), which are then averaged into Mean Opinion Scores (MOSs). This approach has been specified in ITU-T Recommendation P.800.1 [32] and expresses an average quality rating of a group of users by means of standardized scales. For a number of reasons, the use of MOS has been criticized [33] and extended to other ITU recommended subjective assessment procedures classified by type of application and media [34]. An interested reader is referred to the large number of standards which are referenced in [34].

In addition to standardized subjective QoE assessment methods, additional (sometimes complementary) relevant methods used for long-term user experience assessment have been used. In their studies involving QoE evaluations of mobile applications, Wac et al. [35] have collected users' QoE ratings on their mobile phones via an Experience Sampling Method (ESM) [36] several times per day, while a Day Reconstruction Method (DRM) [37] has been used to interview users on a weekly basis regarding their usage patterns and experiences towards the mobile applications. These methods have served to analyze possible relations and causalities between QoE ratings, QoS, and context.

With regards to collection of data and running of QoE experiments, assessments may be conducted in a laboratory setting [38], in a living labs environment [20], or in an actual real world environment [27, 35]. Some performance criteria are modified in a given range in a controlled fashion and subsequently users' opinions regarding the service performance are quantified. As an emerging and very prospective solution focusing on obtaining a large number of ratings in a real world environment, crowdsourcing methodology [39, 40] has been studied and utilized.

2.2.2. Objective QoE Models.

Objective QoE models are defined as the means for estimating subjective quality solely from objective quality measurement or indices [41]. In other words, these models are expected to provide an indication which approximates the rating that would be obtained from subjective assessment methods. Different types of objective quality estimation and prediction models have been developed. Each model has its proper domain of application and range of system or service conditions it has been designed for. Since there exists no universal objective quality assessment approach, proposed ones can be categorized by various criteria in order to determine their application area [34]: (1) application scope; (2) quality features being predicted; (3) considered network components and configurations; (4) model input parameters; (5) measurement approach; (6) level of service interactivity that can be assessed; and (7) level to which psychophysical knowledge or empirical data have been incorporated.

According to the level at which the input information is extracted, there are five types of objective QoE models [34]: (1) media-layer; (2) packet-layer; (3) bitstream-layer; (4) hybrid; and (5) planning models. Media-layer models [42–45] estimate the audio/video QoE by using the actual media signals as their input. In dependence of utilization of the source signal, one can use three different approaches [46, 47]: (1) no-reference (NR) model; (2) reduced-reference (RR) model; and (3) full-reference (FR) model. On the other hand, packet-layer models [48] utilize only the packet header information for QoE estimation, which describes them as in-service nonintrusive quality monitoring approaches. A bitstream-layer model is the combination of the two previously mentioned models, since it utilizes bitstream information as well as packet header information. Similarly, hybrid models [49–51] are conceived as a combination of the previously described three models. Finally, planning models do not acquire the input information from an existing service, but estimate it based on service information available during the planning phase.

In addition to ITU-T standards, ETSI gives a comprehensive guide with generic definitions and test methods for most of the key telecommunication services [52]. There are a number of other standardization bodies that deal with QoE assessment, including VQEG, MPEG, and JPEG.

While most of the current literature considers objective measures in relation to technology oriented collections of data, it is important to note that objective measurements may also refer to objective estimations of user's behavior (e.g., task duration, number of mouse clicks) which is commonly considered only as subjective [53].

2.3. A Survey of General QoE Modeling Approaches.

Besides briefly described subjective assessment methods that may contribute to building objective QoE models, also addressed in the previous subsection, we survey a number of general QoE modeling approaches in order to obtain a "broader picture" on this topic. Therefore, this subsection provides an analysis of several general QoE models that were validated by various types of services. While the listed models are not all strictly limited to wireless environments, they aim to identify numerous QoE IFs and provide mechanisms for relating them to QoE.

Table 1 summarizes these QoE models based on the following comparison parameters: IFs according to categorization in [22], type of service, consideration of wireless aspects, provisioning of the concrete QoE model, and applicability with respect to QoE management. This comparison provides an extension and modification of the analysis given by Laghari et al. in [10]. We consider more concretely QoE models targeted specifically for wireless environments in the following subsection.

Perkis et al. in [54] present a model for measuring the QoE of multimedia services, distinguishing between measurable and nonmeasurable parameters. In other words, the approach does not provide any QoE metric relationship formulae but rather addresses the factors that influence user's QoE. The measurable model parameters are closely related to the technology aspects of the terminal and service, and nonmeasurable entities are closely related to user's perception of a service, his/her expectations, and behavior. Additionally, a framework for quantifying the model parameters is described and validated with Voice on Demand (VoD) and mobile TV services in a mobile 3G environment. Although the authors categorize the parameters by accounting for QoS, QoE, and business aspects, and thereby encompass human and system parameters, the model does not fully include the context dimension. However, the proposed modeling framework gives the input information for the measurement process and thereby contributes to the overall QoE management by aiding the various parties in improving their performance.

A model that does not clearly encompass all QoE dimensions, but rather considers them in a limited manner, is introduced by Kim et al. [55]. The In-service Feedback QoE Framework (IFQF) is a user-triggering scheme aimed at investigating the main reasons of quality deterioration and thereby contributing to the overall QoE management process. The architecture consists of four agents: server, network, user,

TABLE 1: Comparison of QoE modeling approaches.

Modeling approach	Human influence factors		System influence factors				Context influence factors	Type of service	Wireless aspects	Concrete QoE model	QoE management applicability
	Low-level processing	High-level processing	Content	Media	Network	Device					
Perkis et al. [54]	Limited	No	Yes	No	Yes	Yes	No	Voice on demand, mobile TV	Yes	No	(i) Provides the input info for measurement purposes (ii) Most applicable in the context of service optimization
Kim et al. [55]	Limited	Limited	Limited	Not explicitly considered	Yes	Yes	Limited	IP television	Not specified	No	(i) Investigates the reasons for quality deterioration (ii) Most applicable in the context of service optimization
Kilkki [56]	Not explicitly considered	Not explicitly considered	Not explicitly considered	Not explicitly considered	Yes	No	Not explicitly considered	Multimedia	Not specified	No	(i) Proposes a holistic approach to QoE (ii) Most applicable in the context of development of a general QoE management strategy
Möller et al. [57]	Yes	Yes	Not explicitly considered	Not explicitly considered	Yes	Yes	Yes	Multimedia	Not specified	No	(i) Provides a detailed taxonomy of QoE aspects (ii) Most applicable in the context of target-oriented design and system optimization
Geerts et al. [58]	Yes	Yes	Not explicitly considered	No	Yes	Yes	Yes	Not specified	Yes	No	(i) Offers info on measuring different components of QoE (ii) Most applicable in the context of system (service and network) optimization
Laghari et al. [10]	Yes	Yes	Yes	Not explicitly considered	Yes	Yes	Yes	Voice on demand	Not specified	Yes	(i) Establishes the causal relationship between different QoE domains (ii) Most applicable in the context of system optimization

TABLE 1: Continued.

Modeling approach	Human influence factors		System influence factors				Context influence factors	Type of service	Wireless aspects	Concrete QoE model	QoE management applicability
	Low-level processing	High-level processing	Content	Media	Network	Device					
Volk et al. [59]	Yes	Yes	Yes	Yes	Yes	Yes	Yes	Multimedia	Not specified	Yes	(i) Provides the basis for QoE estimation (ii) Most applicable in the context of service estimation and optimization (iii) Most applicable in the context of optimized network resource allocation
De Moor et al. [20]	Limited	Yes	Yes	Yes	Yes	Yes	Yes	Multimedia	Yes	No	(i) Proposes an architecture for QoE monitoring and measurement (ii) Most applicable in the context of service estimation and optimization (iii) Most applicable in the context of optimized network resource allocation
Song et al. [60]	Yes	Yes	Yes	Yes	Yes	Yes	Yes	Video	Yes	No	(i) Enables the development of strategies for QoE improvement (ii) Most applicable in terms of optimizing user experience in a mobile context
Reichl et al. [28]	Yes	Yes	Yes	Yes	Yes	Yes	Yes	Broadband and Internet	Yes	Yes	(i) Provides QoE prediction and root cause analysis—applicable for network planning (ii) Most applicable in the context of service optimization (iii) Most applicable in the context of development of a general QoE management strategy

and management agent that gather information and form a feedback loop to find out the reason and location of faults, and thereby to minimize the difference between QoE value estimated by operators and the real QoE (as subjectively perceived by the user).

In [56], Kilkki proposed a framework that identifies the relationship between QoS and QoE, but does not explicitly consider QoE components in detail. The framework connects different research communities, including engineers, economists, and behavioral scientists. The author makes a strong case for a holistic approach to QoE and suggests the establishment of a multidisciplinary research group which would address the complexity of QoE. Additionally, key terms in the communication ecosystem are stated, but no classification of QoE factors or any details on the taxonomy are provided. However, the framework introduces new concepts such as Quality of User Experience (QoUE) and Quality of Customer Experience (QoCE).

On the contrary to the previous approaches which considered various QoE factors only partially or in a more abstract fashion, Möller et al. [57] have developed a detailed taxonomy of the most relevant QoS and QoE aspects focusing on multimodal human-machine interactions, as well as factors influencing its QoS. The taxonomy consists of three layers: (1) the QoS-influencing factors related to the user, the system, and the context of usage; (2) the QoS interaction performance aspects describing user and system behavior and performance; and (3) the QoE aspects related to the quality perception and judgment processes taking place inside the user. In addition to previously described approaches, this one also does not provide any concrete formulation of QoE metrics relationship but recognizes the need for one with corresponding weights given to QoE IFs in order to contribute to target-oriented design and QoE optimization in future systems. However, it is believed that the developed detailed taxonomy provided in this paper will aid in producing concrete formulation.

As in [56], Geerts et al. [58] have taken a multidisciplinary approach and included researchers from backgrounds such as sociology, communication science, psychology, software development, and computer science in order to create a comprehensive framework. The proposed model consists of four components: user, ICT product, use process, and context. Each component is divided into several subcategories, which then encompass all three aforementioned QoE IF categories. Although the proposed approach does not introduce a weighted QoE formulae, it aims to provide a detailed look at the different components of QoE offering concrete information on how they can be measured.

Another approach accounting for all QoE IF categories is proposed by Laghari et al. [10]. The authors have proposed a high-level QoE model that can be adapted to many specific contexts. It consists of four domains, that is, sets of knowledge, activity, or influence in the proposed model: human, context, technology, and business. Therefore, the model addresses QoE from multiple aspects, while it can be noted that it is more subjectively oriented towards the human domain. Also, the framework defines the main interactions of the domains: human-context, human-technology,

human-business, technology-business, and context-techno-business, as well as presenting causal relationships between domain characteristics. In other words, the presented formulation relates QoE (set of outcome factors) with a "cause-effect" relationship directly affected with the prediction factors (e.g., technological, business, or contextual characteristics) and indirectly with mediating factors (e.g., associations between aforementioned factors). Additionally, by providing a well-structured detailed taxonomy of QoE relevant variables and formulating the causal relationship between them, this approach aids various interested parties in comprehending and managing QoE in a broader manner.

Volk et al. [59] present a novel approach to QoE modeling and assurance in an NGN Service Delivery Environment (SDE). The proposed model is context aware and comprises a comprehensive set of quality-related parameters available throughout various information factories of the NGN and accessible by employing standardized procedures within the NGN SDE. QoS and various human perception components are addressed. Furthermore, parameter selection and mapping definitions are established vertically from the transport layer through the application layer to the end-user layer, and horizontally with concatenation of point-to-point QoS and end-to-end QoE.

De Moor et al. [20] propose a framework that enables the evaluation of multidimensional QoE in a mobile testbed-oriented living lab setting. The model consists of a distributed architecture for monitoring the network QoS, context information, and subjective user experience based on the functional requirement related to real-time experience measurements in real-life settings. The architecture allows the study and understanding of cross-contextual effects, the assessment of the relative importance of parameters, and the development of a basic algorithmic QoE model.

Although Song et al. [60] have not proposed exact formulae for QoE calculation, they have organized QoE IFs into three components: user, system, and context and mapped their impacts upon four elements of the mobile video delivery framework, namely, mobile user, mobile device, mobile network, and mobile video service, since the model is created for a mobile video environment. User-centered design of mobile video may benefit from this model, as well as mobile video vendors that may develop effective strategies to improve user's experience.

Finally, the framework discussed by Reichl et al. [28] is aimed at improved modeling, measurement, and management of QoE for mobile broadband services (e.g., mobile Web browsing, file download). The authors have developed a model for predicting QoE of network services, based on a layered approach distinguishing between the network, application and the user layers. The layered approach derives the most relevant performance indicators (e.g., network performance indicators, user-experience characteristics, and specific application/service related performance indicator) and aims to builds accurate QoE models by combining user studies providing direct ratings, with logged data at the application layer and traffic measurements at the network layer. The employed laboratory setup includes the user's device and two network emulators which model the behavior of a variable UMTS/HSPA network. Participants' network traffic is captured using the METAWIN [61] passive monitoring system that monitors traffic on all the interfaces of the packet-switched core network. Passive network measurements combined with obtained subjective user ratings serve to build reliable QoE models for future QoE estimation. The proposed model provides an interdisciplinary perspective including aspects such as device and application usability, usage context, user personality, emotional issues, and user roles. Thereby, it can be used not only for QoE prediction and management, but also for uncovering functional dependencies between causally relevant performance indicators and the resulting perceived quality.

Based on the comparison given in Table 1, it may be summarized that the majority of discussed approaches [10, 20, 28, 57–60], differing in considered type of service and wireless aspects, address the human IFs at both low-level (i.e., physical, emotional, and mental constitution of the user) and high-level processing (i.e., cognitive ability, interpretation, or judgment). These models also consider system IFs classified into content, media, network, and device factors, as well as context IFs, while a set of them such as [55, 56] do not explicitly address IFs in that fashion. However, although the analyzed approaches address different IFs, most provide a QoE modeling framework, while only a few of them provide a concrete model [10, 28, 59].

In the context of QoE management, all addressed QoE modeling approaches, each in its own way, contribute to this process and may be applied in various contexts such as system or service/application optimization, as well as network resource allocation improvement. Thus several of them have been built to aid monitoring, measurement, and estimation of QoE [20, 54, 58, 59], while others contribute to QoE improvement by diagnosing the main reasons for quality deterioration [55], enabling development of strategies [60], and providing detailed taxonomy [56, 57] and causal relationships [10], as well as QoE prediction mechanisms [28].

2.4. QoE Modeling in the Context of Wireless Networks. QoE modeling becomes even more challenging in the context of wireless and mobile networks due to additional issues posed by this variable environment. Previously analyzed QoE modeling approaches have addressed the points common to both fixed and wireless-mobile environments in terms of system, user, and context IFs. However, in order to gain better understanding of QoE modeling in wireless environments, additional aspects that need to be considered and stressed in addition to common ones have been listed and classified according to the categorization in [22] in Table 2.

Beginning with the environment itself, we address reliability and variability. Wireless channels are more prone to errors than fixed networks because of exposure to various physical phenomena such as noise, fading, or interference. This leads to packet losses, as well as to excessive and variable delays, which consequently affect metrics such as Round Trip Time (RTT), Server Response Time (SRT) or throughput, and integrity and fluency of transmitted data. The wireless infrastructure has been marked as an air bottleneck in data

transmission between the user device and the gateway due to several other features such as wireless capacity in terms of speed, coverage radius, or limited bandwidth, and channel sharing with other users or signal strength which may be affected by temperature, humidity, distance from the antenna, and so forth. Also, regarding the wireless channels' reliability, one must consider security issues and interceptions. In addition, the usage of the multitude of wireless access technologies differing in their characteristics (e.g., bandwidth, capacity and coverage constraints, congestion mechanism) also influences the wireless network performance in many ways and thereby the QoE as well.

In contrast to a fixed environment, mobility (horizontal handover) as well as the freedom of switching between various available wireless access technologies, that is, migration of communication from one network to another (vertical handover), leads to another factor affecting QoE—session establishment delay. Namely, during session establishment, a mobile user passes several steps. Firstly, the user has to wait for the security procedures to be performed in order to be granted access to the network. The user then additionally waits while the signaling procedures are completed in order to establish the session. Therefore, in order to initially establish the session or reestablish one due to interruption caused by handover, these procedures have to be performed [21]. With high users' mobility rate, signaling procedures are performed more frequently, increasing the amount of the signaling traffic. This affects the overall usage of wireless resources and increases the session establishment delay, leading to a negative impact on QoE.

However, the increased amount of signaling traffic exchanged in session set up, modification, or tear down procedure does not only affect radio and signaling resources, but also affects device performance. For example, modern mobile phones have an impressive repertoire of functions and features and support applications that require constant connection with the network [62]. The connectivity is maintained by frequently exchanging signaling traffic, which may dominate in comparison with data traffic. The consequence is the overload of computational resources on the mobile device and faster battery consumption. These factors have been considered neither in the case of laptops where the signaling traffic is not generated that frequently and batteries are bigger and allow longer connection maintenance, nor in the QoE modeling for fixed environments where battery consumption is not an issue. Additionally, battery consumption is not only linked with mobile-device interaction with the network, but also to user-device interaction. Therefore, one may conclude that battery lifetime and its consumption are major factors that need to be considered when modeling QoE in the wireless context.

In addition to battery consumption, a number of mobile device features impact QoE. The size of the mobile device screen, as well as position and location of the keys on the screen, may cause difficulties with resizing or scrolling. The small keyboard can impact overall usability and lead to aggravation when typing. Furthermore, as stated in [2, 35], end-user perceived quality may be affected by a lack of "features," such as flash player, personalized alarm clock, features for

TABLE 2: Aspects to be considered and stressed when modeling QoE in a wireless context.

Category	Aspects impacting QoE to be considered and stressed in the wireless context	
	Network	Device
System	(i) Physical phenomena of wireless channel—variability (affected by noise, fading, and interference)	(i) Signal strength (terminal antenna gain, terminal receiver sensitivity)
	(ii) Wireless channel reliability (interception, security issues)	(ii) Battery lifetime—energy consumption
	(iii) Wireless capacity (speed, coverage, limited bandwidth, shared resources)	(iii) Computational power/resources, storage capacity, processor capability
	(iv) Channel sharing among users	(iv) Screen and keyboard size
	(v) Signal strength (affected by the temperature, humidity, distance from the antenna, base station antenna gain)	(v) Signaling traffic overload
	(vi) Signaling traffic overload	
	(vii) Handover delay	
	Media and Content	
	(i) Adaptation capabilities (e.g., capability to adapt various application parameters to fit the device, network, usage context constraints)	
	(ii) Usability of mobile device	
	(iii) Adjustment to the device power consumption	
	(iv) Data access	
	(v) Offline capabilities	
	(vi) Transparent synchronization with backend systems	
	(vii) Security issues	
	(viii) Lack of add-ons	
User and context	User routine and lifestyle	
	The impact of multiple contexts on user's perception (e.g., mobility, time of day, noisy environment, prior experience)	

privacy settings, Global Positioning System (GPS), and built-in dictionary.

In the context of achieving high QoE, mobile application developers should consider all usage scenarios and address various challenges. Application adaptation capabilities (dynamic or static) are important, in terms of adapting service/application content to fit the device and access network capabilities. Besides usability which is mostly considered in all QoE models, applications should be adjusted to device computational power [63]. Various means of data access, security issues, and offline capabilities as well as transparent synchronization with the backend systems also must be addressed when considering mobile applications.

Finally, user behavior in the wireless context is different as compared to fixed environments. Users are able to access services via various available wireless technologies and different mobile devices, which expose them to dynamic environments. Although addressed in most existing QoE modeling approaches, it is particularly important to address the various usage contexts in wireless environments, since they change the users' perceived quality greatly. The authors in [2] have recognized these important user- and context-related aspects in mobile environments and summarized them in the user routine and lifestyle.

2.5. Summary of QoE Modeling Challenges. There are a number of challenges related to the topic of QoE modeling. Firstly, there is a need to identify a long list of various factors affecting QoE for a given type of service. Secondly, well-planned extensive subjective studies need to be conducted involving human quality perception (including both cognitive and behavioral modeling) in order to model the relationship between identified IFs and (multiple dimensions of) QoE. Some of the main aspects to be considered when planning subjective tests include specification of the methodology to be used, identification of the dependant and independent variables to be considered, user test subjects, testing scenarios, testing environment, and rating scales. Test results analysis leads to identification of the IFs with the most significant impact on QoE and enables the derivation of key QoE IFs. The identification of key QoE IFs and their quality thresholds provide input for relevant QoE optimization strategies. Thirdly, general QoE models should be generic and designed in an elastic way so as to account for fast technology and service advances in converged wireless networks.

While standards specify subjective testing methodologies for multimedia services such as audio, video, and audio-visual services [49, 50, 64, 65], new methodologies are currently being studied for emerging services such as Web and cloud-based services [66–70]. In addition, this section contributes by summarizing the QoE modeling challenges in the wireless context.

3. QoE Measurement and Modeling

As previously stated, QoE is a multidimensional concept which is difficult not only to define in a simple and unified manner, but also to monitor and measure, considering the large number of QoE IFs to be considered. In order to provide accurate QoE assessment, consideration of only one or two QoE IFs is generally not sufficient. On the contrary, QoE should be considered in all its dimensions taking into account as many IFs as possible (and relevant). Knowledge of the key IFs related to a given type of service drawn from QoE models provides input for QoE monitoring purposes.

The QoE monitoring and measurement process encompasses the acquisition of data related to the network environment and conditions, terminal capabilities, user, context, and application/service specific information and its quantification [24]. The parameters can be gathered via probes at different points in the communication system, at different moments, as well as by various methods. A diversity of QoE monitoring and measurement points, moments, and methods together with the selection of the key QoE IFs for a given service additionally increases the complexity of this process.

In order to be able to manage and optimize QoE, knowledge regarding the root cause of unsatisfactory QoE levels or QoE degradations is necessary. As noted by Batteram et al. [71] and also by Reichl. et al. [30], a layered approach relates network-level Key Performance Indicators (KPIs, for example, delay, loss, throughput, etc.) with user-level application specific Key Quality Indicators (KQIs, for example, service availability, usability, reliability, etc.), which then provide input for a QoE estimation model. Additional input to a QoE estimation model may then be provided by user-, context-, and device-related IFs. Knowledge regarding this mapping between KPIs and KQIs (or what we have referred to as quality dimensions) will provide valuable input regarding the analysis of the root causes of QoE degradation. Hence, monitoring probes inserted at different points along the service delivery chain to collect data regarding relevant KPIs are necessary.

When discussing monitoring points, we may roughly distinguish between *network-based* probes and *client side* probes (note that measurements in both cases may be conducted at different layers of the protocol stack). At the client side, we may further distinguish between probes that collect end-user-related data (e.g., objective measures such as user mouse clicks, or data such as user demographics, user motivation, etc.), context data, device-related data, application data, and network traffic data. While monitoring at the client side provides the best insight into the service quality that users actually perceive, a challenge lies in providing QoE information feedback to the network, service/application, content, or cloud provider to adapt, control, and optimize the QoE. As noted by Hoßfeld et al. [24], this client side monitoring point poses the issues of users' privacy, trust,

and integrity, since users may cheat in order to receive better performance. Consequently, collecting data from within the network without conducting client side monitoring (in an either objective or subjective manner), and vice versa, will not generally provide sufficient insight into QoE. Hence, accurate monitoring of QoE needs to employ both: monitoring from within the network and at the client side.

Soldani et al. [72] have used the same conclusions for the monitoring and measurement of QoE, specifically in mobile networks, that is, the need for complementary application of QoE monitoring and measurement methods. Two approaches were proposed: (1) a service-level approach using statistical samples; and (2) a network management system approach using QoS parameters. The former one uses application-level performance indicators and provides the real user opinion towards the used service, while the latter maps QoS performance metrics from various parts of the network onto user-perceptible QoE performance targets. Several similar QoE measurement approaches were standardized by 3GPP in particularly for Real-Time Protocol (RTP) based streaming, Hypertext Transfer Protocol (HTTP) streaming [73], Dynamic Adaptive Streaming over HTTP (DASH), progressive download [74], and Multimedia Telephony (MMtel) [75] for 3GPP devices. Namely, the quality of mobile media is usually degraded due to issues that arise in the last wireless hop, and, consequently, network oriented QoE assessment may not be very reliable. Therefore, it has been reported that the best way to obtain an accurate QoE assessment is to monitor and measure it in the mobile device and report it back to the system [76]. Reported QoE data is combined with other network collected measurements and facilitates the identification of the root causes of quality degradation.

Regarding timing, QoE measurements may be conducted (1) before the service is developed, which includes the consideration of individual quality factors as well as quality planning; (2) after the service is developed, but not delivered; (3) during/after service delivery, which comprises quality monitoring within the network and at the end user side during/after service usage. It has been noted that in the context of closed loop adaptation, there is a growing demand for suitable objective (rather than subjective) QoE evaluation techniques to facilitate optimal use of available wireless resources [23].

As discussed in [71], there are primarily three techniques prevalent in the market today for measuring performance: (1) using test packets; (2) using probes in network elements and user equipment; and (3) using the measurement combination from several network elements. Various approaches involving passive measurements have been reported, based on analyzing the correlations between traffic characteristics and performance criteria [28, 77]. Conducting passive measurements is often cheap and may be used for the evaluation of new applications. However, using network QoS measures for QoE estimation generally implies discerning individual media streams, hence putting additional effort on the monitoring process (involving packet filtering and stream reconstruction) [78].

It is a great challenge today to find a consensus regarding QoE measuring practices. On one hand, QoE has been

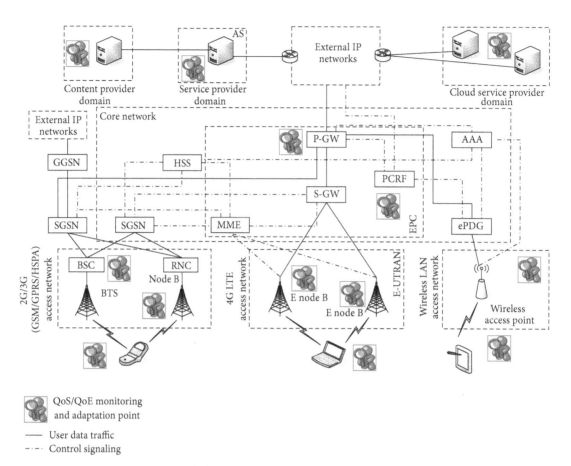

FIGURE 2: QoE/QoS monitoring and adaptation points in a wireless network environment (see Abbreviations).

mainly measured in terms of technical metrics, since it is often interpreted in terms of QoS. This measurement and assessment approach is criticized when stressing the multidimensional character of QoE [20, 54, 56, 79–81]. On the other hand, measuring the subjective dimensions of the experience is often skipped or neglected because of shorter product/service life cycles, time pressure, budgetary reasons, or simply because they are ignored.

3.1. A Survey of QoE Monitoring and Measurement Approaches in Wireless Networks.

Figure 2 illustrates possible QoE/QoS monitoring and adaptation points in a wireless network environment in the context of the 3GPP EPS. The EPS supports multiple access networks and mobility between them via a converged all-IP core network referred to as the previously mentioned EPC [1]. The figure portrays a simplified architecture combining 2G/3G access networks, non-3GPP radio access networks, and the 3GPP LTE access network [6, 82, 83]. As shown, QoE/QoS-related data may be collected from within the network, at the client side, or both. The QoE monitoring and measurement within the network may include data collection at different points such as the base stations within the various access networks, the gateways or routers within the core network, or the servers in the service/application, content, or cloud domains. The acquired parameters may be derived from application level (e.g., content resolution, frame rate, codec type, media type),

network level (e.g., packet loss, delay, jitter, throughput), or a combination thereof, that is, in the cross-layer fashion. This approach of enabling QoS at different layers is required due to the fact that existing QoS support in wireless access technologies (e.g., WiMAX or LTE) focuses only on the access network [84]. Traffic collection closer to the end user will provide input for a more accurate estimate of QoE, as discussed also in [85]. Furthermore, the amount of data to process is greatly reduced as compared to data collected in the core network. While QoS solutions commonly use network egress routers for conducting traffic analysis, there is a need to consider computational load.

The remainder of this subsection provides a discussion of several QoE measurement and monitoring studies that have been conducted with various types of services. The approaches are categorized as focusing on client side or network measurements, or their combination. A summary given in Table 3 compares these approaches based on the QoE monitoring point, QoE estimation point, method of conducting the QoE measurement, metrics (subjective or objective), type of service, and QoE management applicability, as well as deployment challenges in the context of QoE management. We note that while subjective measurements are generally more applicable in the context of building QoE models (or validating monitoring approaches), objective measurements are generally employed for QoE estimation and subsequently optimization purposes.

TABLE 3: Comparison of QoE monitoring and measurement approaches.

Approach	QoE monitoring point	QoE estimation point	QoE management applicability	Measurements environment	Subjective/Objective	Type of service	Deployment challenges
3GPP 26.247 [74]	End user device (technical data)	Network	(i) Dynamic adaptation of service delivery to meet access network capabilities (ii) Applicable in the context of optimization of limited network resource management	Real	Objective	Dynamic adaptive streaming over HTTP	(i) QoE service differentiation and prioritization (ii) Battery consumption (iii) Scalability (iv) Computational complexity (v) Data integrity (vi) User's privacy issues
Ketykó et al. [88]	End user device (technical and user data)	End user device	Applicable in the context of application design improvement (better understanding of content effect)	Semi-real life	Both	Mobile YouTube video streaming	(i) Scalability (ii) User's fairness/correctness (iii) Feedback the estimation output to optimize the network (iv) Data integrity
Wac et al. [35]	End user device (technical, user, and context data)	End user device	Applicable in the context of application design improvement	Real	Both	Wide range of mobile applications	(i) User's fairness/correctness (ii) User's privacy issues (iii) Computational complexity (iv) Feedback the estimation output to optimize the network
Volk et al. [59]	Network	Network	(i) Applicable in the context of service estimation and optimization (ii) Applicable in the context of the network resource allocation optimization	Real	Objective	SDE	(i) User subjectivity (ii) Computational complexity
Varela and Laulajainen [91]	End user device	End user device	(i) Applicable in the context of service estimation and optimization (ii) Applicable in the context of QoE-driven access network selection	Laboratory	Both	Mobile VoIP	(i) Tighter integration with the MIP software (ii) Cost and battery consumption (iii) User's fairness
Hoßfeld et al. [96]	End user device and network	Network	Applicable in the context of network resource optimization	Laboratory	Objective	YouTube video streaming	(i) User's privacy and subjectivity (ii) Limitation of scalability (iii) Additional costs due to DPI

TABLE 3: Continued.

Approach	QoE monitoring point	QoE estimation point	QoE management applicability	Measurements environment	Subjective/Objective	Type of service	Deployment challenges
Menkovski et al. [38]	Network	End user device	(i) Applicable in the context of network resource management (ii) Applicable in the context of content encoding management	Laboratory	Both	Commercial mobile TV	(i) Inability to give information on service perception (ii) Computational complexity
Staehle et al. [97]	End user device (technical data) and network	Network	(i) Applicable in the context of radio resource management (ii) Applicable in the context of service degradation	Laboratory	Objective	YouTube video streaming	(i) Cross-layer information extraction (ii) User's privacy issues (iii) Battery consumption
Ketykó et al. [98]	End user device (technical and user data) and network	End user device	Applicable in the context of service estimation and optimization	Semi-real life	Both	Mobile video streaming	(i) Scalability (ii) User's fairness (iii) Feedback the estimation output to the network optimization (iv) Battery consumption

3GPP: 3rd Generation Partnership Project, DPI: Deep Packet Inspection, HTTP: Hypertext Transfer Protocol, MIP: Mobile Internet Protocol, MMORPG: Massively Multiplayer Online Role-Playing Game, QoE: Quality of Experience, QoS: Quality of service, RRM: Radio Resource Management, SDE: Service Delivery Environment, VoIP: Voice over Internet Protocol.

3.1.1. QoE Monitoring at the Client Side. While 3GPP policy and QoS mechanisms are based on centralized control, there have been complementary efforts to move certain intelligence from the network to the client. In the context of DASH services (Dynamic Adaptive Streaming over HTTP), 3GPP and MPEG standardization bodies have standardized mechanisms for activating QoE measurements at the client device, as well as the protocols and formats for the delivery of QoE reports to the network servers [74]. It is important to note that HTTP adaptive streaming in general provides the client with the ability to fully control the streaming session. This methodology is mostly suitable for mobile wireless environments and proposed as an optional feature on client devices. The QoE monitoring and reporting framework as standardized by 3GPP is composed of the following phases: (1) a server activates QoE reporting, requests a set of QoE metrics to be reported, and configures the QoE reporting framework; (2) a client monitors or measures the requested QoE metrics according to the QoE configuration; and (3) the client sends the QoE report to the network server in Extensible Markup Language (XML) format by using HTTP [86]. In the context of 3GPP LTE systems, it is important to devise and adopt new QoS delivery and service adaption methods targeting DASH services, since they are beneficial in the sense of optimal management of limited network resources and improved QoE provisioning to the end user [87]. The benefits of adaptive streaming have in particular been recognized in the case of high bandwidth-consuming mobile video communications. Figure 3 depicts a possible example of PCC architecture performing end-to-end QoS/QoE delivery for DASH services. As noted in [87], the current 3GPP PCC architecture supports only QoS delivery and service adaptation for RTSP-based adaptive streaming services, with the need for new methods for HTTP adaptive streaming services.

Other work has addressed concrete cases of collecting QoE relevant metrics at the client side, albeit primarily for QoE modeling purposes and not considering QoE reporting mechanisms providing feedback to the network. In their studies of mobile video streaming, Ketykó et al. [88] have introduced an implementation of a QoE measurement approach on the Android platform based on the collection of both objective and subjective parameters. Observed objective parameters are logged by a QoS and context monitor component deployed on an Android device node and include audio and video jitter and packet loss rate, as well as percentage of duration of connection to a specific data network type in relation to the total duration of a video watching session. In addition, observed end user subjective parameters are logged by an *Experience Monitor* component also deployed on the Android device and include test users' ratings of content, picture and sound quality, fluidness, matching to interests, and loading speed. Similar to the procedures in [88], Verdejo et al. [89] discuss the Android-based QoE measurement framework as applied in the context of playing a mobile location-based real-time massively multiplayer online role-playing game (MMORPG). Users' evaluations regarding the feelings of amusement, absorption, or engagement experienced while playing the game are taken into account

and related to a set of objective QoS-related parameters, contextual data, and physiological data obtained from an on-body sensor.

Previously described measurement approaches may contribute to the overall QoE management process in the context of improving the application design, that is, better understanding of content and physical effects. However, if applying such measurement techniques, for example, for optimizing network performance, the challenge lies in reporting QoE feedback obtained at the client side back to the network. Other potential deployment challenges are user related. As previously mentioned, if a user is providing QoE related feedback, they may cheat to improve their performance. Finally, user's privacy may be an issue when it comes to behavioral monitoring.

Besides the previously described subjective data collection methods ESM and DRM, Wac et al. [35] have also addressed technical aspects of QoE in their measurement approach involving a real-life four-week-long study. They have developed an Android Context Sensing Software (CSS) application that unobtrusively collects context and QoS data from users' Android phones. Gathered context data includes current time and user's geographical location, wireless access network technology, cell-ID or an access point name, Received Signal Strength Indication (RSSI), and current used applications with total amounts of application throughput) while the measured network parameter is Round Trip Time (RTT) for an application-level control message sent every minute from a mobile device through the available wireless access network to a dedicated server. As a result of the study, the authors identified a number of QoE IFs for mobile applications, such as user's routine, prior experience, and the possibility to choose between a PC and their mobile device. This approach contributes to the QoE management process in the context of mobile applications design improvement but might experience the same deployment challenges as the two previously described approaches.

With regards to collecting user feedback, a framework proposed by Chen et al. [90] quantifies the users' quality perceptions by having users click a dedicated button whenever he/she feels dissatisfied with the quality of the used application. Hence, the framework is called OneClick and has been demonstrated through user evaluations of different multimedia content in variable network conditions.

Finally, we mention the applicability of client side monitoring in the context of QoE-driven mobility management. Focusing on voice services, Varela and Laulajainen [91] describe QoE estimations for VoIP to improve the existing network-level IP mobility management solutions. The proposed solution performs QoE estimations by passive network QoS monitoring for VoIP traffic, feeding the network's QoS information to a Pseudo-Subjective Quality Assessment (PSQA) tool [92]. The aim is to aid in making access network handover decisions. A presented prototype implementation is tested in scenarios representing real VoIP service usage. We note that VoIP QoE estimation and prediction based on passive probing mechanisms and integrated directly into a mobility management protocol is further addressed by Mitra et al. [93]. Furthermore, a user-centric approach to

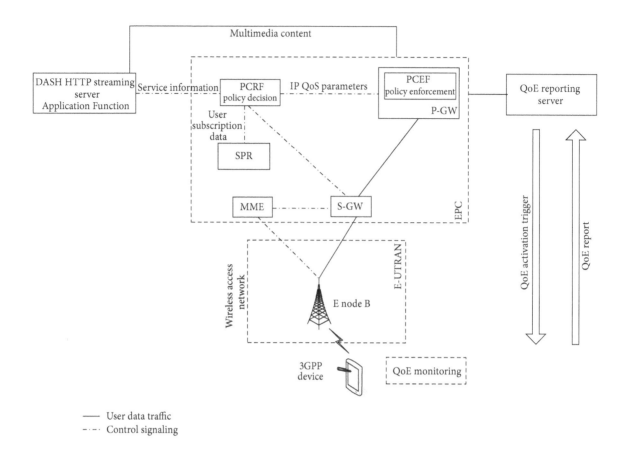

FIGURE 3: Example of possible PCC architecture performing end-to-end QoS/QoE delivery for DASH services (see Abbreviations).

proposing seamless mobility management solutions was one of the key focus areas of the EU FP7 PERIMITER project [94] (available deliverables provide detailed insight into user-centric mobility design).

3.1.2. QoE Monitoring in the Network. Volk et al. [59], whose approach is described in Section 2 in the context of QoE modeling, have focused on an NGN and IP Multimedia Subsystem (IMS) [95] based environment and proposed a solution for QoE assurance which employs an automated proactive in-service algorithm for the user's QoE estimation, rather than relying on regular QoS techniques or acquiring the subjective end-user's feedback. The QoE estimation algorithm is based on context-aware objective end-to-end QoE modeling and is run by a dedicated application server, implemented as a value-added service enabler. The authors argue reasons for conducting centralized QoE estimations in the network as being availability of and access to a wide range of quality-related information, the possibility of non-intrusive in-service QoE estimation, and the potential of proactive in-service quality assurance functionality (e.g., the application server may invoke adaptation/modification of certain quality affecting parameters). While the authors argue that this approach ensures fair interpretation of subjectively perceived quality towards any end user or service, and

operational efficiency in terms of no end-user involvement (guaranteeing universality of the QoE estimation), the notion of user singularity may be considered neglected.

Hoßfeld et al. [96] compare two YouTube QoE monitoring approaches operating at the end user level (described in the following heading) and within the network. A novel YouTube in-network (YiN) monitoring tool is proposed as a passive network monitoring tool. This approach aims at detecting and measuring stalling of the video playback by approximating the video buffer status by comparing the playback times of video frames and the time stamps of received packets. The challenges of this approach are related to the accurate reconstruction of the stalling events that arrive at the application layer which requires additional costs and limits the scalability in terms of the number of YouTube video streaming flows that can be actually monitored by a probe.

Menkovski et al. [38] have presented a method for assessing QoE and developed a platform for conducting the QoE estimation for a service provider. The designed platform estimates QoE of the mobile TV services based on existing QoS monitoring data together with QoE prediction models. The prediction models are built using Machine Learning (ML) techniques from subjective data acquired by limited initial subjective user measurements. Thereby, subjective measurement associated complexities are minimized, while the accuracy of the method is maintained. This platform is currently used for mobile TV systems where it estimates the QoE of the streaming media content and is further used to manage the services and resources. However, the deployed system cannot give any information as to how the service is perceived by the end user.

3.1.3. QoE Monitoring Combining Client Side and Network Measurements. Further focusing on YouTube as one of the most common and traffic intensive mobile applications, Staehle et al. [97] have proposed a previously mentioned YouTube Application Comfort (AC) monitoring tool—*YoMo*, which monitors the QoE at the client's side. The tool detects the YouTube video and determines its buffered playtime. Thereby, the YoMo tool is able to detect an imminent QoE degradation, that is, stalling of the video. The interruption of the video playback is the only considered factor influencing YouTube QoE, as it has been argued that this is the key IF in the given case. Additionally, the tool communicates the stalling information to the network advisor and raises an alarm if the AC becomes bad. What makes YoMo particularly suitable for QoE monitoring and measurement is its ability to predict the time of stalling in advance. Thus, it allows the network operator to react prior to the QoE degradation and to avoid unsatisfied customers.

Ketykó et al. [98] have introduced a measurement concept of QoE related to mobile video streaming in a 3G network environment and semi-real-life context. The data collection, which is based on the Experience Sampling Method, combines objective and subjective data for evaluating user experiences. Observed technical-quality-related QoE parameters, audio and video packet loss and jitter, are obtained at the server-side from the Real-time Transport Control Protocol (RTCP) Receiver Records (RR), while the observed RSSI parameter is obtained from the *MyExperience* in situ measurement tool used at the client side. The subjective assessments parameters have been conducted in two phases: (1) preusage questionnaire (obtaining users' experiences towards mobile applications) and (2) usage phase where users are asked to use the mobile application in six different usage contexts: indoor and outdoor, at home, at work, and on a train/bus. This study has shown that QoE of mobile video streaming is influenced by the QoS and by the context. Additionally, the authors have proposed linear functions for modeling the technical-quality-related QoE aspects and argued that spatial quality and emotional satisfaction are the most relevant QoE aspects for the tested users.

Having surveyed several chosen QoE measurement approaches, we have classified them into ones that aim to perform QoE monitoring by acquiring data only at the client side [35, 74, 88–90], only within the network [28, 38, 59, 91, 96], or by collecting data at both, the client side and within the network [97, 98]. As stated previously, in order to assure accurate QoE estimation and identification of the causes of QoE degradation, measurements collected along the end-to-end service delivery path are needed. The majority of approaches comprise both subjective and objective parameters with end users estimating QoE. While the collection of subjective assessments is generally conducted in the scope of empirical QoE studies targeted towards building accurate

QoE models, objective measurements provide input for QoE prediction mechanisms and are commonly employed for QoE optimization and control purposes. Furthermore, in terms of the measurements environments that have been discussed, several approaches have been illustrated in a laboratory testbed [28, 38, 91, 96, 97], while others were demonstrated in real-life [35, 59, 74, 90] or semi-real-life environments [88, 89, 98].

As it can be observed from the previous analysis, QoE monitoring approaches in the wireless context often measure parameters such as packet loss rate, bandwidth, throughput, delay, and jitter and do not in general differ from ones addressing a fixed environment. However, in order to gain a deeper understanding of QoE IFs in wireless and mobile environments, there is a need to monitor parameters characteristic for such environments (Table 2). For example, RSSI measurements can be utilized for addressing wireless factors such as channel exposure to physical phenomenon, its capacity and sharing among the users, signal strength, terminal antenna gain. Additionally, in order to gain the accuracy regarding the wireless channels, this measurement can be combined with measurements of base station and terminal antenna gain, distance from the antenna, temperature, and so forth. The information obtained by combining the aforementioned measurements can give a clearer picture of which factors impact QoE and to what extent. Another example is the measurement of the radio cell reselection frequency or signaling update frequency which may reveal how these wireless and mobile specific issues can be optimized. Additionally, although not considered in the analysis, it is recommended to measure the mobile device power consumption while using different applications, processor capability, and storage capacity.

3.2. Summary of QoE Monitoring and Measurement Challenges. The previous discussion has shown that the QoE monitoring and measurement process is complex due to the diversity of factors affecting QoE, data acquisition points, and timings, as well as methods of collecting data, and the lack of consensus regarding these issues. The main challenge in this process is to answer the following four questions: (1) *What* to collect?; (2) *Where* to collect?; (3) *When* to collect?; and (4) *How* to collect?

Firstly, one needs to determine *which* data to acquire. The *what/which* clause is specified by the QoE metrics selection which depends on the service type and context. The decision regarding data that should be acquired considering the wide spectrum of QoE IFs is challenging, but it is the prerequisite for any QoE monitoring and measurement approach. Secondly, choosing a location *where* to collect data is another critical issue in the QoE assessment process, that is, determine the location of monitoring probes. As previously mentioned, data can be collected within the network, at the client side, or both (depending also on whether measurements are conducted for QoE modeling purposes or for QoE control purposes). The QoE monitoring and measurement within the network may include data collection at different points such as the base stations within the various access networks, the gateways or routers within the core network, or the servers in the service/application, content, or cloud domains. Additionally, the acquired parameters may be derived from application level, network level, or a combination thereof. Each acquisition location addresses the specific challenges discussed previously. Furthermore, if performing in-service QoE management (e.g., QoE-driven dynamic (re)allocation of network resources), collected data generally needs to be communicated to an entity performing QoE optimization decisions. Hence, the passing of data to a control entity needs to be addressed. Thirdly, one should determine *when* to collect data: (1) before the service is developed; (2) after the service is developed, but not delivered; and (3) after the service is delivered. Additionally, *how often* data should be monitored and measured needs to be considered. Finally, *how* to perform the data acquisition is determined by the *where* and *when* clauses. The QoE monitoring process implies computational operations, hence computational complexity and battery life of mobile devices need to be considered.

It may be concluded, as in the QoE modeling process, that different actors involved in the service provisioning chain will monitor and measure QoE in different ways, focusing on those parameters over which a given actor has control (e.g., a network provider will monitor how QoS-related performance parameters will impact QoE, a device manufacturer will monitor device-related performance issues, while application developers will be interested in how the service design or usability will affect QoE).

Having chosen the proper QoE metrics and monitoring and measurements approach, it is important to provide mechanisms utilizing this information for improving service performance, network planning, optimization of network resources, specification of service level agreements (SLAs) among operators, and so forth. Such issues are addressed as the "final step" in the QoE management process, discussed in the following section.

4. QoE Optimization and Control

Following QoE modeling, monitoring, and measurements, the ultimate goal of QoE management is to control QoE via QoE optimization and control mechanisms. Such mechanisms yield optimized service delivery with (potentially) continuous and dynamic delivery control in order to maximize the end-user's satisfaction and optimally utilize limited system resources. From an operator point of view, the goal would be to maintain satisfied end users (in terms of their achieved QoE) in order to limit customer churn, while efficiently allocating available wireless network resources. QoE optimization as such may be considered a very challenging task due to a number of issues characteristic for converged all-IP wireless environments, including limited bandwidth and its variability, the growth of mobile data, the heterogeneity of mobile devices and services, the diversity of usage contexts, and challenging users' requirements and expectations, as well as the strive to achieve cost efficiency.

4.1. An Overview of QoE Optimization Approaches in Wireless Environment. A number of strategies for optimizing QoE in

a wireless environment that have been proposed differ in the applied approach (network/user oriented), parameters chosen to be adjusted, control location(s) and timing(s), and so forth. Therefore, in this section, Table 4 will provide an overview of the state-of-the-art approaches in terms of QoE optimization point, optimization strategy, considered wireless technologies, and deployment challenges.

Since QoS (and ultimately QoE) provisioning is a key issue in the context of wireless networks, 3GPP has proposed a set of comprehensive QoS concepts and architectures for UMTS [7, 8]. A Policy and Charging Rules Function (PCRF) included in the EPS as part of the 3GPP PCC architecture [9], which is shown in Figure 4, impacts end-user QoE for a particular subscription and service type by providing service-aware network-based QoS. Service requirements may be extracted from the application-level signaling (e.g., based on the Session Initiation Protocol (SIP)) and passed down to the PCRF, responsible for executing policy rules. Execution of policy rules and their enforcement at the network level serves to manage network congestion, provide differentiated service quality based on heterogeneous service requirements, and create a framework for new business models. The bearer- and class-based QoS concept introduces a QoS Class Identifier (QCI) which specifies standardized packet forwarding treatment for a given traffic flow. The standardized QCI characteristics are specified in terms of bearer type (Guaranteed Bit-Rate (GBR) or non-GBR), priority, Packet Delay Budget (PDB), and Packet Error Loss Rate (PELR) [99]. Apart from nine QCIs, QoS parameters defined in the EPS include Allocation and Retention Priority (ARP), Maximum Bit-Rate (MBR), and GBR.

Skorin-Kapov and Matijašević [100] have proposed QoE-driven service adaptation and optimized network resource allocation mechanisms in the context of the 3GPP IMS and PCC architectures (Figure 5(a)). Service requirements and user preferences are signaled in the form of utility functions and serve as input for an optimization process (conducted by a proposed QoS Matching and Optimization Function) aimed at calculating the optimal service configuration and network resource allocation, given network resource, service, and operator policy constraints. The calculation results are passed to the PCRF node and serve as input for resource allocation mechanisms. Ivešić et al. [101] have further built on this approach by focusing on QoE-driven domain-wide optimal resource allocation among multiple sessions. The resource allocation has been formulated as a multiobjective optimization problem with the objectives of maximizing the total utility of all active sessions along with operator profit in the context of the 3GPP EPS.

Further considering a 3GPP environment, an in-service QoE control mechanism has been proposed by Volk et al. [59] and further studied by Sterle et al. [102] (Figure 5(b)). The proposed application-level QoE estimation function running at the application server in the NGN service stratum is based on collection of a comprehensive set of QoE IFs. The authors attempt to maximize QoE by making the adjustments to identified quality performance indicators. As previously discussed in terms of QoE monitoring and measurement, this approach's benefits include the wide range of quality-related

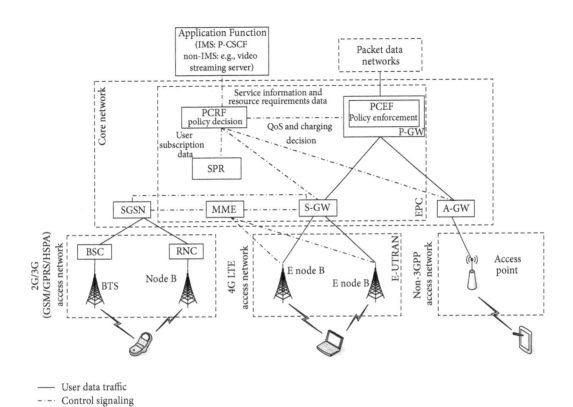

FIGURE 4: 3GPP PCC architecture for EPS (see Abbreviations).

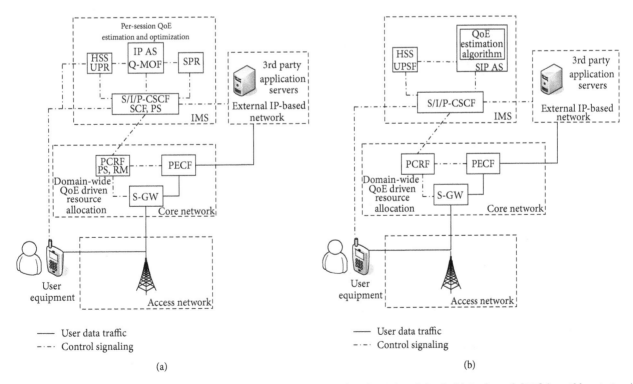

FIGURE 5: QoE control mechanisms: (a) Skorin-Kapov and Matijašević [100] and Ivešić et al. [101]; (b) Sterle et al. [102] (see Abbreviations).

TABLE 4: An overview of QoE optimization approaches in wireless environments.

QoE optimization approach	QoE optimization point	QoE optimization strategy	Wireless technologies considered	Deployment challenges
Skorin-Kapov and Matijašević [100]	SIP application server in IMS domain	(i) Mechanisms for service adaptation (ii) Mechanisms for optimal network resource allocation	3GPP access	(i) Computational complexity (ii) Users subjectivity (iii) Signaling overhead (iv) Scalability
Ivešić et al. [101]	SIP Application server in IMS domain and policy engine in core network (e.g., PCRF)	Mechanisms for domain-wide optimal network resource allocation	3GPP access	(i) Computational complexity (ii) Scalability (iii) Users subjectivity
Sterle et al. [102]	SIP application server in IMS domain	Mechanisms for service optimization	WiMAX and UMTS	(i) Computational complexity (ii) Users subjectivity (iii) Scalability (iv) Extendibility
Thakolsri et al. [103]	Core network (cross-layer based optimization)	(i) Mechanisms for optimal radio resource allocation (ii) Mechanisms for rate adaptation	UMTS (HSDPA)	(i) Users subjectivity (ii) Extendibility
Staehle et al. [97]	Core network (cross-layer based optimization)	(i) Mechanisms for optimal radio resource allocation (ii) Mechanisms for service optimization	WLAN	(i) Computational complexity (ii) Users subjectivity (iii) Scalability
Shehada et al. [112]	Core network (cross-layer based optimization)	Mechanisms for optimal network resource allocation	LTE	(i) Extendibility (ii) Users subjectivity
Amram et al. [113]	Core network (cross-layer based optimization)	(i) Mechanisms for optimal network resource allocation (ii) Mechanisms for optimal handover decision	LTE and WLAN	(i) Extendibility (ii) Cost limitations (iii) Optimal CDN node selection (iv) Users subjectivity (v) Scalability (vi) Modification of scheduling algorithm
Aristomenopoulos et al. [109]	Access network (cross-layer based optimization)	(i) Mechanisms for optimal radio resource allocation (ii) Mechanisms for integration of user's subjectivity	CDMA	(i) User's fairness (ii) Extendibility (iii) Scalability
Wamser et al. [110]	Access network (eNodeB)	Mechanisms for service optimization (prioritized traffic scheduling)	LTE	(i) User's fairness (ii) Signaling overhead (iii) Modification of scheduling algorithm
Piamrat et al. [111]	Access network (user- and network-data collection)	Mechanisms for optimized access network selection	WLAN	(i) Computational complexity (ii) Importing intelligence into base stations (iii) Possible signaling overhead (iv) Extendibility (v) User's fairness
Khan et al. [114]	Sender side (preencoding stage over access network)	(i) Mechanisms for service optimization (ii) Mechanisms for rate adaptation	UMTS	(i) Extendibility (ii) Users subjectivity (iii) Modification of SBR

TABLE 4: Continued.

QoE optimization approach	QoE optimization point	QoE optimization strategy	Wireless technologies considered	Deployment challenges
El Essaili et al. [107]	Distributed on the end user terminal and access network (base station)	(i) Mechanisms for optimal radio resource allocation (ii) Mechanisms for service optimization	LTE	(i) Signaling overhead (ii) Computational complexity (iii) User's privacy
Csernai and Gulyas [115]	End user mobile device	Mechanisms for optimized battery consumption	WLAN	(i) Extendibility (ii) Cost requirements (iii) Modification of scheduling algorithm
Latré et al. [104]	Access network	(i) Mechanism for monitoring the network and building knowledge about it (ii) Mechanisms for analyzing the knowledge and determining QoE actions and enforcing them (iii) Mechanisms for reducing packet loss and switching to different video bit rate to obtain better quality	Not explicitly stated	(i) Scalability (ii) Users subjectivity (iii) Computational complexity
Hassan et al. [106]	Access network	(i) Mechanisms for optimized resource allocation and provider revenue	WLAN (applicable to others)	(i) User's fairness (ii) Scalability (iii) Speech processing

CDMA: Code Division Multiple Access, GPRS: General Packet Radio Service, HSDPA: High-Speed Downlink Packet Access, IMS: IP Multimedia Subsystem, LTE: Long-Term Evolution, QoE: Quality of Experience, RACS: Resource and Admission Control System, SIP: Session Initiation Protocol, UMTS: Universal Mobile Telecommunications System, WiMAX: Worldwide Interoperability for Microwave Access, WLAN: Wireless Access Network.

information sources available in the network and nonintrusive in-service quality assurance and control.

Network-, that is, operator-driven, QoE optimization approaches are primarily concerned with the optimal utilization of available network resources, and in order to maximize QoE, they propose various network resource management mechanisms which rely on the information obtained from the monitoring and measurement process. Therefore, Thakolsri et al. [103] (Figure 6(a)) have applied utility maximization in the context of QoE-driven resource allocation across multiple users accessing different video contents in a wireless network. The proposed scheme allocates network resources and performs rate adaptation such that perceivable quality fluctuations lie within the range of unperceivable changes. Also, the *Aquarema* concept proposed by Staehle et al. [97] (Figure 6(b)) enables application specific network resource management and thereby improves the user QoE in all kinds of networks for all kinds of applications. The authors have achieved the improvement by the interaction of the previously described application comfort monitoring tool—*YoMo*, running at the client side, and a network advisor which may trigger different resource management tools. The tool quantifies how well an application is running and enables prediction of the user experience, thereby allowing the network advisor to act upon an imminent QoE degradation. The principles of these approaches that have placed the resource allocation mechanisms in the core network may be combined. For example, the former one which manages the network resources by prioritizing the users that have better channel conditions and which thereby indirectly assumes the

improvement of the overall QoE can be supplemented with the client information obtained from the monitoring tool. Thereby it would gain more information for the fair prioritizing, that is, network resource allocation, and improvement of individual user QoE.

Additionally, Latré et al. [104] (Figure 6(c)) have defined an autonomic management architecture to optimize the QoE in multimedia access networks using a three-plane approach consisting of (1) a *Monitor Plane* which monitors the network and builds up knowledge about it; (2) a *Knowledge Plane* which analyzes the knowledge and determines the ideal QoE actions; and (3) an *Action Plane* that enforces these actions into the network. The authors have focused on the "smart" Knowledge Plane which consists of two reasoners: an analytical one based on a set of equations and the other one based on neural networks. These reasoners can optimize the QoE of video services with two optimizing actions: applying Forward Error Correction (FEC) to reduce the packet loss caused by errors on a link and switching to different video bit rate to avoid congestion or to obtain a better video quality.

In order to efficiently use limited wireless resources and distribute them among users whose perceived quality should be maximized, QoE-driven resource allocation and scheduling mechanisms should incorporate the sensitivity of the human perceived quality [105] which requires a strategy to include the mapping of users' opinions into resource allocation and scheduling algorithms in various wireless access technologies such as Code Division Multiple Access (CDMA), LTE, UMTS, WiMAX, or Wireless Local Area Network (WLAN). For example, Hassan et al. [106] model the

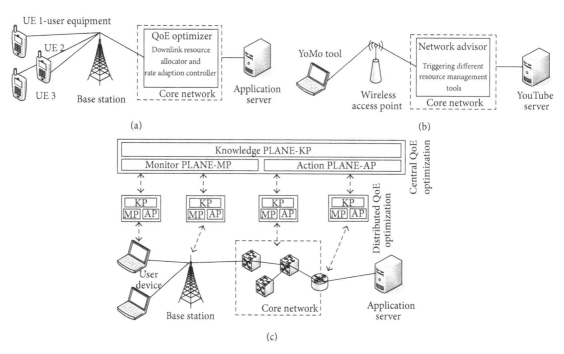

FIGURE 6: QoE optimization mechanisms: (a) Thakolsri et al. [103]; (b) Staehle et al. [97]; (c) Latré et al. [104].

QoE of mobile VoIP services and use this as input for a QoE management scheme employing a game theoretic approach to resource management.

In this context, it is challenging for network elements responsible for resource management to adapt the constrained uplink and downlink wireless resources by assigning or periodically reassigning them to different service providers and users such that all resource competitors are satisfied. Also, QoE-driven resource management that would result in higher users' satisfaction may be performed by implementing QoE-aware routing and packet controllers which give preferential treatment to certain types of packets, according to priority-based policies that may differ depending on operator's interests. However, in resource variable and constrained systems, such as wireless networks, the priority to gain resources is primarily given to users having good channel condition and accessing low-demand applications that result in his/her satisfaction for a small amount of limited resources [103]. Furthermore, one has to account for users that may be given priority for paying more, although they may not have the above mentioned communication conditions. QoE data may be utilized in order to aid and improve decision making in the context of resource allocation and scheduling [103,107], mobility management [91], and so forth.

Further focusing on QoE-driven resource allocation, it can be noted that this process may either be adapted to meet different service requirements (e.g., via 3GPP QoS provisioning mechanisms), or services may be adapted to meet dynamic network resource availability (e.g., adaptive streaming based on MPEG DASH). Additionally, it can be considered in terms of QoE optimization for a single user [91] or multiple users [103] differing in maximization of QoE for a given user or total/average QoE for users, as well as

for single media flow [108] or multiple media flows [100, 101] with different utility functions corresponding to each media component.

However, comprehensive consideration of the various QoE influence factors and their correlations is needed in order to improve and optimize QoE. Depending on the determination of the appropriate QoE IFs which may need to be adjusted for a given service, QoE optimization may be performed at different locations, as depicted in Figure 2. Thus, as summarized in Table 4, the optimization can be conducted by applying various control mechanisms at the base stations within various access networks [109–111] by applying policy management rules at the gateways or routers within the core network [97, 103, 112, 113], by conducting adjustments at the servers in the service/application [104, 113, 114], content or cloud domains, or the combination thereof [107], as well as on end-user device [115]. Since QoE control relies on QoE monitoring and measurement information, usually the control locations are the same as monitoring and measurement points. This does not necessarily mean that QoE optimization is conducted at the location where the data for its activation is collected, since the data gathered at one point in the system may trigger the optimization at another point. Additionally, the optimization may be performed at levels ranging from link- to application-layer [59, 102], as well as in a cross-layer fashion which is most common [97, 103, 108, 112, 113, 116].

The addressed approaches propose various QoE optimization strategies that are aimed at optimal network resource allocation [100, 101, 112, 113]; optimal radio resource allocation [97, 103, 107, 109]; service optimization [97, 100, 102, 107, 110, 114]; optimized handover decision [113]; access network selection [111]; or battery consumption [115].

However, the overall automatic optimization strategies may successfully manage the finite network resources and fulfill general users' requirements, but these may not always be optimal in terms of an individual user's QoE. It has been argued that automated mechanisms may benefit from the user's manual adjustments of the service settings on his/her own device, although it would affect the network resources. For example, Aristomenopoulos et al. [109] have proposed a dynamic utility adaption framework suitable for real-time multimedia services in a wireless environment, which allows users to express their (dis)satisfaction with the service quality and adjust it at their device. This framework provides the seamless integration of users' subjectivity in network utility-based Radio Resource Management (RRM) mechanisms, enabling cross-layering from the application to the Media Access Control (MAC) layer.

With regards to timing when the QoE optimization should be conducted, one may distinguish between in-service and out-of-service approaches. In-service QoE optimization implies the conduction of the process in the system while it is in operation. In other words, it performs the on-line quality prediction/control during service execution. The user-oriented approaches based on quality-related feedback are in-service, since the events that trigger QoE adaptation are coming from the individual user while she/he is using the service [109, 111]. Also, the network-oriented approaches may be in-service, since the resource management functions can be triggered by events happening during the service (e.g., detection of network congestion, operator policy) [59, 97, 102, 103, 110, 113–115]. On the other hand, out-of-service QoE adaptation is performed in an off-line fashion by implementing the control mechanisms for network planning, load balancing, network congestion detection, and so forth [9, 116].

It may be concluded that in most situations the user perceived QoE will depend on the underlying network performance. However, network-oriented QoE optimization processes would clearly benefit from perceived quality feedback data collected at the user's side, since QoE is inherently user-centric. In addition, as previously mentioned, the network decision making process may benefit from the user's adaptations in terms of more efficient resource usage. Therefore, in order to truly optimize and control QoE, both network- and user-oriented issues should be encompassed.

4.2. Summary of QoE Optimization Challenges. As previously discussed, QoE optimization and control is a challenging task considering numerous constraints. Similarly, as related to QoE monitoring and measuring processes, the main challenges that arise with regards to QoE controlling may be summarized in the answers to the following four questions: (1) *what* to control?; (2) *where* to control?; (3) *when* to control?; and (4) *how* to control?

Answering the question of *what* parameters to optimize relates to the issue of determining the key factors whose adjustments would result in improved QoE. Additionally, the impact of those optimizations on other parameters must be considered, since in certain cases improvements of one set of parameters may result in other parameters degradations (e.g., web browsing a high quality media content may prolong a web page response time). The *what* clause determines another critical issue in the QoE optimization process: the location *where* the optimization will be performed. Thus, the QoE may be optimized at various locations as previously discussed. Furthermore, one needs to determine *when* to perform the QoE optimization: during the service, that is, on-line control or in an off-line fashion. Additionally, it needs to be considered *how often* to optimize QoE. Finally, *how* to optimize QoE is determined by all three previously mentioned clauses.

Basically, there are many strategies for QoE optimization and control, and they can be described as being closer to the network or closer to the user. A promising approach appears to optimize QoE by combining the network- and user-oriented approaches by supplementing the drawbacks of one with the advances of the other. Therefore, by combining different approaches in QoE optimization, multiple stakeholders and players involved in the service delivery process would benefit, since the various additional challenges that each of them pose would be addressed. Additionally, the characteristics of wireless and mobile environments that have been discussed in Table 2 (e.g., the constrained and shared network resources, variable and unstable nature of wireless channels, device diversities and capabilities) will pose additional challenges to cope with when allocating limited resources among users.

Therefore, open research issues include applicability across different wireless access technologies (e.g., LTE, WiMAX, WLAN) and implementation on heterogeneous devices; computational issues in terms of complexity of the mechanism or limited computational capacity of a device which may lead to battery consumption; signaling overhead due to increased amount of signaling traffic exchanged between devices and wireless access points (if the optimization mechanism is distributed and combined) and resulting latency; scalability in terms of resulting time-consuming effect and cost when the solution is applied on a large number of users; and so forth. Since a goal of future research is to consider the user's subjectivity in the QoE optimization procedure, user-related issues such as fairness, trust, or privacy must be addressed appropriately.

5. Conclusion

Satisfying user service quality expectations and requirements in today's user centric and upcoming converged all-IP wireless environment implies the challenge of performing successful QoE management. Requirements put forth by standards including 3GPP, ETSI, and ITU include providing support for access to services anywhere and anytime, over any medium and network technology, and across multiple operator domains. In the context of the highly competitive telecom market, the fast development of new and complex mobile multimedia services delivered via various new mobile devices offers a wide scope of choice for the end user, hence increasingly driving operators to put focus on the QoE domain. Studies have shown that the management of QoE as a highly complex issue requires an interdisciplinary view from user, technology, context, and business aspects and flexible cooperation between all players and stakeholders involved in the service providing chain.

This paper gives a survey of the state of the art and current research activities focusing on steps comprising the QoE management process: QoE modeling, QoE monitoring and measurement, and QoE adaptation and optimization. Based on the overview, we have identified and discussed the key aspects and challenges that need to be considered when conducting research in the area of QoE management, particularly related to the domain of wireless networks. Challenges related to QoE modeling include the consideration of various QoE IFs and identification of key ones, as well as mapping the key IFs to QoE dimensions. The main challenges related to QoE monitoring and measurement can be summarized in the questions: *what* to collect?, and *where*, *when*, and *how* to collect data? Similarly, the following questions *what* to improve?, and *where*, *when*, and *how* to improve QoE? summarize the challenges of the QoE optimization process. In the context of wireless networks, QoE management has mostly been considered in terms of resource scheduling, whereby resource allocation decisions are driven to optimize end-user QoE. QoE-driven resource management has become an important issue for mobile network operators as a result of the continuously increasing demand for complex and faster multimedia applications that are adaptable to various devices and require increased network resources (e.g., more bandwidth, less delays, higher link quality), as well as the need for satisfying high user expectations towards continuous communication, mobility, and so forth. Therefore, QoE-driven mobility management solutions have also been presented, as well as QoE-driven service adaptation solutions.

Thus, by approaching various QoE aspects from a wide interdisciplinary perspective, this paper aims to provide a better understanding of QoE and the process of its management in converged wireless environments.

Abbreviations

AAA:	Authentication, authorization, and accounting
A-GW:	Access gateway
AS:	Application server
BSC:	Base station controller
BTS:	Base transceiver station
DASH:	Dynamic adaptive streaming over HTTP
E Node B:	Evolved node B
EPC:	Evolved backet core
ePDG:	Enhanced packet data gateway
EPS:	Evolved packet system
E-UTRAN:	Evolved UMTS terrestrial radio access network
GGSN:	Gateway gprs support node
GPRS:	General packet radio service
GSM:	Global system for mobile communication
HSPA:	High speed packet access
HSS:	Home subscriber service
HTTP:	Hyper text transfer protocol
I-CSCF:	Interrogating call session control function
IMS:	IP multimedia subsystem
IP:	Internet protocol
LAN:	Local area network
LTE:	Long-term evolution
MME:	Mobility management entity
PCC:	Policy and charging control
PCEF:	Policy and charging enforcement function
PCRF:	Policy and charging rules function
P-CSCF:	Proxy call session control function
P-GW:	Packet data network gateway
PS:	Policy server
Q-MOF:	QoS matching and optimization function
QoE:	Quality of experience
QoS:	Quality of service
RM:	Resource manager
RNC:	Radio network controller
SCF:	Session control function
SGSN:	Serving GPRS support node
S-GW:	Serving gateway
SIP AS:	Session initiation protocol application server
SPR:	Subscription profile repository
S-SCSF:	Serving call session control manager
UPR:	User profile repository
UPSF:	User profile server.

Acknowledgments

The authors would like to thank the anonymous reviewers for their valuable comments and suggestions. L. Skorin-Kapov's work was in part supported by the Ministry of Science, Education and Sports of the Republic of Croatia research projects nos. 036-0362027-1639 and 071-0362027-2329.

References

[1] M. lsson, S. Sultana, S. Rommer, L. Frid, and C. Mulligan, *SAE and the Evolved Packet Core: Driving the Mobile Broadband Revolution*, Elsevier, New York, NY, USA, 2009.

[2] S. Ickin, K. Wac, M. Fiedler, L. Jankowski, J. H. Hong, and A. K. Dey, "Factors influencing quality of experience of commonly used mobile applications," *IEEE Communication Magazine*, vol. 50, no. 4, pp. 48–56, 2012.

[3] R. Stankiewicz and A. Jajszczyk, "A survey of QoE assurance in converged networks," *Computer Networks*, vol. 55, no. 7, pp. 1459–1473, 2011.

[4] I. T. U. -T Recommendation Y.2012, "Functional Requirements and Architecture of the NGN Release 1," September 2006.

[5] K. Bogenine, R. Ludwig, P. Mogensen et al., "LTE part II: Radio access," *IEEE Communications Magazine*, vol. 47, no. 4, pp. 40–42, 2009.

[6] 3GPP Technical Report TR 23.882 V8.0.0, "3GPP System Architecture Evolution: Report on Technical Options and Conclusions," December 2008.

[7] 3GPP Technical Specification TS 23.107 V11.0.0, "Quality of Service (QoS) Concept and Architecture," June 2012.

[8] 3GPP Technical Specification TS 23.207 V10.0.0, "End-to-end Quality of Service (QoS) Concept and Architecture," March 2011.

[9] 3GPP Technical Specification TS 23.203 V11.6.0, "Policy and Charging Control Architecture," June 2012.

[10] K. U. R. Laghari and K. Connelly, "Toward total quality of experience: a QoE model in a communication ecosystem," *IEEE Communication Magazine*, vol. 50, no. 4, pp. 58–65, 2012.

[11] ITU-T Recommendation P.10/G.100, "Vocabulary for performance and quality of service. Amendment 2: New definitions for inclusion in Recommendation ITU-T P.10/G.100," July 2008.

[12] ETSI Technical Report 102 643 V1.0.2, "Human Factors (HF); Quality of Experience (QoE) requirements for real-time communication services," October 2010.

[13] K. De Moor, W. Joseph, I. Ketykó et al., "Linking users' subjective QoE evaluation to signal strength in an IEEE 802.11b/g wireless LAN environment," *EURASIP Journal on Wireless Communications and Networking*, vol. 2010, Article ID 541568, 2010.

[14] V. Roto, E. Law, A. Vermeeren, and J. Hoonhout, Eds., "User Experience White Paper. Bringing Clarity to the Concept of User Experience," February 2011, http://www.allaboutux.org /files/UX-WhitePaper.pdf.

[15] A. Van Ewijk, J. De Vriendt, and L. Finizola, *Quality of Service for IMS on Fixed Networks. Business Models and Drivers for Next-Generation IMS Services*, International Engineering Consortium, USA, 2007.

[16] T. M. O'Neill, "Quality of Experience and Quality of Service for IP video conferencing," *Polycom*; 2002.

[17] M. Siller and J. C. Woods, "QoS arbitration for improving the QoE in multimedia transmission," in *Proceedings of the International Conference on Visual Information Engineering*, pp. 238–241, July 2003.

[18] Empirix, "Assuring QoE on Next Generation Networks," Whitepaper, 2001, http://www.whitepapers.org/docs/show/113.

[19] D. Soldani, "Means and methods for collecting and analyzing QoE measurements in wireless networks," in *Proceedings of International Symposium on a World of Wireless, Mobile and Multimedia Networks (WoWMoM '06)*, pp. 531–535, Niagara-Falls, Buffalo-NY, USA, June 2006.

[20] K. De Moor, I. Ketykó, W. Joseph et al., "Proposed framework for evaluating quality of experience in a mobile, testbed-oriented living lab setting," *Mobile Networks and Applications*, vol. 15, no. 3, pp. 378–391, 2010.

[21] S. Baraković, J. Baraković, and H. Bajrić, "QoE dimensions and QoE measurement of NGN services," in *Proceedings of the 18th Telecommunications Forum (TELFOR '10)*, Belgrade, Serbia, November 2010.

[22] P. Le Callet, S. Moller, and A. Perkis, Eds., "Qualinet White paper on Definitions of Quality of Experience (QoE)," May 2012, http://www.qualinet.eu/.

[23] M. G. Martini, C. W. Chen, Z. Chen, T. Dagiuklas, L. Sun, and X. Zhu, "Guest editorial QoE-aware wireless multimedia systems," *IEEE Journal on Selected Areas in Telecommunications*, vol. 30, no. 7, pp. 1153–1156, 2012.

[24] T. Hoßfeld, R. Schatz, M. Varela, and C. Timmerer, "Challenges of QoE management for cloud applications," *IEEE Communication Magazine*, vol. 50, no. 4, pp. 28–36, 2012.

[25] D. Durkee, "Why cloud computing will never be free," *Communications of the ACM*, vol. 53, no. 5, pp. 62–69, 2010.

[26] L. Skorin-Kapov and M. Varela, "A multi-dimensional view of QoE: the ARCU model," in *Proceedings of the 35th Jubilee International Convention on Information and Communication Technology, Electronics and Microelectronics (MIPRO '12)*, Opatija, Croatia, May 2012.

[27] J. Shaikh, M. Fiedler, and D. Collange, "Quality of experience from user and network perspectives," *Annales des Telecommunications/Annals of Telecommunications*, vol. 65, no. 1-2, pp. 47–57, 2010.

[28] P. Reichl, B. Tuffin, and R. Schatz, "Logarithmic laws in service quality perception: where microeconomics meets psychophysics and quality of experience," *Telecommunication Systems Journal*, vol. 55, no. 1, pp. 1–14, 2011.

[29] M. Fiedler, T. Hoßfeld, and P. Tran-Gia, "A generic quantitative relationship between quality of experience and quality of service," *IEEE Network*, vol. 24, no. 2, pp. 36–41, 2010.

[30] P. Reichl, S. Egger, R. Schatz, and A. D'Alconzo, "The logarithmic nature of QoE and the role of the Weber-Fechner law in QoE assessment," in *Proceedings of IEEE International Conference on Communications (ICC '10)*, Cape Town, South Africa, May 2010.

[31] E. H. Weber, *Annotationes Anatomicae et Physiologicae: Programmata Collecta: Fasciculi Tres. de Pulsu, Resorptione, Auditu et Tactu*, Koehler, 1834.

[32] ITU-T Recommendation P.800.1, "Mean Opinion Score (MOS) Terminology," July 2006.

[33] T. Hoßfeld, R. Schatz, and S. Egger, "SOS: the MOS is not enough!," in *Proceedings of the 3rd International Workshop on Quality of Multimedia Experience (QoMEX '11)*, Machelen, Belgium, September 2011.

[34] ITU-T Recommendation G.1011, "Reference Guide to Quality of Experience Assessment Methodologies," June 2010.

[35] K. Wac, S. Ickin, J. H. Hong, L. Janowski, M. Fiedler, and A. K. Dey, "Studying the experience of mobile applications used in different contexts of daily life," in *Proceedings of the 1st ACM SIGCOMM Workshop on Measurements up the Stack (W-MUST '11)*, Toronto, Ontario, Canada, August 2011.

[36] J. M. Hektner, J. A. Schmidt, and M. Csikszentmihalyi, *Experience Sampling Method: Measuring the Quality of Everyday Life*, Sage Publications, 2006.

[37] P. A. Dinda, G. Memik, R. P. Dick et al., "The user in experimental computer systems research," in *Proceedings of the Workshop on Experimental Computer Science*, San Diego, Calif, USA, June 2007.

[38] V. Menkovski, G. Exarchakos, A. Liotta, and A. Cuadra-Sanchez, "Managing quality of experience on a commercial mobile TV platform," *International Journal on Advances in Telecommunications*, vol. 4, no. 1-2, pp. 72–81, 2011.

[39] T. Hoßfeld, M. Seufert, M. Hirth, T. Zinner, P. Tran-Gia, and R. Schatz, "Quantification of YouTube QoE via Crowdsourcing," in *Proceedings of the IEEE International Symposium on Multimedia (ISM '11)*, December 2011.

[40] K. T. Chen, C. J. Chang, C. C. Wu, Y. C. Chang, and C. L. Lei, "Quadrant of euphoria: a crowdsourcing platform for QoE assessment," *IEEE Network*, vol. 24, no. 2, pp. 28–35, 2010.

[41] A. Takahashi, "Framework and standardization of quality of experience (QoE) design and management for audiovisual communication services," *NTT Technical Review*, vol. 7, no. 4, pp. 1–5, 2009.

[42] ITU-T Recommendation P.862, "Perceptual Evaluation of Speech Quality (PESQ): An Objective Method for End-to-End Speech Quality Assessment of Narrow-Band Telephone Networks and Speech Codecs," February 2001.

[43] ITU-T Recommendation P.863, "Perceptual Objective Listening Quality Assessment," January 2011.

[44] ITU-R Recommendation BS.1387, "Method for Objective Measurements of Perceived Audio Quality," November 2001.

[45] ITU-T Recommendation P.563, "Single-ended Method for Objective Speech Quality Assessment in Narrow-Band Telephony Applications," May 2004.

[46] F. Kuipers, R. Kooij, De Vleeschauwer, and K. Brunnstrom, "Techniques for measuring quality of experience," Wired/Wireless Internet Communications, pp. 216–227, 2010.

[47] A. Takahashi, D. Hands, and V. Barriac, "Standardization activities in the ITU for a QoE assessment of IPTV," IEEE Communications Magazine, vol. 46, no. 2, pp. 78–84, 2008.

[48] ITU-T Recommendation P.564, "Conformance Testing for Voice Over IP Transmission Quality Assessment Models," November 2007.

[49] ITU-T Recommendation G.107, "The E-model: A Computational Model for Use in Transmission Planning," December 2011.

[50] ITU-T Recommendation G.1070, "Opinion Model for Video-Telephony Applications," April 2007.

[51] ITU-T Recommendation G.1030, "Estimating End-to-End Performance in IP Networks for Data Applications," November 2005.

[52] ETSI Guide 202 843 V1.1.2, "Definitions and Methods for Assessing the QoS Parameters of the Customer Relationship Stages Other than Utilization," July 2011.

[53] P. Brooks and B. Hestnes, "User measures of quality of experience: why being objective and quantitative is important," IEEE Network, vol. 24, no. 2, pp. 8–13, 2010.

[54] A. Perkis, S. Munkeby, and O. I. Hillestad, "A model for measuring quality of experience," in Proceedings of the 7th Nordic Signal Processing Symposium (NORSIG '06), pp. 198–201, June 2006.

[55] H. J. Kim, K. H. Lee, and J. Zhang, "In-service feedback QoE framework," in Proceedings of the 3rd International Conference on Communication Theory, Reliability, and Quality of Service (CTRQ '10), pp. 135–138, Athens, Greece, June 2010.

[56] K. Kilkki, "Quality of experience in communications ecosystem," Journal of Universal Computer Science, vol. 14, no. 5, pp. 615–624, 2008.

[57] S. Möller, K. P. Engelbrecht, C. Kühnel, I. Wechsung, and B. Weiss, "A taxonomy of quality of service and quality of experience of multimodal human-machine interaction," in Proceedings of the International Workshop on Quality of Multimedia Experience (QoMEx '09), pp. 7–12, July 2009.

[58] D. Geerts, K. De Moor, I. Ketykó et al., "Linking an integrated framework with appropriate methods for measuring QoE," in Proceedings of the 2nd International Workshop on Quality of Multimedia Experience (QoMEX '10), pp. 158–163, Trondheim, Norway, June 2010.

[59] M. Volk, J. Sterle, U. Sedlar, and A. Kos, "An approach to modeling and control of QoE in next generation networks," IEEE Communications Magazine, vol. 48, no. 8, pp. 126–135, 2010.

[60] W. Song, D. Tjondronegoro, and M. Docherty, "Understanding user experience of mobile video: framework, measurement, and optimization," in Mobile Multimedia—User and Technology Perspectives, INTECH Open Access, 2012.

[61] F. Ricciato, "Traffic monitoring and analysis for the optimization of a 3G network," IEEE Wireless Communications, vol. 13, no. 6, pp. 42–49, 2006.

[62] D. Kataria, "Mitigating strategies for smart phone signaling overload," December 2011, http://www.ecnmag.com/articles/2011/10/mitigating-strategies-smart-phone-signaling-overload.

[63] V. Menkovski and A. Liotta, QoE for mobile streaming. Mobile multimedia: user and technology perspectives, InTech Publishing, 2012.

[64] ITU-T Recommendation J.144, "Objective Perceptual Video Quality Measurement Techniques for Digital Cable Television in the Presence of a Full Reference," March 2004.

[65] A. F. Wattimena, R. E. Kooij, J. M. Van Vugt, and O. K. Ahmed, "Predicting the perceived quality of a first person shooter: the Quake IV G-model," in Proceedings of the 5th ACM SIGCOMM Workshop on Network and System Support for Games (NetGames '06), October 2006.

[66] T. Hoßfeld, S. Biedermann, R. Schatz, A. Plazter, S. Egger, and M. Fiedler, "The memory effect and its implications on web QoE modeling," in Proceedings of the 23rd International Teletraffic Congress (ITC '11), San Francisco, California, USA, September 2011.

[67] S. Egger, P. Reichl, T. Hoßfeld, and R. Schatz, ""Time is bandwidth"? Narrowing the gap between subjective time perception and quality of experience," in Proceedings of the IEEE International Conference on Communications (ICC '12), Ottawa, Canada, June 2012.

[68] T. Ciszkowski, W. Mazurczyk, Z. Kotulski, T. Hoßfeld, M. Fiedler, and D. Collange, "Towards quality of experience-based reputation models for future web service provisioning," Telecommunication Systems, vol. 52, no. 2, pp. 1–13, 2013.

[69] M. Jarschel, M. Schlosser, S. Scheuring, and T. Hoßfeld, "An evaluation of QoE in cloud gaming based on subjective tests," in Proceedings of the 5th International Conference on Innovative Mobile and Internet Services in Ubiquitous Computing (IMIS '11), Seoul, Korea, July 2011.

[70] S. Egger, T. Hoßfeld, R. Schatz, and M. Fiedler, "Waiting times in quality of experience for web based services," in Proceedings of the 4th International Workshop on Quality of Multimedia Experience (QoMEX '12), Yarra Valley, Australia, July 2012.

[71] H. Batteram, G. Damm, A. Mukhopadhyay, L. Philippart, R. Odysseos, and C. Urrutia-Valdés, "Delivering quality of experience in multimedia networks," Bell Labs Technical Journal, vol. 15, no. 1, pp. 175–194, 2010.

[72] D. Soldani, M. Li, and R. Cuny, QoS and QoE Management in UMTS Cellular Systems, John Wiley & Sons, USA, 2006.

[73] 3GPP Technical Specification TS 26.234 V11.0.0, "Transparent end-to-end Packet-switched Streaming Service (PSS); Protocols and Codecs," March 2012.

[74] 3GPP Technical Specification TS 26.247 V10.2.0, "Transparent End-to-End Packet-Switched Streaming Service (PSS); Progressive Download and Dynamic Adaptive Streaming Over HTTP (3GP-DASH)," June 2012.

[75] 3GPP Technical Specification TS 26.114 V11.4.0, "IP Multimedia Subsystem (IMS); Multimedia Telephony; Media Handling and Interaction," June 2012.

[76] A. Raake, J. Gustafsson, S. Argyropoulos et al., "IP-based mobile and fixed network audiovisual media services," IEEE Signal Processing Magazine, vol. 28, no. 6, pp. 68–79, 2011.

[77] D. Collange and J. L. Costeux, "Passive estimation of quality of experience," *Journal of Universal Computer Science*, vol. 14, no. 5, pp. 625–641, 2008.

[78] D. Collange, M. Hajji, J. Shaikh, M. Fiedler, and P. Arlos, "User impatience and network performance," in *Proceedings of the 8th Euro-NF Conference on Next Generation Internet (NGI '12)*, Karlskrona, Sweden, June 2012.

[79] K. De Moor and L. De Marez, "The challenge of user- and QoE-centric research and product development in today's ICT environment," in *Innovating for and by Users*, pp. 77–90, Office for Official Publications of the European Communities, Luxembourg, UK edition, 2008.

[80] B. Fehnert and A. Kosagowsky, "Measuring user experience: complementing qualitative and quantitative assessment," in *Proceedings of the 10th International Conference on Human-Computer Interaction with Mobile Devices and Services (Mobile-HCI '08)*, pp. 383–386, September 2008.

[81] M. Andrews, J. Cao, and J. McGowan, "Measuring human satisfaction in data networks," in *Proceedings of the 25th IEEE International Conference on Computer Communications (INFO-COM '06)*, Barcelona, Spain, April 2006.

[82] 3GPP Technical Specification TS 23.402 V11.3.0, "Architecture Enhancements for non-3GPP Accesses," June 2012.

[83] 3GPP Technical Specification TS 22.278 V12.1.0, "Service Requirements for the Evolved Packet System," June 2012.

[84] P. Rengaraju, C. H. Lung, and F. R. Yu, "On QoE monitoring and E2E service assurance in 4G wireless networks," *IEEE Wireless Communications*, vol. 19, no. 4, pp. 89–96, 2012.

[85] R. Serral-Gracià, E. Cerqueira, M. Curado, M. Yannuzzi, E. Monteiro, and X. Masip-Bruin, "An overview of quality of experience measurement challenges for video applications in IP networks," in *Proceedings of the 8th International Conference on Wired/Wireless Internet Communications (WWIC '10)*, pp. 252–263, Lulea, Sweden, June 2010.

[86] R. Fielding, J. Gettys, J. Mogul et al., "Hypertext Transfer Protocol - HTTP/1.1," IETF Technical Report RFC 2616, Jun 1999.

[87] O. Oyman and S. Singh, "Quality of experience for HTTP adaptive streaming services," *IEEE Communications Magazine*, vol. 50, no. 4, pp. 20–27, 2012.

[88] I. Ketykó, K. De Moor, T. De Pessemier et al., "QoE measurement of mobile youtube video streaming," in *Proceedings of the 3rd Workshop on Mobile Video Delivery (MoViD '10)*, pp. 27–32, October 2010.

[89] A. J. Verdejo, K. De Moor, I. Ketyko et al., "QoE estimation of a location-based mobile game using on-body sensors and QoS-related data," in *Proceedings of the IFIP Wireless Days Conference (WD '10)*, October 2010.

[90] K. T. Chen, C. C. Tu, and W. C. Xiao, "OneClick: A framework for measuring network quality of experience," in *Proceedings of the 28th Conference on Computer Communications (INFOCOM '09)*, pp. 702–710, April 2009.

[91] M. Varela and J. P. Laulajainen, "QoE-driven mobility management—integrating the users' quality perception into network-level decision making," in *Proceedings of the Quality of Multimedia Experience (QoMEX '11)*, Mechelen, Belgium, September 2011.

[92] M. Varela, *Pseudo-subjective quality assessment of multimedia streams and its applications in control [Ph.D. thesis]*, INRIA/IRISA, University Rennes I, Rennes, France, Nov 2005.

[93] K. Mitra, C. Ahlund, and A. Zaslavsky, "QoE estimation and prediction using hidden Markov models in heterogeneous access networks," in *Australasian Telecommunication Networks and Applications Conference*, Brisbane, Australia, 2012.

[94] "EU FP7 PERIMITER project," http://www.ict-perimeter.eu/.

[95] 3GPP Technical Specification TS 23.228 V11.4.0, "IP Multimedia Subsystem (IMS)," March 2012.

[96] T. Hoßfeld, F. Liers, R. Schatz et al., *Quality of Experience Management for YouTube: Clouds, FoG and the AquareYoum*, PIK: Praxis der Informationverarbeitung und - kommnikation (PIK)., 2012.

[97] B. Staehle, M. Hirth, R. Pries, F. Wamser, and D. Staehle, "Aquarema in action: improving the YouTube QoE in wireless mesh networks," in *Proceedings of the Baltic Congress on Future Internet and Communications (BCFIC Riga '11)*, pp. 33–40, February 2011.

[98] I. Ketykó, K. De Moor, W. Joseph, L. Martens, and L. De Marez, "Performing QoE-measurements in an actual 3G network," in *Proceedings of the IEEE International Symposium on Broadband Multimedia Systems and Broadcasting (BMSB '10)*, March 2010.

[99] S. M. Chadchan and C. B. Akki, "3GPP LTE/SAE: an overview," *International Journal of Computer and Electrical Engineering*, vol. 2, no. 5, pp. 806–814, 2010.

[100] L. Skorin-Kapov and M. Matijasevic, "Modeling of a QoS matching and optimization function for multimedia services in the NGN," in *Proceedings of the 12th IFIP/IEEE International Conference on Management of Multimedia and Mobile Networks and Services: Wired-Wireless Multimedia Networks and Services Management (MMNS '09)*, vol. 5842 of *Lecture Notes in Computer Science*, pp. 54–68, October 2009.

[101] K. Ivešić, M. Matijašević, and L. Skorin-Kapov, "Simulation based evaluation of dynamic resource allocation for adaptive multimedia services," in *Proceedings of the 7th International Conference on Network and Service Management (CNSM '11)*, pp. 1–8, October 2011.

[102] J. Sterle, M. Volk, U. Sedlar, J. Bester, and A. Kos, "Application-based NGN QoE controller," *IEEE Communications Magazine*, vol. 49, no. 1, pp. 92–101, 2011.

[103] S. Thakolsri, W. Kellerer, and E. Steinbach, "QoE-based cross-layer optimization of wireless video with unperceivable temporal video quality fluctuation," in *Proceedings of the IEEE International Conference on Communication (ICC '11)*, Kyoto, Japan, Jun 2011.

[104] S. Latré, P. Simoens, B. De Vleeschauwer et al., "An autonomic architecture for optimizing QoE in multimedia access networks," *Computer Networks*, vol. 53, no. 10, pp. 1587–1602, 2009.

[105] P. Ameigeiras, J. J. Ramos-Munoz, J. Navarro-Ortiz, P. Mogensen, and J. M. Lopez-Soler, "QoE oriented cross-layer design of a resource allocation algorithm in beyond 3G systems," *Computer Communications*, vol. 33, no. 5, pp. 571–582, 2010.

[106] J. Hassan, M. Hassan, S. K. Das, and A. Ramer, "Managing quality of experience for wireless VoIP using noncooperative games," *IEEE Journal on Selected Areas in Communication*, vol. 30, no. 7, pp. 1193–1204, 2012.

[107] A. El Essaili, L. Zhou, D. Schroeder, E. Steinbach, and W. Kellerer, "QoE-driven live and on-demand LTE uplink video transmission," in *Proceedings of the 13th International Workshop on Multimedia Signal Processing (MMSP '11)*, Hangzhou, China, October 2011.

[108] S. Khan, S. Duhovnikov, E. Steinbach, and W. Kellerer, "MOS-based multiuser multiapplication cross-layer optimization for mobile multimedia communication," *Advances in Multimedia*, vol. 2007, Article ID 94918, 11 pages, 2007.

[109] G. Aristomenopoulos, T. Kastrinogiannis, S. Papavassiliou, V. Kaldanis, and G. Karantonis, "A novel framework for dynamic utility-based QoE provisioning in wireless networks," in *Proceedings of the 53rd IEEE Global Communications Conference (GLOBECOM '10)*, December 2010.

[110] F. Wamser, D. Staehle, J. Prokopec, A. Maeder, and P. Tran-Gia, "Utilizing buffered YouTube playtime for QoE-oriented scheduling in OFDMA networks," in *Proceedings of the 24th International Teletraffic Congress (ITC '12)*, Krakow, Poland, October 2012.

[111] K. Piamrat, A. Ksentini, C. Viho, and J. M. Bonnin, "QoE-based network selection for multimedia users in IEEE 802.11 wireless networks," in *Proceedings of the 33rd IEEE Conference on Local Computer Networks (LCN '08)*, pp. 388–394, Montreal, Canada, October 2008.

[112] M. Shehada, S. Thakolsri, Z. Despotovic, and W. Kellerer, "QoE-based cross-layer optimization for video delivery in long term evolution mobile networks," in *Proceedings of the14th International Symposium on Wireless Personal Multimedia Communications (WPMC '11)*, Le Quartz, Brest, France, October 2011.

[113] N. Amram, B. Fu, G. Kunzmann et al., "QoE-based transport optimization for video delivery over next generation cellular networks," in *Proceedings of the IEEE Symposium on Computers and Communications (ISCC '11)*, Kerkyra, Greece, July 2011.

[114] A. Khan, I. Mkwawa, L. Sun, and E. Ifeachor, "QoE-driven sender bitrate adaptation scheme for video applications over IP multimedia subsystem," in *Proceedings of the IEEE International Conference on Communication (ICC '11)*, Kyoto, Japan, June 2011.

[115] M. Csernai and A. Gulyas, "Wireless Adapter Sleep Scheduling based on video QoE: how to improve battery life when watching streaming video?" in *Proceedings of the 20th International Conference on Computer Communications and Networks (ICCCN '11)*, Maui, Hawaii, USA, August 2011.

[116] A. A. Khalek, C. Caramanis, and R. W. Heath Jr., "A cross-layer design for perceptual optimization of H.264/SVC with unequal error protection," *IEEE Journal on Selected Areas in Communication*, vol. 30, no. 7, pp. 1157–1171, 2012.

11

Angry Apps: The Impact of Network Timer Selection on Power Consumption, Signalling Load, and Web QoE

Christian Schwartz, Tobias Hoßfeld, Frank Lehrieder, and Phuoc Tran-Gia

Institute of Computer Science, University of Würzburg, Chair of Communication Networks, Am Hubland, 97074 Würzburg, Germany

Correspondence should be addressed to Tobias Hoßfeld; hossfeld@informatik.uni-wuerzburg.de

Academic Editor: Pedro Merino

The popularity of smartphones and mobile applications has experienced a considerable growth during the recent years, and this growth is expected to continue in the future. Since smartphones have only very limited energy resources, battery efficiency is one of the determining factors for a good user experience. Therefore, some smartphones tear down connections to the mobile network soon after a completed data transmission to reduce the power consumption of their transmission unit. However, frequent connection reestablishments caused by apps which send or receive small amounts of data often lead to a heavy signalling load within the mobile network. One of the major contributions of this paper is the investigation of the resulting tradeoff between energy consumption at the smartphone and the generated signalling traffic in the mobile network. We explain that this tradeoff can be controlled by the connection release timeout and study the impact of this parameter for a number of popular apps that cover a wide range of traffic characteristics in terms of bandwidth requirements and resulting signalling traffic. Finally, we study the impact of the timer settings on Quality of Experience (QoE) for web traffic. This is an important aspect since connection establishments not only lead to signalling traffic but also increase the load time of web pages.

1. Introduction

Together with the wide-spread usage of smartphones in today's UMTS networks, the popularity of smartphone apps has seen a tremendous growth during the last years [1]. The resulting traffic is expected to exceed half of the global mobile data traffic in the next years [2]. One of the major reasons for this phenomenon is that smartphones are very convenient for users to stay always connected to the Internet. In turn, this has led developers of smartphone apps to the assumption of continuous Internet connectivity. Therefore, many apps such as social network clients, weather forecasts, or instant messengers update their status frequently, which raises a number of problems—in the mobile network as well as on the smartphones.

In contrast to desktops or laptops, smartphones are equipped only with limited battery. Since established connections from the smartphone to the mobile network consume a large amount of energy, some smartphones close these connections soon after the data transmission is finished, that is, after a very short period of no traffic activity, which is controlled by an inactivity timer. This saves energy and prevents battery drain caused by established but unused connections. However, it might also degrade the user experience since the connection start-up delay is in the order of a few seconds. Therefore, users might get annoyed, for example, if the load time of every web page in their browser is increased. Hence, two oppositional effects impact the quality of experience (QoE) perceived by the user: lower energy consumption and short page load times—a tradeoff that we investigate thoroughly in this paper.

From a mobile operator's point of view, each change between connected and disconnected states of the smartphone causes signalling in the network, and excessive signalling load has led to severe problems in the recent past. For example, a large mobile network in Japan suffered from an outage of several hours in January 2012. The operator of this network mentioned a large number of small control messages of certain popular apps (such as keep-alive messages or buddy list updates in VoIP apps) as a probable cause for this outage (Penn-Olson, "Finding a connection: Android, Line, and Docomo's network outage," 2012, available at http://www.penn-olson.com/2012/01/30/docomo-outage-line/). Therefore, we argue that not an overload in data traffic but the high number of establishments and teardowns of wireless connections has brought down the network. As a consequence, the network operator may adjust the timer setting accordingly. A longer timer setting can reduce signalling load and resource costs of the mobile operator, however, at the cost of energy consumption of the user device and an increased consumption of radio resources. Hence, an additional tradeoff exists between battery efficiency on smartphones and signalling load in the mobile network. The proprietary fast dormancy mode as implemented by smartphones (i.e., smartphones tear down the connection earlier than advised by the network) additionally affects the signalling load in the network and is also investigated in this paper. The influence of traffic generated by applications on radio resources is another point of interest of mobile operators which is already well investigated in the literature, for example [5], and out of scope in this paper. In light of current troubles with network outages induced by signalling storms, the interest of mobile operators and equipment vendors has shifted towards signalling generated by the application traffic [6, 7] on which we focus here.

A reason for this signalling storm is the following. UMTS networks are designed to provide wireless, high bandwidth Internet access for mobile users, for example, video telephony. Therefore, high load in terms of data traffic was carefully considered during the design of such networks. However, some currently popular apps such as Aupeo radio streaming or Skype VoIP apps load the mobile network all the time, even if they are only running in the background. They send update and keep-alive messages every few seconds, which is problematic for today's UMTS networks. The reason is that the mobile network usually tears down wireless connections to a user equipment (UE) after an inactivity timeout of a few seconds, that is, when no data was transmitted for this short time. If the time between two such keep-alive messages is slightly above the connection timeout of the mobile network, the wireless connections between the UE and the mobile network are established and torn down every few seconds. This is an issue that UMTS networks have not been designed for.

The contributions of this paper are the following. First, we study the tradeoff between energy consumption at the smartphone and the generated signalling traffic in the mobile network. From the user's point of view, battery efficiency is one of the determining factors for a good QoE due to a very limited energy capacity of smartphones [8]. Thereby, we analyse the impact of the inactivity timer as well as of the fast dormancy mode for exemplary smartphone apps based on measurements in a public 3G network. These apps are selected to cover a wide range of traffic characteristics in terms of bandwidth requirements and resulting signalling traffic. In particular, we consider background applications (like Twitter or Skype in passive mode), bandwidth intensive (like Aupeo radio streaming), and interactive applications

(like Angry Birds). Then, we answer the question whether a mobile operator is able to find optimal values for the inactivity timer for a given application or network configuration. Further, we see which apps (and which traffic characteristics) make the smartphone users and the mobile operators angry, respectively. We compare the results from these different applications and study the impact of choosing one such optimum for one specific application on other applications. This comparison sheds new light on the practice of using network parameters to optimise for power consumption or generated amount of signalling frequency. Furthermore, we discuss new paradigms for the design of mechanisms which try to resolve such conflicts, namely, economic traffic management [9] and design for tussle [10, 11]. Finally, we study the impact of the timer settings on QoE for web browsing based on existing models for web browsing [12]. This is an important aspect since connection establishments do not only lead to signalling traffic but also increase the load time of web pages which is the key influence factor on web QoE.

The remainder of this paper is structured as follows. Section 2 provides the background on UMTS networks and the radio resource control protocol used for connection establishment and teardown. Related work on measurement studies of relevant RRC parameters like the inactivity timer is reviewed. Further, existing optimisation approaches of the resource consumption are revisited. Then, energy consumption as key QoE influence factor of smartphone users is considered. Section 3 describes the measurement setup and the algorithm to infer (connectivity and energy) state transitions of the smartphone from measured IP packets. Then, we calculate signalling frequency and power consumption based on the state transitions. Section 4 presents the numerical results of our analysis. The traffic of the four popular smartphone apps are characterized. Afterwards, we compare the signalling frequency and power consumption depending on the network configuration. Finally, we study the influence of network parameters on QoE for web browsing based on page load times. Section 5 concludes this work with an outlook on open challenges of how to optimise mobile networks without annoying users or operators.

2. Background and Related Work

This section provides background information on the structure of UMTS networks and their components. In addition, it explains the radio resource control (RRC) protocol, which is used for the allocation of wireless transmission resources. Afterwards, it reviews related work on measurement studies of RRC parameters in real networks and on optimisation approaches of such resources, both in the energy and the wireless domain. Finally, we discuss the impact of energy consumption on mobile devices such as smartphones on the QoE of the end user.

2.1. UMTS Networks and the RRC Protocol. UMTS networks consist of the UEs, the radio access network (RAN), and the core network (CN). Their basic structure for packet-switched

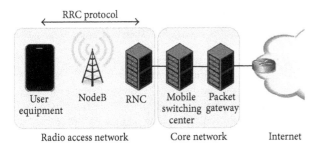

FIGURE 1: Basic structure of a UMTS network for data calls.

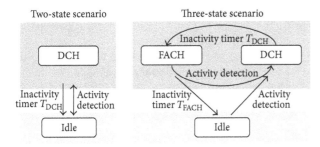

FIGURE 2: RRC state transition diagrams for the two-state and three-state models.

connections is illustrated in Figure 1. UEs are usually cell phones or computers connected using datacards. The RAN connects the UEs to the CN, which is connected to the Internet. The RAN contains the NodeBs in which the UEs are connected to using the air interface. The NodeBs in turn are connected to radio network controllers (RNCs), which among other tasks are responsible for radio resource control using the RRC protocol [3].

For resource management reasons, a UE may be in one of several RRC states, where each state allows the UE a different level of connectivity to the RAN. The RRC protocol specifies five states for the connection between the UE and the RAN: Idle, URA-PCH, CELL-PCH forward access channel (FACH), and dedicated transport channel (DCH).

In the Idle state, the cell is notified of the UE presence, but the UE can neither send nor receive data. The FACH and DCH states allow communication with the RAN, where the DCH state allows for larger bandwidth at the cost of a higher power consumption. For simplicity reasons, we neglect URA-PCH and CELL-PCH in this study. While URA-PCH plays only a role in scenarios of high mobility, CELL-PCH is not yet widely implemented. Our results are still of general nature and do not depend on the limited number of considered RRC states.

State transitions are controlled by the RNC using rules specified in the RRC protocol and timer values set by the network operator [5, 13]. A brief description is given in the following. We consider two different state transition models, depicted in Figure 2. The first model includes the Idle, FACH, and DCH states (cf. the right part of the figure). Therefore, we call it a three-state model. If the UE is in the Idle state and activity is detected (i.e., a packet is sent or received), the connection transits to the DCH state. After

each transmission, a timer T_{DCH} is started, and it is reset whenever a new packet is sent or received. If the timer expires, the connection transits to the FACH state. Upon entering, the T_{FACH} timer is started. If a new transmission occurs, the connection again transits to the DCH state. If T_{FACH} expires, the connection transits to the Idle state.

The second model, denoted as the two-state model, only includes the Idle and DCH states. If the UE is in the Idle mode and a packet is sent or received, the connection transits to the DCH state. Once in the DCH mode, the T_{DCH} timer is started, and it is reset whenever a new packet is sent or received. If the timer expires, the UE transits back to the Idle state.

While the three-state model is closer to the specified RRC protocol, the two-state model is similar to some proprietary fast dormancy implementations used by UE vendors. In these fast dormancy implementations, the UE tears down the connection to the network state as soon as no data is ready to be sent for a certain time, that is, it forces the network to transit to the Idle state. In contrast to the three-state model, there is no transition to the FACH state. If a device disconnects from the network by transitioning to the Idle state, it has to be reauthenticated before another transition to the DCH state occurs. This results in additional signalling traffic and causes more load on the network [6] due to frequent reestablishments of the RRC connection. These proprietary fast dormancy algorithms do not adhere to the RRC specification [14] but, nonetheless, exist in the real world and have been identified as possible causes for signalling storms. The major reason for fast dormancy implementations is the decrease in power consumption on the UE, since the transmission unit of the UE consumes only 1%–2% of the energy in the Idle state compared to the DCH state. Thus, both models warrant further investigation.

2.2. Related Work on Measurements of RRC Parameters and Optimisation of Resource Consumption. The increased use of mobile broadband networks has caused radio resource management to become a hot research topic. In particular, a considerable research effort is spent on measurements of RRC configurations observed in real UMTS networks. The authors of [13] present a measurement tool exactly for that purpose. They use round-trip times of data packets to infer the RRC state of the connection. This is possible since the latency in the FACH is significantly higher than in the DCH state. This allows the authors to measure RRC state transition parameters such as T_{DCH} and T_{FACH}, channel setup delays, and paging delays in different networks. They find that the settings vary by network and give values of 1.2 seconds for the DCH release timer and values of more than one minute for the Idle timer. To validate their method of inferring the RRC states from the round-trip times, they compare the actual energy consumption of the device with the expected energy consumption in a specific RRC.

A similar approach is applied by the authors of [5]. They reach comparable conclusions but report timer values of 5 seconds for T_{DCH} and 12 seconds for T_{FACH}. Furthermore, the authors identify sets of RRC state transitions from two network providers. We used these results to define the state models in Section 2.1.

In [15], the authors propose the tail optimisation protocol. The main idea is that the applications on the UE can accurately predict whether traffic will soon be transmitted or not. This knowledge permits to avoid the unused tail of DCH periods if no further data has to be sent. If traffic activity is expected within a short time frame, the UE stays in the DCH state to avoid frequent connection reestablishments and the associated signalling load. The same authors extend this idea in [4] and propose ARO, an application resource optimiser, together with an implementation for Android 2.2. This tool also includes additional features such as batching up data or increasing the update rate of application to optimise their resource consumptions.

Finally, the 3GPP has released a technical report [16] about the adverse impact of mobile data applications. This report states that frequent connection reestablishments due to small data packets caused, for example, by status updates of social network or instant messaging apps, can lead to problems of increased signalling load. This highlights the importance of this topic.

2.3. Smartphone Energy Consumption and Quality of Experience. In [8], the authors performed a 4-week long study with 29 participants to identify factors influencing QoE of mobile applications. The study comprises (1) data from context sensing software, (2) user feedback using an experience sampling method several times per day, and (3) weekly interviews of the participants. To determine the factors of influence, the authors analyse the frequency of specific keywords in the interviews and the surveys. It turns out that the term *battery* has the highest frequency. According to [8], this is reasonable since the battery efficiency has a strong impact on the user perceived quality, in particular, when it is nearly discharged.

As a consequence of this finding, we investigate the energy consumption of a smartphone as one of the main indicators for QoE. In addition, we show that the energy consumption of the transmission unit of a smartphone can be reduced if the state of wireless connection between the UE and the RNC is set to Idle shortly after data transmission. However, this can lead to frequent connection reestablishments since some apps send or receive small status updates very often. The signalling load produced by such issues is one of the major problem in today's UMTS networks. Hence, this is clearly a tradeoff between battery efficiency on the side of the end user and the network load for the network operators.

There are different approaches to cope with such tradeoffs in the design of specific mechanisms. The two most prominent ones are economic traffic management (ETM) [9] and design for tussle [10, 11]. The ETM paradigm suggests that the different stakeholders collaborate and exchange information so as to permit a joint optimisations of the tradeoff. This can achieve better results than separate optimisation since these tend to work in opposite directions. Design for tussle focuses more on conflicting interests than on cooperation. It means that mechanisms should be able to adapt the outcome of a certain *tussle* at run time and not at design time, for example, by giving the sole control of essential entities to a certain stakeholder.

3. Inferring Signalling Frequency and Power Consumption from Network Trace

However, RRC state transitions are triggered by the UE's firmware. While solutions exist to capture RRC state transitions on specific hardware [17], they are not available for all modern smartphone platforms. Other options to measure the required information include using costly hardware and specific UEs, usually not available to researchers and developers. This prevents the application developers from evaluating the effect their applications have on the overall health on the network. Consequently, they cannot take measures to prevent the harmful behaviour of their applications. However, it is possible to infer the RRC state transitions for a given packet trace if the network model is known.

In this section, we first describe the setup used to capture network packet traces for arbitrary apps. Then, we give an algorithm to infer the RRC state transitions for a given packet trace. Based on these state transitions, we can calculate the number of signalling messages generated by the packet trace. Finally, we use the information of the RRC state of the UE at every given point in time to calculate the power consumption of the UE's radio interface.

3.1. Measurement Procedure and Setup. To investigate the behaviour of the application under study, we capture traffic during a typical use of the application on a smartphone. The smartphone runs the Android operating system and is connected to the 3G network of a major German network operator. To obtain the network packet traces, we use the *tcpdump* application. This application requires *root* privileges which are obtained by rooting the device and installing the custom *cyanogenMod* ROM (http://www.cyanogenmod.org/). Once *tcpdump* is installed and running, we start the application under study and capture packet traces while the application is running. Then, the *android debugging bridge* is used to copy the traces to a workstation. The traces contain Internet Protocol (IP) packets as well as Linux Cooked Captures. We only require the IP packets; thus, we filtered the traces for IP packets which are used during the following analysis.

3.2. Inferring Network State. In this section, we study the influence of the application traffic on RRC state transitions and signalling messages. Since RRC state transitions cannot be captured using commonly available tools, we introduce an algorithm to infer RRC state transitions from IP packet traces. Using this algorithm, we analyse the RRC state transition frequency and signalling message load for the two-state model and the three-state model.

Traffic below the network layer cannot be measured without specific equipment which is often out of reach for developers interested in assessing the impact of their applications on the network. Based on the two-state and the three-state models introduced in Section 2.1, we process *tcpdump* captures of the application traffic. However, it should be noted that this method is not restricted to a specific network model but can be extended to any other network model as well. Using these captures, we extract the timestamps when IP packets are sent or received. Furthermore,

```
Input: Packet arrival timestamps ts
    DCH to FACH timer T_DCH
    FACH to Idle timer T_FACH
Output: Times of state transition state_time
    New states after state transitions state
    interarrival(i) ← ts(i + 1) − ts(i)
    index ← 0
    for all ts(i) do
        if state(index) = Idle then
            index ← index + 1
            state(index) ← DCH
            state_time (index) ← ts(i)
        end if
        if interarrival(i − 1)> T_DCH then
            index ← index + 1
            state (index) ← FACH
            state_time (index) ← ts(i) +T_DCH
        end if
        if interarrival(i − 1)> T_DCH + T_FACH then
            index ← index + 1
            state(index) ← Idle
            state_time (index) ← ts(i) + T_DCH + T_FACH
        end if
    end for
```

ALGORITHM 1: Inferring RRC state transitions based on IP timestamps.

TABLE 1: Number of signalling messages per RRC state transition perceived at the RNC (taken from [3]).

From/to	Idle	FACH	DCH
Idle	—	28	32
FACH	22	—	6
DCH	25	5	—

TABLE 2: Power consumption of the UE radio interface depending on current RRC state (taken from [4]).

RRC state	Power consumption (mW)
Idle	0
FACH	650
DCH	800

we require the timer values of the transition from the DCH state to the FACH state, T_{DCH}, and the timer for the transition between the FACH and the Idle states, T_{FACH}. Based on this information, Algorithm 1 infers the timestamps of state transitions according to the 3GPP specification [3] for the three-state model. This algorithm can be simplified to also work for the two-state model. Alternatively, a way to postprocess the results of the algorithm to obtain results for the two-state model is given at the end of this section. The algorithm first computes the interarrival times for all packets. Then, each timestamp is considered. If the UE is currently in the Idle state, a state transition to DCH occurs at the moment the packet is sent or received. If the interarrival time exceeds the T_{DCH} timer, the UE transits to the FACH, T_{DCH}, seconds after the packet was sent or received. Similarly, if the interarrival time exceeds both the T_{DCH} and T_{FACH} timers, a state transition to Idle occurs, T_{FACH}, seconds after the state transits to the FACH.

UE vendors always search for ways to decrease energy consumption of their devices. A straightforward way to achieve this, if only the wellbeing of the UE is considered, is to transit from the DCH to Idle states as soon as no additional data is ready for sending. While this transition is not directly available in the 3GPP specification for the RRC protocol [3], a UE may reset the connection, effectively transitioning from any state to Idle. This behaviour can be modelled using the two-state model introduced in Section 2.1.

State transitions for the two-state model can be calculated using a similar algorithm. Alternatively, the behaviour of the two-state model can be emulated using Algorithm 1 if T_{FACH}

is set to 0 seconds and all state transitions to FACH are removed in a postprocessing step.

3.3. Calculating Signalling Frequency and Power Consumption.

In reality, the number of state transitions is not the metric of most importance if network load should be evaluated. Each state transition results in a number of RRC messages between the UE and different network components. For this study, we consider, the number of messages perceived at the RNC, which can be found in [3] and is summarized in Table 1. It can be seen that transitions from or to the Idle state are especially expensive in terms of number of messages sent or received. This is due to the fact that upon entering or leaving, the Idle state authentication has to be performed. Note that for the two-state model, only transitions from or to the Idle state occur. This results in the fact that for the same network packet trace, the number of signalling messages occurring in the two-state model is generally higher than in the three-state model. To obtain the total number of signalling messages, we weight the number of state transitions with the number of messages sent per state transitions. Then, we average the number of state transitions over the measurement duration to obtain a metric for the signalling load at the RNC. The inference algorithm does not differentiate between state changes caused by upstream or downstream traffic. State changes caused by downstream traffic usually generate some additional signalling messages, as paging is involved. The inference algorithm can be easily enhanced to support this behaviour. However, the results discussed in the next section would only change quantitatively. Furthermore, the inference of signalling messages can be easily adapted to new networking models or signalling numbers.

From users' point of view, the signalling message frequency is not important. The user is interested in a low power consumption because this increases the battery time of the device. To calculate the battery time, we use the time when state transitions occurred, and the new RRC state of the UE to calculate the relative amount of time that was spent in each state. Given the relative time spent in each state, we use Table 2 (taken from [4]) to compute the power consumption of the radio interface during the measurement phase. To obtain the energy consumption, the power consumption can

TABLE 3: Qualitative characterization of applications under study.

Application	Traffic characteristic	Application use	Required bandwidth
Angry Birds	Interactive	Foreground	Low bandwidth
Aupeo	Interactive	Background	High bandwidth
Twitter	Periodic, low frequency	Background	Low bandwidth
Skype	Periodic, high frequency	Background	Low bandwidth

be multiplied with the duration of the measured network packet trace. We only focus on the power consumption of the radio interface, as it is possible to measure the aggregated power consumption using out-of-the-box instrumentation techniques provided by the hardware vendor.

4. Numerical Results of Measurement Study

In the measurement study, we apply the methods introduced in Section 3 to four popular smartphone applications to infer signalling traffic and energy consumption. In Section 4.1, we characterize the applications in terms of traffic patterns, application usage, and bandwidth requirements. In Section 4.2, we study the signalling frequency and power consumption caused by these applications, if inactivity timers such as T_{DCH} or T_{FACH} are modified. Finally, we analyse in Section 4.3 the influence of network parameters on web QoE in terms of mean opinion score (MOS) depending on page load times which are influenced by the network settings.

4.1. Characterization of Traffic Patterns for Selected Applications. For this study, we chose four specific applications in order to cover a broad spectrum of traffic characteristics, as described in Table 3. First, we discuss said characteristics for these applications. We differentiate between applications, where the user interaction causes the generation of traffic, and such where the application periodically sends or receives traffic. Finally, we consider the amount of bandwidth used by the application.

Angry Birds for Android is a popular *interactive* free-to-play game and runs in the *foreground*. To finance the game, an advertisement is shown once the player starts or restarts a level. Advertisements are downloaded on demand by the application but require *low bandwidth*. Thus, the time between two advertisements depends on the frequency of the player advancing to the next level or deciding to restart the current one.

Aupeo is an Internet radio application, allowing a user to listen to content from personalised radio stations while running in the *background*. Content is not streamed but downloaded at the beginning of the track. The exact duration depends on the radio stations chosen by the user and is thus *interactive*. This results in large times of inactivity during the

playback of the track itself. Due to the fact that audio files are downloaded, there is a *high bandwidth* requirement.

The Twitter client is used to send and receive new short messages from the user's Twitter account. Transferring these messages requires relatively *low bandwidth*. To this end, the user can specify an update frequency when to pull new messages in the *background*. Thus, the downloads occur with a *periodic behaviour of low frequency*, where the client sends an HTTPS request to the Twitter server and in return receives new Tweets for the user's account. We do not consider an active user who is publishing new Tweets. Such behaviour would manifest as additional traffic to the periodic one generated by the status updates. Due to the fact that publishing updates occurs relatively infrequently and updating the feed occurs more often, the traffic generated by publishing updates is dominated by that occurring due to updates and thus can be neglected.

Finally, we consider the Skype application. We do not consider any Voice over IP (VoIP) calls but the application's Idle behaviour, that is, when the application is running in the *background*. During this time, the application sends keep-alive messages to the network. These keep-alive messages are sent with *high frequency* and require *low bandwidth*.

In addition to the applications considered, there exist other categories of applications which are running in the *foreground* and *interactively* require a *high bandwidth*. One example for such an application is Skype while taking a VoIP call. These applications are not considered in this study because this kind of behaviour causes the UE to be always online. This results the minimal amount of signalling messages to be sent and a maximal power consumption at the UE, independent of network model, or used parameters. Other combinations of traffic criteria also exist. However, from both a signalling load as well as a power consumption point of view, they can be mapped to one of the discussed cases. For example, if an application is sending periodic updates with low bandwidth without user interaction, then the fact that the application is running in the foreground or the background is without consequence for the generated signalling load or power consumption. However, these cases should be considered when the optimisation strategies for message sending are under study. For example, background applications could allow for the batching of messages because the transmission is usually not urgent, while foreground applications do not allow for such behaviour because it would decrease QoE.

Next, we describe the applications under study in more detail. For each application, we show the cumulative distribution function (CDF) of the interarrival times in Figure 3(a) and give information about the mean values and standard deviation of both interarrival times and bandwidth in Table 4, respectively.

Let us again begin with the Angry Birds application. We see that there are no distinct peaks in interarrival time, which would hint at periodic behaviour. Furthermore, we see that 5% of all interarrival times are greater than 1 second. As we consider only T_{DCH} values above 1 second, those are candidates for triggering state transitions. The mean interarrival time is 0.66 seconds, with a relatively high standard deviation

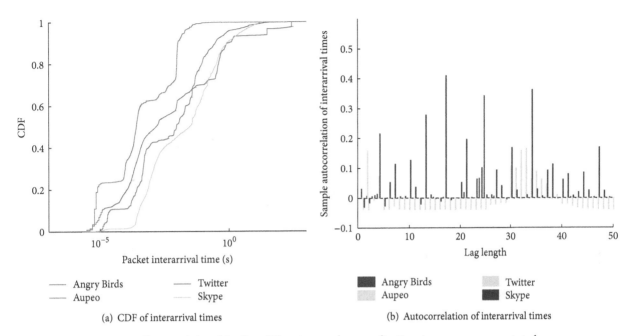

(a) CDF of interarrival times   (b) Autocorrelation of interarrival times

FIGURE 3: Characteristics of the four different smartphone applications in our measurement study.

TABLE 4: Mean and standard deviation of interarrival time and bandwidth for considered apps.

Application	Mean interarrival time (seconds)	Standard deviation of interarrival time (seconds)	Mean bandwidth (kilobit/second)	Standard deviation of bandwidth (kilobit/second)
Angry Birds	0.66	15.90	4.42	4.50
Aupeo	0.06	3.06	129.76	482.63
Twitter	8.91	44.09	0.27	0.04
Skype	0.55	1.95	1.30	1.84

of 15.90 seconds. This is caused by the low interarrival times in one advertisement request and the relatively large interarrival times between two advertisements. Mean bandwidth is relatively low with 4.42 kbps and a high standard deviation of 4.5 kbps. These differences can be explained by considering the behaviour of the application. During long phases of use, no traffic is sent, and, after a level is restarted, a new advertisement has to be obtained, causing the transmission of data.

Next, we study the behaviour of the Aupeo application. We see that the application generates packets with relatively small interarrival times. This finding is backed up by the small mean interarrival time of 0.06 seconds. The high standard deviation of 3.06 seconds is caused by the wait between two tracks. Furthermore, we see a high mean bandwidth of 129.76 kbps and a standard deviation of 482.63 kbps. This is caused by the difference in traffic activity between times when tracks are either downloaded or not.

For Twitter, we see that 90% of all transmissions occur with an interarrival time of 1 seconds. Also, we can observe a high mean interarrival time of 8.91 seconds and a high standard deviation of 44.49 seconds. Additionally, the mean bandwidth is low with only 0.27 kbps and a low standard deviation of 0.04 kbps due to the fact that Twitter text

messages are only 140 characters in length, and thus only a low volume of traffic needs to be transmitted.

Finally, we consider the Skype application. Similar to the Twitter application, we see that 90% of all packets occur with an interarrival time of less than 1 second. However, in contrast to Twitter, we see a low mean interarrival time of 0.55 seconds with a standard deviation of 1.95 seconds. Further, we observe a relatively low mean bandwidth of 1.30 kbps and a standard deviation of 1.8 kbps.

To further study the traffic patterns of the applications, we study the autocorrelation of the packet interarrival time with regard to the lag length in Figure 3(b). We note that all studied applications present completely different autocorrelations for the interarrival times. This is one of the reasons that the applications under consideration will display different signalling behaviour in the next section.

4.2. Influence of Application Characteristics on Optimisation with Network Timers. This section studies the impact of traffic generated by applications on both the network and the QoE of the user. We consider two metrics. First, we consider the *frequency of signalling messages* perceived at network components such as an RNC. In light of network outages caused by the so called *signalling storms* (a large number of signalling messages leading to overload at network equipment), it is in the interest of a network operator to reduce the number of signalling messages arriving at the RNC. One possible way to reduce the signalling frequency is to modify network timer values like T_{DCH} and T_{FACH}. As discussed in Section 2.3, the QoE a user perceives while using his device is influenced by the battery life of the UE. Thus, the second metric considered is the influence of the used network model and associated timer settings on the device's *power consumption*. As described in Section 3.3, based on a measurement trace for an application, we use Algorithm 1 to infer the state transitions occurring during the use of the application. Then, we calculate the relative time spent in each state and use Table 2 to compute the mean power consumption of the radio interface during the measurement. We study both metrics: first on its one and then aggregated for both network models introduced in Section 2.1. First, we consider the three-state model in Section 4.2.1, which describes the default behaviour in 3G networks. Then, we describe the influence of the two-state model in Section 4.2.2. Here, we model a network behaviour similar to that if proprietary fast dormancy algorithms are used. These algorithms have been identified as one of the causes of a signalling storm [6]. Finally, we summarize the results and discuss the possible ramifications of using network timer values to reduce the signalling frequency in Section 4.2.3. More numerical results and details can be found in [18].

4.2.1. Three-State Model: Signalling Frequency versus Power Consumption.

First, we investigate the signalling frequency generated by the studied applications for the three-state network model. Figure 4(a) shows the signalling frequency with regard to the T_{DCH} timer. For all studies of the three-state model, the FACH timeout is set to $T_{FACH} = 2 \cdot T_{DCH}$, a realistic value, as shown in [4]. We see that for T_{DCH} timers shorter than 6 seconds, the Skype application in Idle mode generates the highest signalling message frequency. The Angry Birds application generates the second highest frequency of signalling messages, followed by the Aupeo application. The Twitter application generates the smallest signalling load. If the T_{DCH} value is longer than 15 seconds, this order changes. However, in general, the signalling message frequency for higher T_{DCH} timeouts is lower than for shorter T_{DCH} timeouts. Now, the Aupeo application has the highest signalling frequency, followed by the Twitter application. The signalling message frequency for the Angry Birds application takes the third place. The application which generated the highest signalling message frequency generates the lowest frequency for higher timeout values. This behaviour can be explained by the fact that the Skype application sends keep-alive messages with an interval of less than 20 seconds. If the timer is greater than the interval time of the keep-alive messages, the UE stays always connected and thus generates almost no signalling.

These results show that the traffic patterns of the application have a large influence on the generated signalling load. Signalling is generated for every pause in sending or receiving larger than the configured timeouts. If such pauses occur frequently, this increases the signalling load as shown on the examples of Skype and Angry Birds. Applications with more time between the sending or receiving of data cause less signalling, as shown by Aupeo and Twitter. Furthermore, we can observe that the signalling load can be reduced by increasing the DCH timeout, with the minimum being reached as T_{DCH} approaches infinity. From a signalling load perspective, a value of 20 seconds would probably be sufficient; however, if other metrics such as radio resource consumption are considered, 10 seconds would be acceptable for a network operator.

Based on this finding, we see that increasing the T_{DCH} timer decreases the signalling frequency at the RNC. However, the actual signalling frequency depends on the application running at the UE. From a network operator's point of view, the three-state model should always be preferred to the two-state model because it generates less signalling messages per second, thus decreasing the load at the RNC. This view however does not consider the additional radio resources which are kept in use for a longer time if larger T_{DCH} values are used. Additionally, it should be noted that the choice of the network model is sometimes outside of the domain of the network operator. Proprietary fast dormancy algorithms, as the considered two-state model, are enabled on the UE by the user.

In Figure 5(a), we consider the power consumption if the network uses the three-state model, that is, if the fast dormancy mode of the UE is disabled. The figure shows the mean power consumption of the device with regard to the T_{DCH} timeout. Possible values range between 0 mW if the UE was in Idle state during the whole measurement and 800 mW if the UE was in DCH state during the complete measurement. We see that the least power over all considered T_{DCH} values is consumed by the Twitter application. The second least power consumption is required by Aupeo, followed by Angry Birds. Finally, the most power is consumed by Skype. Here, we see that the maximum value of 800 mW is reached at a T_{DCH} timeout of 20 seconds. This is because, due to the periodic traffic behaviour of Skype, the device is always in the DCH state. Again, we see that the traffic characteristics of the applications impact the power consumption. Applications with more network activity are forced to stay in more power consuming states for a longer time. We see that for very small network timers, the power consumption is minimal. However, as seen in the last section, small timers increase the signalling load at the RNC. Again, a choice of 10 seconds for the T_{DCH} timer can be seen as a compromise between signalling load and power consumption.

Finally, we aggregate both metrics in Figure 6(a). The x-axis of the figure gives the signalling message frequency. On the y-axis, we show the power consumption. Different T_{DCH} values are shown by different colors as specified by the colorbar. First, we consider Angry Birds. We observe that as the signalling frequency approaches zero, the power consumption rapidly increases, even if only small gains in signalling frequency reduction can be achieved. The Aupeo application presents a completely different picture. Here, we can see multiple almost horizontal lines of markers. If T_{DCH} is chosen in this range, each increase of T_{DCH} brings a small

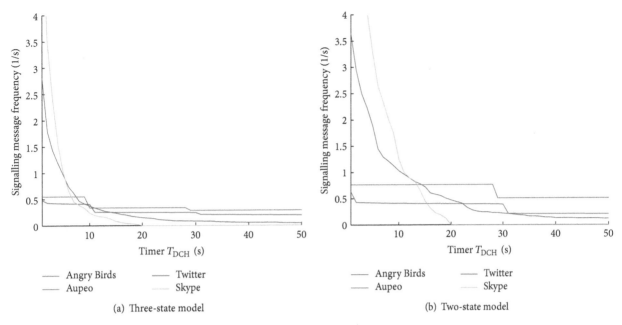

FIGURE 4: Signalling messages frequency for varying T_{DCH} timers.

decrease in signalling frequency for an increase in power consumption. However, some points of discontinuity exist. If, for example, the DCH timer is increased from 10 seconds to 11 seconds, a decrease in power consumption of 40% can be achieved by only suffering from a small increase of power consumption. These points of discontinuity would present themselves to be suitable targets of optimisation. Next, we consider the Twitter application. It displays a similar behaviour as the Aupeo application, with multiple points of discontinuity. Note that Twitter exhibits a different point of discontinuity, and the T_{DCH} value of 10 seconds, which provided good results for Aupeo, is not optimal for Twitter. Finally, Skype shows a completely different picture. First, note that due to the large signalling frequency of Skype for small values of T_{DCH}, $T_{\text{DCH}} = 1$ second is not displayed in the figure. Furthermore, as the T_{DCH} timer increases above 20 seconds, the signalling frequency does not decrease any further, and the power consumption remains at the maximum value. We observe that there is no common optimal value for all applications which would result in an acceptable tradoff.

4.2.2. Two-State Model: Signalling Frequency versus Power Consumption.
Now, we study the consequences of the application traffic in a network using the two-state model. The two-state model occurs in reality if fast dormancy implementations are considered. Here, the UE disconnects from the network if for a certain time no traffic is sent or received in order to reduce power consumption. As for the three-state model, Figure 4(b) shows the signalling frequency with regard to the setting of the T_{DCH} timer. We see the same general behaviour as with the three-state model; however, the signalling frequency generated by each of the applications for the two-state model is usually higher. For example, even for

relatively high T_{DCH} timeout values of 10 seconds, the Angry Birds application causes 270% of the signalling frequency as in a network using the three-state model.

Next, we consider the changes in the power consumption of the UE if the user decides to enable fast dormancy, that is, switch to a two-state model, in Figure 5(b). As with the signalling frequency, we only see a quantitative differences to the three-state model. Again, we compare the differences between the two-state model and the three-state model on the example of the Angry Birds application. For the same considered T_{DCH} timeout of 10 seconds, we see a decrease of 81% in power consumption when compared with the 3-state model.

Finally, we compare the influence of changes of the T_{DCH} timeout on both signalling frequency and power consumption for the two-state model in Figure 6(b). As for the three-state model, we see that there is no tradeoff between power consumption and signalling frequency that would be acceptable for all application. Even for single applications, T_{DCH} values such as 11 seconds which was an acceptable tradeoff for Angry Birds is no longer a good choice in the two-state model.

4.2.3. Consequences of Tradeoff: Signalling Frequency versus Power Consumption.
To illustrate the ramifications of the behaviour discussed in the previous section, we compare the influence of the T_{DCH} timer on an application with different traffic characteristics, for example, the Aupeo application as shown in Figure 7(b). The signalling load before the increase of the DCH timer was 0.55 messages per second; after the change to $T_{\text{DCH}} = 8$ seconds, the load remains unchanged. Thus, the policy change based on one application brings no significant gain to other applications. However, from a user's point of view, the power consumption increased

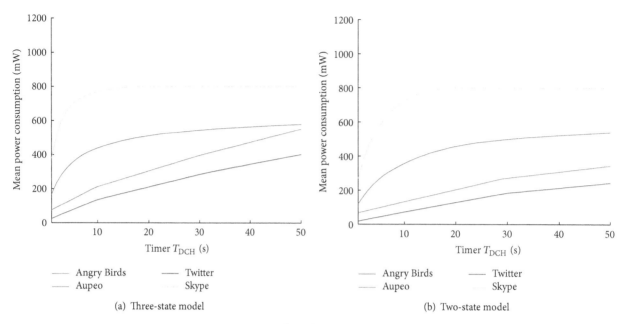

FIGURE 5: Power drain for varying T_{DCH} timers.

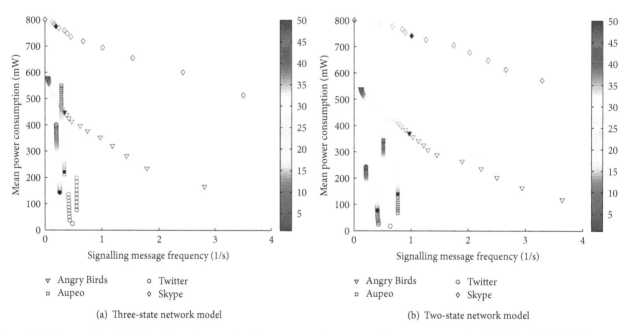

FIGURE 6: Influence of manipulating T_{DCH} timer on signalling message frequency and power consumption. Filled marker highlights $T_{DCH} =$ 11 seconds.

from 121 mW to 183 mW. Again, we assume that the user activates fast dormancy to deal with the increase in power consumption of more than 50%. This results in a decrease of power consumption to 117 mW and an increase of overall signalling frequency to 0.76 signalling messages per second. By changing the value without considering all applications, the network operator has decreased the QoE for other users and worsened their overall situation. Thus, due to the large number of applications, it seems impossible to optimise the DCH timeout to reduce the signalling message frequency

without negatively impacting the users QoE in unexpected ways.

There exist applications, like Twitter and Aupeo, where optimisation by modifying the T_{DCH} values can provide acceptable results. However, these optimisations are only successful if a single application or network model is considered. For other applications, like Angry Birds or Skype, this optimisation approach does not seem to be successful. A reduction of signalling load and power consumption is possible, if the application developers are incentivised to

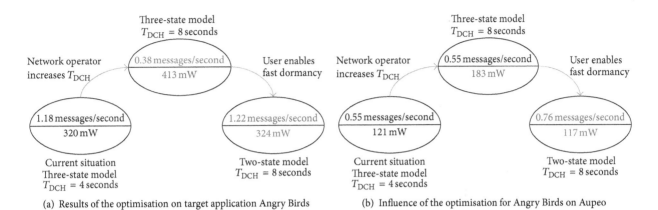

(a) Results of the optimisation on target application Angry Birds   (b) Influence of the optimisation for Angry Birds on Aupeo

FIGURE 7: Influence of manipulating T_{DCH} timer on different applications.

optimise their applications in these regards. In [4], the authors suggest methods to achieve this optimisation, for example, batch transfer of advertisements for applications like Angry Birds or decreasing the refresh rate in applications like Skype. However, at the moment, neither application developers are receiving incentives to optimise applications in this way, nor hardware vendors do provide interfaces to facilitate such optimisation. Such interfaces would allow application developers to schedule their data transmissions in such a way that both signalling and battery drain would be reduced. Additionally, these interfaces would need to allow the application developer to specify if sending the transmission is urgent because the application is being actively used by the user and requires the feedback of the transmission or if the data is being sent as a regular update, while the application is running in the background and can be scheduled for later transmission as suggested by [19, 20].

To bring network operators, hardware vendors, and application developers together and allow for global optimisation of all relevant metrics, holistic approaches like Economic Traffic Management or Design for Tussle, as described in Section 2.3, are required.

4.3. Impact of Network Configuration and Background Traffic on Web QoE.
So far, we have discussed only power consumption as a QoE influence factor. For applications like web browsing, one relevant QoE influence factor is page load times. Therefore, we consider a web QoE model which quantifies the impact of page load times on mean opinion scores [12]. We distinguish here between web QoE and QoE as no QoE models are currently existing which consider page load times as well as power consumption. In this section, we study the impact of background traffic as well as network timer settings on the page load time of an image and the resulting MOS. For this study, we only consider the three-state network model, but the results can be applied to the two-state model as well.

We assume a scenario where a user is running a background application like Twitter or Skype. Then, while the application is in the background, the user begins to download an image from a website. Due to the background traffic, and depending on the network model and associated timer values,

the UE may be currently either in Idle, FACH, or DCH state. We give the probability of a random observer encountering the system in FACH state by p_{FACH} and the probability of a random observer encountering in Idle state by p_{Idle}. If the device is currently not in DCH state, it takes some time to connect. This promotion time depends on the current state and is according to [15] 2 seconds if the UE is in Idle state and 1.5 seconds if the device is in the FACH state. For this study, we assume that the user randomly chooses a time to begin downloading an image. The time until the image is displayed consists of the time to load the page t_p as well as the time to go online t_o, where t_o is the mean time to go online, given as

$$t_o = p_{\text{Idle}} \cdot 2.5\,\text{s} + p_{\text{FACH}} \cdot 1.5\,\text{s}. \qquad (1)$$

Thus, the total time t that is required to download the image is given by $t = t_o + t_p$.

The authors of [12] give a function to calculate the MOS based on the required page load time as $\text{QoE}(t) = a \cdot \ln t + b$, where a and b depend on the type of content being downloaded. For our scenario, picture download and values of $a = -0.8$ and $b = 3.77$ are suggested. It has to be noted that for different websites, the logarithmic function was still observed, but different values for a and b were obtained as given in [12]. These values depend for example on the type of web page as well as the size of the content. Nevertheless, the results presented in this section are therefore generalizable for web browsing to various pages. This allows us to give an expected MOS for downloading pictures while a background application is influencing the probability of a device already being in DCH state or still having to be promoted to DCH state.

Using this methodology, we study the influence of background traffic on the QoE for two background applications with different traffic characteristics. In Figure 8(a), we assume that the user is running the Twitter application as a background process. The application is set to update the users' status feed every 5 minutes. In Figure 8(b), the user is running the Skype application as a background application. This application sends keep-alive messages every 20 seconds. For each application, we assume that the three-state network model with T_{DCH} settings of 1, 4, 8, and 16 seconds is used. We always set $T_{\text{FACH}} = 2 \cdot T_{\text{DCH}}$. In both figures, we show the

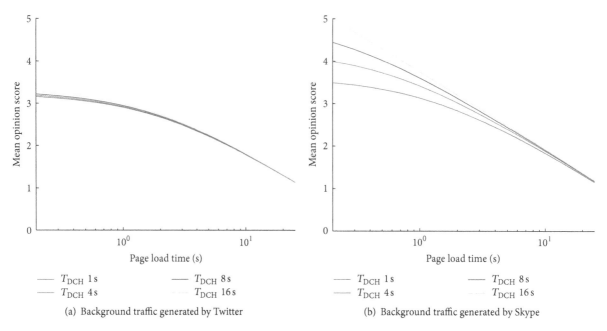

FIGURE 8: Perceived QoE for loading a page with existing background traffic.

assumed page load time, as provided by the network, on the *x*-axis for values from 0.2 seconds to 25 seconds. We assume that 0.1 seconds is a lower bound because page load times lower than 0.1 seconds are not distinguishable [21] by humans. The calculated MOS values are given on the *y*-axis.

The picture downloads with the background traffic generated by the Twitter application result in MOS values beginning at 3.15 for $T_{DCH} = 1$ second, 3.18 for $T_{DCH} = 4$ seconds, 3.21 for $T_{DCH} = 8$ seconds, and 3.27 for $T_{DCH} = 16$ seconds, respectively. With increasing page load time, the MOS again decreases. This behaviour is due to the fact that the Twitter application periodically sends traffic every 5 minutes. Then, no further activity occurs until the next refresh occurs. In this time, the UE transits to Idle state. This traffic characteristic causes an high probability of a user encountering the device in an Idle state. In contrast, downloading pictures with the Skype application generating background traffic causes different MOS values. For a page load time of 0.2 seconds, the MOS value with $T_{DCH} = 1$ second is 3.49, with $T_{DCH} = 4$ seconds is 3.99, with $T_{DCH} = 8$ seconds is 4.44, and finally with $T_{DCH} = 16$ seconds is 4.99, respectively. For increasing page load times, the MOS decreases. This increased MOS values occur because of the high frequency of traffic sent by the Skype application. Here, every 20 seconds, traffic is sent. This means that even for relatively low values of T_{DCH}, the user has a high probability of encountering a state where no promotion delay is required before the actual page load time can begin.

From these studies, we can conclude that, when considering QoE on mobile devices, not only the page load time caused by the network but also additional delays caused by the state of the device should be considered. As shown on two examples, this state can be affected by other applications which are running in the background and generate traffic.

5. Conclusion

In this study, we investigate the influence of both application traffic characteristics and network configuration on the signalling load at the RNC as well as the QoE for the user. We consider two different influence factors on QoE: power consumption and page load times for web browsing.

First, we consider the power consumption at the UE. The network operator can reduce the signalling load at the RNC by increasing a network parameter, the T_{DCH} timer, which determines the time a UE remains connected to the network. However, increasing this timer also increases the battery drain at the UE. While it is possible to find a tradeoff between signalling load and battery drain for any single application, we show that for a set of applications, this is not possible. A network parameter, which might be optimal for one application, may cause another application to generate either a high signalling load or an increased battery drain. Additionally, we consider the influence of background applications on the web QoE. For mobile applications, the page load time may be increased if the UE is currently disconnected and has to connect to the network before obtaining the requested content. If another application is already running, the device may, depending on the traffic pattern of the application, already be online, that is, connected to the radio access network. We suggest to consider this when performing QoE studies for mobile users.

When considering ways to improve mobile networks, many different players, metrics, and tradeoffs exist. We highlighted one examples of such a tradeoff, that is, signalling frequency versus power consumption, and discussed the influence of the current optimisation parameters and the network timers on another. However, many additional tradeoffs exist. For example, the mobile operator has to balance the use of radio resources with the number of generated signalling frequencies. Furthermore, application providers seek to improve the user experience which usually results in a higher frequency of network polls, creating additional signalling traffic. The high number of tradeoffs and involved actors in this optimisation problem indicates that the current optimisation technique used by operators is no longer sufficient.

Approaches like *Economic Traffic Management* or *Design for Tussle* could be applied to find an acceptable tradeoff for all parties. In economic traffic management all, participating entities share information in order to enable collaboration. This collaboration allows for a joint optimisation of the tradeoff. Design for tussle aims to resolve tussles at run time, instead of design time. This prevents the case that one actor has full control over the optimisation problem, which would likely result in the actor choosing a tradeoff only in its favour, ignoring all other participants.

One example of an actor providing information for another in order to optimise the total system would be UE vendor could provide interfaces for application developers to use when sending data. These interfaces would schedule data to be transmitted in such a way that signalling load and battery drain would be reduced, if the application's requirements allow for it. Until such interfaces exist, application developers could consider the effect of the traffic their applications produce both on the UE and the network. To this end, we will provide a web application as future work, which will allow application developers to upload and analyse their applications' traffic according to different network models.

Acknowledgments

This work was partly funded by the Deutsche Forschungsgemeinschaft (DFG) under Grants HO 4770/1-1 and TR257/31-1. The authors would like to thank Florian Wamser for the fruitful discussions. The authors alone are responsible for the content.

References

[1] F. Cuadrado and J. Dueñas, "Mobile application stores: success factors, existing approaches, and future developments," *IEEE Communications Magazine*, vol. 50, no. 11, pp. 160–167, 2012.

[2] Cisco, "Cisco visual networking index: global mobile data traffic forecast update, 2011–2016," White Paper, 2012.

[3] TS 25.331, "Radio Resource Control (RRC); Protocol specification," 3GPP Std., 2012.

[4] F. Qian, Z. Wang, A. Gerber, Z. Mao, S. Sen, and O. Spatscheck, "Profiling resource usage for mobile applications: a cross-layer approach," in *Proceedings of the 9th International Conference on Mobile Systems, Applications, and Services (MobiSys '11)*, pp. 321–334, July 2011.

[5] F. Qian, Z. Wang, A. Gerber, Z. M. Mao, S. Sen, and O. Spatscheck, "Characterizing radio resource allocation for 3G networks," in *Proceedings of the 10th Internet Measurement Conference (IMC '10)*, pp. 137–150, Melbourne, Australia, November 2010.

[6] Nokia Siemens Networks, "Understanding smartphone behavior in the network," White Paper, 2011.

[7] C. Yang, "Huawei communicate: weather the signalling storm," White Paper, 2011.

[8] S. Ickin, K. Wac, M. Fiedler, L. Janowski, J. Hong, and A. Dey, "Factors influencing quality of experience of commonly used mobile applications," *IEEE Communications*, vol. 50, no. 4, pp. 48–56, 2012.

[9] T. Hoßfeld, D. Hausheer, F. Hecht et al., "An economic traffic management approach to enable the TripleWin for users, ISPs, and overlay providers," in *Towards the Future Internet—A European Research Perspective*, G. Tselentis, J. Domingue, A. Galis et al., Eds., pp. 24–34, IOS Press Books Online, May 2009.

[10] D. D. Clark, J. Wroclawski, K. R. Sollins, and R. Braden, "Tussle in cyberspace: defining tomorrow's internet," *IEEE/ACM Transactions on Networking*, vol. 13, no. 3, pp. 462–475, 2005.

[11] Trilogy Project, "D2—lessons in "designing for tussle" from case studies," Deliverable of the Trilogy Project ICT-216372, 2008.

[12] S. Egger, P. Reichl, T. Hoßfeld, and R. Schatz, "Time is bandwidth? Narrowing the gap between subjective time perception and quality of experience," in *Proceedings of the International Conference on Communications (ICC '12)*, p. 1325, Ottawa, Canada, June 2012.

[13] P. H. J. Perälä, A. Barbuzzi, G. Boggia, and K. Pentikousis, "Theory and practice of RRC state transitions in UMTS networks," in *Proceedings of the Global Communication Conference (GLOBECOM '09)*, pp. 1–6, Honolulu, Hawaii, USA, December 2009.

[14] GSMAssociation and others, "Network efficiency task force fast dormancy best practices," White Paper, May 2010.

[15] F. Qian, Z. Wang, A. Gerber, Z. M. Mao, S. Sen, and O. Spatscheck, "TOP: tail optimization protocol for cellular radio resource allocation," in *Proceedings of the 18th IEEE International Conference on Network Protocols (ICNP '10)*, pp. 285–294, Kyoto, Japan, October 2010.

[16] TR 22.801, "Study on non-MTC Mobile Data Applications impacts (Release 11)," 3GPP Std., 2011.

[17] A. Díaz Zayas and P. Merino Gómez, "A testbed for energy profile characterization of IP services in smartphones over live networks," *Mobile Networks and Applications*, vol. 15, no. 3, pp. 330–343, 2010.

[18] C. Schwartz, T. Hoßfeld, F. Lehrieder, and P. Tran-Gia, "Performance analysis of the trade-off between signalling load and power consumption for popular smartphone apps in 3G networks," Tech. Rep. 485, University of Würzburg, January 2013.

[19] M. Calder and M. K. Marina, "Batch scheduling of recurrent applications for energy savings on mobile phones," in *Proceedings of the 7th Annual IEEE Communications Society Conference on Sensor, Mesh and Ad Hoc Communications and Networks (SECON '10)*, pp. 1–3, Boston, Mass, USA, June 2010.

[20] E. Vergara and S. Nadjm-Tehrani, ""Energy-aware cross-layer burst buffering for wireless communication," in *Proceedings of the Conference on Future Energy Systems: Where Energy, Computing and Communication Meet*, p. 24, Madrid, Spain, May 2012.

[21] S. Egger, T. Hoßfeld, R. Schatz, and M. Fiedler, "Waiting times in quality of experience for web based services," in *Proceedings of the Workshop on Quality of Multimedia Experience (QoMEX '12)*, pp. 86–96, Yarra Valley, Australia, July 2012.

12

Selective Forwarding Attacks against Data and ACK Flows in Network Coding and Countermeasures

Yuanyuan Zhang[1,2] **and Marine Minier**[1]

[1] *CITI laboratory, INSA-Lyon, INRIA, Université de Lyon, 69621 Lyon, France*
[2] *Department of Computer Science and Technology, East China Normal University, No. 500 Dongchuan Road, Shanghai 200241, China*

Correspondence should be addressed to Yuanyuan Zhang, yyjess@gmail.com

Academic Editor: Gildas Avoine

Network coding has attracted the attention of many researchers in security and cryptography. In this paper, a well-known attack *selective forwarding attack* will be studied in network coding systems. While most of the works have been dedicated to the countermeasures against pollution attacks where an attacker modifies intermediate packets, only few works concern selective forwarding attacks on data or acknowledgment (ACK) packets; those last ones are required in network coding. However, selective forwarding attacks stay a real threat in resource constraint networks such as wireless sensor networks, especially when selective forwarding attacks target the acknowledgment (ACK) messages, referred to as *flooding attack*. In the latter model, an adversary can easily create congestion in the network and exhaust all the resources available. The degradation of the QoS (delay, energy) goes beyond the capabilities of cryptographic solutions. In this paper, we first simulate and analyze the effects of selective forwarding attacks on both data flows and ACK flows. We then investigate the security capabilities of multipath acknowledgment in more details than in our original proposal (Zhang et al., 2011).

1. Introduction

Network coding is a very active field of both information theory and networking for information dissemination. It consists in encoding a message into several packets and transmitting those packets in an oriented multicast way through the network to the destination. The intermediate nodes can also combine the received packets. It has been shown that network coding could reach the maximum possible information flow in a network. Network coding is also very interesting for security. Many works have been interested in demonstrating the security capacity of network coding. Two security worlds coexist, and the border is delimited by the adversary capabilities. Network coding can be used to bring secrecy if the adversary eavesdropping capabilities are bounded (see [1–3]). Otherwise, cryptography and security must be used to defeat more powerful adversaries [4–6]. This paper falls in the second class of works related to network coding and security.

In network coding, two information flows are identified: the data flow and the acknowledgment (ACK) flow. Both flows can be targeted by an adversary with different consequences. An adversary attacking the data flow wants to affect the messages produced by different sources and decoded by the destinations. An example of such an attack is *pollution attacks* [6]. Many works have proposed countermeasures against *pollution attacks* [4, 5, 7–10]. Another classical attack on data flow is selective forwarding attack where an adversary drops/delays all or part of the data packets he receives. As shown in [11], this kind of attacks is defeated by network coding due to its intrinsic multipath nature. In this paper, we first show by simulations this result; selective forwarding attacks on the data flow are inefficient when network coding is employed in the network.

Finally, attacks against the ACK flow have less attracted the attention of the security community. It does not mean that threats against the ACK flow are less dangerous than those on the data flow, quite the contrary. Threats against the

ACK flow can be partially defeated by some cryptographic techniques. But it is not enough to prevent attacks against the quality of services (QoS). Attacking the ACK flow can create congestion or exhaust the nodes energy by flooding the network with useless packets. Up to our knowledge, Dong et al. [6, 11] are the only ones referring to attacks against the ACK flow in network coding with the DROP-ACK attack [6]. The threats considered in this paper have all the same consequence: flooding. Unfortunately, the solutions found against flooding in classical networks [12] are all dedicated to TCP and cannot be applied in our context.

In this paper, we first give simulation results concerning the effects on selective forwarding attacks first targeting the data flow and second the ACK flow. From those simulations, we observe that first and as expected selective forwarding attacks targeting the data flow are inefficient when network coding is activated in the network and second that attacks against the ACK flow could be really efficient. We then propose a dedicated mechanism based on multipath routing of ACK packets to discard flooding attacks when the adversary drops or delays the ACK packets. We then provide some results concerning global evaluation of the security of network coding when selective forwarding attacks on data and on ACK flows are combined.

In Section 2, network coding and selective forwarding attacks are described as well as related works. Section 3 presents our network and adversary models and describes our multipath ACK back strategy to prevent flooding attacks together with some implementation issues. Section 4 gathers all our simulation results concerning selective forwarding attacks and flooding attacks against first classical network coding (without our multipath strategy) and second network coding with our multipath strategy. We finally show that classical network coding is efficient against selective forwarding attacks and that our network coding multipath ACK strategy is efficient against flooding attacks and sum up those results in Section 5.

2. Preliminaries

In this section, we remind the basic elements on network coding and the related work on flooding attacks.

2.1. Network Coding. The seminal work on network coding was done by Ahlswede et al. in [13]. The main aim of network coding is to find optimal information dissemination in a network. It has been shown that network coding can also improve the network resilience against communication failure, for example, erasure, [14, chapter 1]. Wireline and wireless networks can benefit from network coding. For more details on network coding and on the problems solved by this technique, the readers can consult [14–16].

An important topic in network coding is linear codes: packets exchanged by the nodes are linear combinations of the data to be transmitted over a given finite field. Random linear network coding [17] has particularly attracted attention. The coding process is as follows. Let us assume a network viewed as a graph with a source node and some destination nodes. Let us denote $D = (d_1, d_2, \ldots, d_n)$ a data of kn bits viewed as a vector of n fragments $d_i \in \mathbb{F}_{2^k}, i \in [1, n]$. The messages $m_j = h_j \| p_j$ transmitted by the source and the relaying nodes in a scheme using random linear network coding consist in a header h_j and a payload p_j:

$$p_j = \sum_{i=1}^{n} \alpha_{i,j} d_i, \tag{1}$$

where the coefficients $\alpha_{i,j}$ are chosen randomly over $\mathbb{F}_q$ with $q = 2^u$ the favorite choice in the literature. The header h_j contains all the coefficients $\alpha_{i,j}$ which describe the payload:

$$h_j = \left(\alpha_{1,j}, \ldots, \alpha_{n,j} \right). \tag{2}$$

The source and the relaying nodes apply the coding process infinitely until they receive an acknowledgment (ACK) from all destinations. All destinations run the decoding process: a Gaussian elimination or any other methods for solving linear systems of equations (not described here). In network coding, we have an implicit *"data flow"* which transmits data from the sources to the destination and a *feedback/acknowledgment flow* which carries the ACK from the destination to the sources.

Finally, network coding problems are divided into two classes: *intra-flow* and *inter-flow*. Intraflow network coding corresponds to the example described above: a single message and one or several sources. Interflow network coding combines different messages from different sources at the level of intermediate nodes. This problem is also known as source network coding.

Classically, network coding is used with an oriented multicast strategy that could be compared with a partial flooding of information. This partial flooding allows to obtain the maximum possible information flow in the network.

Generally, in most network environments, the mechanism of transmission of the ACK packets usually employs the routing protocol at the lower routing layer by default. This simplified treatment is enough for most of the upper layer transmission demands in most networks such as TCP/IP because the retransmission will compensate the loss of ACK. However, in network coding environments, the source node continues sending encoding packets until it receives an ACK to confirm the correct decoding at the sink node, so it is crucial to guarantee its arrival.

2.2. Classical Attacks against Network Coding. Three attacks are dedicated to network coding in the security literature: *packet pollution attack* [6, 11], *drop-data packets attack* [11] (also known as selective forwarding attack), and DROP-ACK *attack* [6]. In a pollution attack, an adversary injects invalid packets into the data flow. The adversary exploits the capacity of network coding to spread information at his own advantage. The invalid packets are carried through the network to be only discarded by the destination in the best case. The resources, for example, bandwidth, energy used to carry these packets are lost. Such an attack is extremely powerful in resource-constrained networks such as wireless sensor networks (WSNs). Many papers are devoted to find countermeasures to pollution attacks [4, 5, 7–10].

Selective forwarding attack is a well-known and very harmful attack in wireless multihop networks for example described in [18]. In a selective forwarding attack, a compromised node refuses to forward some of the packets in its outstanding buffer, such as control information or data packets in order to cut off the packets propagation. An extreme example of this attack is a two-step attack where first a malicious node attracts most of the local traffic using, for example, false neighbors information, and then the malicious node completely suppresses the received packets transmission provoking what is usually known as a *black hole attack*. Selective forwarding attacks will not always happen on the data flow but also on controlling packets such as HELLO packets or acknowledgment packets. When it is applied on ACK, we talk here about *flooding attacks.*

Selective forwarding attacks have been studied [11] in the context of network coding where the adversary drops or delays packets of the data flow. By its intrinsic nature, network coding process uses several routes to transmit a message, and the consequences of this attack will be essentially to introduce a delay as shown in [11] but not to prevent the data to reach the destination. Some additional methods [19] coming from the routing world can also help improving the damaged throughput and to decrease the delay.

A DROP-ACK attack [6, 11], or flooding attacks as it is referred throughout the paper, targets the ACK flow. Everything happens after a destination successfully decodes D and starts to forward an ACK. Attacking the ACK flow can be particularly interesting for the adversary: preventing the ACK to reach the source can increase the congestion in the network, prevent a given source to transmit new information, or exhaust the energy of all nodes forwarding the packets (see Figure 1).

From the perspective of the classical man-in-the-middle adversary model, three attack strategies are possible against the ACK flow: injecting/modifying ACK, dropping/removing ACK, and delaying ACK. The last two attacks are the ones leading to a flooding attack.

(a) Injecting/Modifying ACK. Charlie attempts to forge an ACK packet and sends it to Alice. She can believe that Bob has received enough information to recover D. Such attacks can be prevented by a proper use of cryptography, that is, by using a message authentication code (MAC) [20–22] and key distribution [23].

(b) Dropping/Removing ACK. Charlie is seen as a black hole attacker by destroying any ACK packet. Charlie can also just modify the ACK delivery path to prevent the packet to reach Alice. As a result, Alice continues indefinitely sending encoded packets to Bob and so wastes resources. This attack is very difficult to detect.

(c) Delaying ACK. In this case, instead of dropping the ACK packet, Charlie has just to delay the delivery of the

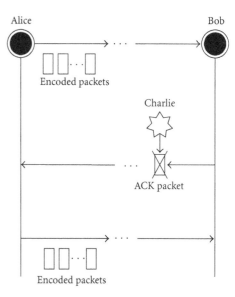

FIGURE 1: An example of flooding attack. Alice is the source who attempts to send encoded packets to the destination, Bob. Bob is supposed to forward an ACK to Alice once he successfully decodes a message. The adversary, Charlie, drops or delays the ACK: Alice never stops to transmit packets to Bob.

packet. This behavior is difficult to distinguish from the selfishness behavior when nodes want to reduce their own energy consumption. As a result, this attack increases the time needed to pass to the next set of packets, and it implies a node energy waste and additional transmission delay.

3. General Assumptions, Implementation Aspects, and Our Proposal

In this section, we provide all the hypotheses made concerning the network, the adversary models, and the implementation of the network coding process. We also provide in Section 3.3 our multipath ACK back strategy to discard flooding attacks.

3.1. General Network Assumptions and Adversary Models. In our proposal, we focus on large-scale static wireless sensor networks as case study with two types of nodes: low-power sensor nodes and a single collecting point which we call the sink.

In our approach, all low-power sensor nodes are exactly the same. In our implementation, we use a general multistream unicast scenario as a network coding mechanism. Every sensor node has 100 raw messages to be encoded and delivered to a single destination which is the sink. So, from this point, we talk about the destination or the sink without distinction. A source sensor node continuously sends one encoded packet per second until it receives the ACK from the sink, and then it starts sending the encoded packets of the next raw message. Meanwhile, all the sensor nodes also play the role of forwarding nodes in the network. The encoded packets are computed using XOR network coding [24]. XOR network coding is a special case of linear network coding where the coefficients $\alpha_{i,j}$ belong to $\mathbb{F}_2$. Because the coefficients are chosen between 0 and 1, the decoding procedure is much simpler. The destination nodes add the received linear combinations until they recover a single message slice. Repeating the procedure, all slices will be calculated and the original message comes out. In this work, the original message is cut into 10 slices and encoded by XOR network coding method.

In this paper, we assume that the adversary goal is to selectively drop packets in two flows, data, and ACK flows after a communication has begun in the network between a source node and the sink. We also assume that the adversary is an insider; that is, it can capture and corrupt sensor nodes, and then he launches those selective forwarding attacks from those compromised nodes. For the sake of simplicity and as previously mentioned, we distinguish these two attacks, on data and ACK flows, by naming them, respectively, *selective forwarding attack* and *flooding attack*.

Our security goal is to prevent selective forwarding attack depressing the performances of network coding. Specifically, we want to be able to preserve a high probability of successful decoding, to prevent *selective forwarding attack* and *flooding attack* from prolonging the average message decoding time, *flooding attack* from wasting the energy of the network (i.e., the energy cost must stay reasonable), preventing a network coding session from finishing (i.e., to decrease the average decoding time consumption).

3.2. Implementation Aspects.

Classically, network coding is implemented using an oriented multicast as routing protocol. However, even if this method guarantees the maximum flow in the network, it is very expensive in terms of energy when considering constrained networks such as sensor networks. To preserve the diversified nature of the neighbors choice of network coding and to limit the energy consumption, we first have based all our implementations at the routing layer level and we decided to use a random version [25] of the gradient-based routing (GBR) protocol [26]— a multihop and multistream unicast routing protocol— underneath the network coding. The choice of the random GBR, as explained in [25], allows to maintain the diversified nature of the next hop neighbor required by network coding and also allows to create at the end of a multipath routing protocol useful for network coding. In all the simulations provided in this paper, we have made those implementation choices for network coding.

3.2.1. Gradient-Based Routing (GBR).

GBR was first proposed in [26]. It uses a natural gradient as a metric to forward the query towards source. The metric can be regarded as physical distance, hops, or others. In this work, a query is forwarded based on the hop gradient in the sensor nodes. A node forwards the query to its neighbors including its information level about the queries. After a certain period, every sensor node builds up a *gradient table* (GTable) which indicates the distance to its sinks.

When a source node outwards a packet, it chooses a nexthop node which has the smallest gradient in GTable.

Thus, each forwarder node will choose their nexthop in the same way. Finally, the path from source to sink is established ideally.

3.2.2. Random GBR.

As the network coding process is only efficient if many forwarders combine/forward the encoded packets, we need to modify the original GBR proposal from single path routing to multipath routing from the source to the sink. To do so, we use [25] where the original version of GBR is randomized. This mechanism works as follows: when a source node outwards a packet, it randomly chooses a nexthop node which has a smaller gradient than him in GTable. So, at each packet sent, the choice for the source node for the next hop is randomly made leading to generate multipath routing as soon as many packets are sent which is the case for the network coding process. In the same way, each forwarder node will choose their own nexthop nodes in the same manner (at each new packet, the next hop is randomly chosen leading to create multipath when the network coding process is used). Notice that, we only allow the packets generated from the same data flow to belong to the encoding process. Each packet traversing through the network will record its path for future use because when the sink has correctly decoded the message, then it sends back through the shortest single path the ACK message. Finally, we will have multipath GBR protocol.

3.3. Our Multipath ACK Strategy against Flooding Attacks.

In this section, we describe our multipath ACK scheme strategy and how we have implemented this scheme for the simulations presented in Section 4.

The algorithm we propose to prevent flooding attacks in the network is really simple.

(i) The source node Alice wants to send the data D to Bob. First, she encodes D into a certain number of m_j messages as explained in Section 2.1, and then she sends to r_1 of her neighbors the encoded packets m_j for $j = 1, \ldots$ until she receives an ACK packet.

(ii) Each of the forwarders (i.e., intermediate nodes) forwards and/or combines the received packets m_j sent by Alice to r_2 of its neighbors (note that the process for a forwarder to encode intermediate packets is the same as the one previously described) until the packets reach the sink Bob.

(iii) The sink, after having received at least n encoded packets, begins to try to decode the message D. When Bob receives a sufficient amount of data, he decodes D and sends the ACK packet through p different routes. Those p routes are selected among all the routes received by the sink: each packet m_j brings with it all the intermediate nodes from the source to the destination.

(iv) As soon as the source Alice has received one ACK packet, she stops sending combination of data of D.

The principle of this algorithm is rather simple; however, its implementation is more tricky and depends on the way the network coding process is performed. In our case, as the network coding is implemented with the help of the random GBR protocol, we derive multipath from it for the ACK flow.

As previously defined, each sensor in the network continuously transmits encoded packets according to network coding scheme. Each encoded packet could choose several nexthop nodes by random GBR protocol. The forwarding nodes generate new encoded packets from the packets buffers and then forward to next-hops.

When the sink collects enough encoded packets of the same data flow, the data flow will be successfully decoded and recovered. Then, the sink must send back an ACK to the source to notify it to stop sending more encoded packets. Using random GBR, we can obtain several paths from the source to the sink. In random GBR, every packet records its route. So, when it arrives at the sink, the route is stored for ACK backsending. The sink maintains a routing table of distinct candidate ACK paths collected from incoming packets. Meanwhile, these paths also satisfy the condition of "the least hop counts" from the sink to the source. Therefore, the sink has many paths to send back ACK; thus the opportunity of ACK being blocked by flooding attackers is reduced.

Multipath ACK scheme is supposed to provide more opportunity to avoid the hijacking of ACK on the paths. The sink is able to choose more than one path from the candidate paths to send ACK.

4. Simulation Results without and with the Multipath ACK Strategy

In this section, we present all our simulation results concerning selective forwarding attacks and flooding attacks, first against classical network coding (without our multipath ACK strategy) and second using our solution after having shortly introduced our simulation environment.

4.1. Simulation Assumptions. All the simulations performed in this paper are carried out using the simulator WSNet [27], an event-driven network and physical layer simulator.

Our simulation results are observed in several scenarios. The result of each scenario is averaged on 20 times simulations run with n sensor nodes, where $n \in [50, 200]$ randomly distributed over a square field of 100 m by 100 m. Each sensor node has a radio range equal to 20 m. We assume that energy consumption of transmitting a packet is twice that of receiving a packet, and each sensor does not expire during the simulation duration time.

In this work, the negative influence by packet loss rate caused by signal degradation or collision in MAC layer is not taken into account, which implies that the source nodes do not retransmit the lost encoded packets but just continue sending encoding packets until the ACK arrives from the sink. The simulation duration time is 150 s. Packet transmission rate at each sensor node is one packet per second.

(a) Adversary Strategy. Our adversary is specialized on dropping/removing all data packets and/or all ACK packets passing through him. To do so, he compromises nodes in the network. We assume that he chooses randomly the nodes to compromise. Our adversary is not really clever in the sense that he does not take into account his position in the network. In our simulation, the number of compromised nodes is between 10% and 30% of the total.

(b) Metric. We focus essentially on evaluating the *average probability of successfully decoded messages*. This event occurs when the decoding process is successful for a given message D and when the source node stops forwarding encoded packets for this message; that is, the source receives the ACK. The *decoding rate* denotes this event, that is, the proportion of successfully decoded packets. The *average decoding time* represents the time interval, at the source node, between the moment where a raw message is generated and an ACK packet is received. The *energy consumption* represents the gain in terms of energy between the most expensive solution and the considered solution (a scale between 0 and 1).

4.2. Attacks under Study with Classical Network Coding. In this part, we give simulation results concerning the way the network coding reacts when confronting to first selective forwarding attacks and second flooding attacks when only single ACK path is considered. For comparison purpose, we also give the results for the dummy example "single path network coding strategy" which means that the network coding process works on a single path using classical GBR. In Section 4.2.1 we give the results concerning selective forwarding attacks whereas in Section 4.2.2 we give results concerning flooding attacks. In Section 4.2.3 we give the results concerning the combination of the two previous attacks.

4.2.1. Analysis for Selective Forwarding Attacks. We sum up in Figure 2 the simulation results when the network is confronted to selective forwarding attackers (from 0% to 30% of attackers), considering both network coding used with a single path (i.e., classical GBR) and network coding used with multipath (random GBR). Note that network coding with single path is only a case study which is not really interesting in concrete applications of network coding.

First, it is important to notice that the decoding rate never reaches 100% even when there is no attacker in the network. This is due to the way the simulations are processed: the simulation time is bounded and the simulations stop when the network still works. We do not wait for the successful decoding of all packets. So, all decodings are not completed; this is why the decoding rate never reaches 100%. This fact is more visible on small networks because less packets are sent in the network, leading to reduce the proportion of well-decoded packets (in the sense of our metric). Moreover, XOR network coding is not always a solution for large networks where operations on bigger finite fields are more efficient. Indeed, the number of packets that must be sent in XOR network coding must be more

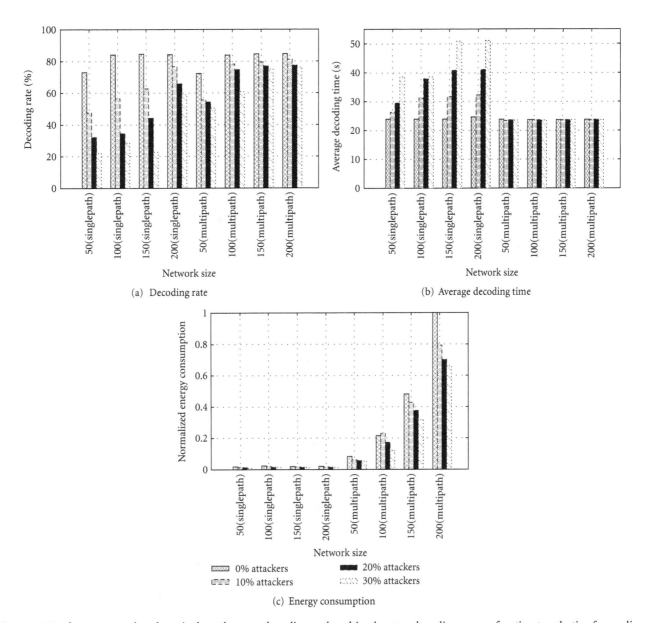

FIGURE 2: Performance results when single path network coding and multipath network coding are confronting to selective forwarding attackers.

important than in other cases to guarantee a correct decoding at the destination (as shown in [28]). However, we compare the different results performed in the same conditions.

So, we observe in Figure 2(a) that the decoding rate drastically decreases for the single path case when the number of attackers increases whatever the size of the network. For example, whereas the decoding rate is more than 80% when no attackers are present in a 150 nodes network, the decoding rate decreases to about 40% when 20% of the nodes are compromised and down to around 20% when 30% of the nodes are compromised. The degradation is clearly less important when the multipath strategy is used (the worst case is observed for a 50 nodes network where the decoding rate passes from 70% with 0% of attackers down to around 50% when 30% of attackers are present in the network). And larger the network is, less the degradation

is important (this remark also holds for the single path case). This is due to the previous remark concerning the bounded simulation time and because, in a larger network, the opportunities of finding more paths are greater.

The average decoding times presented in Figure 2(b) clearly increase in all cases when considering single path GBR whereas the average decoding time (equal to 24 seconds) stays about the same in all cases when considering multipath scheme. This means that when multipath strategy is enabled in a sufficiently dense network, it erases all the negative effects brought by the selective forwarding attackers and makes the average time approaching the ideal value when no attackers are present in the network.

When looking at energy consumption results presented in Figure 2(c), we define the norm value equal to 1 as the biggest energy consumption which is the multipath

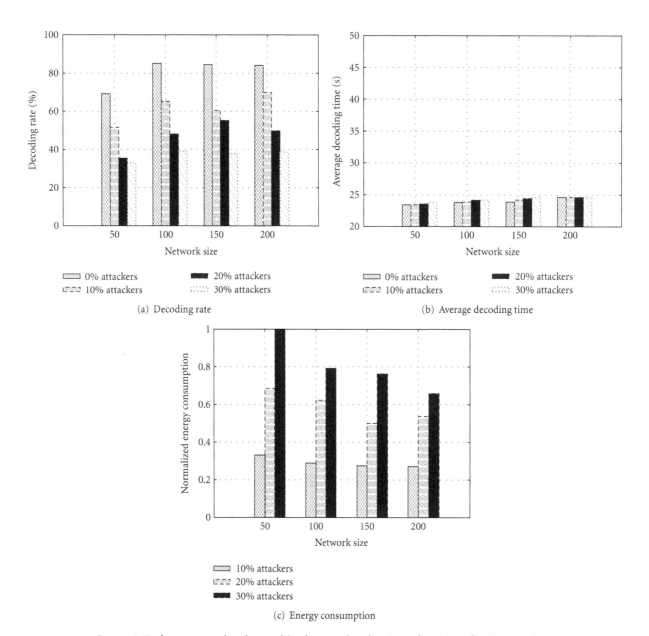

FIGURE 3: Performance results when multipath network coding is confronting to flooding attackers.

scenario for a 200-node network in Figure 2(c). We observe that, in single path scenarios, the energy consumption is about the same in all cases and is equal to 5% of the normalized value. This is due to the fact that the energy consumption only linearly depends on the length of the path from the source node to the sink. Moreover, in single path scenarios, the energy consumption slightly decreases when the number of attackers increases because the attackers make some packets to disappear as the energy linked with those packets. Multipath scenarios are of course much more energy consuming because several paths are in use. Moreover, bigger the network is, exponentially greater the energy consumption is. This also comes from the previous remark where the possible number of paths exponentially increases according to the size of the network.

In conclusion, we finally state that, as expected, classical multipath network coding strategies are efficient in terms of decoding rate and of average decoding time to defeat selective forwarding attackers on data flows even if the energy cost to pay can be important and even prohibitive when energy preservation is crucial for the considered network (e.g., for highly constrained networks).

4.2.2. Analysis for Flooding Attacks. As the flooding attack concerns the suppression of packets in the ACK flow, we only provide the results for the multipath scheme applied on the data flow.

As in the previous case and for the same reason, when there is no attacker in the network, the decoding rate does not reach 100%. However, concerning the decoding

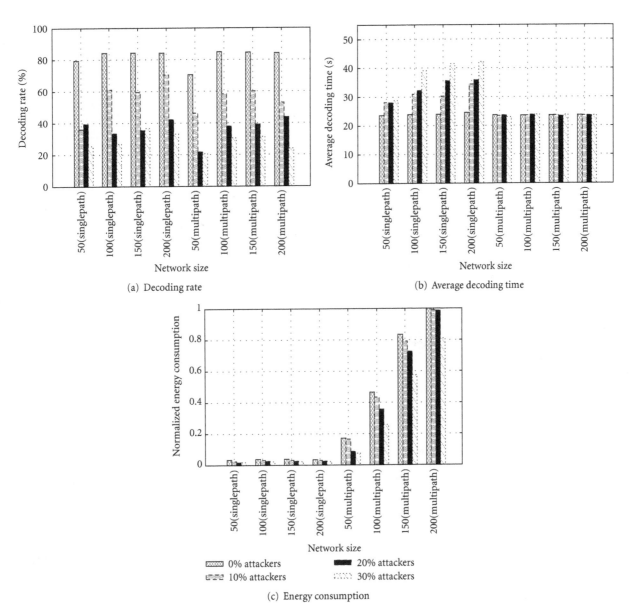

FIGURE 4: Performance results when single path and multipath network coding are confronting to selective forwarding attackers and to flooding attackers.

rate, the portion of successfully decoded packets, presented in Figure 3(a), we notice a clear degradation of this rate: passing, for a 200 nodes network, from more than 80% when no attackers are present in the network to less than 40% when 30% of attackers are present. This means that many source nodes will continue to send encoded packets until they die. Thus, the success of the attacker is clear in this case.

Comparing those values with the ones of the previous section where no degradation is observed when multipath network coding is confronting to selective forwarder attackers, we deduce that flooding attack affects the network coding process in terms of decoding rate.

When looking at average decoding time shown in Figure 3(b), this value remains about the same for all cases: equal to 24 seconds. This result is exactly the same as the ones given in the previous section. This is due to the fact that the decoding time only concerns messages that have been successfully decoded, that is, messages that have been correctly sent and where the ACK has been correctly received by the source node. In other words, this value only concerns messages that have not encountered any attacker. So, this value remains normally the same.

When ACK is hijacked by flooding attackers, even after the successful decoding process at the sink, the source node continues sending encoded packets, and others receive and forward these packets. *Energy consumption* measured in this section is the sum of these extra consumptions. Scenario with a 50-node network fronting 30% attackers is used as the norm value, and the others are normalized according to this norm, as shown in Figure 3(c). The results concerning the

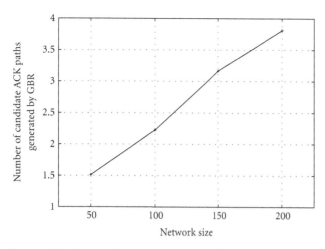

FIGURE 5: Evolution of the average number of ACK paths generated by GBR as a function of the network size.

case of 0% attackers do not appear on Figure 3(c) because they are all too close to 0. So, the most expensive case is the 50-node network with 30% of attackers. It means that the energy wasted in the network due to the absence of ACK back is huge. The results for 30% of attackers and other network sizes proportionally imply less degradation because the diversity of possible ACK paths is more important leading to waste less energy due to source nodes that continue to send packets. In the same way, with fewer attackers present in the network (10% and 20%), the energy waste is less important because more ACK messages reach their destinations.

In conclusion, and as observed in our simulations, the flooding attack is clearly an efficient attack against the network coding process because network coding does not provide intrinsic mechanisms to prevent attacks against the ACK flow. This is why we propose such a mechanism in our paper.

4.2.3. Analysis for Combining Attacks. A critical question for network coding security is to combine all the solutions dedicated to a given attack and to evaluate the performances in the presence of all kind of adversaries. Our results include both selective forwarding attacks on the data flow and flooding attacks. Those results are presented in Figure 4: the percentage $x\%$ of compromised nodes corresponds to $x\%$ of flooding nodes on the ACK flow and of $x\%$ of selective forwarding nodes in the data flow.

As in Section 4.2.1, we present the results for the dummy example "network coding with single path and single ACK back path" for comparison purpose. In Figure 4(a), we observe that the decoding rate, with respect to the number of attackers, always degrades for all the network sizes and all the strategies. The degradation for the single path strategy comes essentially from the selective forwarding attackers even if the presence of flooding attackers increases the degradation (when compared with Figure 2(a)). Figure 4(a) exactly reflects the severe impact of the flooding attack on the network. The influence is so significant that it overwhelms all the advantages brought by multipath data forwarding. As we can see in Figure 2(a), the multipath data forwarding

method is applied against selective forwarding attacks, so the performance results of 10%, 20%, and 30% attackers are close to the ones with 0% attackers. We assume that the multipath method almost compensates all the negative influences from selective forwarding attacks. And we release two attacks in Figure 4(a) scenario: the selective forwarding attack and the flooding attack. The selective forwarding attacks impose great performance degradation onto the data flow from the source to the sink, but the multipath data forwarding method helps the network to overcome the performance loss, according to Figure 2(a). The flooding attacks impose performance degradation on the ACK flow. It is obvious that the performances brought down by flooding attacks are dominant in this scenario. That means that the advantages of multipath data forwarding strategy are totally overwhelmed by the flooding attacks.

Concerning the average decoding time presented in Figure 4(b), surprisingly, the times for the single path strategies are better than the ones in Figure 2(b) for all network sizes. This is due to the fact that less packets arrive at the sink, and less ACKs are returned to the source nodes. So, messages that are correctly decoded are less numerous and require less time to be correctly decoded. As already observed in Figures 2(b) and 4(b), in the case of multipath strategies, there is no significant degradation of decoding time for the same reasons as the ones exposed in Sections 4.2.1 and 4.2.2 This essentially comes from the fact that the decoding time only concerns packets well received at the sink and well acknowledged at the source nodes.

In Figure 4(c), we observe the energy consumption results where the norm value is for 0% attackers, a network with 200 nodes and multipath network coding as in the case of Figure 2(c). Anyway, Figures 4(c) and 2(c) have the same main characteristics. However, the energy consumption for multipath strategies is worst in all cases when both attacks are combined due to the flooding attacks effect. For single path strategies, surprisingly the energy consumption is about the same proportion as in Figure 2(c) (the values are also about to be the same). These surprising results come from the combining effects of flooding attacks that discard the acknowledgements and make the source nodes to continue to send packets and effects of selective forwarding attacks that discard a part of those exceeded packets sent. More generally, the energy consumption of the single path strategies is small when compared with all multipath strategies.

When combining both attacks, clearly the simulation results also combine the worst performances of each attack so the decoding rate for single path strategies has about the same behavior (in worst) as in the case of selective forwarding attackers whereas the decoding rate and the decoding time for multipath strategies have about the same behavior (in worst) as in the case of flooding attackers.

4.3. Attacks under Study with Multipath ACK Network Coding Strategy. In this part, we sum up our simulation results and the corresponding analysis when our multipath ACK network coding strategy is used in the network. All simulations are performed using the same experimental

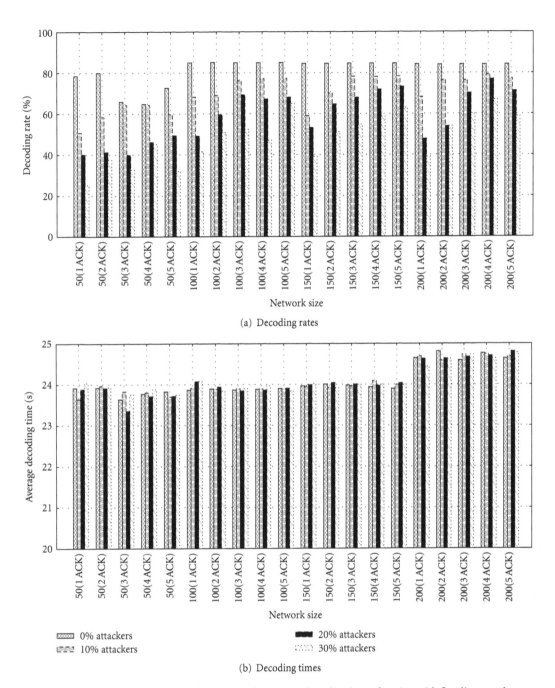

(a) Decoding rates

(b) Decoding times

FIGURE 6: Decoding rates and decoding times when network coding is confronting with flooding attackers.

conditions and the same metrics than the ones described in Section 3. We first study the evolution of the number of paths available in the network to send back the ACK, as this parameter is critical in our problem.

4.3.1. Average Number of Paths from Random GBR. As explained in Section 3.3, the successful transmission of the ACK depends essentially on the capabilities and the opportunity to send back the ACK packets to the source node. Intuitively, it should be accomplished by using as many paths as possible. In fact, the ideal number of ACK paths is

not "the bigger the better," as this will be bounded by the routing protocol parameters. Our simulation results show, in Figure 5, that, for GBR and for the network sizes considered here, the average number of established ACK paths is always less than 4.

This average value becomes constant as the network grows as shown by other simulations not drawn in Figure 5 where a clear logarithmic effect appears. So in this case, it however remains better to use 4 or 5 paths to send back ACK packets rather than 2 or 3. Those results can also be seen in Figure 6(a).

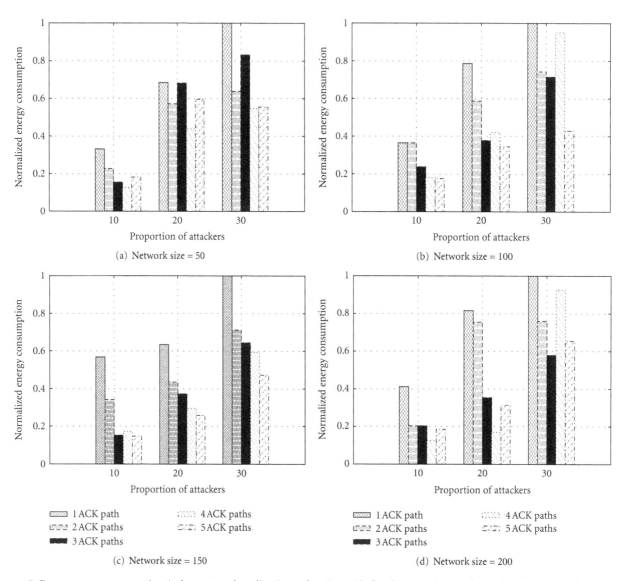

FIGURE 7: Extra energy consumption *when network coding is confronting with flooding attackers *when ACK is intercepted, the source node still sends encoded packets. The sending and receiving of these packets cause extra energy consumption. *Refers to all figures presesnted in this figure.

4.3.2. Results Concerning Flooding Attackers. The results in Figure 6(a) also show that even if our multipath ACK strategy is not so efficient in small networks, it becomes interesting (increasing the rate of successfully decoded packets) as soon as the network is sufficiently large, that is, dense. For example, for 5 ACK and 200 nodes, the decoding rate is equal to 79% when 10% of attackers are present into the network and decreases to 62% when 30% of nodes are malicious which gives better rates and better digressions than with only one ACK path.

The results are more significant in larger networks because smaller networks have fewer paths (as shown in Figure 5) available for the sink to send back ACK packets. Therefore, multipath ACK strategy is much more suitable for networks with larger size, that is, dense networks. On the other side, we should notice that using more ACK paths does not always help improving the performances, as we already explained in Section 4.3.1 and as shown in Figure 6(a). We

can see in every figure that the performance gap among scenarios with one ACK path, two ACK paths, and three ACK paths is larger than others; that is, the number of packets successfully decoded in scenarios with two ACK paths and three ACK paths is 28% and 47% more than for the scenario with one ACK path approximately, while scenarios with four and five ACK paths have improvements of 45% and 53%, respectively. Employing many ACK paths is interesting only when numerous paths are available which is not always the case even for dense networks as shown in Section 4.3.1.

The worst case possible scenario to occur is when attackers are inserted on all different paths between the sink and the source node. This can happen when we deal with very clever attackers (this is not the case here where the attackers are randomly picked among all the nodes). Those particular attackers have an excellent analysis of the network traffic. However, our proposal stays efficient because the routes are at each time taken as random (due to the design of

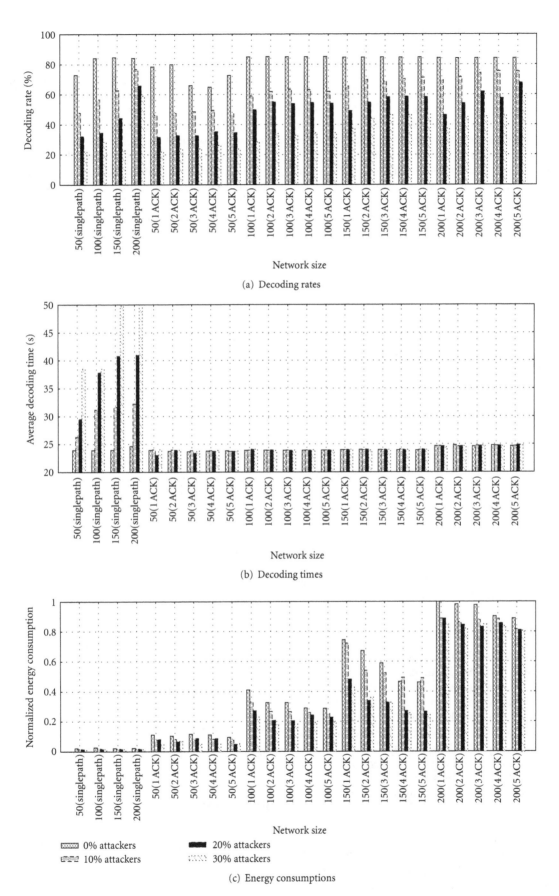

(a) Decoding rates

(b) Decoding times

(c) Energy consumptions

FIGURE 8: Combined flooding and selective forwarding attackers: comparison of the number of decoding rates, decoding times, and energy consumptions in case of 1 ACK path, 2 ACK paths, 3 ACK paths, 4 ACK paths, and 5 ACK paths.

the random GBR protocol described in Section 3.2.2) where an attacker could not know all the random routes used by the encoded packets from a source to the destination as explained in [25].

In Figure 6(b), we present the results concerning the average decoding time. This time stays about the same in all cases even if the cases with 4 and 5 ACK paths seem to give the best decoding time. In all cases, the values observed stay around 24 seconds and do not seem to generate a big degradation of performances. However, the decoding time for a 200 nodes network is a little bit greater due to the size of the network. We have implemented the same scenario with bigger network sizes and have noted that the decoding time growth steepens from network size 200 and above.

In Figure 7, we present the results concerning energy consumption gain. When ACK flow is hijacked by flooding attackers, even after the successful decoding process at the sink, the source node continues sending encoded packets, and others receive and forward these packets. Figure 7 highlights those extra consumptions. The norm value of our figures equal to 1 (which is the most energy consuming one) is for each network size, the energy consumed when 30% of attackers are present in the network and when only one ACK path is used. This corresponds with the case where the most of energy is dissipated in the network due to the source nodes that continue to send encoded packets as already mentioned.

It is interesting to notice here that even if multiplying the ACK paths consumes energy, this consumption is marginal when compared to the flooding provoked by the disappearance of the ACK packets. So, in terms of energy consumption, our multipath ACK solution is really efficient when compared with the single ACK path (e.g., when 30% attackers are present in the network, 5 ACK paths solution only consumes half of the energy of the 1 ACK path solution). Indeed, with only one ACK path, the probability that the ACK packets are thwarted by the attackers is high; thus the source and intermediate nodes continue sending and forwarding packets, which is exactly the cause of unnecessary energy waste.

4.3.3. Results When Combining Selective Forwarding Attackers and Flooding Attackers. As already mentioned in Section 4, it is really important when a security solution is proposed to combine possible attacks and to evaluate the performances in the presence of all kinds of adversaries. The results presented in this section include both selective forwarding attacks on the data flows and flooding attacks. Those results are presented in Figure 8: as previously, the percentage x% of compromised nodes corresponds to x% of flooding nodes on the ACK flow and of x% of selective forwarding nodes in the data flow.

When we bring two attacks into the network, as shown in Figure 8, the performances of single path scenarios do not vary from results of Figure 4. When we switch on the multipath option, *average decoding time* keeps up with the good results of Figures 2(b) and 6(b), but *decoding rate* has been drawn back by flooding attackers. Because the attacks take effects on different flows, analysis on separated attacks

is much more effective and clearer to unveil the advantages brought about by multipath method.

All the results presented in Figure 8 are always worse than those presented in Figures 6 and 7. This comes from the fact that selective forwarding attackers on the data flows introduce a delay for a correct decoding of the packets, and as the simulations made here hold the same time in all cases, the portion of correctly decoded packets is worse. Those effects are less significant for larger networks because the delay induced by selective forwarding is less important. Note also that for dense networks our multipath ACK strategy against flooding attackers stays efficient.

This combined attacks scenario also highlights the fact that our strategy is more efficient in cases of dense networks as shown in Figure 8(a). Moreover and as expected, the impact of selective forwarding is not efficient due to the intrinsic nature of the network coding.

5. Conclusion

We have considered selective forwarding attacks against both data flows and ACK flows in network coding applications. The impact of those attacks has been studied when the adversary randomly compromised the nodes.

Due to its intrinsic multipath nature, network coding is resilient against selective forwarding attackers even if this kind of attacks introduces a little delay in the network. This is the first step we want to demonstrate in this paper. We do not develop here a dedicated mechanism to identify and avoid attackers in the network because we only want simple mechanisms that could be added to the routing layer complementary with network coding to bypass the attackers at a reasonable cost.

Against flooding attacks, our countermeasure is based on multipath ACK, and it is a randomized variant of GBR that allows to build several backward paths we use for the ACK sent. Our simulation results have shown that our solution is efficient as soon as we have a sufficient number of distinct backward paths. Such condition is easily obtained in dense networks.

The choice of the routing protocol is critical, and the key feature is the capacity to generate randomly many paths: greater are the paths of the ACK, higher is the probability to thwart flooding attacks.

Acknowledgment

This work is supported by the National Natural Science Foundation of China (no. 61103040).

References

[1] L. Lima, J. Barros, and M. Médard, "Random linear network coding: a free cypher?" in *Proceedings of the IEEE International Symposium on Information Theory (ISIT '07)*, pp. 176–180, Nice, France, July 2007.

[2] N. Cai and R. W. Yeung, "Secure network coding," in *Proceedings of the IEEE International Symposium on Information Theory (ISIT '02)*, p. 323, July 2002.

[3] S. Y. El Rouayheb and E. Soljanin, "On Wiretap networks II," in *Proceedings of the IEEE International Symposium on Information Theory (ISIT '07)*, pp. 551–555, Nice, France, June 2007.

[4] Z. Yu, Y. Wei, B. Ramkumar, and Y. Guan, "An efficient scheme for securing XOR network coding against pollution attacks," in *Proceedings of the 28th IEEE Communications Society Conference on Computer Communications (IEEE INFOCOM '09)*, pp. 406–414, Rio de Janeiro, Brazil, April 2009.

[5] Z. Yu, Y. Wei, B. Ramkumar, and Y. Guan, "An efficient signature-based scheme for securing network coding against pollution attacks," in *Proceedings of the 27th IEEE Communications Society Conference on Computer Communications (IEEE INFOCOM '08)*, pp. 2083–2091, Phoenix, Ariz, USA, April 2008.

[6] J. Dong, R. Curtmola, and C. Nita-Rotaru, "Practical defenses against pollution attacks in intra-flow network coding for wireless mesh networks," in *Proceedings of the 2nd ACM Conference on Wireless Network Security (WiSec '09)*, pp. 111–122, ACM, March 2009.

[7] A. Apavatjrut, W. Znaidi, A. Fraboulet, C. Goursaud, C. Lauradoux, and M. Minier, "Energy friendly integrity for network coding in wireless sensor networks," in *Proceedings of the 4th International Conference on Network and System Security (NSS '10)*, pp. 223–230, IEEE, September 2010.

[8] D. Charles, K. Jain, and K. Lauter, "Signatures for network coding," *International Journal in Information and Coding Theory*, vol. 1, no. 1, pp. 3–14, 2009.

[9] D. Boneh, D. Freeman, J. Katz, and B. Waters, "Signing a linear subspace: signature schemes for network coding," in *Proceedings of the 12th International Conference on Practice and Theory in Public Key Cryptography (PKC '09)*, vol. 5443 of *Lecture Notes in Computer Science*, pp. 68–87, Springer, Irvine, Calif, USA, 2009.

[10] S. Agrawal and D. Boneh, "Homomorphic MACs: MAC-based integrity for network coding," in *Proceedings of the 7th International Conference on Applied Cryptography and Network Security (ACNS '09)*, vol. 5536 of *Lecture Notes in Computer Science*, pp. 292–305, Paris, France, 2009.

[11] J. Dong, R. Curtmola, and C. Nita-Rotaru, "Secure network coding for wireless mesh networks: threats, challenges, and directions," *Computer Communications*, vol. 32, no. 17, pp. 1790–1801, 2009.

[12] C. L. Schuba, I. V. Krsul, M. G. Kuhn, E. H. Spafford, A. Sundaram, and D. Zamboni, "Analysis of a denial of service attack on TCP," in *Proceedings of the IEEE Symposium on Security and Privacy*, pp. 208–223, IEEE Computer Society, Oakland, Calif, USA, May 1997.

[13] R. Ahlswede, N. Cai, S. Y. R. Li, and R. W. Yeung, "Network information flow," *IEEE Transactions on Information Theory*, vol. 46, no. 4, pp. 1204–1216, 2000.

[14] T. Ho and D. Lun, *Network Coding: an Introduction*, Cambridge University Press, 2008.

[15] R. W. Yeung, S.-Y. R. Li, N. Cai, and Z. Zhang, *Network Coding Theory*, NOW Publishers, 2005.

[16] J. Cannons, R. Dougherty, C. Freiling, and K. Zeger, "Network routing capacity," *IEEE Transactions on Information Theory*, vol. 52, no. 3, pp. 777–788, 2006.

[17] T. Ho, M. Médard, R. Koetter et al., "A random linear network coding approach to multicast," *IEEE Transactions on Information Theory*, vol. 52, no. 10, pp. 4413–4430, 2006.

[18] C. Karlof and D. Wagner, "Secure routing in wireless sensor networks: attacks and countermeasures," *Ad Hoc Networks*, vol. 1, no. 2-3, pp. 293–315, 2003.

[19] S. Marti, T. J. Giuli, K. Lai, and M. Baker, "Mitigating routing misbehavior in mobile ad hoc networks," in *Proceedings of the 6th Annual International Conference on Mobile Computing and Networking (MOBICOM '00)*, pp. 255–265, ACM, Boston, Mass, USA, August 2000.

[20] H. Krawczyk, "LFSR-based hashing and authentication," in *Proceedings of the Annual International Cryptology Conference (CRYPTO '94)*, vol. 839 of *Lecture Notes in Computer Science*, pp. 129–139, Springer, Santa Barbara, Calif, USA, 1994.

[21] H. Krawczyk, M. Bellare, and R. Canetti, "HMAC: Keyed-Hashing for Message Authentication," 1997, rFC 2104.

[22] J. Black and P. Rogaway, "CBC MACs for arbitrary-length messages: the three-key constructions," *Journal of Cryptology*, vol. 18, no. 2, pp. 111–131, 2005.

[23] L. Eschenauer and V. D. Gligor, "A key-management scheme for distributed sensor networks," in *Proceedings of the 9th ACM Conference on Computer and Communications Security (CCS '02)*, pp. 41–47, ACM, Washingtion, DC, USA, November 2002.

[24] S. Katti, H. Rahul, W. Hu, D. Katabi, M. Medard, and J. Crowcroft, "XORs in the air: practical wireless network coding," *IEEE/ACM Transactions on Networking*, vol. 16, no. 3, pp. 497–510, 2008.

[25] O. Erdene-Ochir, M. Minier, F. Valois, and A. Kountouris, "Toward resilient routing in wireless sensor networks: gradient-based routing in focus," in *Proceedings of the 4th International Conference on Sensor Technologies and Applications (SENSORCOMM '10)*, pp. 478–483, Venice, Italy, July 2010.

[26] J. Faruque and A. Helmy, "Gradient-based routing in sensor networks," *ACM SIGMOBILE Mobile Computing and Communications Review*, vol. 7, no. 4, pp. 50–52, 2003.

[27] A. Fraboulet, G. Chelius, and E. Fleury, "Worldsens: development and prototyping tools for application specific wireless sensors networks," in *Proceedings of the 6th International Symposium on Information Processing in Sensor Networks (IPSN '07)*, pp. 176–185, ACM, April 2007.

[28] M. Médard and R. Koetter, "Beyond routing: an algebraic approach to network coding," in *Proceedings of the IEEE Communications Society Conference on Computer Communications (IEEE INFOCOM '02)*, pp. 122–130, IEEE, New York, NY, USA, June 2002.

13

Experimental Evaluation of a SIP-Based Home Gateway with Multiple Wireless Interfaces for Domotics Systems

Rosario G. Garroppo, Loris Gazzarrini, Stefano Giordano, and Luca Tavanti

Dipartimento di Ingegneria dell'Informazione, Università di Pisa, 56126 Pisa, Italy

Correspondence should be addressed to Luca Tavanti, luca.tavanti@iet.unipi.it

Academic Editor: Gildas Avoine

In modern houses, the presence of sensors and actuators is increasing, while *communication services* and *entertainment systems* had long since settled into everyday life. The utilization of wireless communication technologies, such as ZigBee, Wi-Fi, and Bluetooth, is attractive because of their short installation times and low costs. The research is moving towards the integration of the various home appliances and devices into a single domotics system, able to exploit the cooperation among the diverse subsystems and offer the end-user a single multiservice platform. In this scenario, the paper presents the experimental evaluation of a domotics framework centered on a SIP-based home gateway (SHG). While SIP is used to build a common control plane, the SHG is in charge of translating the user commands from and to the specific domotics languages. The analysis has been devoted to assess both the performance of the SHG software framework and the negative effects produced by the simultaneous interference among the three widespread wireless technologies.

1. Introduction

Domotics refers to a system that controls several (or all) home "services," such as lighting, HVAC (heating, ventilation, and air conditioning), communications, security, healthcare, and entertainment, in a integrated and automatic or semi-automatic way, allowing the user to manage them from a series of heterogeneous devices (e.g., touch panels, remotes, mobile handsets, and smartphones), either at home or from anywhere in the world. In the domotics archetype, all subsystems are able to talk to each other and interact in a seamless manner, realizing an intelligent structure that improves the quality of life, reduces the costs, and achieves energy savings. To put this paradigm into practice, the communication among the single devices and between the various subsystems is the fundamental operation. Hence, wired and wireless networks will be one of the building blocks of the present and future domotics solutions. On top of this somewhat "physical" element, a common control plane is also necessary, in order to unify the management operations into a single and portable user interface.

One of the major components of a domotics system is the set of sensors and actuators. These usually come in the form of one or more networks, backed either by a single technology or by different ones. Not always, however, do the specifications define a common control plane that is suitable to contemporarily manage devices belonging not only to different standards, but even to different application profiles. As a result, the burden of coordinating and making devices interoperate is often left entirely to the system implementer. Indeed, a scenario with mixed profiles and technologies is not so uncommon, especially in those environments where multiple services might be requested. One such example is exactly the "smart home" or domotics concept, in which several profiles and technologies (e.g., ZigBee's home automation, smart energy, and telecom services, or KNX's lighting, heating, and energy management—just to cite the most appealing ones) might all be present.

From the user perspective, the devices belonging to the diverse subsystems of the home services platform can be typically controlled through dedicated appliances located in the house (e.g., a touch panel, a smart telephone, a TV remote). However, this paradigm no longer holds for remote control operations that occur when the user is far from home. In this case the user would normally have a single device at hand, such as a notebook or a smartphone, by means of which he/she would like to control any device in the home, not just those belonging to a specific profile or technology, and possibly without complex configuration or selection procedures.

In addition to the need for a coordinating system for the DSANs, in today's houses we already find interpersonal communication and multimedia entertainment systems. Hence, the design of a domotics platform should also consider the integration of communication and multimedia applications with the DSAN-based services.

In this scenario, we describe an architecture designed to gain interoperability among devices belonging to different technologies and profiles. In our vision, the common control plane is realized through the Session Initiation Protocol (SIP) [1], while a *SIP-based home gateway* (SHG) translates the user commands from and to the specific DSAN language, thus allowing the user to control all domotics devices either at home or away from it, using his mobile terminal or his favorite SIP client, in a transparent, uniform, and simple way. The SHG, which is the major enabler of the envisioned system, is also devised to retain the compatibility with the existing SIP infrastructure and the deployed SIP clients, which can therefore be exploited in full.

Among the various domotics sensor and actuator networks (DSANs), wireless sensor networks (WSNs—note that the term "sensor" is often used for both sensors in the strict sense and for actuators too) are the version that is growing faster, due to shorter deploying times and simplified configuration. Several technologies and standards are nowadays available for the implementation of a WSN [2]. Especially the ones based on open or widely adopted standards, such as ZigBee, Bluetooth, Z-Wave, and KNX-RF, can undeniably be regarded as the most interesting ones. This is because they allow the deployment of large and almost self-configuring networks in relatively short times and at reduced costs. Two of these standards, ZigBee and Bluetooth, have been embedded into the SHG.

On the other hand, the current trend in multimedia and communication home systems is to move the physical transport services over the Wi-Fi technology. Thus, we have equipped our SHG also with a Wi-Fi interface, used for providing the above-mentioned "wideband" services.

The majority of these wireless standards operate into the unlicensed 2.4 GHz ISM band, which can be exploited by multiple users and networks at the same time. However, due to the mutual interference, the coexistence of different devices operating in proximity of each other can be troublesome. As proved by many authors [3, 4], this is especially true for ZigBee networks, whose performance is heavily influenced by the presence of Wi-Fi devices. While it is sometimes feasible to avoid the interference among devices sharing the same spectrum and implementing the same standard (e.g., collision avoidance schemes might work across separate networks), the use of incompatible modulations and channel access schemes makes it virtually impossible to

ensure the coexistence among devices belonging to different technologies.

In summary, the design and implementation of a domotics gateway must face two key issues: integrating heterogeneous indoor devices and networks, allowing the composition of dynamic and pervasive services (including interpersonal communications and multimedia), and assuring the physical coexistence of the interfaces located on the gateway apparatus.

1.1. Contribution. We present a working prototype of the SHG, which is used to build a complete proof-of-concept of our SIP-based domotics architecture. A customized SIP event package and a notification server have also been developed to validate a possible extension to new services. The SHG was interfaced with an actual ZigBee network and a Bluetooth PAN, in addition to a generic Wi-Fi connection. We experimentally evaluated the performance of the SHG prototype, proving its ability to support large domotics systems.

In describing our SIP-based system, we also present the aspects that make it innovative. We arranged for the SHG to be the sole entity to have a SIP address, thus avoiding the overhead of having a SIP address for each home device. We designed and implemented a functional addressing and a control scheme to ease the user interaction with the system and an abstraction layer to decouple the implementations on the SIP and DSAN sides. We also show how we exploited some features of ZigBee to improve the integration with the SIP and the SHG.

Then, the paper reports an experimental study involving Wi-Fi, ZigBee, and Bluetooth networks. The goal of this study is to characterize the performance of the SHG in terms of the coexistence of the three systems, especially because they are all active in the same time and space, that is, in the prototype SHG board, and thus subject to strong mutual interference.

2. Related Work

In this section we just draw a sketch on the current state of the art in domotics systems and interference studies, with specific focus on the works whose topic is most similar to ours. The differences that make our contribution innovative are also pointed out.

Starting from the domotics area, some authors approached the integration between WSNs and control plane protocols by bringing customized or reduced versions of SIP or REST on the sensor nodes. For example, Luckenbach et al. [5] employed REST to provide clients connected to the Internet with the ability to directly interact with MICAz sensors. Similarly, Krishnamurthy and Lange [6, 7] proposed TinySIP, an architecture to offer to multiple clients the access to sensor-based information via SIP.

These kinds of approaches suffer from a series of drawbacks. Since the device is resource constrained, the protocols must be stripped of many functionalities. Due to the particular operative system running on the sensor nodes, the development times might be nonnegligible. Also, given the high heterogeneity of the devices, it might be necessary to repeat and modify the customization and development steps for every technology that is going to be integrated into the system. Finally, compatibility with deployed hardware and software is not retained. Conversely, our framework moves the development effort to a single high-end device (the SHG), allowing faster implementation times and full compatibility with both existing sensor and actuator devices and also with the SIP.

An approach that follows the philosophy of making an open and flexible service platform can be found in [8], whose authors started their work from an architecture similar to ours.

Acker et al. [9] presented a concept of ubiquitous home and facility control that exploits the IP Multimedia Subsystem (IMS), a SIP-based control architecture considered by mobile network operators.

The work closest to ours is perhaps the one by Bertran et al. [10, 11], who tested SIP as a universal communication bus for home automation environments. A SIP gateway and a series of SIP adapters and interpreters have been implemented and deployed to make all devices SIP compliant. However, there are some aspects that may put our framework one step ahead.

Bertran et al. did not consider the issues with addressing and reachability of the single DSAN devices. Conversely, we designed a functional addressing scheme that greatly simplifies the user interaction and does not require the DSAN nodes to register to any SIP server or other additional entities. Then, we devised a way of keeping the compatibility not only with the DSAN elements, but also with the user terminals. This allowed us to provide the user also with functionalities that are not natively supported by his/her device. This paradigm can even be extended to ensure forward compatibility with new domotics services. Conversely, Bertran et al. did not pay much attention to this aspect. A third distinguishing point is in the adaptation between the SIP and the DSAN worlds. While Bertran et al. design a single software module to be put in the gateway, we perform this operation in two steps, via the DFA layer. This allows to decouple the implementation of the two domains, making the system more flexible. Finally, we studied in much more detail the integration with two possible DSANs, namely, ZigBee and Bluetooth, and showed how it is possible to exploit their features to simplify the integration into the system. In [11], the main focus of the experimental platform was on the performance figures of the gateway (which, if we consider the current hardware technology, might not be the most relevant hurdle to the domotics development, as proved by our tests in Section 7.2).

A major disadvantage that is common to proposals like [8–10] is the need for every home device to register with its own URI. When the number of devices increases (heavily monitored and automated buildings may have hundreds of nodes), the user capability of handling them through their URIs is clearly hampered. The same shortcoming applies to the zone manager solution proposed by [6], in which the

majority of the communications are possible only by knowing the address of each gateway to which the sensors of interest refer. On the other hand, in our system the sole SHG must register to an external SIP server (unless the SHG itself implements a registrar) and we can mask the multitude of DSAN nodes by means of the "functional addressing" method.

As for the coexistence of multiple wireless interfaces, we can find numerous analytical and simulation studies, especially about the performance of ZigBee under the interference of Wi-Fi and Bluetooth (such as [12], just to cite one). The major shortcoming of these approaches is that due to the very complex nature of the wireless channel and environment, there is no measure of their agreement with the reality, and thus their actual utility is somehow limited.

Sikora and Groza experimentally obtained the PER of a ZigBee system under the interference of Wi-Fi devices, Bluetooth devices, and also a microwave oven [4]. However, the study is limited to a single source of interference (e.g., either Wi-Fi or Bluetooth), and also the analysis of the coexistence of ZigBee and Bluetooth is not complete, since the (actually very few) results have been collected in one direction only (i.e., Bluetooth over ZigBee). Nevertheless, an interesting observation in Sikora and Groza's paper is about the presence of notable discrepancies between the collected experimental data and the simulation results provided by the IEEE 802.15.4 task group.

A similar experimental study was led by Musaloiu-Elefteri and Terzis, who evaluated the loss rate of a ZigBee system under Wi-Fi interference [3]. Starting from this result, they developed interference estimators and distributed algorithms to dynamically change the ZigBee operating channel. This approach was proved to drastically reduce the loss rate of ZigBee networks.

The authors of [13] present the results of an empirical study on the coexistence between IEEE 802.11b and Bluetooth devices. However, the primary objective was to develop an analytical model to estimate the mutual interference, rather than characterizing it in real world scenarios. Hence, to build such models, the experiments were controlled through the use of attenuators, signal generators, and coaxial cables, thus resulting in a rather idealistic environment.

From the analysis of the cited works, it emerges that in all cases, even in [4], the authors studied the interference of no more than two systems at a time. A two-way experimental analysis of the simultaneous interference among Wi-Fi, Bluetooth, and ZigBee can be found in [14], which confirms the weakness of ZigBee and also shows that some supposed interference-free ZigBee channels are in fact affected by the presence of Wi-Fi transmissions.

However, in all cited works, the interfering sources are always placed in physically disjoined devices. On the contrary, devices such as the domotics gateways are expected to embed several wireless interfaces onto the same board. In such cases, the interference effect might be even greater, due to the electrical couplings on the board. The experimental measurement we carried out over our prototype SHG was aimed at filling this gap.

3. Domotics Requirements and the SIP Control Plane

The complexity of the domotics system demands for a series of requirements that allows an easy integration among the subsystems and the development of a "friendly" and always available user interface. A set of the major requirements is represented by the following list (see also [8, 15] for similar surveys).

(i) The domotics system must implement and provide a *request/response* paradigm to allow the user to send commands to the DSAN devices and possibly have a feedback. Commands can also be exchanged among the various domotics entities.

(ii) Both the user and the system should be promptly notified when events of some importance occur in the environment. Thus, the network is expected to support asynchronous and/or periodic *event notification*.

(iii) Commands and events suit the need of exchanging small amounts of data in very short times. The use of *sessions* would instead allow the streaming of various types of data over a period of time (e.g., audio and video, but also fast varying sensor readings or large file transferrals).

(iv) The extensive adoption of mobile devices such as smartphones and tablets has made the connection to the global network available everywhere. As a consequence, the user should be regarded as a *mobile user*, who would want to control his/her home from different places and via diverse access technologies (e.g., wireless LAN, cellular, ADSL).

(v) Despite the heterogeneity of the various domotics subsystems, the user would hardly be keen on using several and different human interface devices (HIDs), remembering the network addresses of every DSAN device, or learning technology-specific aspects of its domotics system. Conversely, it would be beneficial if the user could interact with a unique interface layer and associate mnemonic names to the devices and their functions (i.e., what we later call "functional addresses", e.g., the room where they are placed and/or the action they perform). Therefore, the domotics system should *integrate the subsystems* at both the technical and the user interface level.

(vi) While the domotics idea is slowly gaining field, *communication services* and *entertainment systems* had long since settled into everyday life. Therefore, the design should seamlessly include these services into the domotics platform (see [10] for some interesting examples).

Among the many options for realizing the common control plane (see, e.g., [15–19]), we selected the Session Initiation Protocol for its numerous advantages. From the conceptual point of view, which relates to the operations that are to be carried out by the control plane, SIP provides a set of *methods* that fit well the necessities of DSAN control and management as follows.

(i) The low overhead of the MESSAGE method (no set-up phase is needed) perfectly matches the requirements of the *request/response* operations.

(ii) A publish/subscribe-notify semantic is available in SIP specifications and allows the user to be promptly notified of events that occur in the network. This allows an almost direct mapping of asynchronous and/or periodic *event notifications* to SIP methods.

(iii) SIP has been natively designed to offer *session management* capabilities (i.e., session creation, modification, and tear down).

(iv) The core SIP infrastructure exploits the REGISTER method to transparently manage the movement of the user between different points of attachment to the network.

From a more practical and implementation perspective, we can identify the following key points.

(i) SIP is a text-based protocol: message building and parsing is a relatively simple task. SIP parsers and interpreters are widely available. Hence, the development effort is greatly reduced.

(ii) The body of SIP messages is flexibly structured and can contain a wide variety of information. This allows an easy extension of the protocol to support customized DSAN-related data and commands.

(iii) A huge SIP infrastructure is already deployed and working; hence, there is no need to deploy new infrastructural elements (either servers or core-network software).

(iv) SIP works at the application layer, being transparent to the underlying physical and networking technologies. It can thus work as a gluing layer for heterogeneous systems.

A further valuable asset of SIP is the use of *mnemonic names*. Every SIP resource is associated to a URI (uniform resource identifier), a mnemonic text pattern based on the same syntax established for web services. This allows the user to remember names rather than complex numeric addresses. A way of exploiting this feature is presented later on in the paper.

Despite its numerous advantages, employing SIP for the control plane of our domotics system does not come for free. There are several issues that must be solved as follows.

(i) SIP is defined by a series of RFCs that provide only general indications on the use of the standardized procedures. The application to practical cases is left to the implementer, and it clearly depends on the specific scenario. Hence, the usage of SIP might require a preliminary phase to map the existing methods and design complementary procedures that fit the application requirements. One such example is the Event Notification Framework, a standardized but empty framework in which we have defined a new package to be used in our domotics architecture (see Section 6.3).

(ii) To be effective, a control plane must be pervasive and its procedures supported by all devices forming the system. However, porting SIP on devices with minimal processing and/or storage capabilities, such as the sensors and actuators, is a nontrivial task that is often reduced to porting just a subset of the original methods and features (see, e.g., [6]). Clearly, this approach is not optimal and should be avoided in favor of a complete transposition of the available paradigms and/or capabilities.

(iii) Though SIP is a mature and relatively widespread technology, the majority of end-user devices employ SIP to support very few services. Designing a system under the assumption that all user devices can support all SIP methods is undoubtedly appealing, but quite unrealistic as well. Conversely, defining the procedures to allow the users to take advantage of these paradigms by means of their current terminals is a harder but definitely more sensible task.

3.1. Selected SIP Methods. In this subsection we provide a brief description of the SIP methods we used and how we integrated them into the domotics system. Note that the integration mode is not univocal and other mappings can be implemented. Therefore, particular attention is paid to the reasons that drove our choice, how these methods have been exploited, and how they interact with the other elements of the system.

3.1.1. Instant Messaging. The SIP MESSAGE method [20] is used to supply the real-time dispatch of short text messages where each message is independent from the others. A MESSAGE transaction requires no session setup and does not establish a dialog. The UA receiving a MESSAGE must send an immediate reply to the sender to inform it about the successful or failed reception of the message—in case of success, the answer is 200 OK.

We used this real-time and low-overhead method to implement the *request/response* paradigm (see Section 3). In detail, the *request* is mapped to a first MESSAGE transaction, and the *response* is mapped to a second MESSAGE transaction. Therefore, four SIP messages are necessary to realize the *request/response* paradigm. A typical usage case of this method is illustrated in Figure 1.

A very important aspect of the MESSAGE method is its compatibility with all existing SIP clients. Since every SIP client must support this method, this ensures that the basic managing functions of our system are also supported.

3.1.2. Publish/Subscribe-Notify Paradigm. The SIP Event Notification Framework (ENF), defined in [21], provides a way for SIP elements to learn when "something interesting" has happened somewhere in the network. The procedures to

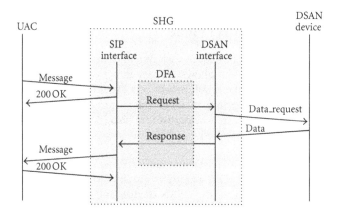

FIGURE 1: The *request/response* paradigm implemented via the MESSAGE method.

allow for the prompt distribution of such events are known as the Publish/Subscribe-Notify paradigm.

Briefly, an initial SUBSCRIBE message is sent by the subscriber (the user that is interested in the event) to the notifier (the node that is first aware of the event). If the subscription is accepted, a 200 OK answer is sent to the subscriber. Then, the events are reported from the notifier to the subscriber by means of the NOTIFY method. Notifications can be sent either periodically or when the specific event occurs (or both).

SIP also provides a framework for the publication of event states on a notification server, called Event State Compositor (ESC). This task is accomplished using the PUBLISH method [22]. The ESC is then responsible for managing and distributing this information to the interested parties through the ENF.

The mapping of the complete Publish/Subscribe-Notify paradigm to the domotics architecture is shown in Figure 2. The figure shows both periodical and event-driven notifications.

Note that the ESC is a logical entity, which can physically reside in diverse parts of the system; in our prototype the ESC functions are provided by the SHG. In particular, the SHG is the only entity that publishes the events. DSAN devices are thus preserved from knowing anything about the SIP existence. In addition, the SHG can filter and compose events that are not available in the single DSAN domains.

3.1.3. Registration. In the proposed domotics architecture, just two elements must be registered: the user and the SHG. All sensors and actuators of the various subsystems are managed by the SHG via the specific DSAN interfaces. Thus they can be completely unaware of the SIP control plane. On the other side, the user can interact with the system by knowing just the SIP URI of the SHG and can refer to the DSAN devices through what we have called the "functional addressing" scheme (see Section 4.2), that is, a set of mnemonic names (such as the room names and the device functions). This makes the system extremely user-friendly and also highly scalable. No matter how many devices are in the house, the user can control them invariably

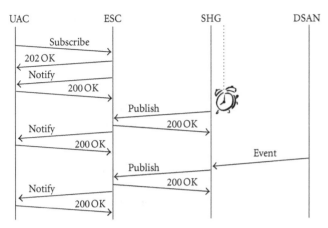

FIGURE 2: SIP message flow for publish, subscribe, and notify operations over the domotics system.

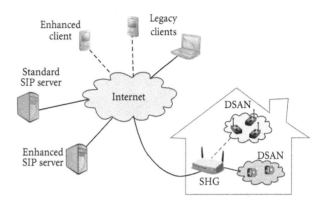

FIGURE 3: Reference architecture of the SIP-based domotics system.

through the same URI (the SHG one), from anywhere he/she is and from any SIP-enabled device he/she is using.

4. System Architecture

The general architecture of the conceived domotics system is illustrated in Figure 3. We can identify four major physical elements: the clients, the SIP servers, the SHG, and the DSANs.

The expert reader may have noticed that this kind of architecture is not completely novel: a similar picture has been presented, for example, by [8, 10]. This means that the scenario in which the domotics system is going to operate can be considered quite settled. Nevertheless, though addressing a similar architecture, the various works, and ours in particular, differ in several aspects, such as how the SIP is integrated into the framework and exploited by the designer, what semantics are taken into account, how they interact with the other components of the system, and how they can be beneficial to the user. Specifically, our approach targets a more scalable, transparent, and painless integration, both from the user perspective and from the DSANs' point of view.

The new and distinguishing elements of the architecture are described in the following.

4.1. SIP-Based Home Gateway. The SIP-based home gateway (SHG) is the key element of the system. It enables the remote control of the various DSANs by translating the messages and procedures from the SIP world to the specific DSAN technology and vice versa. Furthermore, it performs "intelligent" operations, such as piloting devices of a DSAN in response to events from another DSAN (e.g., turn on a KNX-enabled heater after a ZigBee sensor has reported a temperature/humidity change) and interpreting generic user commands and mapping them to device-specific actions.

The complete description of the SHG prototype is reported in Section 6.1.

4.2. Domotics Facility Abstraction. An intermediate entity, named domotics facility abstraction (DFA), has been introduced with a double goal: disjoin the implementation of the

two domains of the system (i.e., the SIP and the DSANs) and create a single and user-friendly service abstraction. The former goal is meant to ease the development of the SIP and the DSAN interfaces, which may be carried on separately. The abstract definition of the domotics services enables the *functional addressing and control* paradigm employed for the user interface, leaving SIP on the pure transport layer, which is thus hidden to the user.

A pictorial description of the framework can be seen in Figure 4. The user is immersed into the functional service abstraction, which is implemented through the user interface on the client, and is understood and processed at the SHG. As it will be detailed in Section 6.1, the DFA is realized for the most part in the SHG, which stores the set of actions and performs the necessary tasks to accomplish the user's directives.

An example application of this framework can be swiftly provided. Imagine a user at a remote place (e.g., returning from a travel abroad) wishing to find the home at a comfortable temperature. He/she can then issue a simple command, such as "set home temperature 20." The client then wraps the command into the proper SIP procedure and conveys it to the SHG, where it is mapped to a DFA service. The SHG then cares for translating it into a proper set of DSAN operations, such as starting the HVAC system and setting an alarm threshold on the temperature sensors deployed in the house. When the desired temperature is reached, the SHG will automatically stop the HVAC system.

We can see from this example that the user demands a specific operation to be performed, but he/she is clearly ignoring all the technical processes of the domotics system, which are transparently handled by the SHG by means of the DFA layer.

4.2.1. System Configuration and Reconfiguration. Clearly, to unleash the capabilities of the DFA layer and the functional addressing and control scheme, a configuration phase must take place. In our vision, this phase can be split into two steps.

In the first step, occurring during the system development, the set of actions and user keywords must be defined and implemented. With reference to the previous example, the developer should make the SHG aware of the keywords "set," "home," and "temperature" and implement

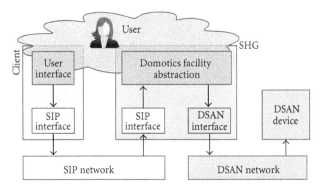

FIGURE 4: The functional paradigm implemented via the domotics facility abstraction.

the procedures that transform these keywords into real actions (such as sending a command to a HVAC actuator). Yet, these procedures cannot address a specific device, since the set of available devices will only be known at deployment time. Therefore the procedures can define just generic commands that become actual technology-specific actions once the DSAN devices are connected. For example, typical general HVAC actions could be "heat," "ventilate," and "cool." The completion of this phase defines the set of keywords and paradigms the user can take advantage of.

The second configuration step takes place at deployment time. Having a look at Figure 7, which shows the SHG internals, might help making the concept clearer. The installation-specific details, such as the plan of the house and the room names, are stored into the SHG database and/or file system. This task can be performed either by the installer or by the user. Offering a GUI to let the user install and/or configure the SHG might be a commercial choice. At the same time, the DSAN managers detect the connected devices and populate the SHG database, inserting information such as the device types, capabilities, and the actions they can perform. The physical position of the devices is inserted by the user/installer, after the devices have been registered with the SHG.

The system is now ready to work. When a user request is received, the SHG will map it to the appropriate action, search its database for the device(s) supporting that action, and issue the command(s) towards those DSAN devices. The full workflow of the SHG and its internals are described in Section 6.1.

Obviously, the information entered during the deployment phase can be modified later on, for example, as a consequence of device movement, replacement, or addition. Though being a more delicate operation, also the set of keywords and actions available to the user can be changed, for example, by upgrading the SHG firmware.

5. Wireless Technologies in the SHG

In this section we give a quick overview of the three wireless technologies, that is, Wi-Fi, ZigBee, and Bluetooth, that we have selected for the Home Network and hence, integrated onto the SHG prototype board. We also outline how these standards exploit the 2.4 GHz band and interact in this region of the spectrum.

5.1. Wi-Fi. The latest IEEE 802.11 standard [23] defines a CSMA/CA (carrier sense multiple access with collision avoidance) scheme as the mandatory medium access scheme. According to CSMA/CA, every Wi-Fi device shall listen to the medium before transmitting. The transmission is allowed only if the medium has been sensed idle for a predefined time period. In case the medium is sensed busy or after a collision, the device shall refrain from transmission for a period whose length is determined by a random variable (exponential backoff).

An IEEE 802.11 network can operate over one of the 11, 13, or 14 channels defined for the 2.4 GHz ISM band (the exact number depends on the local regulations). Each channel is 22 MHz wide, and the channels are partially overlapped (since the overall ISM bandwidth is just above 80 MHz). Therefore, no more than three networks can be contemporaneously operated in the same area in order to keep the transmissions of each free from interference from the others.

The operative channel and the transmission power are generally set statically (e.g., by the manufacturer or by the user at configuration time), even though dynamic channel selection (DCS) and transmit power control (TPC) routines have been defined for operations in the 5 GHz band. In the 2.4 GHz band, the maximum transmission power is 100 mW (20 dBm) in Europe and 1 W (30 dBm) in North America; in Japan, where power is measured in relation to bandwidth, the maximum allowed power is 10 mW/MHz.

Finally, the modulation scheme is either a DSSS (direct sequence spread spectrum) for the lower bit rates or an OFDM (orthogonal frequency division multiplexing) for the higher ones.

5.2. ZigBee. The IEEE 802.15.4 standard [24] specifies the physical and medium access control layers for low-rate wireless PANs, targeting a 10-meter communication range with a transfer rate of up to 250 kb/s.

Similar to Wi-Fi, 802.15.4 devices employ a CSMA/CA channel access algorithm and the DSSS modulation (actually, the latest release of the standard defines four modulation schemes, but in the 2.4 GHz band only the DSSS modulation is allowed).

Sixteen channels are defined for worldwide use in the 2.4 GHz band. However, differently from 802.11, they are much narrower (just 2 MHz) and do not overlap, so that up to sixteen 802.15.4 networks can easily coexist in the same area. When starting a new network, an energy detection (ED) functionality is used to determine the activity of other systems and thus decide the operating channel; yet there is no support for dynamic channel selection.

The latest ZigBee release has introduced the support for frequency hopping in the "ZigBee Pro" standard. In this way a PAN coordinator can move the whole PAN to another channel if the one in use is overloaded. However, this is not a fast, reliable, and energy saving way to solve the problem. In addition it is not mandatory to implement.

5.3. Bluetooth.

Bluetooth is a standard communication protocol designed for connection-oriented services such as voice, with low power consumption and short-range operations. The output power depend on the device class, spanning from 1 to 100 mW. Accordingly, the expected range should go from 1 to 100 meters, even though the practical range is highly variable.

Bluetooth transmits on up to 79 channels in the 2402–2480 MHz range. Each channel is 1 MHz wide, and one guard channel is used at the lower and upper band edges. In order to reduce the interference from external sources, frequency hopping (FHSS) is used to spread the signal across all channels. Thus a single Bluetooth network uses the full available 2.4 GHz ISM band. Different networks can coexist in the same area by employing different hopping patterns or a time-shifted version of the same pattern. Since Specification v1.2, Bluetooth also includes an adaptive frequency hopping (AFH) scheme, which reduces the number of employed channels to improve its robustness against the interference.

The Bluetooth channel access procedure is based on a master-slave scheme, which is built on the top of a time division duplex (TDD) transmission scheme. The basic modulation is Gaussian frequency-shift keying (GFSK), which allows a transfer rate of up to 1 Mb/s. Since the introduction of the enhanced data rate (EDR) with specification v2.0, $\pi/4$-DQPSK (differential quadrature phase shift keying) and 8-DPSK modulations may also be used, bringing the data rate to 2 and 3 Mb/s, respectively.

5.4. Channels, Frequencies, and Modulations.

Figure 5 shows the allocation of the ZigBee and Wi-Fi channels over the 2.4 GHz ISM band. Note that a single 802.11 channel completely overlaps with four ZigBee channels. Bluetooth channels are not reported, as the FHSS covers the whole available spectrum.

The three most used nonoverlapping Wi-Fi channels are 1, 6, and 11. In this case, two ZigBee channels should be free from interference from Wi-Fi transmissions, that is, channels 25 and 26 (the two rightmost ones). However, there is no assurance that using channels 25 and 26 solves the interference problem. For example, two channels might not be enough to allow the coexistence among several geographically overlapping PANs. In addition, though in North America ZigBee channels 25 and 26 can be really assumed free from Wi-Fi transmissions, in other regions such as Europe and Asia all Wi-Fi channels can be used, thus covering the complete set of ZigBee channels.

A further aspect making the coexistence of Wi-Fi and ZigBee difficult is the different allowed transmission power. In fact, the maximum Wi-Fi output power can be up to 100 times higher than the maximum allowed ZigBee transmission power (100 mW versus 1 mW). The same consideration holds for Wi-Fi and Bluetooth devices belonging to Classes 2 and 3.

6. Proof of Concept

To put the ideas expressed in the previous sections into practice, we have realized a small testbed involving all the elements of the architecture. The SHG, being the core and most innovative element, has been built from scratch. Two DSANs have been implemented using two sets of ZigBee and Bluetooth devices. Finally, to illustrate the potentials of expansion and customization of our architecture, we have defined and implemented the "home automation" package, a specific SIP event package for the domotics framework.

6.1. SIP-Based Home Gateway.

The only requirements for building the SHG are the sufficient processing power and memory to run the software and the capability to interface with the technologies of the particular sensor networks to control.

With regard to the former aspect, we used a generic single-board computer (SBC) with a Texas Instrument AM 3730 processor (ARM Cortex-A8) running at 720 MHz with 256 MB of DRAM and 256 MB of NAND flash memory. As it will be shown in Section 7.2, this hardware is more than adequate. To give the SHG the physical interfaces towards the wireless networks, a ZigBee module has been embedded into the board and connected to the main processor via a serial interface; then a Hama Bluetooth adapter and a Wi-Fi card were inserted into the two USB ports. Figure 6 shows the prototype SHG.

The SHG software was built on top of Linux (with kernel 2.6.36), which provides the necessary support and development tools (e.g., a SIP library, the interface drivers). The software that implements the SHG functionalities has been written from scratch using the C++ language and then cross-compiled for the ARM platform. A multithreaded approach has been followed. Each user request is handled in parallel by a different thread. This helps improving the scalability performance of the SHG.

The internal software architecture of the SHG is reported in Figure 7. Starting from the top, the first object we meet is the SIP interface. This is nothing more than the SIP software (the GNU oSIP and eXosip libraries), which extracts the user's commands from the SIP messages and passes them to the next module in the form of plain text strings. These are then translated into the proper DFA actions by the translation module, which fetches the set of available DFA actions from the DFA Library. The output of this module is fed to the SHG engine, where we have placed the intelligence for executing the user's directives in the proper way. This is typically achieved via the creation of a series of elementary DSAN commands to be delivered to the various DSAN elements. The set of available elements and commands is retrieved from the device database. The SHG engine then passes the DSAN commands to the various DSAN managers, which are in charge of translating them into the technology-specific commands and performing all the operations to ensure that the specified actions are fulfilled. Finally, the ZigBee, Bluetooth, and Wi-Fi interfaces are the software modules (a custom software for ZigBee, the BlueZ stack for Bluetooth, and the Linux drivers and tools for Wi-Fi) that

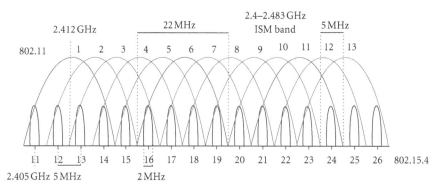

FIGURE 5: Channel occupancy of 802.11 and 802.15.4 systems.

FIGURE 6: A photo of the SHG prototype, with the indication of the main components.

pilot the physical objects that are connected to the various sensors and actuators.

The device database (DdB) holds the set of available DSAN objects, with the related properties (e.g., commands, location, technology). The DdB is filled and kept up to date by the DSAN managers, which are aware of the number and types of devices connected through the various DSAN interfaces. Further information, such as the physical location of each device, can be inserted at configuration time either by the user or by the service provider.

The operations in the reverse direction, that is, from the DSAN networks to the SIP interface, are analogous to the ones mentioned above. The notifications from the sensors are passed, by means of the DSAN managers, to the SHG engine, which decides what actions are to be taken. For example, a new command might be issued towards the DSAN, or an information message can be sent to the user (or both). In the latter case, the message is passed to the translation module and finally to the SIP interface.

6.2. The Wireless Networks. This section briefly describes the setup of the two DSANs and of the Wi-Fi local area network. A few essential technical details are also given.

6.2.1. The ZigBee DSAN. The nodes of the ZigBee sensor network are based on the Freescale MC1322x board, which integrates a 32-bit ARM-7 MCU and a low-power 2.4 GHz transceiver. The fully compliant ZigBee stack provided by Freescale was installed on the nodes.

A custom application that supports environmental data collection (temperature and pressure), remote light control, and message routing has been developed on top of the ZigBee stack by means of the ZigBee Cluster Library (ZCL) functions. The APS ACK feature (an end-to-end acknowledgment mechanism) was enabled to make the ZigBee transmissions reliable.

Ambient data is retrieved both on regular time basis and on demand, and both approaches are available to the user, who can either subscribe to this event or ask the SHG to check a specific sensor value. As for remote light control, the MC1322x boards are equipped with an array of LEDs, which was used to mimic a multilevel light. For both ambient data collection and light control, we defined a set of textual commands. Combining them with the name of a room allows the user to set the desired light level or retrieve the sensor reading.

An important aspect of the ZigBee system is that it provides for a mechanism, known as *binding*, to connect endpoints (an "endpoint" is a logical wire connecting distributed applications residing on different nodes). Binding creates logical links between endpoints and maintains this information in a binding table. The binding table also has information about the services offered by the devices on the network. The ZigBee coordinator (ZC) typically holds the binding table for the whole network. A notable advantage of this structure is that it allows the implementation of the *service discovery* procedure via bindings. The services available inside the ZigBee network can thus be discovered directly within the ZigBee domain, without resorting to any additional software or external entities. With specific reference to the SIP control plane, this means that there is no need to port the SIP registration procedure to the ZigBee network, since this would be a duplication of the ZigBee service discovery.

6.2.2. The Bluetooth DSAN. The Hama Bluetooth adapter connected to the SHG board embeds a version 2.0 compliant

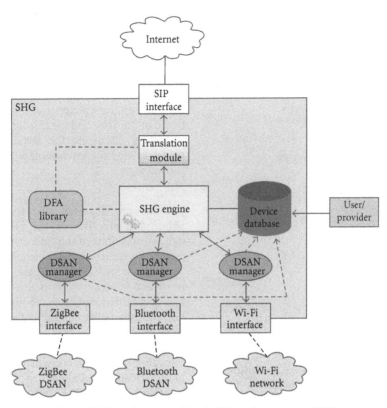

FIGURE 7: The software modules building the prototype SHG.

chipset supporting the EDR feature. It is a Class 2 device, with 2.5 mW (4 dBm) of output power allowing for an approximate range of 10 meters and a physical bit rate of 3 Mbps. To operate this device, we took advantage of the Bluetooth Linux stack (BlueZ), which gives support for basic operations such as scanning and pairing. On top of these basic functionalities, we built the Bluetooth interface, which is capable of listing and managing the connected devices.

For the purposes of validating the domotics system, we set up an audio streaming test. A Bluetooth-enabled headset (Sony DR-BT101) was used as the client device. The audio streaming was handled directly by the BlueZ (on the SHG side) and the headset, by means of the A2DP profile.

On the SIP-based control plane, we defined and implemented some simple commands, such as listing of the available content and playing an audio stream on the Bluetooth headset.

6.2.3. The Wi-Fi Local Area Network.
To build the Wi-Fi LAN, we used two adapters based on the Ralink RT3572 chipset, a IEEE 802.11a/b/g/n compliant card. One of the adapters was installed on the SHG and the other on a common laptop PC. The drivers from the latest "compat-wireless" package have been used to pilot the card.

We set up a private IBSS network on one of the 2.4 GHz channels. The use of an IBSS topology rather than an "infrastructure" one is justified by the shorter set-up times (mostly in terms of driver and software configuration) but has no impact neither on the traffic at the transport and application layers nor on the physical layer mechanisms. The SHG and the PC are therefore two "peer" stations.

Traffic on the Wi-Fi connection has been generated by means of common test applications, such as FTP or iperf.

6.3. A Domotics Event Framework.
The SIP Event Notification Framework (ENF) standardized in RFC 3265 [21], and later augmented by RFC 3903 [22], provides just the procedures that enable notification of events (as outlined in Section 3.1) but do not define any specific "event package." Indeed, a few packages for the SIP ENF have currently been ratified. Among them, the Presence package [25] is probably the most popular and also the one that is implemented in some widely available SIP clients. However, this package does not suit well the needs of a domotics environment, as it provides just a single elementary functionality (the presence of a given user) and refers to the bare ENF, without taking advantage of the PUBLISH method.

To test our domotics system with a complete and flexible Publish/Subscribe-Notify paradigm, we built a new package, named "home automation." The basic features of home automation are similar to the ones of Presence, but our package employs the PUBLISH method too. We designed it to embed a customized XML text, like the one illustrated in Figure 8, which contains domotics specific data (such as the values read by some ambient sensors). In this particular example, the XML snippet is sent from the SHG to an *enhanced client* to report about the readings of the sensors in the *Lab* room and also the current light level. Note that

```
<device room = "Lab"
        name = "dimmablelight">
    <attrib name = "Level"
            value = "33">
    </attrib>
</device>
<device room = "Lab"
        name = "ambientsensor">
    <attrib name = "Temperature"
            value = "20">
    </attrib>
    <attrib name = "Pressure"
            value = "308">
    </attrib>
</device>
```

FIGURE 8: Figure 8: Sample XML for the home automation event package.

the tags implement a possible functional naming abstraction of the DFA layer. Clearly, this XML scheme can be replaced with any other kind of text format, like REST or SOAP (the ones employed by the ZigBee Gateway [26]).

In order to correctly handle this package, we also built a customized ESC server. We employed Kamailio, an open-source SIP server released under GPL, to which we made some modifications. The changes mainly consisted in adding the specific home automation keywords to let it recognize the home automation package in a similar fashion to any other package.

Note that the XML text is not touched by the ESC (only a formal check is done) but is passed directly to the subscribers by means of the NOTIFY messages. Hence, SIP is immediately able to deliver this information using the existing infrastructure.

6.4. SIP Clients. We developed a test SIP client that supports the full Publish/Subscribe-Notify paradigm and the Home Automation package described in Section 6.3. One such client is in all aspects a SIP-compliant software, but with the extra feature that can control the DSAN with its native semantic.

6.5. SIP Servers. Servers build the necessary infrastructure for SIP to work properly. In our proof of concept, we employed two different servers. An external registrar and a proxy server provided by *iptel.org* were used as a sample of a preexisting SIP network element. This server is compliant to existing SIP standards and is completely unaware of the nature of our domotics testbed.

A customized SIP server was built in our lab by means of the Kamailio open-source software. As explained in Section 6.3, this was necessary to provide support for our home automation event package. Hence, this server is representative of a domotics-aware element in the SIP infrastructure. We called this server the enhanced notification server (ENS).

7. Performed Tests

The performed tests can be divided in two sets. The first series was aimed at assessing the performance of the prototype SHG in terms of capacity, scalability, and processing delay. The objective of the second set instead was to verify the amount of interference among the wireless interfaces on board of the SHG and the impact on the SHG performance.

Before discussing the tests, we outline the deployed networks and the environment where the tests have been carried out.

7.1. Network Topology. All tests have been carried out within the premises of the Dipartimento di Ingegneria dell'Informazione of the University of Pisa, Italy. This might indeed constitute a good environment for both kinds of tests: applications such as smart energy, building automation, and intrusion detection systems fit well this kind of structures, and we might indeed expect to find in the department several devices using different radio technologies working at the same time.

The realized testbed is made of five ZigBee sensor nodes, including the ZigBee coordinator (ZC), which is embedded in the SHG board as already shown in Figure 6. The physical location of the nodes is illustrated in Figure 9. All ZigBee nodes have a wireless path to the ZC. Due to the indoor environment, the nodes *Stairs*, *Office*, and *Corridor* use a multihop path. The Bluetooth headphones (*bths*) are placed in the same room of the SHG, approximately 8 meters apart; the PC acting as a Wi-Fi station (*sta1*) is placed in a room adjacent to the one with the SHG. We checked that the Bluetooth and Wi-Fi devices, as well as the *Lab* node, are within the operation range of the SHG. *sta0* represents the Wi-Fi adapter connected to the USB port of the SHG.

7.2. Performance of the SHG. We assessed the performance of the SHG in terms of two metrics: the number of served user requests per second (in short: SURPS) and the average response time.

To compute the first metric, we connected the SHG to a varying number of clients through our 100 Mbps local area network. Every client was programmed to send a continuous flow of 100 requests using the MESSAGE method. Each request is cast as soon as the previous response is received from the SHG (we recall that a response is implemented with a distinct MESSAGE transaction). In this way the SHG always has a pending request to process for each client. The auxiliary SIP procedures, such as registration, have been excluded in order to measure the raw SHG capacity. For the same reason, we did not connect the SHG to any real DSAN but implemented a fake interface that returns a response as soon as it receives a command. In practice, with reference to Figure 7, the processing path stops at the ZigBee interface. The Bluetooth and Wi-Fi networks were left inactive.

The collected numbers of total SURPS and mean SURPS per client, averaged over ten experiments, are reported in Figure 10 as a function of the number of connected clients. Focusing on the red lines (labeled "eXosip"), we can see that

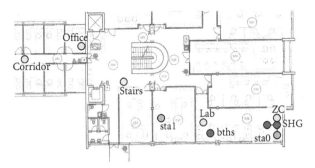

FIGURE 9: Map of the Dipartimento di Ingegneria dell'Informazione with the position of the ZigBee, Bluetooth, and Wi-Fi nodes (yellow, blue, and green discs, resp.); the SHG is also shown (red disc).

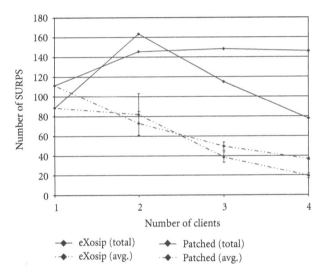

FIGURE 10: Total and average number of user requests per second served by the SHG; the standard deviation among the clients is also reported.

when a single client is connected, this can enjoy a service rate that is around 89 requests per second. This number can undoubtedly be deemed adequate not only for any human-based activity but also for any sensible automated application (see, e.g., [11]). In case of two clients, the number of total SURPS is almost doubled, but when further clients are added, there is a sudden performance drop. When four clients are connected, the total SURPS are even less than the single client case.

We have explored the reasons for such a tremendous degradation and found that it was due to the eXosip library integrated into the SHG. Without delving into the software details, this library presents some structures and timeouts that slow down the entire system when eXosip is called to serve many requests at the same time. We thus devised a simple patch that bypasses these shortcomings and repeated the SURPS test.

The results for the amended version are also shown in Figure 10 (the blue lines, labeled "patched"). The performance of the SHG has improved for almost any number of connected clients (it has slightly worsened for the two-client

case only). More remarkable, however, is the fact that the trend in the number of SURPS is now much smoother and, above all, that the total number of SURPS reaches a stable level—it floors to about 146 SURPS. This means that the performance of the SHG is not appreciably influenced by the number of clients. Hence, we can reasonably affirm that the SHG can scale to serve many requests from different clients at the same time.

With the second performance test, we analyzed the behavior of the SHG from an internal point of view. We measured the time that elapses between the reception of a request MESSAGE and the issue of the response MESSAGE. The measurement was carried out with a single client, with the auxiliary SIP procedures at work, but still with the Bluetooth and Wi-Fi networks kept idle. We used two configurations. The first one is still based on the fake interface, whereas the second setting is an operative scenario with a real ZigBee DSAN attached. To keep the things simple, however, the ZigBee DSAN is composed of two nodes only: the coordinator (physically soldered to the SHG board) and a device node in direct communication range. The ZigBee network operated on channel 25, which is the most free from external interference sources.

The first row of Table 1 shows the processing times of the SHG in the two configurations. The difference is apparent, with them being apart by almost two orders of magnitude. This result does not leave much room for speculation and clearly identifies the bottleneck of the system with the domotics sensor network.

In the second row of Table 1, we have reported the performance of the SHG software when run on a generic PC based on an Intel Core i3 processor running at 2.66 GHz with 4 GB of RAM. The purpose of these figures is to provide a comparison with a "high-end" hardware. The PC is somewhat slower in running the software but is faster when the actual ZigBee network is attached. The "software" gap can be ascribed to the scarce optimization of both the code and the hardware, whereas the "DSAN" gap comes from the different connection with the ZigBee coordinator: serial (slower) on the SHG prototype and USB (faster) on the PC.

7.3. Effect of Interference. To check the effect of the interference on the domotics system, we set up a sort of "use-case" scenario. We assumed that the Wi-Fi and Bluetooth networks are used to deliver different but massive data to the user(s). Specifically, a FTP or HTTP transfer is conveyed over the Wi-Fi connection, whereas an audio streaming is performed by means of the Bluetooth devices. The SHG thus acts as the source of the data, and its Wi-Fi and Bluetooth interfaces work mainly as transmitters. Such a scenario can be mapped, for example, to a file download from the Internet (the FTP transfer) and a user listening to a song retrieved from a local repository (the audio streaming). As for the ZigBee DSAN, this is used to send commands to the sensors spread across the house. We exploit the *request/response* paradigm implemented via the double SIP MESSAGE transactions (as illustrated in Section 3.1.1). Hence, the SHG and the sensors alternate the roles of source and destination of the traffic.

TABLE 1: Processing delay of the SHG.

Hardware	Fake interface	Real ZigBee DSAN
SHG prototype	11.0 ms	177 ms
i3-based PC	34.8 ms	103 ms

TABLE 2: Interference performance of the SHG.

Metric	Test 0	Test 1	Test 2	Test 3
Service delay	179.4 ms	202.0 ms	835.9 ms	937.5 ms
Execution delay	176.5 ms	197.2 ms	824.4 ms	913.6 ms
Peak delay	181.4 ms	1268 ms	5538 ms	5291 ms
Lost commands	0	0	0	0

Since the weak link in the chain is the ZigBee connection, our effort was mostly targeted at measuring the effect of the two "stronger" technologies, that is, Wi-Fi and Bluetooth, on the performance of the ZigBee subsystem and consequently on the capability of the user to control and have feedback from the ZigBee DSAN.

The test was organized in a similar manner as the performance experiment described in the previous section. A SIP client sends a continuous flow of 100 requests to the SHG via the local 100 Mbps Ethernet LAN. Each request is sent as soon as the previous response is received. No requests nor responses are lost in this segment of the system. The auxiliary SIP procedures (registration, publish, etc.) have been disabled, as they do not have any influence on the radio interference. The SHG then translates and casts the requests over the ZigBee network. Only one ZigBee sensor node is used for the test. This is sufficient for the purposes of the test, as the interference mostly occurs in the first wireless hop.

As for the wireless segment, we placed the Wi-Fi network on channels 1 or 11 and the ZigBee DSAN either on channel 25 or on channel 15. We did not test the system under overlapped ZigBee and Wi-Fi channels because we believe it is logical to assume that a deployed system will be smart enough to avoid such clearly troublesome kind of allocation. Also, we did not test the full range of possible combinations, which is not the purpose of the present work—the reader interested in this kind of analysis can refer to [14].

We collected four performance parameters: the average command service time registered on the client (in short: service delay), the average and the peak command execution time on the ZigBee interface (in short: execution delay and peak delay), and the number of lost commands (i.e., either lost requests or lost responses; we made ourselves certain that the losses can only occur on the ZigBee network).

To monitor the activity on the 2.4 GHz spectrum, including possible external interference sources (e.g., other Wi-Fi networks), we used the AirView2-EXT ISM-band spectrum analyzer (http://www.ubnt.com/airview). A screenshot of the power level in the test area has been taken before performing every experiment, to check whether strong external interferences are present and thus avoiding biased results.

Table 2 reports the outcome of the tests. The first test, labeled "0", is a preliminary test, used to benchmark the system when solely the ZigBee network is active (on channel 25). We can see that no commands are lost and that the peak execution delay is just a few milliseconds greater than the average. This indicates that the behavior of the ZigBee network is quite stable. Also, the average service and the execution delays differ only by 3 ms.

In the next test (1), we activated both the Bluetooth and the Wi-Fi networks, with Wi-Fi placed on channel 1, that

is, the farthest possible from the ZigBee one. In this case, the interference is mostly due to Bluetooth, which covers the whole 2.4 GHz band. The performance drop is apparent, with an increase of 12% in the average time. The peak delay is the value that changed most, as it is now almost seven times the average execution delay. Thus, the ZigBee network can still bring all commands to completion, but its response time has become quite unpredictable. In absolute terms, however, even the highest values (1.268 s) can be deemed acceptable.

In test (2) we moved the Wi-Fi emissions closer to the ZigBee ones; that is, we put Wi-Fi on channel 11. In theory, there is still no overlapping between the ZigBee and the Wi-Fi channels. But in fact the ZigBee segment is heavily penalized, as proved by the values in Table 2. The average delays reach almost 1 second, with the peak execution delay going beyond 5 seconds. For some applications these values might be critical, for the user annoying. Note, however, that no commands are lost.

The reason for these figures lies in the long timeouts and the numerous retries that are allowed at the ZigBee application and MAC layers. For example, the default application retry timeout is 1.5 seconds, and the allowed number of retries is 3, both at the MAC and at the application layer. Thus, the ZigBee network, which is highly hampered by Wi-Fi, can take advantage of several attempts to deliver each packet, and consequently the overall transmission time grows very large.

To have a confirmation that Wi-Fi interferes with ZigBee even in nonoverlapping channels, we repeated the test by moving Wi-Fi to channel 1 and ZigBee to channel 15. The numbers of this test (3), which are very similar and even worse than the previous ones, indeed corroborate this fact.

8. Conclusions

The paper presented an architecture and a home gateway for realizing a domotics system with heterogeneous devices and user terminals. The architecture is based on the use of SIP as the common control plane and is centered on the SIP-based home gateway. A functional addressing scheme and an abstract translation layer (called DFA) are used to make the underlying technology transparent to the user. The DFA is the glue between the DSAN domain and the SIP world and simultaneously allows to separate the implementation of the SIP and DSAN interfaces. In addition, by choosing to expose a single SIP URI to the user (the SHG one), the system increases the user-friendliness and can be easily extended to large deployments. Note that this single-URI approach is neither an intrinsic feature of SIP nor of the domotics concept itself. Rather, it is a notable advantage of the way we built our architecture and the SHG. The positive impact of this approach is greater as the network grows larger.

We have built a proof of concept that includes the prototype SHG, three standard ZigBee, Bluetooth, and Wi-Fi networks, a newly defined SIP event package, and a customized event state compositor.

The performance of the SHG has been assessed in terms of served user requests per second, processing delay, and average and peak service delay. The effect of having the three wireless interfaces on the same board that operate on the same frequency band has also been evaluated.

The results proved the SHG ability to support a considerable number of requests per second, also from a different number of clients. Thus, the developed prototype can indeed be employed for large deployments, as it does have the ability to scale to any realistic requirement.

On the interference side, it emerged that ZigBee suffers the presence of both Bluetooth and Wi-Fi. Yet, while the former technology produces just a relatively small performance degradation, the presence of Wi-Fi is definitely more cumbersome, as the ability of the ZigBee network to accomplish its task in short times is heavily hampered. Though the weakness of ZigBee is well known, it is remarkable that this occurs even when Wi-Fi and ZigBee operate on channels that are nominally separated from each other. Our experiments showed a tremendous performance degradation when ZigBee and Wi-Fi are on adjacent channels. Nevertheless, by means of a proper configuration, we have also proved that it is possible to avoid command losses.

Acknowledgments

This work was supported by the Italian Ministry of Instruction, University and Research (MIUR) under the PRIN 2009 Research Project GATECOM. The authors would like to thank Luca Boggioni and Alessio Del Chiaro for their help in developing the prototypes and running the tests.

References

[1] J. Rosenberg, H. Schulzrinne, G. Camarillo et al., "SIP: session initiation protocol," RFC 3261, Internet Engineering Task Force, 2002.

[2] K. Sohraby, D. Minoli, and T. Znati, *Wireless Sensor Networks: Technology,Protocols, and Applications*, John Wiley and Sons, 2007.

[3] R. Musaloiu-Elefteri and A. Terzis, "Minimising the effect of WiFi interference in 802.15.4 wireless sensor networks," *International Journal of Sensor Networks*, vol. 3, no. 1, pp. 43–54, 2008.

[4] A. Sikora and V. F. Groza, "Coexistence of IEEE802.15.4 with other systems in the 2.4 GHz-ISM-band," in *Proceedings of the IEEE Instrumentation and Measurement Technology Conference*, vol. 3, pp. 1786–1791, May 2005.

[5] T. Luckenbach, P. Gober, S. Arbanowski, A. Kotsopoulos, and K. Kim, "TinyREST: a protocol for integrating sensor networks into the internet," in *Proceedings of the Workshop on Real-World Wireless Sensor Networks (REALWSN '05)*, June 2005.

[6] S. Krishnamurthy, "TinySIP: providing seamless access to sensor-based services," in *Proceedings of the 3rd Annual International Conference on Mobile and Ubiquitous Systems: Networking and Services, MobiQuitous*, July 2006.

[7] S. Krishnamurthy and L. Lange, "Enabling distributed messaging with wireless sensor nodes using TinySIP," in *Ubiquitous Intelligence and Computing*, J. Indulska, J. Ma, L. Yang, T. Ungerer, and J. Cao, Eds., vol. 4611 of *Lecture Notes in Computer Science*, pp. 610–621, 2007.

[8] M. Alia, A. Bottaro, F. Camara, and B. Hardouin, "On the design of a SIP-based binding middleware for next generation home network services," in *Proceedings of the OTM 2008 Confederated International Conferences, CoopIS, DOA, GADA, IS, and ODBASE*, pp. 497–514, 2008.

[9] R. Acker, S. Brandt, N. Buchmann, T. Fugmann, and M. Massoth, "Ubiquitous home control based on SIP and presence service," in *Proceedings of the 12th International Conference on Information Integration and Web-Based Applications and Services (iiWAS '10)*, pp. 759–762, November 2010.

[10] B. Bertran, C. Consel, P. Kadionik, and B. Lamer, "A SIP-based home automation platform: an experimental study," in *Proceedings of the 13th International Conference on Intelligence in Next Generation Networks (ICIN '09)*, Bordeaux, France, October 2009.

[11] B. Bertran, C. Consel, W. Jouve, H. Guan, and P. Kadionik, "SIP as a universal communication bus: a methodology and an experimental study," in *Proceedings of the IEEE International Conference on Communications (ICC '10)*, May 2010.

[12] S. Y. Shin, H. S. Park, S. Choi, and W. H. Kwon, "Packet error rate analysis of zigbee under WLAN and bluetooth interferences," *IEEE Transactions on Wireless Communications*, vol. 6, no. 8, pp. 2825–2830, 2007.

[13] I. Howitt, V. Mitter, and J. Gutierrez, "Empirical study for IEEE 802.11 and bluetooth interoperability," in *Proceedings of the IEEE Vehicular Technology Conference (VTS SPRING '01)*, pp. 1109–1113, May 2001.

[14] R. Garroppo, L. Gazzarrini, S. Giordano, and L. Tavanti, "Experimental assessment of the coexistence of wi-fi, zigbee, and bluetooth devices," in *Proceedings of the 12th IEEE International Symposium on a World of Wireless, Mobile and Multimedia Networks (WOWMOM '11)*, pp. 1–9, Lucca, Italy, june 2011.

[15] H. Schulzrinne, X. Wu, S. Sidiroglou, and S. Berger, "Ubiquitous computing in home networks," *IEEE Communications Magazine*, vol. 41, no. 11, pp. 128–135, 2003.

[16] D. Bonino, E. Castellina, and F. Corno, "Automatic domotic device interoperation," *IEEE Transactions on Consumer Electronics*, vol. 55, no. 2, pp. 499–506, 2009.

[17] F. Genova, M. Gaspardone, A. Cuda, M. Beoni, G. Fici, and M. Sorrentino, "Thermal and energy management system based on low cost wireless sensor network technology, to monitor, control and optimize energy consumption in telecom switch plants and data centres," in *Proceedings of the 4th International Conference on Telecommunication-Energy Special Conference (TELESCON '09)*, May 2009.

[18] A. Brown, M. Kolberg, D. Bushmitch, G. Lomako, and M. Tthew, "A SIP-based OSGi device communication service for mobile personal area networks," in *Proceedings of the 3rd IEEE Consumer Communications and Networking Conference, CCNC 2006*, pp. 502–508, January 2006.

[19] D. J. Cook, J. C. Augusto, and V. R. Jakkula, "Ambient intelligence: technologies, applications, and opportunities,"

Pervasive and Mobile Computing, vol. 5, no. 4, pp. 277–298, 2009.

[20] B. Campbell, J. Rosenberg, H. Schulzrinne, C. Huitema, and D. Gurle, "Session initiation protocol (SIP) extension for instant messaging," RFC 3428, Internet Engineering Task Force, 2002.

[21] A. B. Roach, "Session initiation protocol (SIP)-specific event notification," RFC 3265, Internet Engineering Task Force, 2002.

[22] A. Niemi, "Session initiation protocol (SIP) extension for event state publication," RFC 3903, Internet Engineering Task Force, 2004.

[23] "IEEE Standard 802.11-2007," December 2007.

[24] "IEEE Standard 802.15.4-2006," September 2006.

[25] J. Rosenberg, "A presence event package for the session initiation protocol (SIP)," RFC 3856, 2004.

[26] The Zigbee Alliance, "ZigBee Gateway Standard," 2010, http://zigbee.org/Standards/ZigBeeNetworkDevices/Overview.aspx.

14

Usage of Modified Holt-Winters Method in the Anomaly Detection of Network Traffic: Case Studies

Maciej Szmit[1,2] and Anna Szmit[3]

[1] *Computer Engineering Department, Technical University of Lodz, 18/22 Stefanowskiego Street, 90-924 Lodz, Poland*
[2] *Corporate IT Security Agency, Orange Labs Poland, 7 Obrzezna Street, 02-691 Warsaw, Poland*
[3] *Department of Management, Technical University of Lodz, 266 Piotrkowska Street, 90-924 Lodz, Poland*

Correspondence should be addressed to Maciej Szmit, maciej.szmit@gmail.com

Academic Editor: Yueh M. Huang

The traditional Holt-Winters method is used, among others, in behavioural analysis of network traffic for development of adaptive models for various types of traffic in sample computer networks. This paper is devoted to the application of extended versions of these models for development of predicted templates and intruder detection.

1. Intruder Detection Systems

Intruder Detection Systems (IDSs) are software or hardware solutions aimed at detection of intrusion attempts to a protected network or a host. This is done by monitoring network traffic, usage of the resources of a protected computer system or by the analysis of system logs in order to detect suspicious actions and then take appropriate actions, which in the majority of cases is the generation of an alert informing about the detected danger. In the literature, the following are usually distinguished: Intruder Detection Systems, Active Response Systems, and Intruder Protection Systems (IPSs).

The next generation of security devices is the so-called Unified Threat Management (UTMs), which integrate, apart from the traditional IPS, also mechanisms such as Gateway Antivirus, Gateway Antispam, Content Filtering, Parental Control, Load Balancing, Bandwidth Management, and On-Appliance reporting, while obviously not every UTM system must have all of the above mechanisms implemented.

Another type of specialized security solutions, which can be implemented in UTM systems or constitute standalone solutions, is Information Leak Prevention systems, also known as Data Loss Prevention, Data Leak Prevention (DLP), or Information Loss Prevention (ILP),

Book [1, page 179] presents a listing of Intruder Detection Systems and Intruder Protection Systems, which includes more than 60 systems. Issues relating to IDS are also presented in many other research works (see e.g., [2–4]).

Anomaly detection is one of the three groups of methods, including misuse detection systems and integrity verification, used in Intruder Detection Systems.

Misuse detection is the detection of specific behaviours which confirm that an attack occurred, whereas anomaly detection involves predictive pattern of behaviours, deviations from which instances of an attack on a protected system are considered. Misuse detection has, in the majority of cases, deterministic character (the rules matching the observed phenomena or action is found or not), and it is easier to algorithmize, whereas anomaly detection necessarily refers to uncertain observations and has to use statistical methods (statistical methods have been used in IDS systems since 1987, and the first IDS in which they were implemented was the "Haystack" project conducted in Los Alamos National Laboratory (see e.g., [5, page 432]).

Paper mentioned in [6] describes the application of the traditional Holt-Winters method in behavioral analysis of network traffic for development of adaptive models for various types of traffic in four sample computer networks. The next obvious step, after evaluation of the model, is the development of and predicted pattern and alert generation algorithm (see e.g., [5, 7, 8, page 419]).

2. Holt-Winters Model: Brutlag's Anomaly Detection Algorithm

The Holt-Winters model, called also the triple exponential smoothing model, is a well-known adaptive model used to modeling time series characterized by trend and seasonality (The Holt model was formulated in 1957 and the Winters model in 1960. See [9, 10, page 248], a comprehensive review of the literature about this and other models based on exponential smoothing is given in [11]). In its additive version, it presents the smoothed variant of the y_t time series as the sum of three constituents

$$\hat{y}_t = L_t + T_t + S_{t-r}, \tag{1}$$

where $\hat{y}_t$ is the value estimated by the model of the variable in moment t, r is the length of the seasonal periodicity,

$$L_t = \alpha(y_t - S_{t-r}) + (1 - \alpha)(L_{t-1} + T_{t-1}) \tag{2}$$

is the constituent smoothing out the level of the time series,

$$T_t = \beta(L_t - L_{t-1}) + (1 - \beta)T_{t-1} \tag{3}$$

represents the increase of the time series resulting from the trend,

$$S_t = \gamma(y_t - L_t) + (1 - \gamma)S_{t-r} \tag{4}$$

is the seasonal component of the time series, α, β, and γ are smoothing parameters, estimated for the particular time series, while y_t is the real value of the variable in moment t, and the parameters α, β, and γ belong to $[0; 1]$ interval.

Estimation of model parameters is iterative, usually though minimization of arbitrarily selected measures of error (e.g., the Mean Squared Error of expired estimations or the sum of absolute values of the residuals of the model see e.g., [12, page 187], [13, page 226], [14, page 77], and [6, 15], [16, page 223]).

Holt-Winters method was used to detect network traffic anomalies as described in [17]. In the paper concept of "confidence bands" was introduced. As described in the paper, confidence bands measure deviation for each time point in the seasonal cycle, and this mechanism bases on expected seasonal variability.

The estimated deviation of the real value of the dependent variable is

$$d_t = \gamma|y_t - \hat{y}_t| + (1 - \gamma)d_{t-r}, \tag{5}$$

where d_t is the estimated deviation of the real value of the dependent variable y in moment t from the estimated value $\hat{y}_t$, where the value of parameter γ is the estimated value in the model described above in (4). The event when the real value of the dependent variable y_t differs from the estimated value $\hat{y}_t$ by more than d_t multiplied by the scaling factor m is considered an anomaly (an alert is triggered in the IDS system). In [17] the extension of the RRDtool is presented, covering real-time determination and marking of values $\hat{y}_t + md_t$ and $\hat{y}_t - md_t$ on the chart and generating information on occurring anomalies. The author assumed an arbitrary

method of determining the initial values of parameters α, β, and γ as well as the iterative method of adapting only parameter α (see: [17]), which, from a statistical point of view, may provoke doubts, as it leads to development of suboptimal models from the perspective of minimization of the value of any measure of error. Additionally, in the Brutlag method, the calculated value of the parameter d_t for the purposes of determining the value above or below which anomalies will be reported is multiplied by intuitively selected scaling factor m of value between 2 and 3, which makes the model even more arbitrary (see e.g., [18]).

Thirdly, an important feature of the Holt-Winters model is the assumption on single seasonality (periodicity) of the given series, while in the case of network traffic one could expect double seasonality: daily and weekly. Anyone intending to use the Holt-Winters model to develop an anomaly detection system needs to select which periodicity should be used in the model.

3. Adaptative Models with Double and Triple Seasonality (Taylor Models)

In, [19] a suggestion is made to extend the Holt-Winters method to cover series with double, while in [20] with triple seasonality. In [21] the Taylor model with double seasonality was used to modelling internet traffic. Obviously it is theoretically possible to develop analogous models for time series with multiple periodicity; however, issues are raised in the literature (see [22]) concerning the unstable behaviour of such models, as well as the doubtful impact of third and further seasonalities on the calculated value of the predicted variable. Similar reservations also apply to double-seasonal Taylor models, in which the duration of the first period is considerably longer than that of the second one.

Double-seasonal Holt-Winters-Taylor model (referred to as HWT2 in subsequent sections) is determined by the following equations:

$$\hat{y}_t = L_{t-1} + T_{t-1} + D_{t-r1} + W_{t-r2}, \tag{6}$$

where r_1 is the length of the seasonal 1 (day) periodicity, r_2 is the length of the seasonal 2 (week) periodicity,

$$L_t = \alpha(y_t - D_{t-r1} - W_{t-r2}) + (1 - \alpha)(L_{t-1} + T_{t-1}) \tag{7}$$

is the constituent smoothing out the level of the series,

$$T_t = \beta(L_t - L_{t-1}) + (1 - \beta)T_{t-1} \tag{8}$$

corresponds to the increase of the series resulting from the trend,

$$D_t = \gamma(y_t - L_t - W_{t-r2}) + (1 - \gamma)D_{t-r1} \tag{9}$$

is a seasonal component of the series for seasonality 1 (day), and

$$W_t = \delta(y_t - L_t - D_{t-r1}) + (1 - \delta)W_{t-r2} \tag{10}$$

is a seasonal component of the series for seasonality 2 (week).

The initial values of components were arbitrarily set as

$$L_1 = y_1,$$
$$T_1 = 0,$$
$$D_1 = D_2 = \cdots = D_{r1} = 0,$$
$$W_1 = W_2 = \cdots = W_{r2} = 0.$$

(11)

4. Application of Brutlag's Anomaly Detection Algorithm in the HWT2 Model

In order to identify indications of anomalies in the modelled system, an analogous solution to the one presented in [17] can be used. In view of the double seasonality in the Taylor model, one might imagine two types of scatter permitted for the value of the predicted variable—one based on the parameter γ, and the other on δ

$$d_t = \gamma |y_t - \hat{y}_t| + (1 - \gamma)d_{t-r1},$$
$$w_t = \delta |y_t - \hat{y}_t| + (1 - \delta)d_{t-r2}.$$

(12)

The initial values of components were arbitrarily set as

$$w_{r2+1} = d_{r2+1} = |y_{r2+1} - \hat{y}_{r2+1}|.$$

(13)

One needs to remember that the parameters of the exponential smoothing models may be interpreted as a measure of the impact of the last measurement (parameters α, β, γ, and δ) or earlier measurements (values $1 - \alpha$, $1 - \beta$, $1 - \gamma$, and $1 - \delta$) on predicted values. Contrary to descriptive models, where the estimated values of parameters given the appropriate dependent variable has an intuitive meaning (in the case of single-equation additive model, the impact of the explanatory variable on the value of the dependent variable), and the criterion of minimizing the adopted measure of adjustment is decisive, the parameters of adaptive models of time series with exponential smoothing may be interpreted as a measure of smoothing—the greater the values of γ and δ, the greater the impact of values of the last measurements (i.e., measured correspondingly one day and one week earlier), the lower the values of the parameters, the better the model "remembers" the previous values (whose impact is weighted with $1 - \gamma$ and $1 - \delta$ coefficients). One might, at least to a certain extent, that is if does not have too great an influence on the adopted measure of adjustment, decide to arbitrarily change the values of smoothing parameters, especially if the given series displays periodicity.

The existence of two types of permitted scatter results in the necessity of distinguishing between two types of alerts: the first one related to exceeding the thresholds determined by the parameters of daily seasonality and the second one— of weekly seasonality. As the thresholds may intertwine it is necessary to distinguish in the alerts (see Figure 1) all three possible events ("daily" threshold exceeded, "weekly" threshold exceeded, both thresholds exceeded).

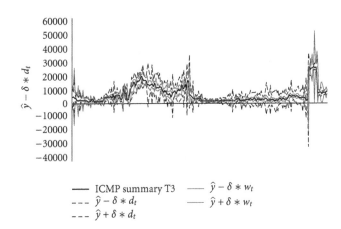

FIGURE 1: Sample fragment of series (308 observations, that is, 2.14 hours) ICMP in T3 network (from [6]) with daily thresholds and weekly thresholds for the scaling factor = 2.5.

5. Results and Conclusions

For the networks described in [6], the HWT2 model analysis was carried out for which the parameters were estimated through minimization of the expression

$$\frac{\text{Mean\_Absolute\_Error}}{\text{Mean}},$$

(14)

where

$$\text{Mean} = \frac{\sum_{t=1}^{n} y_t}{n},$$

(15)

where n is the length of the data series.

We decided to use MAE rather than mean squared error (MSE)-based measure because there were a lot of so-called outliers noted in the analysed samples and MSE-based measure that can be oversensitive in those cases (see, e.g., [21]).

In the referenced article network traffic for aggregated series was modelled (hourly data) and in the case of smaller-scale research series resulting from measurements of traffic every 10 minutes were used.

The obtained results and the number of alerts generated on exceeding the data threshold ("gamma" alert and "delta" alert) is presented in Table 1. For comparison, the table also contains the number of alerts obtained in modelling traffic using the classic Holt-Winters model (analogous to [6], this is with an iterative estimation of the value of parameters with minimization of MAE/M error, however, for 10-minute interval measurement, which is a departure from the referenced article).

As compared to the traditional Holt-Winters model, the magnitude of error is virtually unchanged (the table presents results with accuracy down to one per cent. In reality, there were differences between models in adjustment measures, at no more than one thousandth percentage point, which in practice is insignificant) whereas in all cases the number of alerts generated for the same scaling factor has lowered.

TABLE 1: Parameters of the HWT2 model for particular types of traffic.

Network	Protocol	Alpha	Beta	Gamma	Delta	MAE/M	Number of gamma alerts	Number of delta alerts	Number of gamma and delta alerts	Number of Brutlag's Holt Winters alerts
T3	TCP	0,999497	0,00224	0,487092	0,492391	4,11%	0	0	0	1052
T3	UDP	0,887382	0,007949	0,006263	0	15,45%	1413	2056	717	1377
T3	ICMP	0,999501	0,004789	0,487093	0,492397	8,69%	0	0	0	944
W1	TCP	0,968618	0,005005	0,002687	0,00513	45,92%	918	2193	714	1070
W1	UDP	0,997541	0,001291	0	0,15	30,19%	2743	1358	1047	3293
W1	ICMP	0,8433	0,002486	0	0,2	31,27%	2743	2504	1687	3247
T2	TCP	0,999385	0,00449	0,616195	0,499587	4, 20%	0	0	0	1014
T2	UDP	0,884039	0,000771	$3,54E{-}05$	0	15,87%	4562	4685	2806	4562
T2	ICMP	1	0,006488	0,5	0,5	8,53%	0	0	0	1174

Source: own research.

The potential application of the HWT2 model with the so-determined two types of thresholds may prove useful for reducing the number of false positives.

The application of the parameters γ and δ as weights determining the permissible scale makes the model have a relatively "short memory." Therefore, if the present value of the periodical constituent is closely related to its previous value, the extent of permitted thresholds will be relatively high. In the case of models with "better memory," they will be more sensitive to unitary changes in traffic. In the analyzed network traffic series, together with the high value of parameter α, the usually estimated value of parameter γ was relatively low (10^{-2} or less), the consequence of which was a relatively high number of alerts, the vast majority of which, as it would seem, would be deemed false positives. In the examined series, noted was greater sensitivity of the model to changes in the α level parameter than the seasonality impact (γ and δ), that had relatively low values. One might thus consider, instead of increasing the scaling factor, to arbitrarily increase the value of these parameters to the maximum values which do not cause significant deterioration of the model-matching score (e.g., below 1 percentage point). As it would seem, this is an approach which is better substantiated from a statistical point of view than manipulating the value of the scaling factor (an interesting challenge of the method adopted in [17] for determination of the values not provoking alerts contained [18]).

6. Further Actions

Among the methods used in anomaly detection, the following may be mentioned:

   (i) entropy measurement—see, for example, [23, 24],

   (ii) the so-called correlation of packets—see [25, 26]—where algorithms of simulated annealing were used,

   (iii) principal components analysis—see, for example, [27, 28],

   (iv) support vector machines—see, for example, [4],

   (v) adaptive threshold algorithm and the cumulative sum algorithm—see, for example, [29–31],

   (vi) data clustering—see also [32],

   (vii) k-nearest neighbors method—see [33], decision trees—see, for example, [34],

   (viii) artificial neural networks (ANNs)—see, for example, [35].

   (ix) distributed ANN—see, for example, [35, 36],

   (x) decision rule induction—see, for example, [37],

   (xi) immune algorithms—see, for example [38],

   (xii) genetic algorithms—see, for example, [39],

   (xiii) fuzzy logic—see, for example [40, 41],

   (xiv) zero-one models—see [42] and so forth.

As presented in [6] the characteristics of various networks or even the various types of network traffic in the same network are very different. Therefore, even if one of the widely used models of traffic or methods for their creation finds even the slightest application in test trials, its research work is practically useful.

Presently, our works are carried out on implementing both models (traditional Winters and HWT2) in the Anomaly Detection preprocessor, referred to in articl [6].

References

[1] A. Fadia and M. Zacharia, "Network intrusion alert. An ethical hacking guide to intrusion detection," in *Proceedings of the Thomson Source Technology*, Boston, Mass, USA, 2008.

[2] S. Sooyeon, K. Taekyoung, J. Gil-Yong, P. Youngman, and H. Rhy, "An experimental study of hierarchical intrusion detection for wireless industrial sensor networks," *IEEE Transactions on Industrial Informatics*, vol. 6, no. 4, pp. 744–757, 2010.

[3] E. A. Patkowski, "Mechanizmy wykrywania anomalii jako element bezpieczeństwa," Biuletyn Instytutu Automatyki i Robotyki nr 26/2009, Wydawnictwo Wojskowej Akademii Technicznej, Warsaw, Poland, 2009.

[4] F. Palmieri and U. Fiore, "Network anomaly detection through nonlinear analysis," *Computers and Security*, vol. 29, no. 7, pp. 737–755, 2010.

[5] J. Pieprzyk, T. Hardjono, and J. Seberry, *Teoria Bezpieczeństwa Systemów Komputerowych*, Helion, 2005.

[6] M. Szmit and A. Szmit, "Use of holt-winters method in the analysis of network traffic: case study," *Communications in Computer and Information Science*, vol. 160, pp. 224–231, 2011.

[7] L. Fillatre, D. Marakov, and S. Vaton, "Forecasting seasonal traffic flows," in *Proceedings of the Workshop on QoS and Traffic Control*, Paris, France, December 2005.

[8] I. Klevecka, "Forecasting network traffic: a comparison of neural networks and linear models," in *Proceedings of the 9th International Conference "Reliability and Statistics in Transportation and Communication" (RelStat '09)*, Riga, Latvia, October 2009.

[9] P. Goodwin, "The holt-winters approach to exponential smoothing: 50 years old and going strong," in *Proceedings of the FORESIGHT Fall*, pp. 30–34, 2010, http://www.forecasters.org/pdfs/foresight/free/Issue19_goodwin.pdf.

[10] B. Guzik, D. Appenzeller, and W. Jurek, *Prognozowanie i Symulacje. Wybrane Zagadnienia*, Wydawnictwo AE w Poznaniu, Poznań, Poland, 2004.

[11] E. S. Gardner, "Exponential smoothing: the state of the art-Part II," *International Journal of Forecasting*, vol. 22, no. 4, pp. 637–666, 2006.

[12] J. Gajda, *Prognozowanie i Symulacja a Decyzje Gospodarcze*, C. H. Beck, Warsaw, Poland, 2001.

[13] A. Zeliaś, B. Pawełek, S. Wanat et al., *Prognozowanie Ekonomiczne. Teoria, Przykłady, Zadania*, Wydawnictwo Naukowe PWN, Warszawa, Poland, 2004.

[14] M. Cieślak, Ed., *Prognozowanie Gospodarcze*, Wydawnictwo AE Wrocław, 1998.

[15] P. J. Brockwell and R. A. Davis, *Introduction to Time Series and Forecasting*, Springer, New York, NY, USA, 2nd edition, 2002.

[16] R. J. Hyndman, A. B. Koehler, J. K. Ord, and R. D. Snyder, *Forecasting with Exponential Smoothing: The State Space Approach*, Springer, Berlin, Germany, 2008.

[17] J. D. Brutlag, "Aberrant behavior detection in time series for network monitoring," in *Proceedings of the 14th System Administration Conference*, pp. 139–146, New Orleans, Fla, USA, 2000.

[18] E. Miller, "Holt-Winters Forecasting Applied to Poisson Processes in Real-Time," August, 2010, http://www.scribd.com/doc/35521051/Miller-Automated-Error-Detection-in-Web-Production-Environment.

[19] J. W. Taylor, "Short-term electricity demand forecasting using double seasonal exponential smoothing," *Journal of Operational Research Society*, vol. 54, pp. 799–805, 2003.

[20] J. W. Taylor, "Triple seasonal methods for short-term electricity demand forecasting," *European Journal of Operational Research*, vol. 204, pp. 139–152, 2010.

[21] S. Gelper, R. Fried, and C. Croux, "Robust forecasting with exponential and holt-winters smoothing," *Journal of Forecasting*, vol. 29, no. 3, pp. 285–300, 2010.

[22] R. Lawton, "On the Stability of the Double Seasonal Holt-Winters Method," http://forecasters.org/submissions09/LawtonRichardISF2009.pdf.

[23] G. Nychis, V. Sekar, D. G. Andersen, H. Kim, and H. Zhang, "An empirical evaluation of entropy-based traffic anomaly detection," in *Proceedings of the Association for Computing Machinery (ACM '08)*, 2008.

[24] Y. Gu, A. McCallum, and D. Towsley, "Detecting anomalies in network traffic using maximum entropy estimation," in *Proceedings of the IMC Conference*, http://conferences.sigcomm.org/imc/2005/papers/imc05efiles/gu/gu.pdf.

[25] SPADE 092200, http://rpmfind.net/linux/RPM/mandriva/9.2/i586/Mandrake/RPMS/snort-2.0.1-3mdk.i586.html.

[26] T. J. Kruk and J. Wrzesień, "Korelacja w wykrywaniu anomalii," in *Proceedings of the Materiały Konferencji CERT Secure*, Warsaw, Poland, 2003.

[27] H. Ringberg, A. Soule, J. Rexford, and C. Diot, "Sensitivity of PCA for Traffic Anomaly Detection," San Diego, Calif, USA, 2007, http://www.haakonringberg.com/work/papers/pca_tuning.pdf.

[28] A. Lakhina, M. Cronvella, and C. Diot, "Diagnosis network-wide traffic anomalies," in *Proceedings of the ACC SIGCOMM*, February 2004, http://citeseerx.ist.psu.edu/viewdoc/download?doi=10.1.1.93.7011&rep=rep1&type=pdf.

[29] V. A. Siris and F. Papaglou, "Application of anomaly detection algorithms for detecting syn floodinfg attacks," in *Proceedings of the IEEE Global Telecommunications Conference*, vol. 4, pp. 2050–2054, 2004.

[30] R. Mbabazi, *Victim-based defense against ip packet flooding denial of service attacks*, M.S. thesis, Makerere University, 2009.

[31] R. Blazek, H. Kim, B. Rozovskii, and A. Tartakovsky, "A novel approach to detection of "Denial-of-Service" attacks via adaptive sequential and batch-sequential change-point detection methods," in *Proceedings of the IEEE Systems, Man, and Cybernetics Information Assurance Workshop (West Point '01)*, June 2001.

[32] O. Siriporn and S. Benjawan, "Anomaly detection and characterization to classify traffic anomalies case study: TOT public company limited network," *Proceedings of World Academy of Science, Engineering and Technology*, vol. 37, pp. 706–714, 2009.

[33] A. Sharma, A. K. Pujari, and K. K. Paliwal, "Intrusion detection using text processing techniques with a kernel based similarity measure," *Computers and Security*, vol. 26, no. 7-8, pp. 488–495, 2007.

[34] S. O. Al-Mamory and H. Zhang, "New data mining technique to enhance IDS alarms quality," *Journal in Computer Virology*, vol. 6, no. 1, pp. 43–55, 2010.

[35] D. Tian, Y. Liu, and Y. Xiang, "Large-scale network intrusion detection based on distributed learning algorithm," *International Journal of Information Security*, vol. 8, no. 1, pp. 25–35, 2009.

[36] Snort+AI, http://snort-ai.sourceforge.net/.

[37] R. Cichocki, "Algorytmy indukcji reguł decyzyjnych w Systemach Wykrywania Intruzów," in *Proceedings of the XII Konferencja Sieci Komputerowe*, Zakopane, Poland, 2005.

[38] D. Dasgupta, "Immunity-based intrusion detection system: a general framework," in *Proceedings of the 22nd National Information Systems Security Conference (NISSC '99)*, 1999.

[39] W. Li, "Using genetic algorithm for network intrusion detection," in *Proceedings of the United States Department of Energy Cyber Security Group 2004 Training Conference*, Kansas City, Mo, USA, 2004.

[40] J. Luo, S. Bridges, and R. Vaughn, "Fuzzy frequent episodes for real time intrusion detection," *International Journal of Intelligent Systems*, vol. 15, no. 8, pp. 687–704, 2000.

[41] S. Bridges and R. Vaughn, "Fuzzy data mining and genetic algorithms applied to intrusion detection," in *Proceedings of the National Information Systems Security Conference (NISSC '00)*, Baltimore, Md, USA, October 2000.

[42] M. Szmit, Využití nula-jedničkových modelů pro behaviorální analýzu síťového provozu, [w:] Internet, competitiveness and organizational security, Tomas Bata University Zlín, pp. 266–299, 2011.

15

The Concept of the Remote Devices Content Management

Miroslav Behan and Ondrej Krejcar

Department of Information Technologies, Faculty of Informatics and Management, University of Hradec Kralove, Rokitanskeho 62, 50003 Hradec Kralove, Czech Republic

Correspondence should be addressed to Ondrej Krejcar, ondrej.krejcar@remoteworld.net

Academic Editor: Peter Brida

Modern mobile communication devices which are often used as remote access to information systems bring up many advantages for user. Unfortunately in some cases when user has several different mobile devices for the same remote access, a problem of multiplatform and multivendor environment fragments productivity by user knowledge in principals of approach to possible services, controlling or management of devices as well as features is available. The customizable interface of remote device management benefits by the control of all owned, authorized, or publically accessible devices from single point of user perspective. We propose a concept of such information system which takes into account mobile devices and their content. Concept is suitable not only for Apple iOS or Google Android, but also it covers all mobile platforms as well as the sensors capabilities of mobile devices which can turn such mobile Smart Device to Smart and mobile sensor concentrator.

1. Introduction

Future resource-based economy will dramatically shape current daily processes in many parts of human activities. The consumer society will face the effective artificial self-responsible subsystems with behaviour where cost-effectiveness and nature-related responsibility would be on first place. Global acquirements of devices power used for developing smart environments, that could dramatically increase human productivity as a side effect, would be recognized as a middle step of oncoming technology evolution. We acknowledged that nowadays the current market with mobile devices is more and more fragmented cross-vendors or platforms where different users approach could be confusing. As an alternative we would present future vision of Remote Device Management (RDM) which could positively shape human productivity and could be simply used for actual and future user centric multidevice environment as a convenient interface. Our Remote Device Management is designed as a productivity concept for users who prefer centralized management point and confident approach to multiplatform types of devices in comprehensive way. The future user content management challenges will have to take into account multidevice environment where

different User Interfaces (UI) and platform are and device-specific features [1].

1.1. Multidevice Environment. As a device, we define all the devices which are able to connect to network, that is, to the internet resources using an online or offline mode. The multidevice environment from single person point of view naturally underlines future realistic scenario where user would own or have to manage more than one device. We acknowledge multivendor environment and multiplatform environment as Android [2], iOS, Mango, and so forth. Every common user has currently at least more than one device which would be as an interface to cyberspace or which would be an extension to visualization of electronic world. The scenario would be about connectivity to cyberspace where user prefers conventional way more and more. The basic idea of the multiple-device management is based on simplify user friendly environment, where the same User Interface (UI) is presented for different devices or types of devices from multiple vendors or manufactures. What could happen when user reclaims the same type of device interface; for instance, mobile phones, where the same functionality and content exist? The user has to know as many device interfaces as possible many types of platforms exist. What if there exists one customizable device interface which accesses the most common features of different devices. Is that a good experience in evaluation of human productivity? What if user could be independent on platforms and type of devices and in case of device crash or device lost, it could be easily recovered by one button click? Even more when user realizes that there is a possibility to manipulate content of different devices which is accessible from single interface. Of course it is all about capability of devices which could in the future lead more and more to massive usage of smart solutions and could make mobile device as natural connection between human and groups of devices (e.g., car, fridge, or boat).

1.2. Mobile Device Apple Platform. The Apple platform provides for developers fundamental and well-prepared design support with framework named COCOA, which is basically using Object-C as programming language. There are other extensions from point of developer view where Java or other scripting languages could be used. The mobile devices are used as operation systems the iOS and the most convenient way for developing an application is at using common system calls as application interfaces, application services, and core services [3]. The advantages of the Apple platform are basically comprehensive, publishable, and distributive application channels over Internet.

Another plus of this platform architecture [4] is one-vendor device based on a solution where the certainty of proper system calls and their behaviour is well defined and supported. As well as device hardware access in terms of mobile device development the screen resolution where as ratio between height and width constantly $5:3$ could be announced another beneficial aspect in Rapid Application Development (RAD). Apple platform establish fundamentals of mobile application ecosystem environment. The increase of usability of mobile device is enormous. Identity of application is consisting of small image and short-term expression with remote update framework possibility known as an application market.

1.3. Mobile Device Android Platform. The mobile platform as Android is due to self-interopen ability suitable for the 3rd party solutions where partial problems are solved [5]. The security and stability of the system which is based on an Open Source concept is outstanding [6]. A device types which are currently running under Android platform are well-known for smartphones and tablets but also for other device types [7] due to suitability of platform design for, instance laptop, netbooks, smart books, e-book readers, smart TVs, wristwatches, headphones, car players, smart glasses, vehicle navigating systems, refrigerators, home automation systems, games consoles, mirrors, cameras, or portable media players. The architecture of Java-based platform fully provides multi-threading environment where gathering of precise data form sensors are required. The architecture [8] allows services which are running on background as a provider or as a consumer of external services [9].

2. Problem Definition of Remote Device Management

In this chapter we summarized problematic areas in device management in consideration of possible remote use. We focused on cross-device features which are mainly based upon the management that provides measurement, controlling, and maintenance over sensors or content of device. Other point of view would consider the platform aspects which are supportive to some key benefits in the Remote Device Management (RDM). At last the focus would consider the network access and its capabilities in terms of usability and sustainable processing. For better overview we outline ideas expressed in the mind map on the following figure (Figure 1) which are described in more details bellow in this chapter.

The aim of Remote Device Management is about to provide consistent cloud service where key benefits are open framework accessibility with simple to use Application Program Interface (API), social connectivity, content consistency, and security policies. Let starts with identity connector (Figure 1) problematic which is bound by correct user identification over native account provided and where all user data are mounted on.

2.1. Identity Problematic. The identity is nowadays spread over web application mostly and therefore we include into account the main of them which are divided into Social Networks, Emails, Mobile, and Desktop devices identity providers. The Social Networks are considered only the main ones such as Facebook, G+, Twitter, and LinkedIn. The identity from most of them is provided over inner-defined application which after user authorization by Open Access (OAuth 2.0) process acquired user permission on specific tasks and is able to process user's information and establish secure 3rd side authentication for login session. The other way of user identification used world widely is email authorization where over the provided user email in registration process is authorization link sent and after user activation we assume the email is correct as communication channel or current browser is authorized for login session temporary or permanently. Another case is about mobile devices where the authorization channels are SMS, Voice Call, or Native Application. The identity acquired is Mobile Number or Device Identity where each provides authorized secure channel. The last one case is desktop which uses for access browser or native client in terms of specific platform (iOS, Windows, Linux), and where user identity is acquired over registration process with or without any parts mentioned before.

2.2. Content Problematic. The core feature of Remote Device Management is multiply, sync, or backup content over different types of devices. Content is any kind of information related to user and in terms of device management, we consider content as an end-user data which are important to keep safe on devices due to daily usage even in offline mode of the device connectivity and also accessible from

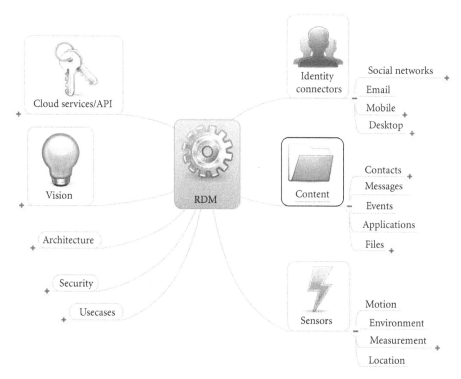

FIGURE 1: Mind map-Remote Device Management.

different mobile or desktop devices. As representative types of user content we recognized Contacts, Messages, Events, Applications, and Files. These kinds of content would be smart distributed and synchronized over user owned devices or be backed up automatically in terms of lost or broke accident. Management of content would be more convenient on desktop device rather than small screen mobile device. On the other hand in time or in location tasks are required event from nonconforming user interfaces for specific tasks of content management. Contacts are very specific content which requires correct personal identification and actual communication channels availability resolving therefore supportive part is Social Networks, Email Contacts and Phone Contact list in terms of distributive social knowledge. Messages are consists of SMS, Voice mail or IMs which provides open access to 3rd sides. Also the problematic is mounted by personal identification based on contacts. Events represents all activity provided by device or user action. Applications are content which in mobile point of view is mostly provided over platforms dedicated applications web or desktop (iTunes-iOS, Play-Android, MarketPlace-Windows Phone) therefore at least the list of application resources with time spent monitoring is considerable for sync. The last one kind of content we assume as files where the requirements are limited to amount of date and share purposes. The file content is achieved by implemented Camcorder, Camera, Microphone, or Universal Serial Bus (USB) for other types file content. The main reason for defined file content is to share further postprocessing on desktop.

2.3. Sensor Problematic. As the sensors we define all measureable informational providers of devices which are accessible and are enabled for gathering motion or environment data such as wireless signals, sensorial data, or long-term indicators. There are more types of sensors and therefore we divide them into Motional, Environmental, and Locational-based sensors [1, 10–12]. The motional types are connected to movements of device or its position in space for instance Accelerometer, Magnetic field, or Gyroscope sensor (Table 1).

The environmental types are associated with conditions of current location such as pressure or temperature and also knowledge-based measurable information which are gathered over long-term time period where for instance the home environment is recognizable as the most occupied place of device where the sleeping time of user is recognized by motion or microphone sensor inactivity [13, 14].

And the location-based sensors we consider as Global Positioning System (GPS) sensor, Global System for Mobile communication (GSM) signal sensor, or Wireless Local Area Networks (WLAN) signal receiver which in cooperation establish precise measurement of device location accordingly to energy efficiency. The way of gathering sensor data is over allowed platform system calls where access is authorized by an end-user or by device management provided for platform or by overriding manufactured firmware within dedicated customized distribution of opened platforms which would be available as an Open Source. We are focusing on allowed 3rd party sensor access which is available through framework API, for example, in Android (Table 1).

TABLE 1: Android sensors [18] for smart and ambient environments—overview.

Type	Functionality
Accelerometer	Sensor calculate acceleration without gravity acceleration $g = 9.81$ m/s^2 as following equitation: $Ad = -g - \sum F/mass$ The reason is user centric-suspected behaviour for an end-user where device in a stable position placed on the table should have acceleration 0 instead of +9.81
Ambient temperature	Ambient (room) temperature in degree Celsius
Gravity	A three-dimensional vector indicating the direction and magnitude of gravity. Units are m/s^2. The coordinate system is the same as is used by the acceleration sensor
Gyroscope	Values are in radians/second and measure the rate of rotation around the device's local X-, Y-, and Z-axis
Light	Ambient light level in SI lux units
Linear acceleration	A three-dimensional vector indicating acceleration along each device axis, not including gravity. All values have units of m/s^2. The coordinate system is the same as is used by the acceleration sensor The output of the accelerometer, gravity and linear-acceleration sensors must obey the following relation: acceleration = gravity + linear-acceleration
Magnetic field	Values are in micro-Tesla (uT) and measure the ambient magnetic field in the X-, Y-, and Z-axis
Orientation	All values are angles in degrees
Pressure	Atmospheric pressure in hPa (millibar)
Proximity	Proximity sensor distance measured in centimeters
Relative humidity	Relative ambient air humidity in percent
Rotation vector	The rotation vector represents the orientation of the device as a combination of an angle and an axis, in which the device has rotated through an angle θ around an axis $\langle x, y, z \rangle$

The measurement requires at least separate thread to perform precise measured result therefore architecture suites to producer and consumer concept. In case of remote consumer the results would not be influenced by dilation of time of transport or transaction. With consideration of network latency the result would be notified or expected in correct time form. We recognized two groups of sensors where one of them is real-time changed and the other one consists of state long-time sensor changes.

The following article [15], where the domain of sensors data gathering is well defined, was considered as contributory for our solution design. The informational system as extension would provide user status resolution over sets of gathered sensor data, where sleeping, sitting, running, walking, or driving have informational value in current context point of view. Also the environment context is valuable in terms of user productivity for instance vacation, work, or distance movement.

2.4. Universal Platform Approach. The most significant aspect which influences usability of mobile devices is platform based solution. All positive and negative user experience leads to platform evolution where useless platforms are terminated. Therefore platform survival dependents on scalability and open mind accessibility where openness to new solutions and approach both technical and future ideas predetermine the platform success. The accesses to device features as well as technical capabilities which are not user invasive are essential to be included in our universal solution where native client on device is realized as connector between user and platform.

3. Solution Design Concept

This paper describes solution concept of remote device management focused mainly on server side architecture. Designed concept is variable in terms of technology use case. We suppose to use as development framework all Java based technology because of effectiveness in productivity, scalability and reuse of available Open Source components. The following figure (Figure 2) highlights important parts of architecture which are required for specific needs especially from network connectivity characteristics [16]. The informational system consists of three main parts which are remote client part, core system part and end-user interface part. We start to describe remote part where all possible devices potentially could be connected to the system. The devices are highly fragmented hardware area due to competition of manufactures and vendors about end-user's goodwill. We recognize basically two sets of devices from system point of view.

The first contains all mobile devices which have to care about power supply management and without power-saving management the unnecessarily draining battery would lead to uselessness of developed application. The second group of devices is an independent of power supply where for instance we classify cars because of their external power supply. For these reasons each group would behave differently in terms of kind of connectivity mode. The devices which could be connected to the system over any kind of network and could provide peer-peer internet connectivity instantly or for exact amount of time we called as active devices. The others we called as passive where which would not be all time online or connected to a dedicated server. The passive mode would respect user's defined network connectivity due to cost effectiveness or power management. Next figure

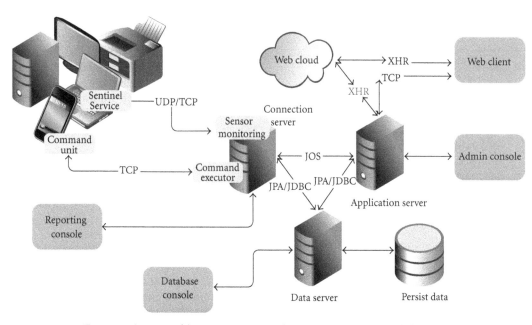

FIGURE 2: System architecture-Remote Device Management (using gliffy UML).

(see Table 2) overviewed connectivity of devices and their statuses according to an active or passive device policy.

Explicitly defined states of connectivity would not get rid of some cases where the uncertain behaviour of network connectivity could appear. The problem would be eliminated by control queuing management based on messages. The messages of events and data would be handled on a client side as well as on a server side in correct time frame. In case of network unavailability the queue substitute consumer and when network status changed and reconnects the message queue processed all First In First Out (FIFO) messages in time order. The sentinel measurement data which are with low level importance and are not supposed for real-time processing are lastly consumed. From technical point of view the messages are sent from client to server by User Datagram Protocol (UDP) in such low level importance cases and where high measurement precision is not required but is preferred speed of delivery or amount of transmitted data. Otherwise the Transport Control Protocol (TCP) is used for confident types of measurement or data delivery of content [17]. The connection server consists of datagram resolver and socket transport object resolver where socket resolver due to usage with sensor monitoring and also with command executor is practically core functionality of connection server. The socket resolver either being client or server is providing communication between device and system. The main responsibilities are maintenance of connection and transportation of data objects between both sides. Objects are transported over serialization Java technology where content is fast serialized or de-serialize on binary code and sent over network.

The second part called as system part basically handles core features of informational system from device monitoring, device command execution and device management with predefined device or user policies up to the system external data storing, system content providing, and system authorized access ability for all kinds of requests from front or background processing. Also as a connection server we would use Java programing language for implementation due to object interserver exchange. The application server and client application service decides what and when would be transported. Device execution commands are initiated also by application server where are authorizations of requests dispatched from an end-user actions or device routines with associated permissions. Application server is responsible for all other types of requests from the device or the end-user. The calls consist of group with data visualization calls, group of background routine calls based on the time triggering settings and maintenance group or administration group of calls. All calls are related to specific tasks or concrete device or group of devices therefore also security and authorizations are part of responsibility of application server. Last component is data management of informational system based on Java Persistence Application Programing Interface (JPA) technology which is being used due to extraordinary developing capability and time development saving. The data objects are defined in Java classes and relations between entities are expressed as a member of concrete class with specific annotation which specific cardinality and type of relation. The objects are transformed to database though persistent commands and after the commitment are saved to hard file on disk.

The last part of the system is focused on web content delivery and interactions with an end-user. The web content is hosted on external web server as a cloud solution where the user identity and cloud services could be used. The web client is connected to the web cloud services either to the application server over secure channel. Web cloud is used due to implicit network traffic monitoring tool and cost-effective load balancing for web clients with minimal

TABLE 2: Table of connection modes.

Device mode	Connectivity/status	Initiator	Purpose
Active	Persistent/live	Server	After client registration server establishes peer-peer connection for live command requests channel triggered by web user interface
			Client sentinels could send event change statuses
Active	Interval/command routine	Server/client	In defined interval on server side based on configuration or policy system connects and performs commands on background
			Client sends interval defined sentinel updates
Active	Zero-base/online	Server	Heart beat protocol for devices in active mode to maintain stable persistent connection
Active/Passive	Session/online	Server/client	Requested commands related to established session by web user interface where in passive mode explicit authorization is required
			Registration request of client with meta data for system connection
			Batch updates of sentinels in passive mode
Active/Passive	Not available/offline	Server/client	Connection with client or server is lost or could not be established. Data or tasks are queuing and waiting for the connection to be established

impact on the maintenance. Web cloud is basically used as secured fast traffic response container for web client which mainly communicates with application server in global world scale where continental redistribution is a case. Web client itself implements data visualization and requests posting and corresponding response handling. The client is based on HyperText Markup Language (HTML) version 5 and JavaScript (JS) concept. Communication with an application server is performed over Transmission Control Protocol (TCP) by Web Socket technology due to convenient and fast responsive way in comparisons to classical Asynchronous JavaScript and Xml (AJAX) technology. The Web Socket technology provides persist communication channel over a well-known port 80 with advantages of socket connectivity. Therefore the reaction time of committed commands in live online mode increases usability of the entire system where round trip time (RTT) to server is multiple times faster than common Xml Http Request (XHR) for short messages.

4. Conclusions

Over the current multiple device environmental interfaces and subsidized functionality we would decrease human time spent with maintenance of an authorized, owned or public group of devices in terms of content, settings, policy or gathering sensor information and to increase human productivity accordingly to comprehensive user's interface for multiple devices and within comfortable working space. The fragmentation of devices is more increasing in time due to the technological innovations and therefore Remote Content Device Management would be convenient also for nongeek personalities. The advantages of proposed system concept are single user interface customizable by user-centric behaviour undependable on platforms or vendors settings and recovery optionality over uniform or nonuniform devices with a user synchronized content delivery.

Acknowledgments

The work and the contribution were partially supported by the Project (1) "SMEW-Smart Environments at Workplaces," the Grant Agency of the Czech Republic, GACR P403/10/1310; (2) "Smart Solutions in Ambient Intelligent Environments," University of Hradec Kralove under the Project SP/2012/6.

References

[1] P. Mikulecky, "Remarks on ubiquitous intelligent supportive spaces," in *Proceedings of the 15th American Conference on Applied Mathematics/International Conference on Computational and Information Science,*, pp. 523–528, University of Houston, Houston, Tex, USA, 2009.

[2] A. Loukas, D. Damopoulos, S. A. Menesidou, M. E. Skarkala, G. Kambourakis, and S. Gritzalis, "MILC: a secure and privacy-preserving mobile instant locator with chatting," *Information Systems Frontiers*, vol. 14, no. 3, pp. 481–497, 2012.

[3] S. P. Hall and E. Anderson, "Operating systems for mobile computing," *Journal of Computing Sciences in Colleges*, vol. 25, no. 2, pp. 64–71, 2009.

[4] Apple Developer Site, iOS, http://developer.apple.com/library/ios/#documentation/Miscellaneous/Conceptual/iPhoneOSTechOverview/IPhoneOSOverview/IPhoneOSOverview.html.

[5] M. L. Murphy, *Android Programming Tutorials*, CommonsWare, 2009.

[6] T. Yamakami, "Foundation-based mobile platform software engineering: implications to convergence to open source software," in *Proceedings of the 2nd International Conference on Interaction Sciences: Information Technology, Culture and Human (ICIS'09)*, pp. 206–211, November 2009.

[7] D. Vybiral, M. Augustynek, and M. Penhaker, "Devices for position detection," *Journal of Vibroengineering*, vol. 13, no. 3, pp. 531–535, 2011.

[8] J. P. Espada, R. G. Crespo, O. S. Martínez, B. Cristina Pelayo G-Bustelo, and J. M. C. Lovelle, "Extensible architecture for context-aware mobile web applications," *Expert Systems with Applications*, vol. 39, no. 10, pp. 9686–9694, 2012.

[9] N. Radia, Y. Zhang, M. Tatipamula, and V. K. Madisetti, "Next-generation applications on cellular networks: trends, challenges, and solutions," *Proceedings of the IEEE*, vol. 100, no. 4, pp. 841–854.

[10] P. Brida, J. Machaj, J. Benikovsky, and J. Duha, "An experimental evaluation of AGA algorithm for RSS positioning in GSM networks," *Elektronika ir Elektrotechnika*, no. 8, pp. 113–118, 2010.

[11] N. Chilamkurti, S. Zeadally, A. Jamalipour, and S. K. Das, "Enabling wireless technologies for green pervasive computing," *Eurasip Journal on Wireless Communications and Networking*, vol. 2009, Article ID 230912, 2 pages, 2009.

[12] N. Chilamkurti, S. Zeadally, and F. Mentiplay, "Green networking for major components of information communication technology systems," *Eurasip Journal on Wireless Communications and Networking*, vol. 2009, Article ID 656785, 7 pages, 2009.

[13] R. Brad, "Satellite image enhancement by controlled statistical differentiation," in *Innovations and Advances Techniques in Systems, Computing Sciences and Software Engineering*, Proceedings of the International Conference on Systems, Computing Science and Software Engineering, ELECTR NETWORK, pp. 32–36, 2007.

[14] O. Krejcar, J. Jirka, and D. Janckulik, "Use of mobile phones as intelligent sensors for sound input analysis and sleep state detection," *Sensors*, vol. 11, no. 6, pp. 6037–6055, 2011.

[15] G. G. Blazquez, A. Berlanga, and J. M. Molina, "InContexto: multisensor architecture to obtain people context from smartphones," *International Journal of Distributed Sensor Networks*, vol. 2012, Article ID 758789, 15 pages, 2012.

[16] S. Conder and L. Darcey, *Android Wireless Application Development*, Addison-Wesley, 2009.

[17] V. Kasik, M. Penhaker, V. Novák, R. Bridzik, and J. Krawiec, "User interactive biomedical data web services application," *Communications in Computer and Information Science*, vol. 171, pp. 223–237, 2011.

[18] Android Developer Site, Sensors, http://developer.android.com/reference/android/hardware/Sensor.html.

16

Adaptive Probabilistic Proactive Routing for Dense MANETs

Abdelfettah Belghith,[1] Mohamed Amine Abid,[1] and Adel Ben Mnaouer[2]

[1] *HANA Research Group, Ecole Nationale des Sciences de l'Informatique (ENSI), University of Manouba, La Manouba 2010, Tunisia*
[2] *College of Computer Engineering and IT, Dar Al Utoum, Al Mizan, Al Falah, Riyad 13314, Saudi Arabia*

Correspondence should be addressed to Abdelfettah Belghith, abdelfattah.belghith@ensi.rnu.tn

Academic Editor: Liansheng Tan

Conventional proactive routing protocols, due to their inherent nature based on shortest paths, select longer links which are amenable to rapid breakages as nodes move around. In this paper, we propose a novel adaptive probabilistic approach to handle routing information in dense mobile ad hoc networks in a way to improve the proactive routing pertinence as a function of network dynamics. We first propose a new proactive routing framework based on probabilistic decisions and a generic model to compute the existence probabilities of nodes and links. Then, we present a distributed algorithm to collect the cartography of the network. This cartography is used to instantiate the existence probabilities. Conducted simulations show that our proposal yields substantially better routing validity. Nonetheless, it amounts to much longer routes. We proposed then a bounding technique to adapt and overcome this side effect and defined two probabilistic proactive routing variants. Conducted simulations show that our proposed bounded probabilistic proactive routing schemes outperform conventional routing protocols and yield up to 66 percent increase in throughput.

1. Introduction

Mobile ad hoc networks (MANETs) are spontaneous networks that do not require any infrastructure for their operations. The task of routing packets from a source to a destination is the sole responsibility of all participating nodes and is distributed among them, where a node can serve as a traffic source, a destination, or a relaying router. All nodes should cooperate, under normal conditions, to fulfill such a requirement. In these networks, nodes and links can appear and disappear spontaneously as a consequence of several facts such as the behavior of users, the depletion of energy resources, but more inherently and subtly the underlying random mobility of the different nodes. These aspects imply a dynamic and randomly evolving topology in both time and space making the routing a real challenging task.

A host of routing protocols and algorithms were proposed, though, only very few of them are actually standardized. The standardized routing protocols are classified into reactive and proactive protocols. Reactive protocols, such as DSR [1] and AODV [2], calculate routes only when needed, and as such they are supposed to generate low signaling overhead. Proactive protocols, like the Optimized Link State

Routing protocol (OLSR [3]) and the Destination Sequenced Distance Vector routing protocol (DSDV [4]), establish paths for all known source-destination pairs in advance by periodically exchanging topological information, and, as a result, they are stipulated to generate more control traffic than reactive protocols. Routing overhead, nevertheless, depends on many factors such as topology, number of nodes (i.e., density), number of hops, degree and type of mobility, number of flows, and the rate at which traffic streams are established within the network.

Numerous simulation studies were conducted on different scenarios to evaluate the performance of both proactive and reactive routing protocols [5–7]. Nevertheless, due to the large number of relevant and complex events that can happen in mobile wireless ad hoc networks and their effects on the performance of the underlying protocols, the results do not necessarily agree as to which family of protocols yields better performances and lower control traffic overhead.

In this paper, we restrict our attention to proactive routing where a periodic exchange of topological messages provides each node with a certain image of the network at the beginning of each routing period. Once the routing table is updated, it will be maintained and used during the entire current routing period. As a result and as the elapsed time since the start of the routing period gets farther, the topological information collected at the beginning of the routing period becomes inaccurate leading patently to invalid paths. In such mobile networks, there is certainly a need to consider paths composed of nodes and links having large remaining residual lives. The question naturally arises as to how should we select and decide on these links and routes. Finding the most stable path must anticipate or predict topological changes. We propose a novel probabilistic approach that would improve the routing pertinence of proactive routing protocols as a function of the network dynamics. Conducted simulations confirm that our proposed probabilistic scheme improves the accuracy of proactive routing and hence yields much larger throughput.

The paper is organized as follows. In Section 2, we present some of the relevant research work done in the field. In Section 3, we define our probabilistic general framework for selecting stable routes. Section 4 presents a Markovian model which provides a simple, yet an effective mean for the computation of the probabilities of existence of network links and nodes. In Section 5, we present our network cartography collecting algorithm that is required to instantiate the existence probabilities of network links and nodes. In Section 6, we investigate, through extensive simulations, the suitability of the proposed probabilistic framework and its instantiation. We finally summarize our work in Section 7.

2. Related Work

Conventional protocols use in general the hop-count metric to compute shortest paths towards destinations. However, shortest paths are not always reliable especially in case of dynamic networks. Finding stable routes is rather the main concern for dynamic multihop ad hoc networks. Several works established already that choosing routes based on positions, battery level, and so forth of the nodes would make selected paths more resilient to topological changes. A new routing approach has then come out considering the route stability or resiliency as a fundamental routing metric. Stability-based routing is a new emergent approach which allows routing to withstand the network dynamics. It aims essentially at choosing routes which are more stable in time and hence more resilient to dynamic changes in the network topology.

The stability of a path relies on the stability of its composing links. Authors in [8] proposed to classify links based on the mobility behavior of their end point nodes. Links between stationary or very slowly moving nodes are considered as stationary links. Links which exist only for a short period of time are handled as transient links. Newly formed links are also considered to be transient as they are more likely to break down. Routing should use then stationary links whenever this is possible. A ticket-based probing procedure is proposed to find stable routes. Classification of links is previously adapted in [9] where authors used the strength of the received signal from each neighboring node to determine whether the associated link is either weak or strong. Routing is then made through paths maximizing the received signal strength.

Associativity-based routing (ABR) [10] used a new metric called associativity which defines the stability of the link between two given nodes. ABR considers that the longer the two nodes have being neighbors, the longer they would stay connected. To express its associativity, each node broadcasts periodically a Beacon to indicate its presence. Upon the reception of a Beacon, a counter associated to the generating node is updated. The counter is reset to zero if the associated node is no longer accessible. The optimal route towards a destination is the one maximizing its cumulative associativity metric. Further stability-based routing techniques can be found in [11–18]. In contrast to all of these research proposals, our present work thrives to select the appropriate links composing a given path based on an adaptive procedure that calibrates the stability of chosen links and consequently yields shorter paths.

Furthermore, few probabilistic techniques were proposed although they seem to better cope with the unpredictable behavior of ad hoc topologies. In [19], a probabilistic technique is proposed to estimate the residual lifetime of routes. Routing is then made through the ones with maximum residual lifetime. Lifetime of a route is computed as a function of the existence probability of each link which is derived from the distribution governed by the underlying mobility model. In contrast, our present work focuses rather on the existence probability of complete routes. Mobility is represented through a generic and simple behavioral analytical Markovian model based on the network cartography collected at the start of each routing period. This cartography is then used to instantiate the existence probabilities. Our probabilistic proposal yields substantially better routing validity, but it amounts to much longer routes. A simple route bounding technique is then proposed to overcome this side effect.

3. Probabilistic Framework for the Selection of Stable Routes

Throughout the paper, we consider that links are symmetric. We model a mobile multihop ad hoc network by an undirected complete graph $G = (V, E)$, where V is the set of vertices and E represents the set of undirected edges. We stress here the fact that the graph is complete but this does not mean that all nodes are mutually within transmission range of each other. Links in $G = (V, E)$ will be partitioned into two disjoints groups as defined and explained in the following paragraph.

We define two states Up (U) and $Down$ (D) for the links and nodes of $G = (V, E)$. A vertex (i.e., a node) in V is said to be in state U at time t if it is *actively* connected to the network; notice that a node can be connected but not active when, for instance, it is forced to be in a dozing state by a power saving mechanism. A vertex is said to be in state D at time t if it is not active independently of being connected or not. An edge in E is said to be in state U when its end point vertices are within propagation range of each other independently of the states in which they are; otherwise, the edge is said to be in state D. An edge is said to be in state U means only that its end points are within propagation range independently of whether they are active or not. We note here that E is indeed partitioned into two groups of edges: a group of U edges and a group of D edges. The actual topology of the network at time t is then provided by the subgraph of $G = (V, E)$ that contains only the U nodes and their corresponding U edges. This subgraph may surely not contain some U edges exactly those not having both of their end point vertices in the U state.

3.1. Probability of Link Existence.

In ad hoc networks, a link exists whenever its two end point nodes exist (i.e., they are in the U state) yet they are within transmission range (i.e., the link is in the U state). Let x and y be the end vertices of edge e, the probability of existence of e at time t is then given by

$$P(e, t) = P_U(x, t) \cdot P_U(y, t) \cdot P_U(e, t), \tag{1}$$

where $P_U(x, t)$ is the probability that node x is in state U at time t, $P_U(y, t)$ is the probability that node y is in state U at time t and $P_U(e, t)$ is the probability that nodes x and y are within transmission range at time t. We note here that we are tacitly assuming the independence between the different nodes and links. This might not be the case in real-life networks. However, later we shall focus solely on the dynamics of the links and assume that all nodes in the network are kept permanently active. In this case, there is no need of such an assumption as links are independent.

3.2. Probability of Path Existence.

We define a path (s, d) as a sequence of n undirected links from a source s to a destination d. A path exists if all its nodes and its links are in state U. Let $S_v = \{n_0 = s, n_1, \ldots, n_i, \ldots, n_n = d\}$ be the sequence of $n + 1$ vertices and $S_e = \{e_1, e_2, \ldots, e_i, \ldots, e_n\}$ the sequence of n edges composing path (s, d). The probability of existence of the path from a source s to a destination d at time t is then given by

$$P((s, d)) = \prod_{n_i \in S_v} P_U(n_i, t) \prod_{e_i \in S_e} P_U(e_i, t). \tag{2}$$

Here again, we assumed a complete independence among links, among nodes, and between links and nodes. Our objective is to find the optimal path between any two given nodes. The optimal path is the one having the greatest probability of existence among all possible paths. Let $T_{s,d}$ be the set of all possible paths from source s to destination d. We call $T_{opt}(s, d)$ the most stable path (i.e., having the greatest probability) from a source s to a destination d, that is

$$T_{opt}(s, d) : \arg \max_{T \in T_{s,d}} P(T), \tag{3}$$

and, consequently

$$T_{opt}(s, d) : \arg \max_{T \in T_{s,d}} \ln P(T), \tag{4}$$

using now (2), we obtain

$$T_{opt}(s, d) : \arg \max_{T \in T_{s,d}} \left(\ln \left(\prod_{n_i \in T} P_U(n_i, t) \prod_{e_i \in T} P_U(e_i, t) \right) \right). \tag{5}$$

which leads to

$$T_{opt}(s, d) : \arg \min_{T \in T_{s,d}} \left(\sum_{n_i \in T} - \ln P_U(n_i, t) + \sum_{e_i \in T} - \ln P_U(e_i, t) \right). \tag{6}$$

The solution to (6) may be readily provided by any shortest path algorithm executed on the corresponding valued graph where every edge e has a weight $- \ln P_U(e, t)$ and every vertex has a weight $- \ln P_U(n, t)$ (see for instance [20]).

The above represents a generic framework to compute probabilistic optimal paths. It remains to devise how the probability for a node or a link to be in the U or D state is calculated. In the following section, we present a novel method to compute these probabilities.

4. Markovian Model for the Existence of Network Elements

According to the dynamics of the network, nodes and links of our complete graph $G = (V, E)$ switch between state U and state D in a completely independent manner (by our independence hypothesis stated above). At any instant, the actual network is the one composed of the U vertices and the corresponding U edges. To model this dynamic behavior, we propose to view each node and each link of the complete graph $G = (V, E)$ as a Markovian two state automaton.

4.1. Probability of Existence of Vertices and Edges.

Let x be a vertex or an edge of $G = (V, E)$. We model state changes of x by a 2-state continuous time Markov chain where the residence time in state U, respectively, in state D, is exponentially distributed with parameter λ, respectively, with parameter μ. Let $P_U(x, t)$ denote the transient probability of element x being in state U at time t. Let also $P_D(x, t)$ denote the transient probability of element x being in state D at time t. Our objective is to obtain the transient probability $P_U(x, t)$. The solution to this transient probability should then obey to the following differential equations [21]:

$$P_U(x, t) + P_D(x, t) = 1,$$
$$\frac{dP_U(x, t)}{dt} = \mu P_D(x, t) - \lambda P_U(x, t). \tag{7}$$

The solution of these equations is of the form

$$P_U(x, t) = \frac{\mu}{\lambda + \mu} + B \exp^{-(\lambda + \mu)t}. \tag{8}$$

Let us see the time axis divided into intervals representing the routing periods. At the beginning of a routing period, that is at time $t = 0$, we assume that the state of each and every element of the complete graph is known. This indeed necessitates the complete knowledge of the network cartography. For now, we suppose that a certain oracle is there to give us this cartography, we will develop on that later on. As a result, we readily have

$$P_U(x, at\ t = 0) = 1, \quad \text{if } x \text{ is } U \text{ at } t = 0,$$
$$= 0, \quad \text{if } x \text{ is } D \text{ at } t = 0, \tag{9}$$

if we define

$$\delta = \frac{\mu}{\lambda + \mu}, \tag{10}$$

then, the final solution for $P_U(x,t)$ will be

$$P_U(x,t) = \delta + (1-\delta)\exp^{-(\lambda+\mu)t}, \quad \text{if } x \text{ is } U \text{ at } t = 0,$$
$$= \delta - \delta\exp^{-(\lambda+\mu)t}, \quad \text{if } x \text{ is } D \text{ at } t = 0. \tag{11}$$

The steady state probabilities of having element x in state U denoted by $P_U(x)$ or in state D denoted by $P_D(x)$ are readily given by

$$P_U(x) = \delta, \qquad P_D(x) = 1 - \delta. \tag{12}$$

In the rest of the paper, we shall focus solely on links' dynamics and assume that all nodes are kept permanently active. We are then restricting the network dynamics to be solely driven by the mobility of the nodes. Our aim is then to investigate the impact of node mobility on proactive routing tables and at the same time demonstrate the efficiency of our probabilistic model. Recall that there is no need here to consider the aforementioned independence assumption.

4.2. Computing Links Parameters. Link stability depends on the actual distance separating its end points and their relative mutual mobility. Let R denote the adopted transmission range. Let d_e denote the distance separating two given nodes. These two nodes are capable of communication only if d_e is less than or equal to R. However, the shorter is d_e, the more stable is the corresponding link. Such a stability, as a function of time, depends necessarily on their relative speeds and the adopted mobility model. For a given predefined mobility, this amounts to consider λ and μ of any link as functions of the distance separating their corresponding end points. The question here is what functions of d_e should we use for λ and μ. To answer this question, we rely on the tacit observation that the transient state of a Markov process decays rather very rapidly to reach its steady state [21]. Consequently, we can discuss our functions by considering and relying on the steady state probabilities given by (12).

Consider a link that is known to be in state U at the beginning of the routing period. That is d_e for this link is not larger than R at the start of the routing period. Its transient probability of being Up starts equal to one and then will decay rapidly to δ its steady state probability. This steady state probability should tend to one as the distance d_e gets smaller; yet it should tend to one half as d_e approaches R.

Now, let us consider a link in state D at the beginning of the routing period, that is, its d_e is larger than R. Its transient probability of being in state D starts equal to one (its transient probability of being in state U starts equal zero) and then will decay rapidly to $(1 - \delta)$ its steady state probability. The later should tend to one as d_e gets farther and should equal one half as d_e approaches R.

The previous discussion amounts to consider λ as an increasing function (resp., μ as a decreasing function) of d_e/R. The rate at which λ increases (resp., μ decreases) as a function of d_e/R is of utmost concern since it reflects the degree at which shorter hops are preferred in the selection process. The larger such a rate of increase of λ (resp., such a rate of decrease of μ), the more we select shorter hops. Extensive experiments and tests dictate the usefulness of the following equations where we adopt the value $k = 4$:

$$\lambda = \left(\frac{d_e}{R}\right)^k, \qquad \mu = \left(\frac{R}{d_e}\right)^k. \tag{13}$$

5. Cartography-Augmented DSDV

Now, we turn to our earlier assumption about the oracle that provides us, at the start of each routing period, with the actual real network cartography which gives us the different distances separating the different nodes. Our aim here is then to design a distributed algorithm that collects the cartography of the network at the beginning of each routing period. The network cartography can be collected by any proactive routing algorithm by appropriately integrating the cartography information in its signaling messages. More specifically, we here propose to augment the Destination Sequenced Distance Vector routing DSDV protocol [4] that uses the distributed BellmanFord [22, 23] algorithm to calculate paths. It requires that each node in the network periodically generates and sends a Hello message to inform its neighbors of any detected topology changes.

First of all, we intend to get a correct and valid cartography, and, therefore, we will not tolerate delayed routing information. As such, we propose to distinguish between control (i.e., Hello) messages and data packets. Hello messages are to be transmitted as soon as possible before any other data packets. As such, received or locally generated Hellos are put at the head of the IP sending queue in front of any awaiting data packets. Secondly, we assume that each node is capable of knowing its own geographical location. Recent availability of small and inexpensive low-power GPS receivers and approaches for inducing relative coordinates based on signal strength provides a justification for such an assumption [24]. For instance, the APS protocol [25] is a distributed hop by hop positioning algorithm that approximates the absolute positions of all nodes given that only a small fraction of nodes possess a self-positioning capability. The APS algorithm works as an extension to a distance vector proactive routing protocol, and, as such, it can be assumed for this current work. Consequently, before forwarding a Hello or sending its locally generated Hello message, a node includes its own perceived position. Note in particular that a forwarded hello contains both its originating node's position and its forwarding node's position.

The cartography capable augmented DSDV protocol works as follow.

(1) It is through Hello messages that a node can maintain its routing table up to date. The routing table includes entries to already heard destinations. Each entry includes a creation date (i.e., the period's number), the entry local start instant (recall that an entry is deleted after a maximum duration period

(Max_duration_period)), the current perceived position of the destination node, and the current perceived position of the next hop node.

(2) Each node generates locally a Hello message every Hellomsgperiod_DSDV period. The Hello message contains the following fields.

  (i) Source address: the address of the node that originated this Hello.

  (ii) Current period number: works as a sequence number since synchronization is supposedly maintained throughout the network.

  (iii) Next hop address: the next hop to reach the source address, this is just the address of the node that sent this Hello.

  (iv) Number of hops: representing the cost.

  (v) Source position: the source node coordinates at the Hello generation instant.

  (vi) Next hop position: the sender node coordinates at the forwarding instant.

(3) Upon receiving a Hello message, a node first consults the sender's relative fields (they necessarily contain new information). If no entry exists in the routing table to reach the node pointed by the next hop address field, then an entry is added in the table. Otherwise, if the entry is relative to a previous period, then the entry is updated accordingly. A Hello is automatically created to advertise this new entry to other nodes in the network.

(4) Then, the node checks whether it is the originator of this Hello, in which case it just discards the message. If the Hello is relative to an older period, it will be discarded too. Otherwise, the node tests the usefulness of the received hello: if its routing table contains already an entry for the *Source Address* (which represents the destination to be reached), the creation time of the entry and the sequence number included in the Hello are compared. The entry is updated if it is older, or when the two sequence numbers are equal, but the message proposes a better cost. A new entry is automatically created in the routing table, if the message offers a path to a destination not yet known.

(5) If the received message is useful, the node forwards it to its neighbors. It puts its address in the *Next hop Address* field, puts its position in the corresponding field, increments the *Number of hops*, and then broadcasts it to its neighbors.

From the above discussion, we readily observe that our cartography is solely based on the underlying routing protocol in effect; namely, here the DSDV protocol. More interestingly, we do not require any additional control traffic to build the network cartography. The exact control traffic of DSDV is sufficient, but where each Hello message is augmented to include the originator and the forwarder positions.

5.1. Cartography Validity Definition. The network cartography is built by every node through the dissemination of geographic information integrated in the routing announcements as described above. What we need, for our current purpose, is a collected cartography that reflects, the best possible, the actual real network cartography at the start of the routing period. To evaluate the correctness of the collected cartography, we compared it against the real actual cartography of the network. Note that the actual instantaneous cartography of the network can be extracted from the simulator but it cannot be known in practice. This is of no concern to us here since all what we are searching for is to be confident that the collected cartography does represent adequately the real actual cartography at the start of the routing period.

Consider a target node N. When N advertised itself (i.e., sent its own generated Hello), it was at position (x_0, y_0). In the routing table of a node A that had already heard N's Hello, a new entry for N was created, showing (x_0, y_0) as N's coordinates. Since node N is mobile, its position varies as a function of time, and, consequently, it will be at position (x_t, y_t) at time t during the same current routing period. We say that N's position, as indicated by A's current cartography, is valid as long as the distance between the recorded position (x_0, y_0) and the actual current position (x_t, y_t) is less than a tolerated predefined value denoted by d. That is $\sqrt{(x_t - x_0)^2 + (y_t - y_0)^2} \leq d$. The validity of the cartography, as perceived by any given node, say node A, represents the percentage of nodes having valid positions among all nodes. d is a tuning parameter whose value is relative to the transmission range used and is in general a small fraction of this range.

5.2. Simulation Set up. To ascertain the validity of the cartography as a function of the mobility, the traffic load, and the elapsed time since the start of the current routing period, we conducted an extensive set of simulations. We have considered a simulation area of 400 m by 400 m with 120 mobile nodes using the Random Way Point mobility model [17]. We used a transmission range of 100 m, a tolerance d of 10 meters that is a tolerance equals to one tenth of the used transmission range, a network capacity of 11 Mbps, and a maximum MAC retransmission count equals to 7. We used a priority IP module at the network layer to enforce that Hellos are treated before any awaiting data packet. The priority queue maximum size is 100 packets. Furthermore, this queue is handled such as a locally generated IP data packet is only accepted if less than 70 packets (data and Hellos) are present in the queue; otherwise, it is rejected at the IP level. Hello messages are only rejected (dropped) if the queue is completely full. This enforces a further layer for the priority handling of the Hello messages as they are the responsible for the cartography dissemination. The routing updating period is set to 10 seconds. Finally, the *Max_duration_period*, representing the life time of an entry in the routing table, is set to 15 seconds. All required modifications are ported on the OMNET++ network simulator.

5.3. Observations. Figure 1 portrays the validity of the cartography as a function of the elapsed time since the start of the routing period and for different node speeds. Recall that we are using a priority IP handling, and, therefore, the network load has a very little impact on the validity of the cartography. For a null node speed (no mobility), we get a validity of one hundred percent. For speeds higher or equal to 1 m/sec, the validity of the cartography gets at its maximum around instant 1.5 sec which is the time required to get the maximum of Hellos throughout the network. Consequently, if we launch the routing updating process around 1.5 seconds before the start of the period, we get the maximum cartography validity just at the start of the routing period. Moreover, as we see on Figure 1, the validity reaches one hundred percent for all considered speeds but 10 m/sec. For the later, the validity is sufficiently high and equals nearly ninety seven percent.

6. Suitability of the Proposed Probabilistic Model

To experiment our new probabilistic proposal, we conducted a set of simulations using the OMNET++ simulator where we integrated the proposed probabilistic framework, the cartography collecting algorithm, and the Priority IP handling. Our simulation set up is as defined previously; that is a simulation area of 400 m × 400 m, 120 mobile nodes, a transmission range of 100 meters, a tolerance of 10 meters, and the Random Way Point mobility model [17]. The time axis is seen divided into consecutive routing periods each of length T seconds. For the conventional proactive routing; namely, the DSDV, each node generates a Hello message just at the start of the routing period. However, for the probabilistic routing protocol and its derivatives which will be introduced next, each node generates a Hello message one second and a half before the end of the current period. As such, the cartography with the maximum validity is readily available just at the start of the next routing period. The initial topology of 120 nodes is chosen randomly, and the period size T is fixed to 10 seconds.

Before we can proceed further, we require here to recall that probabilistic routing inherently thrives to select shorter hops as the elapsed time from the start of the routing period gets farther. As a result, probabilistic routes are much more resilient to breakages caused by the mobility of nodes, but they are much longer than the routes used by the common proactive routing. The upper curve in Figure 2 represents the average route length in number of hops provided by the probabilistic routing, for a null speed and a null traffic load, as a function of the elapsed time since the start of the routing period. At the start of the routing period that is at instant 0, the network collected cartography provides the distances between the nodes, and, consequently, we readily get the initial probabilities for all links as given by (9). At time instant 1 second, we reach the steady state and the link probabilities are now rather governed by (12). As such, the probabilistic route average length starts around 2.8 which is the same average route length as given by both the

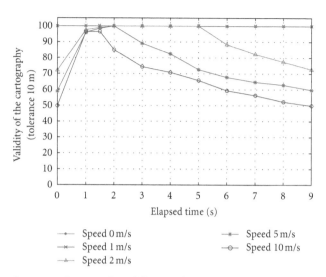

FIGURE 1: Cartography validity as a function of the elapsed time.

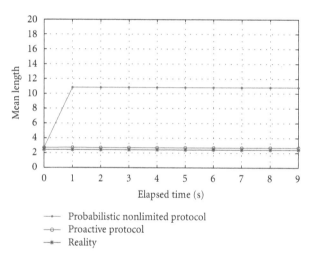

FIGURE 2: Average route length as a function of the elapsed time, $V = 0$ m/sec.

conventional proactive routing and the real actual topology. From instant one second, the probabilistic average route length stabilizes at around 11 hops which is a rather very large value.

We clearly observe that probabilistic routing amounts to much longer routes than both the real optimal routes given by the actual network and those delivered by the conventional proactive routing. This is quite expected since the crux of the probabilistic routing is its preference and greed for short stable links. Conventional proactive routing, however, amounts to a slightly larger average route length than the real optimal case which can be clearly observed on Figure 3. Indeed, some Hello messages may arrive through longer paths due to collisions. This will not affect the cartography validity which remains at its optimum validity of one hundred percent but do slightly affect the proactive routing tables.

This very large average route length hinders any practical use of our probabilistic routing unless some definite action is undertaken to impose on it an upper limit. To mitigate the

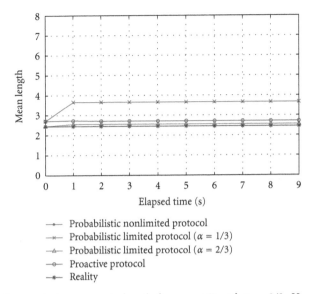

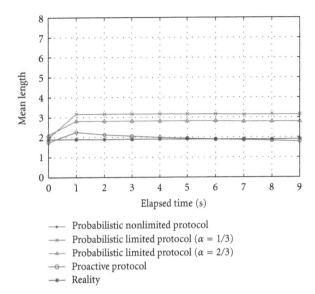

FIGURE 3: Average route length for $\alpha = 1/3$ and $\alpha = 2/3$, $V = 0$ m/sec.

FIGURE 4: Average route length as a function of the elapsed time, $V = 5$ m/sec.

down side of probabilistic routing, we propose to integrate a bounding function. Let αR be a fraction of the transmission range where $(0 < \alpha \leq 1)$ and d_f be the flying distance between a source node S and a destination node D. Let $L(S, D)$ be the bounding number of hops that can be used to reach node D from node S. We readily have $L(S, D) = d_f/\alpha R$. Note here that when α goes to zero then no bounding is used and when α goes to one then only hops of length R can be used. Consequently, α is an adequate tuning parameter that can be used in conjunction with the probabilistic routing to limit the length of its provided routes. Let $L_s(S, D)$ be the length of the shortest path between S and D. Then, we readily adopt the following bounding equation governing the route length of the probabilistic routing:

$$L(S, D) = \max\left(\frac{d_f}{\alpha R}, L_s(S, D)\right). \tag{14}$$

The question naturally arises as to how to calculate now the shortest routes within our probabilistic framework. Earlier, we have just to execute a shortest path algorithm on the valued graph provided by the network cartography seen at the start of the routing period. But now, we have to further restrict these routes according to the bounding function just defined. We solved this by using the Extended Bellman-Ford Algorithm (EBFA) for shortest paths computed with 2 metrics [11]. A probabilistic route must now have the greatest probability of existence among all possible routes, yet its length should not exceed (in terms of the number of hops) the maximum threshold given by 11. In the remaining, we shall consider the value $\alpha = 1/3$ to approach the pure probabilistic routing and the value $\alpha = 2/3$ to approach rather the common proactive routing.

Figure 3 represents the average route length as a function of the elapsed time since the start of the routing period, the same as Figure 2 but without the curve corresponding to the unlimited probabilistic routing. First, we observe

that the probabilistic limited $\alpha = 1/3$ provides an average route length equals to 3.8 hops which amounts to just and only one additional hop compared to the conventional proactive routing (2.8 hops) but much less than the pure probabilistic routing (11 hops, see Figure 2). This is normal since the probabilistic limited $\alpha = 1/3$ is armed to choose longer routes than the proactive routing as $\alpha = 1/3$. More interestingly, we observe that the probabilistic limited $\alpha = 2/3$ provides lower average route length than even the conventional proactive routing. To explain this, recall that this probabilistic limited protocol selects large hops as the conventional proactive routing. However, being based on the network cartography, it has a much better and comprehensive view of the network and consequently can use routes that the conventional proactive routing does not even realize and know about.

We conducted many simulations for different mobility levels. We observed that the probabilistic limited incurs a very small increase in the average route length but still remains much more efficient than the pure probabilistic protocol. For instance, Figure 4 represents the average route length but for a speed of 5 m/sec. It is interesting to note here that, as the network is dynamic, the validity of the proactive routing loses as time progresses and consequently only stable paths specially those within the closer vicinity will stay valid. As such, we notice that the average route length of the proactive routing may even get smaller than the actual real average route length. For the same exact reason, the average route length provided by the probabilistic $\alpha = 2/3$ is higher now than that given by the proactive routing. This takes us to investigate the correctness or validity of the routes given by each protocol against the actual real network.

The routing period is divided into T equally spaced observations points; namely, an observation point each second. At each observation time point, we have then five different views of the network: the actual real view provided by the underlying mobility model used in our OMNET++

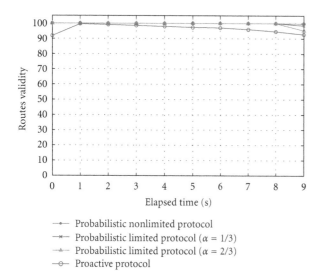

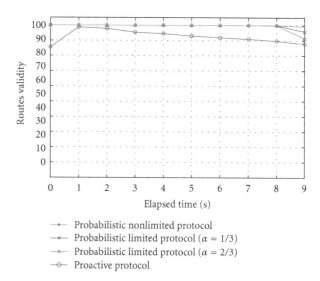

FIGURE 5: Percentage of valid probabilistic routes as a function of the elapsed time, $V = 1$ m/sec.

FIGURE 6: Percentage of valid probabilistic routes as a function of the elapsed time, $V = 2$ m/sec.

simulator, the DSDV routing table computed in the common conventional proactive way, the probabilistic nonlimited routes computed by our pure probabilistic proposed model, the probabilistic limited $\alpha = 1/3$, and the probabilistic limited $\alpha = 2/3$. A route from a source node to a destination node is termed valid if it exists in the real network regardless whether it is optimal (a shortest route) or not. To ascertain the efficiency of our proposed probabilistic routing algorithms, we first compute the percentage of valid routes from a designated node (node 1) to all the other 119 destinations given by each one of the four protocols. Figures 5, 6, 7, and 8 portray the percentage of the validity of the routes as a function of the elapsed time since the start of the routing period for all the four defined protocols when no load is applied to the network and, respectively, for the speeds 1 m/sec, 2 m/sec, 5 m/sec, and 10 m/sec. Obviously, for a speed of 0 m/sec, all four protocols provide a constant validity of one hundred percent.

We observe that as node speed gets higher, the conventional proactive routing starts losing its efficiency by delivering the lowest route validity percentage. Most interestingly, we notice that the probabilistic limited $\alpha = 1/3$ outperforms even the pure unlimited probabilistic protocol under high mobility. While this is remarkable and might not be expected, it surely needs some explanations. The crux of this phenomenon resides mainly in three different facts. Firstly, recall that the probabilistic routing chooses the path having the largest product of the links weights (the product of the probabilities of existence of the links). As a result, it selects the largest number of very short hops. The probabilistic limited, especially using $\alpha = 1/3$, provides a path comprising much less hops, and, at the same time, this path can have a very close value of the product of the links weights. For instance, the probabilistic routing selects a path with four hops, each one having a weight 3/4, while the probabilistic limited selects a path having just two hops each of which has a weight of 1/2. Secondly, the probabilistic limited inherently uses different paths for

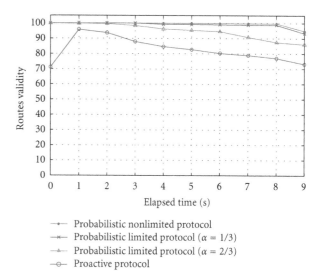

FIGURE 7: Percentage of valid probabilistic routes as a function of the elapsed time, $V = 5$ m/sec.

different destinations, while the probabilistic not limited is restricted to pass through the same longest path's segments as dictated by the well-known principle of optimality. Least but not last, when mobility gets higher, a breakage of just one link brings down all the probabilistic paths passing through it which are numerous according to previous observations, but very few paths in the case of the probabilistic limited. In other terms, all three probabilistic protocols provide resilient paths at the beginning of the routing period. As we get farther from the start of the routing period and as the mobility gets stronger, the probabilistic limited stands out to provide better resiliency.

Let us now investigate the betterment brought by this probabilistic framework in terms of the network throughput. We consider the same network scenario used previously; however, we also consider 8 traffic flows emanating from 8 different sources chosen randomly and destined to 8 other

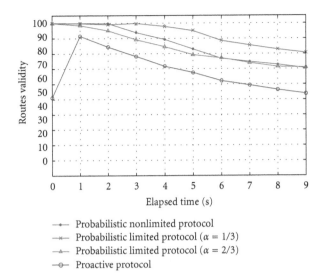

FIGURE 8: Percentage of valid probabilistic routes as a function of the elapsed time, $V = 10$ m/sec.

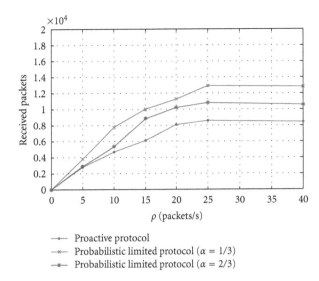

FIGURE 9: Throughput as a function of the traffic load, $V = 5$ m/sec.

destination nodes also chosen randomly. We fix the nodes' speed to 5 m/sec. The data packet size used is 200 bytes. Figure 9 portrays the average number of received packets per flow as a function of the traffic load per flow. We observe that the probabilistic limited $\alpha = 1/3$ outperforms both the conventional proactive and the probabilistic limited $\alpha = 2/3$ in delivering more throughput. The probabilistic limited $\alpha = 1/3$ stands out even for light traffic loads, for moderate traffic, for instance, 15 packets per second, it delivers around 67 percent more than the conventional proactive routing. For a higher traffic load, for example, at 40 packet per second, it delivers 50 percent more than the conventional proactive protocol. The probabilistic limited $\alpha = 2/3$ outperforms also the conventional proactive protocol; however, it delivers much less than its $\alpha = 1/3$ counterpart.

7. Conclusion

In this paper, we proposed a new probabilistic proactive routing framework that selects the most stable links to construct routes towards their destinations. A network element being a node or a link is represented as a two-state simple Markovian automaton. Furthermore, a network cartography collecting algorithm is proposed to provide distances between nodes at the start of each routing period. The cartography is then used to instantiate the required probabilities of existence of each element in the network.

Extensive simulations are conducted to demonstrate the efficiency of both the proposed probabilistic framework and the cartography collecting algorithm. Our probabilistic proposition bases its decision rather on link stability and consequently selects shorter and more resilient links. However, such an inherent behavior has a side effect of increasing the average route length. To mitigate this down side, we adopted a simple hop bounding approach that limits the number of hops within probabilistic routes. Conducted simulations showed that this is an effective

technique yielding substantially much more valid routes and amounting to a substantial increase in network throughput.

References

[1] D. B. Johnson, D. A. Maltz, and Y.-C. Hu, "The dynamic source routing protocol for mobile Ad Hoc Networks (DSR)," Internet-Draft. IETF MANET Working Group, 2004.

[2] C.E. Perkins, E.M. Royer, and I.D. Chakeres, "Ad Hoc On demand distance vector routing protocol," Internet Draft, MANET Working Group, 2003.

[3] T. Clausen and P. Jacquet, "Optimized link state routing protocol (OLSR. m inus 0.4em Request for Comment 3626)," MANET Working Group, 2003.

[4] C.E. Perkins and P. Bhagwat, "Highly dynamic destination-sequenced distance-vector routing (DSDV) for mobile computers," in *Proceedings of the ACM Conference on Communications Architectures, Protocols and Applications (SIGCOMM'94)*, 1999.

[5] T. Clausen, P. Jacquet, and L. Viennot, "Comparative study of routing protocols for mobile Ad Hoc networks," in *Proceedings of the The 1st Annual Mediterranean Ad Hoc Networking Workshop*, 2002.

[6] J. Novatnack, L. Greenwald, and H. Arora, "Evaluating ad hoc routing protocols with respect to quality of service," in *Proceedings of the IEEE International Conference on Wireless and Mobile Computing, Networking and Communications, (WiMob'05)*, pp. 205–212, August 2005.

[7] C. Mbarushimana and A. Shahrabi, "Comparative study of reactive and proactive routing protocols performance in mobile ad hoc networks," in *Proceedings of the 21st International Conference on Advanced Information Networking and ApplicationsWorkshops, (AINAW'07)*, pp. 679–684, May 2007.

[8] W.-H. Chung, "Probabilistic analysis of routes on mobile ad hoc networks," *IEEE Communications Letters*, vol. 8, no. 8, pp. 506–508, 2004.

[9] R. Dube, C. D. Rais, K. Y. Wang, and S. K. Tripathi, "Signal stability-based adaptive routing (SSA) for ad hoc mobile networks," *IEEE Personal Communications*, vol. 4, no. 1, pp. 36–45, 1997.

[10] C.-K. Toh, "Associativity-Based Routing for Ad-Hoc Mobile Networks," *Wireless Personal Communications*, vol. 4, no. 2, pp. 103–139, 1997.

[11] M. A. Abid and A. Belghith, "Stability routing with constrained path length for improved routability in dynamic MANETs," *The International Journal of Personnal and Ubiquitous Computing*, vol. 15, no. 8, pp. 799–810, 2011.

[12] R. Beraldi, L. Querzoni, and R. Baldoni, "A hint-based probabilistic protocol for unicast communications in MANETs," *Ad Hoc Networks*, vol. 4, no. 5, pp. 547–566, 2006.

[13] H. Dubois-Ferriere, M. Grossglauser, and M. Vetterli, "Age matters: efficient route discovery in mobile ad hoc networks using encounter ages," in *Proceedings of the 4th ACM International Symposium on Mobile Ad Hoc Networking and Computing (MOBIHOC '03)*, pp. 257–266, Annapolis, Md, USA, June 2003.

[14] M. Roth and S. Wicker, "Termite: emergent ad-hoc networking," in *Proceedings of The 2nd Mediterranean Workshop on Ad-Hoc Networks*, Mehdia, Tunisia, 2003.

[15] M. A. Abid and A. Belghith, "Period size self tuning to enhance routing in MANETs," *International Journal of Business Data Communications and Networking*, vol. 6, no. 4, pp. 21–37, 2010.

[16] D. Yu, H. Li, and I. Gruber, "Path availability in ad hoc network," in *Proceedings of the 10th International Conference on Telecommunications (ICT'03)*, vol. 1, pp. 383–387, 2003.

[17] T. Camp, J. Boleng, and V. Davies, "A survey of mobility models for Ad Hoc network research," *Wireless Communication and Mobile Computing*, vol. 2, no. 5, pp. 483–502, 2002.

[18] H. Zhang and Y.-N. Dong, "A novel path stability computation model for wireless ad hoc networks," *IEEE Signal Processing Letters*, vol. 14, no. 12, pp. 928–931, 2007.

[19] Y. C. Tseng, Y. F. Li, and Y. C. Chang, "On route lifetime in multihop mobile ad hoc networks," *IEEE Transactions on Mobile Computing*, vol. 2, no. 4, pp. 366–376, 2003.

[20] R. Marie, M. Molnar, and H. Idoudi, "A simple automata based model for stable routing in dynamic Ad-Hoc networks," in *Proceedings of the 2nd ACM International Workshop on Performance Monitoring, Measurement, and Evaluation of Heterogeneous Wireless and Wired Network(PM2HW2N '07)*, Crete Island, Greece, 2007.

[21] L. Kleinrock, *Queueing Systems*, vol. 1: Theory, 1975, Wiley Interscience.

[22] T. H. Cormen, C. E. Leiserson, Ronald L. Rivest, and C. Stein, *Introduction to Algorithms*, MIT Press, Cambridge, Mass, USA, 2nd edition, 2001.

[23] D. Bertsekas and R. Gallager, *Data Networks*, Prentice-Hall, Englewood Cliffs, NJ, USA, 1987.

[24] S. Giordano and I. Stojmenovic, *Position-Based Ad Hoc Routes in Ad Hoc Networks*, CRC Press, Inc, Boca Raton, FL, USA, 2003.

[25] D. Niculescu and B. Nath, "DV Based Positioning in Ad Hoc Networks," *Telecommunication Systems*, vol. 22, no. 1-4, pp. 267–280, 2003.

Permissions

The contributors of this book come from diverse backgrounds, making this book a truly international effort. This book will bring forth new frontiers with its revolutionizing research information and detailed analysis of the nascent developments around the world.

We would like to thank all the contributing authors for lending their expertise to make the book truly unique. They have played a crucial role in the development of this book. Without their invaluable contributions this book wouldn't have been possible. They have made vital efforts to compile up to date information on the varied aspects of this subject to make this book a valuable addition to the collection of many professionals and students.

This book was conceptualized with the vision of imparting up-to-date information and advanced data in this field. To ensure the same, a matchless editorial board was set up. Every individual on the board went through rigorous rounds of assessment to prove their worth. After which they invested a large part of their time researching and compiling the most relevant data for our readers. Conferences and sessions were held from time to time between the editorial board and the contributing authors to present the data in the most comprehensible form. The editorial team has worked tirelessly to provide valuable and valid information to help people across the globe.

Every chapter published in this book has been scrutinized by our experts. Their significance has been extensively debated. The topics covered herein carry significant findings which will fuel the growth of the discipline. They may even be implemented as practical applications or may be referred to as a beginning point for another development. Chapters in this book were first published by Hindawi Publishing Corporation; hereby published with permission under the Creative Commons Attribution License or equivalent.

The editorial board has been involved in producing this book since its inception. They have spent rigorous hours researching and exploring the diverse topics which have resulted in the successful publishing of this book. They have passed on their knowledge of decades through this book. To expedite this challenging task, the publisher supported the team at every step. A small team of assistant editors was also appointed to further simplify the editing procedure and attain best results for the readers.

Our editorial team has been hand-picked from every corner of the world. Their multi-ethnicity adds dynamic inputs to the discussions which result in innovative outcomes. These outcomes are then further discussed with the researchers and contributors who give their valuable feedback and opinion regarding the same. The feedback is then collaborated with the researches and they are edited in a comprehensive manner to aid the understanding of the subject.

Apart from the editorial board, the designing team has also invested a significant amount of their time in understanding the subject and creating the most relevant covers. They scrutinized every image to scout for the most suitable representation of the subject and create an appropriate cover for the book.

The publishing team has been involved in this book since its early stages. They were actively engaged in every process, be it collecting the data, connecting with the contributors or procuring relevant information. The team has been an ardent support to the editorial, designing and production team. Their endless efforts to recruit the best for this project, has resulted in the accomplishment of this book. They are a veteran in the field of academics and their pool of knowledge is as vast as their experience in printing. Their expertise and guidance has proved useful at every step. Their uncompromising quality standards have made this book an exceptional effort. Their encouragement from time to time has been an inspiration for everyone.

The publisher and the editorial board hope that this book will prove to be a valuable piece of knowledge for researchers, students, practitioners and scholars across the globe.

List of Contributors

Federica Paganelli and David Parlanti
CNIT, Research Unit at the University of Firenze, Via S. Marta 3, 50139 Firenze, Italy

Jung-Shyr Wu and Chen-Chieh Huang
Department of Communication Engineering, National Central University, Chung-Li 32001, Taiwan

Shun-Fang Yang
Department of Communication Engineering, National Central University, Chung-Li 32001, Taiwan
Telecommunication Laboratories, ChungHwa Telecom Co., Ltd., Yang-Mei 32601, Taiwan

Alireza Shameli-Sendi, Julien Desfossez, Michel Dagenais, and Masoume Jabbarifar
D´epartment de Genie Informatique et Genie Logiciel, Ecole Polytechnique de Montreal, P.O. Box 6079, Succ. Downtown, Montreal, QC, Canada H3C 3A7

Kaustubh Dhondge, Hyungbae Park and Baek-Young Choi
University of Missouri-Kansas City, 546 FlarsheimHall, 5110 Rockhill Road, Kansas City, MO 64110, USA

Sejun Song
Texas A&M University, Fermier Hall 008, 3367 TAMU, College Station, TX 77843, USA

Gerardine Immaculate Mary and Z. C. Alex
School of Electronics Engineering, VIT University, Vellore, Tamilnadu 632014, India

Lawrence Jenkins
Department of Electrical Engineering, IISc, Bangalore, Karnataka 560012, India

Alireza Shameli-Sendi, Masoume Jabbarifar and Michel Dagenais
D´epartment de Genie Informatique et G´enie Logiciel, ´Ecole Polytechnique de Montr´eal, P.O. Box 6079, Succ. Downtown, Montreal, QC, Canada H3C 3A7

Mehdi Shajari
Department of Computer Engineering & Information Technology, Amirkabir University of Technology, 424 Hafez Avenue, Tehran, Iran

Patrick Loschmidt, Reinhard Exel, and Georg Gaderer
Institute for Integrated Sensor Systems, Austrian Academy of Sciences, 2700 Wiener Neustadt, Austria

Rajesh K. Sharma, Anastasia Lavrenko and Reiner S. Thomä
International Graduate School on Mobile Communications, Ilmenau University of Technology, Helmholtzplatz 2, 98684 Ilmenau, Germany

Dirk Kolb
Reconnaissance Research & Development (RRD) Division, MEDAV GmbH, Gr¨afenberger Straβe 32-34, 91080 Uttenreuth, Germany

Jussi Turkka
Department of Communications Engineering, Tampere University of Technology, 33720 Tampere, Finland
Department of Mathematical Information Technology, University of Jyv¨askyl¨a, 40014 Jyv¨askyl¨a, Finland

Fedor Chernogorov, Kimmo Brigatti and Tapani Ristaniemi
Department of Mathematical Information Technology, University of Jyv¨askyl¨a, 40014 Jyv¨askyl¨a, Finland

Jukka Lempiäinen
Department of Communications Engineering, Tampere University of Technology, 33720 Tampere, Finland

Sabina Barakovic
Ministry of Security of Bosnia and Herzegovina, Trg BiH 1, 71000 Sarajevo, Bosnia andHerzegovina

Lea Skorin-Kapov
Faculty of Electrical Engineering and Computing, University of Zagreb, Unska 3, 10000 Zagreb, Croatia

Christian Schwartz, Tobias Hoßfeld, Frank Lehrieder and Phuoc Tran-Gia
Institute of Computer Science, University of Wurzburg, Chair of Communication Networks, Am Hubland, 97074 Wurzburg, Germany

Yuanyuan Zhang
CITI laboratory, INSA-Lyon, INRIA, Universite de Lyon, 69621 Lyon, France
Department of Computer Science and Technology, East China Normal University, No. 500 Dongchuan Road, Shanghai 200241, China

Marine Minier
CITI laboratory, INSA-Lyon, INRIA, Universite de Lyon, 69621 Lyon, France

Rosario G. Garroppo, Loris Gazzarrini, Stefano Giordano, and Luca Tavanti
Dipartimento di Ingegneria dell'Informazione, Universit`a di Pisa, 56126 Pisa, Italy

Maciej Szmit
Computer Engineering Department, Technical University of Lodz, 18/22 Stefanowskiego Street, 90-924 Lodz, Poland
Corporate IT Security Agency, Orange Labs Poland, 7 Obrzezna Street, 02-691 Warsaw, Poland

Anna Szmit
Department of Management, Technical University of Lodz, 266 Piotrkowska Street, 90-924 Lodz, Poland

Miroslav Behan and Ondrej Krejcar
Department of Information Technologies, Faculty of Informatics and Management, University of Hradec Kralove, Rokitanskeho 62, 50003 Hradec Kralove, Czech Republic

Abdelfettah Belghith and Mohamed Amine Abid
HANA Research Group, Ecole Nationale des Sciences de l'Informatique (ENSI), University of Manouba, La Manouba 2010, Tunisia

Adel Ben Mnaouer
College of Computer Engineering and IT, Dar Al Utoum, Al Mizan, Al Falah, Riyad 13314, Saudi Arabia

Printed in the USA
CPSIA information can be obtained
at www.ICGtesting.com
JSHW051441221024
72173JS00006B/1541